# Sotheby's

## ART AT AUCTION 2000–2001

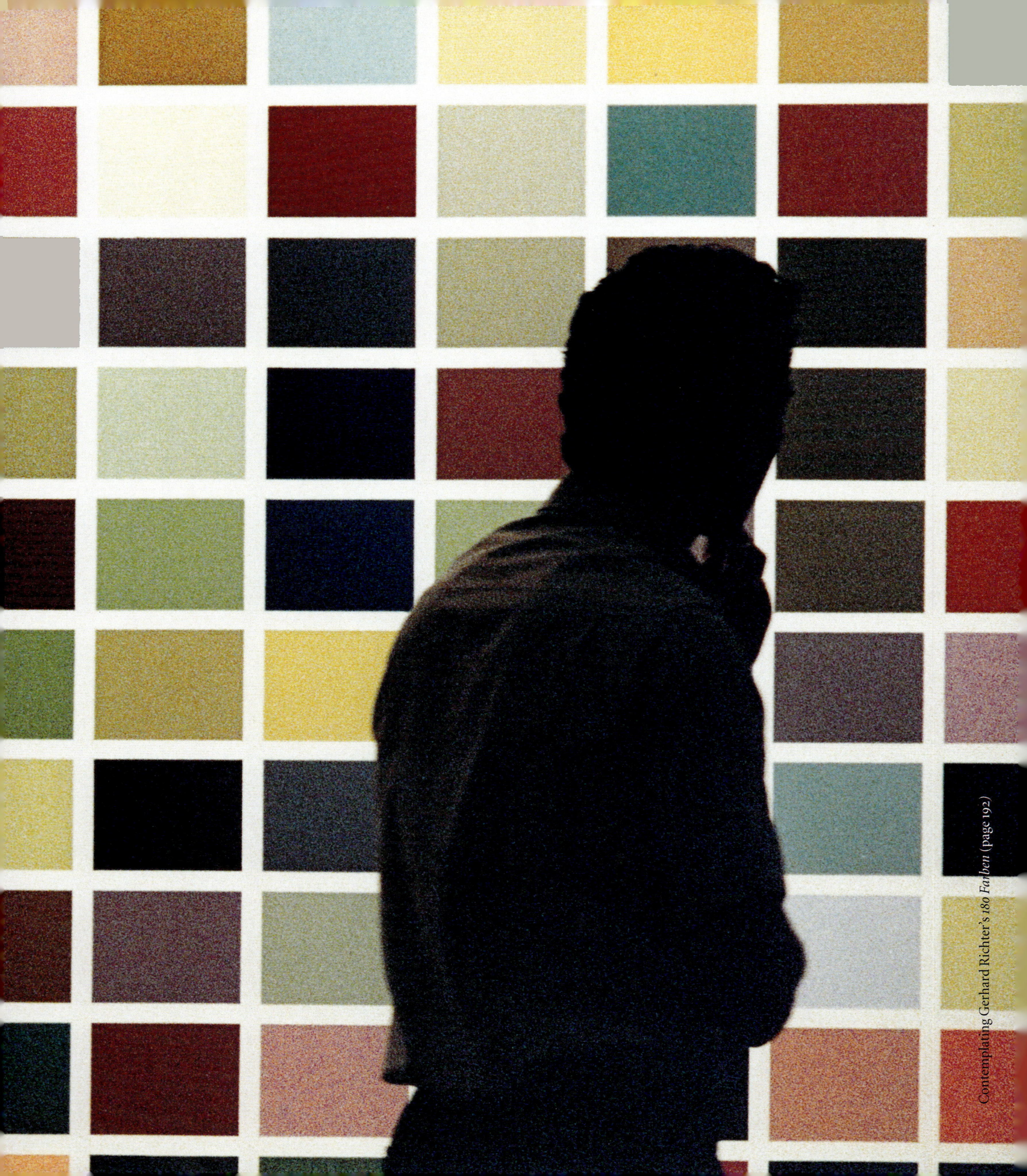

Contemplating Gerhard Richter's *180 Farben* (page 192)

# Contents

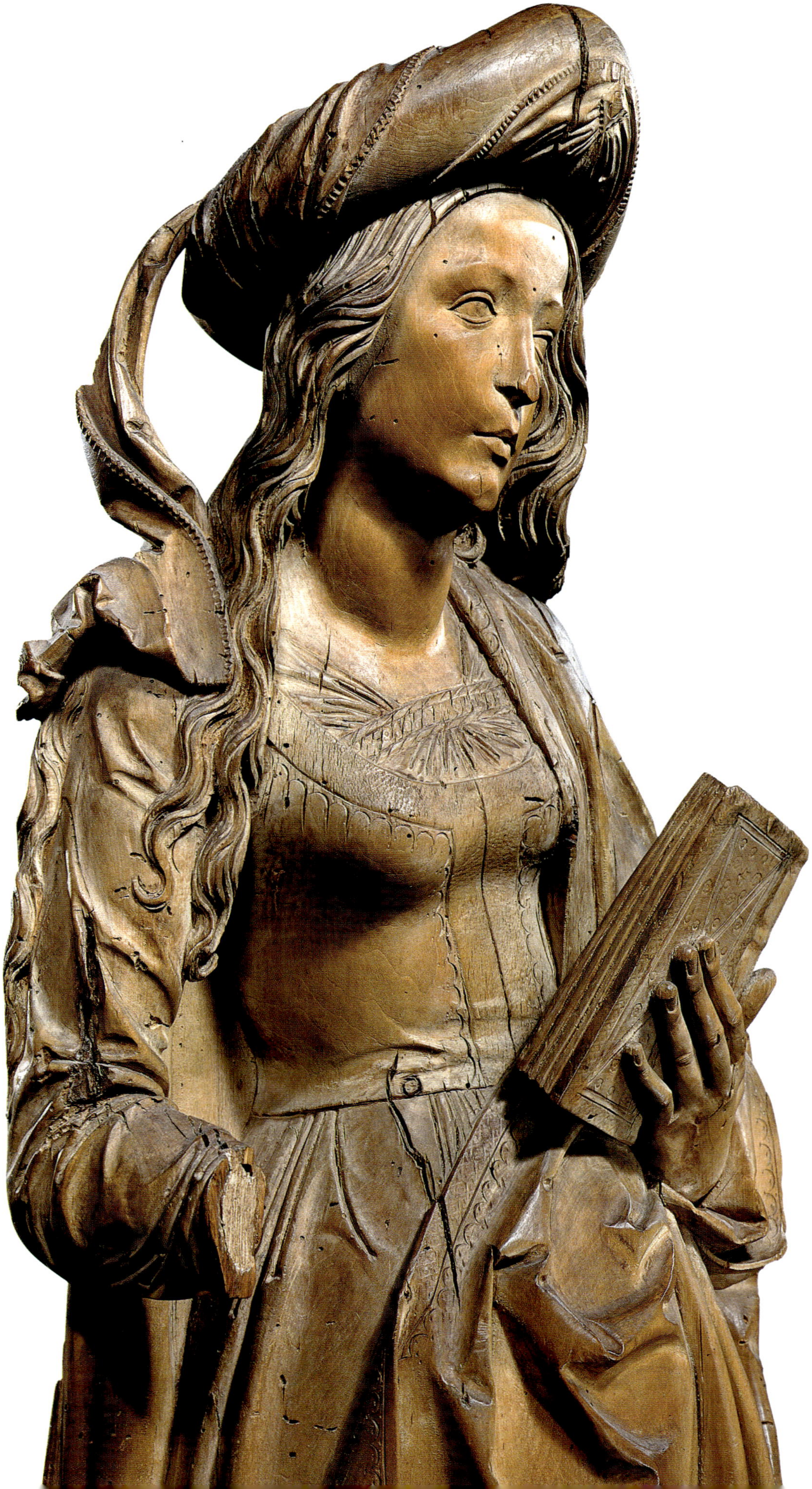

# Introduction

William F. Ruprecht

As I write this introduction in late September, it is the beginning of a new auction season and, like all beginnings, it is full of promise. But this beginning is also different. We have begun to resume our lives after the tragic events of 11th September and there is uncertainty in the air.

It is with particular pleasure, therefore, that I turn to the certainty of the past season. For Sotheby's, while there were indeed challenges on the corporate front, the year was filled with wonderful art and objects, as well as treasured experiences with our clients and at the podium. From Hong Kong to London, Geneva to New York, exceptional works of art were the distinguishing feature. Many achieved record-breaking prices; many others were memorable for the sheer joy they provided – to us as temporary guardians, to the many people who attended our exhibitions and, most importantly, to their new owners.

Without question, Max Beckmann's haunting *Self-portrait with Horn* stands out – in this or any season. Resonant and powerful, it is a compelling statement of 20th-century artistic independence under oppression. We are fortunate that a museum is its new owner. Monet's *Meules, derniers rayons de soleil*, a work of outstanding beauty, had not been seen publicly since 1895. Michelangelo's *Study of a Mourning Woman*, a previously unrecorded drawing, was discovered by a Sotheby's expert – a significant art historical event. As the following pages illustrate, these three examples are but a few of the extraordinary paintings and objects that Sotheby's has been privileged to sell this season.

We are also privileged to have the best exhibition space in the art auction world. The presentation of art is something we take seriously and our stunning and recently completed galleries in New York, where our brand-new York Avenue facility is now complete, are without equal. In London, we have just opened our new auction facility at Olympia, where a continuous flow of art, antiques and collectibles will be presented in an accessible and flexible environment, allowing our elegant and historic Bond Street headquarters to focus on the high end. And our beautiful Paris premises at the Galerie Charpentier will soon be home not just to exhibitions but also to auctions, which we expect, finally, to begin this season.

As we look forward to the promise of the season ahead, there is indeed much we do not know. But there is also much we do. We know that we have the best art experts anywhere. We know we have a responsibility as a market leader to provide informed and honest advice and to be a voice of reason and perspective. And we know that our premises around the world will be filled with wonderful paintings and works of art. That has only happened with your support, which is more meaningful and appreciated than ever. We will do our best to deserve it.

This sculpture of a female saint by Tilman Riemenschneider (1460–1531) was sold at Sotheby's New York in May for $2,975,750 (£4,312,681) to benefit the Leo and Karen Gutmann foundation.

# Sotheby's Year in Europe

Robin Woodhead and
Henry Wyndham

Any year that contains the sale of great works by Michelangelo, Claude Monet, Salvador Dalí and Johann Zoffany was bound to be interesting. To be involved with art of this calibre, which encompasses such a breadth of style and media, is one of the greatest pleasures and privileges of being at Sotheby's. Looking back over the year across Europe one of the most salient features is the consistent quality of the works that have appeared in our salerooms.

The drama of major discoveries within country-house collections was highlighted last year when a Sotheby's expert on a valuation in the library of Castle Howard in Yorkshire discovered a unique drawing by Michelangelo (pages 28–29). That this important work was discovered within one of the most important collections of art in the United Kingdom is a testament to the tenacity and knowledge of our experts.

The Impressionist and Modern Art department at Sotheby's London has offered some outstanding works over the past year. Particularly memorable is the powerful work by Claude Monet, *Meules, derniers rayons de soleil*. This painting, explored more fully on pages 18–19, combined art-historical importance with impeccable pedigree. Prior to the exhibition of the work in London in July, the painting had never left France and had not been on public display since 1895. The technique and use of colour gives the painting an extraordinary emotional and intellectual power.

The innovation of holding Impressionist auctions in February proved to be a resounding success. *Portrait of Anton Peschka* by Egon Schiele (page 84), created a new record for the artist at auction. The success of this German work had been preceded in October by a sale devoted to German and Austrian artists. The auction included an array of Expressionist works by Ludwig Meidener, from the Marvin and Janet Fishman Collection. It was one of a number of themed sales held over the last year; another was the first ever auction devoted to the Surrealist movement. This new departure contained sculpture, paintings and photographs, and saw a new world auction record achieved for Salvador Dalí's portrait of his wife, Gala (page 88).

Contemporary Art sales held throughout the year maintained their pre-eminence and included some outstanding works, not least the beautiful *180 Farben* by Gerhard Richter (page 4). The work is the culmination of a series of experiments in colour conducted by the artist in the late 1960s and early 1970s.

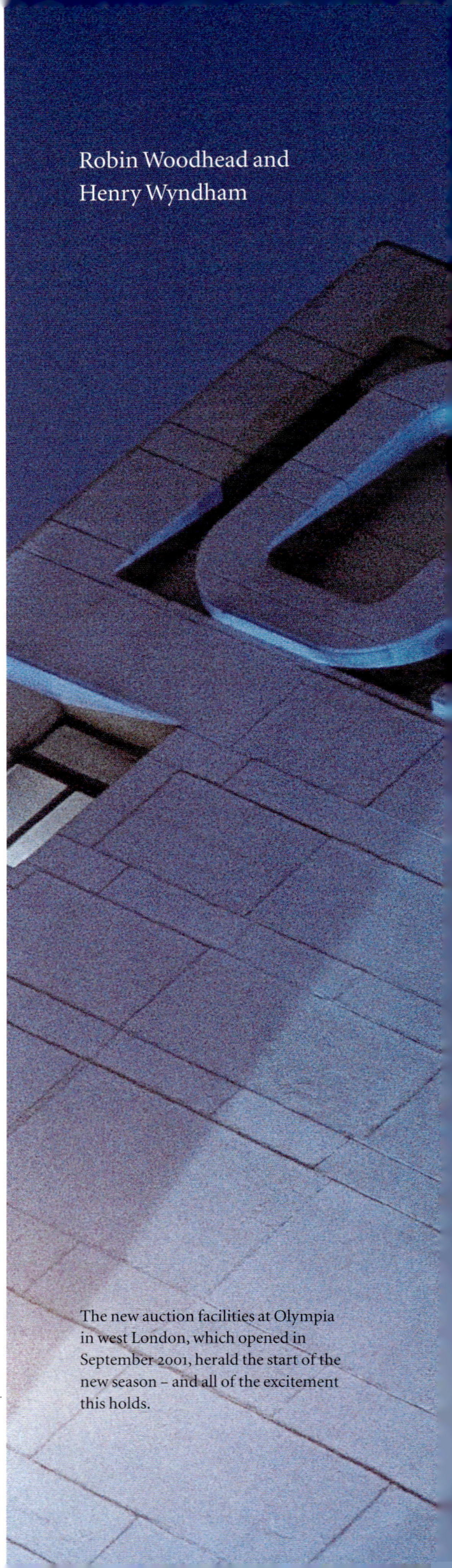

The new auction facilities at Olympia in west London, which opened in September 2001, herald the start of the new season – and all of the excitement this holds.

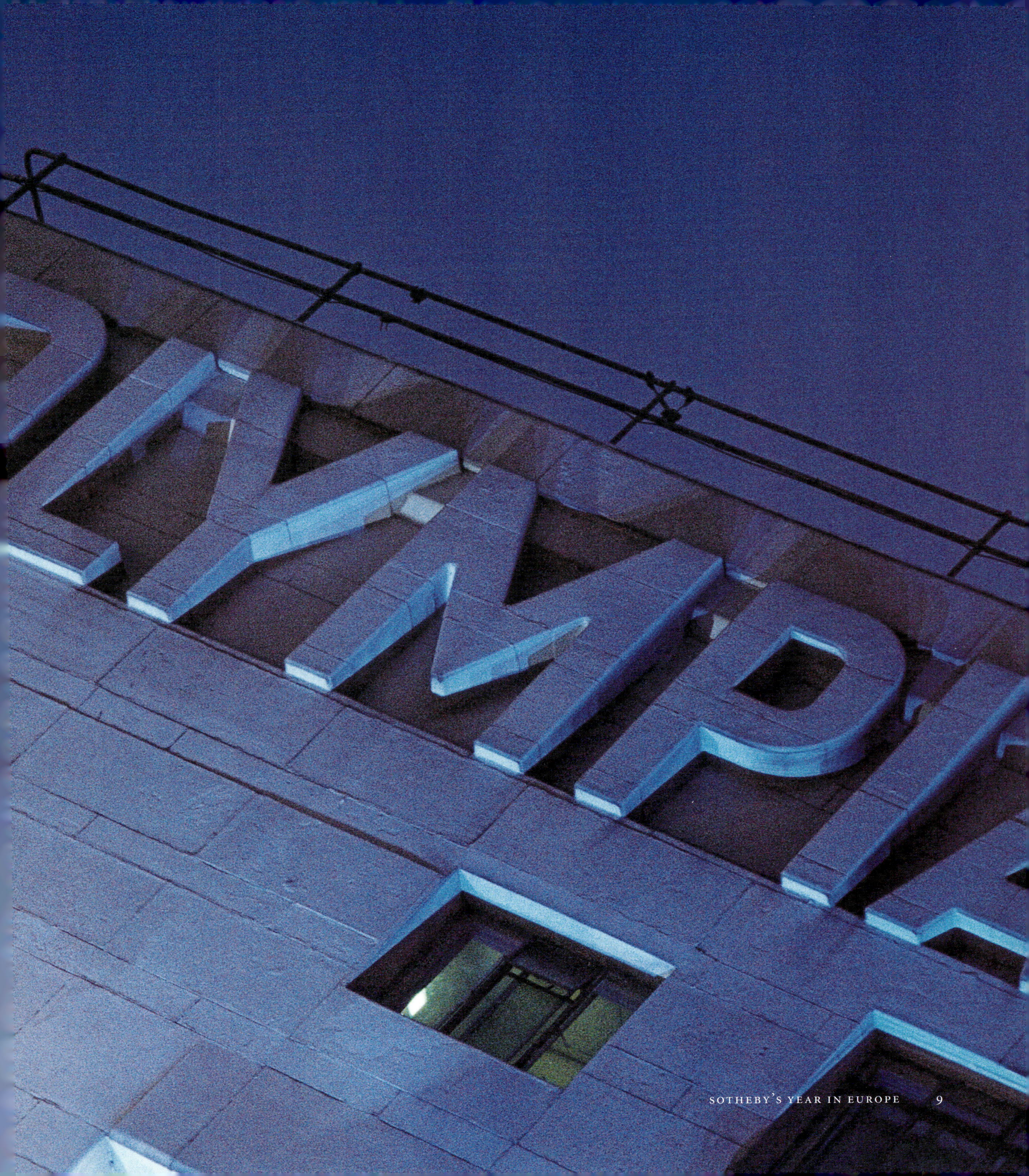
OLYMPIA

Such power and control of colour was exhibited in quite a different way in a fascinating watercolour sold in the British Sale in June. In an auction filled with so many highlights, the depiction of sunlight after a rainstorm by J. M. W. Turner in his *Heidelberg with a Rainbow* (page 31) was phenomenal. The same sale also included a fascinating conversation piece by the 18th-century artist Johann Zoffany, *The Dutton Family* (right), and encompassed Modern works, such as Stanley Spencer's *From Up the Rise* (page 63), an evocation of his home village of Cookham in Berkshire. A selection from the Collection of Stanley J. Seeger preceded this June sale. Part of the collection had sold in New York in May (page 22–23), and the sale of British works in London saw a number of world auction records established, including one for Patrick Heron's *Lux Eterna* (page 2).

Across Europe Sotheby's has had a successful year. There was understandable excitement at the prospect of sales at the Galerie Charpentier, Sotheby's office in Paris (page 40–1). As a precursor to selling in our own rooms, a series of successful auctions were held in association with French auctioneers Poulain Le Fur, including two single-owner collections that epitomize French style: the furniture and decorations from the dealer–collector Luigi Anton Laura and his wife, and the library of Charles Hayoit. The persistence of Sotheby's, aided by the patience of Monsieur Laura, has finally seen the law changed to allow us to hold auctions in our own galleries, and Paris will undoubtedly become a regular venue for similarly impressive sales.

Paris was not the only focus for sales in Europe, with Sotheby's in Amsterdam, Milan and Zurich all selling works of diverse history and exceptional quality. Geneva and St Moritz sold some magnificent pieces of jewellery over the course of the year, some of which are pictured on pages 104–111. The successful book sales in Paris were complemented by those in London. The sale of books, manuscripts and photographs from the collection of Alice Liddell, the little girl who inspired the *Alice in Wonderland* stories was particularly fascinating (pages 20–1).

Looking back over these sales, we have a great sense of achievement and satisfaction. Sotheby's maintains a leading role in the art market through the reservoir of knowledge and skill provided by our expert departments. There is great anticipation regarding the opening of our state-of-the-art facility in Olympia, west London, giving the opportunity for more sales to be held both there and at our established site in New Bond Street. Sotheby's now has unparalleled facilities around the world that will enable us to continue to make the historical and high-profile sales that characterized the 2000–2001 auction season.

Painted in 1771, at the height of the artist's powers as a painter of conversation groups, portraits and royal commissions, Johann Zoffany's *The Dutton Family in the Drawing Room of Sherborne Park, Gloucestershire* sold in London for £3,523,500 ($4,968,135), a world auction record for the artist.

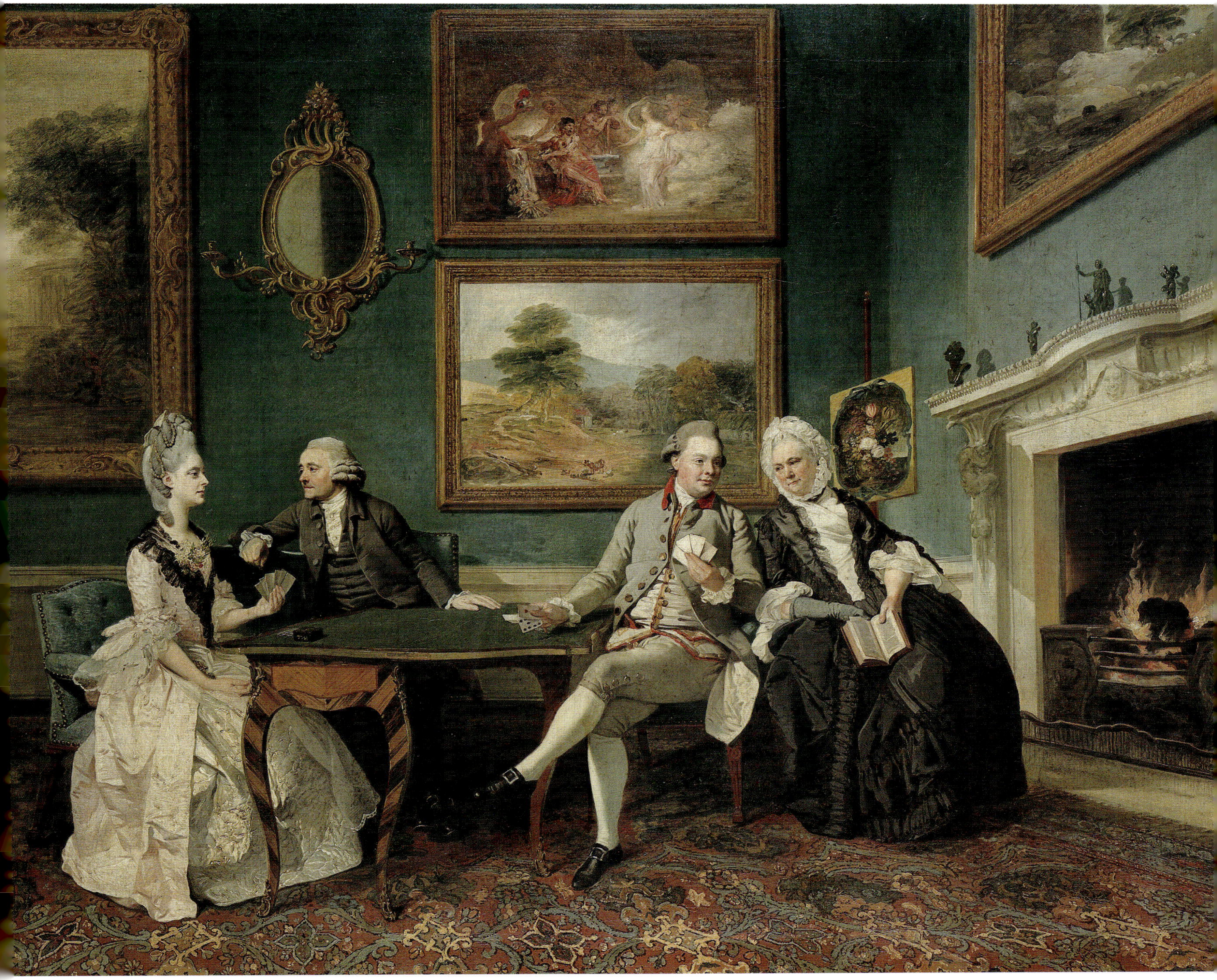

# Sotheby's Year in North America

Warren P. Weitman, Jr.

Raised bidding paddles in the main saleroom of Sotheby's headquarters are not an uncommon sight. Yet when all but one had lowered on 28th June, and the auctioneer brought his hammer down for the winning bid on the last lot, it signalled more than just the end of another sale in New York, it marked the end of the first auction year of the 21st century. Revisiting the successes of the 2000–2001 season not only reflects North America's continued strength in an expansive global art market, but Sotheby's continued leadership in the world of fine and decorative arts.

Long considered the barometer of the art market and the benchmark for an auction house's accomplishments, Impressionist, Modern and Contemporary Art sales in the past year delighted collectors and art enthusiasts alike. Anchored by a classic group of paintings and sculpture from the Estate of Ronne and Joseph Wohl, Sotheby's evening sale of Impressionist and Modern art in November brought a remarkable $123,055,000 (£86,379,239) – the third highest total for a various owners sale in a decade. While the auction's top seller was a rare and beautiful work by Edouard Manet entitled *Jeune fille dans un jardin*, shown on page 83, new world auction records were set for Henri Matisse, Aristide Maillol and Berthe Morisot. The following week, sales of Contemporary Art displayed similar strength with an offering that included Mark Rothko's striking *No. 2 (Blue, Red and Green)* featured on page 93. The same auction witnessed Alexander Calder's mighty stabile, *Stegosaurus* (page 90), lead a group of new artist records at auction that also included Brice Marden and Isamu Noguchi.

By spring, even stronger results were achieved in our May sales of Impressionist, Modern and Contemporary Art that realized an impressive $222.3 (£155.3) million, leading all other competitors in these fields. Without question, the season's triumph was the Collection of Stanley J. Seeger, a highly personal yet powerful group of works, which brought an extraordinary total of $54,020,500 (£37,762,050) (pages 22–3). Max Beckmann's important and powerful *Self-portrait with Horn* topped the regular sales of Impressionist and Modern art, and Jeff Koon's massive sculpture of *Michael Jackson and Bubbles* was one of the many highlights of the summer Contemporary Art sales achieving $5,615,750 (£3,931,025).

Other key sectors of the fine arts market also achieved strong results.

The refurbished New York headquarters of Sotheby's at 72nd Street and York Avenue provides museum-quality exhibition galleries and state-of-the-art auction facilities.

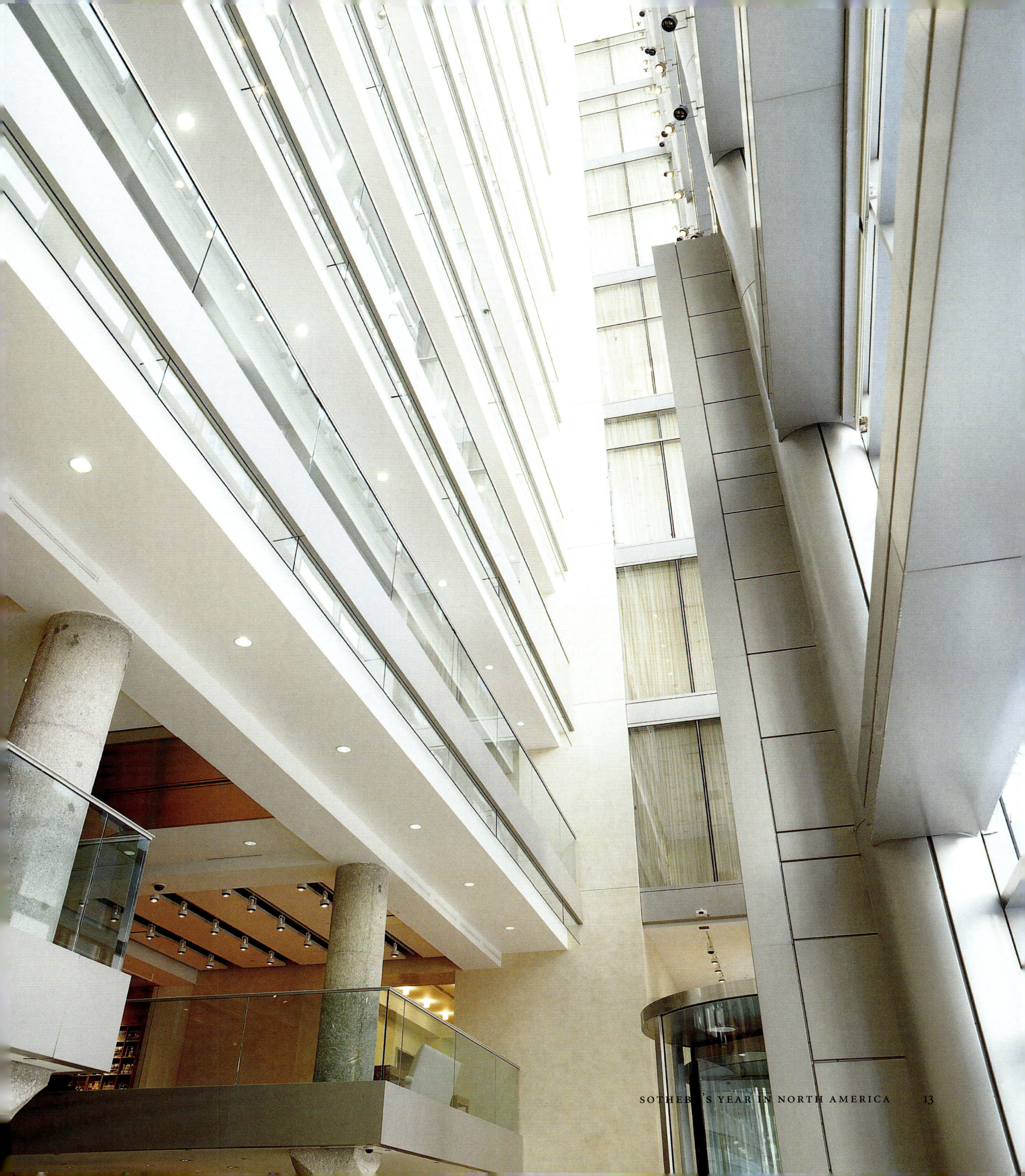

December's American Paintings sale brought a total of $41,162,250 (£28,860,473), highlighted by the record-breaking price of $2,975,750 (£2,083,025) paid for Thomas Moran's *Mount Moran, Teton Range* (page 71). In May, John Singer Sargent's *Rosina in Capri* took centre stage when it sold for $5,395,750 (£3,777,025) (page 70). Collectors of Latin American Art watched Rufino Tamayo's masterpiece *Sandias* – last seen at auction in 1978 – sell for $1,215,750 (£851,025) in the autumn (pages 78–9), and Frida Kahlo's *Portrait of Cristina, My Sister* bring $1,655,750 (£1,159,025) in the spring (page 76). The first important fine art auction of 2001, January's Old Master Paintings sale, totalled $32,320,475 (£21,652,358). The auction featured Hans Hoffman's *Hare in the Forest* (page 44), which was purchased by the J. Paul Getty Museum.

While this past auction year was distinguished by Sotheby's traditional calendar of fine arts sales, the world of decorative arts exhibited a dazzling assortment of precious objects and the richness of several extraordinary single-owner collections. The sale of Important Chinese Export Porcelain and Works of Art from the Collection of the Late Mildred and Rafi Y. Mottahedeh held in October soared to an outstanding $4,283,640 (£2,928,144), nearly double pre-auction high estimates. The next month, the Americana Library of Laird U. Park, Jr. was the first of two remarkable collections presented by the New York Book and Manuscript department. Following the $5,220,360 (£3,497,260) success of this wide-ranging collection of documents relating to all aspects of American history was January's sale of the Magnificent Scientific Library and Mineral Collection of Joseph A. Freilich, explained in greater detail on pages 38–9. That same month, the Americana Week showcased 11 lots of Colonial American silver consigned by the Church of the Presidents in Quincy, Massachusetts. Totalling an exceptional $3,027,875 (£2,028,455), the collection included the Richard and Alice Brackett Cup illustrated on page 116.

In March, it was Sotheby's privilege to feature *The Life and Art of Toulouse-Lautrec.* Totalling $3,170,400 (£2,194,595), the auction was the first in America devoted to the post-Impressionist artist. Formerly the Collection of Herbert Schimmel, the sale offered posters, prints, drawings, manuscripts and photographs including *Ambassadeurs* (right), one of four posters Lautrec created of his close friend Aristide Bruant.

The first week of April began with an exhibition and sale devoted to the Collection of Gianni Versace. This outstanding assemblage of fine art, furniture and fashions from the late designer and the subsequent three-day sale are explained in greater detail on pages 32–3. Later that month, Photographs from the Museum of Modern Art were featured in a record-breaking two-day auction that is described on pages 34–5.

Toulouse-Lautrec's *Ambassadeurs, Aristide Bruant* was part of the successful sale of property from the collection of Herbert Schimmel. This lithograph is a classic example of the artist's characteristic style. It sold in New York for $170,750 (£119,525).

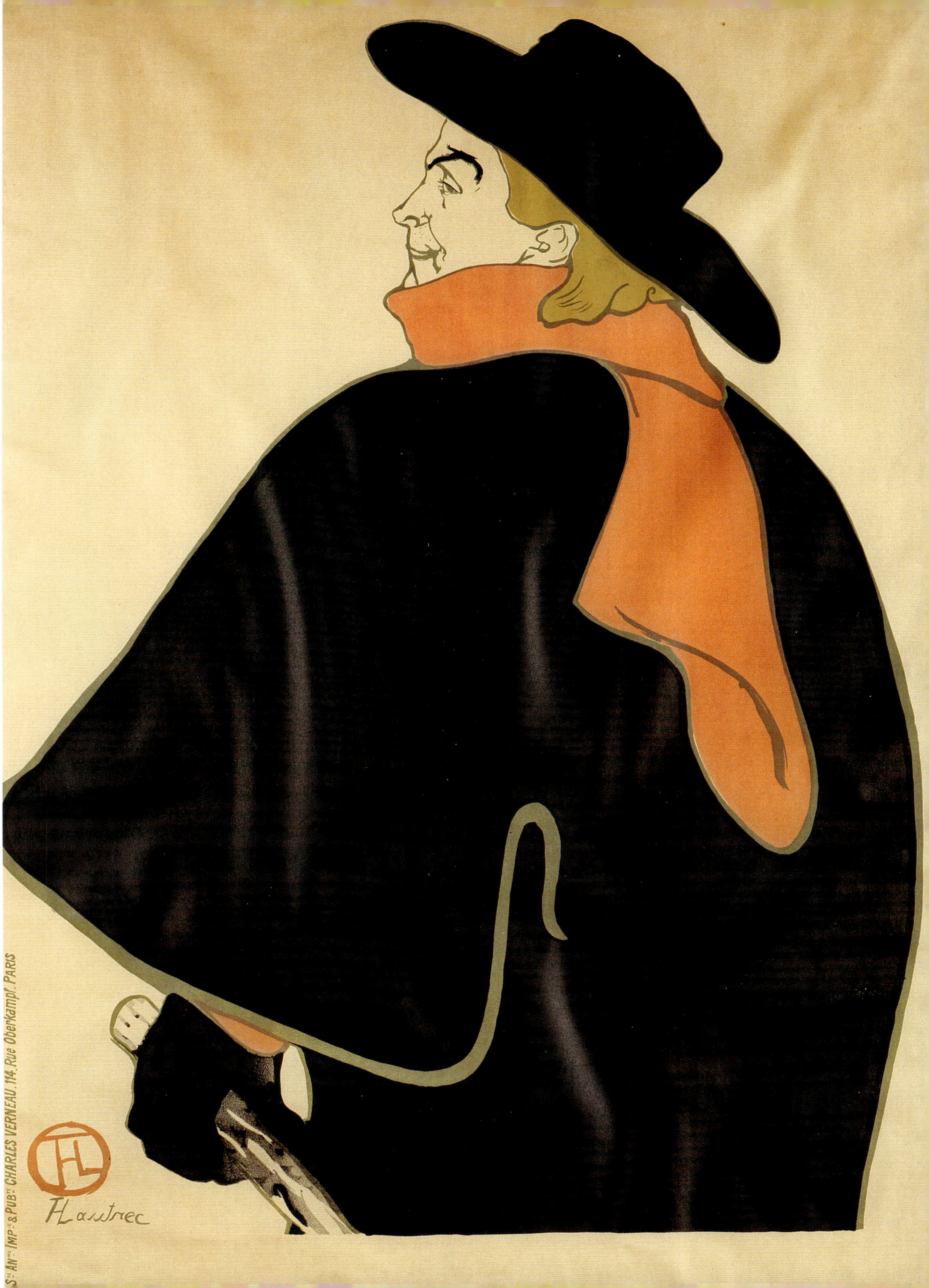
Ste Anme Impie & Pubté CHARLES VERNEAU. 114, Rue Oberkampf. PARIS
HLautrec

# Sotheby's Year in Asia

Henry Howard-Sneyd

This has been an exciting and eventful year for Sotheby's in Asia; the art market has flourished, resulting in record prices for objects and record sales results. Most notable of the individual sales was the Collection of Ming and Qing Porcelain from a Private Trust, sold in October. The 'star' of the show was undoubtedly the Jiajing period polychrome 'fish' jar, which repeated its 1992 feat of breaking the world record for any piece of Chinese porcelain at auction (page 42). Another world record was broken by a *falangcai* ('foreign colour') enamel-decorated glass vase, and a third for the gilt-bronze Buddha (right). In the same sale the Guo'An Collection of Snuff Bottles sold almost every lot for a total of HK$14.8 million ($1,924,000; £1,332,000).

The Chinese porcelain and works of art sale in April showed renewed interest in the great porcelains of the early Ming period, a group that has been neglected in recent years. A beautiful blue and white 'moonflask' from the Yongle period sold for HK$8,624,750, ($1,121,218; £776,228) and an extremely rare 'powder-blue' dice bowl reached HK$4,444,750 ($577,818; £400,028).

Classical and Modern Chinese paintings continue to attract interest. October saw an extraordinary opportunity to acquire works by Zhang Daqian, kept by his wife as among her favourites. In the same sale a record was set for the Ming artists Shi Lu (HK$2,354,750; $306,118; £228,128) and Xie Zhiliu (HK$1,034,750; $134,518; £93,128). Spring saw further exciting prices when a unique work, *Comic Entertainers At Lantern Festival*, by the previously unknown 13th-century artist Zhu Yu, sold for HK$7,524,750 ($978,218; £677,228).

In Singapore Sotheby's held successful sales in the growing field of South-East Asian paintings. The world record for Walter Spies was twice shattered; in September for *Desadurchblick* (S$889,550; $507,043; £346,924) and in March for *Rehlandschaft In Djembrana* (S$1,549,550; $867,748; £588,829).

Asia is rapidly becoming one of the most important markets for jewellery. Of particular appeal was a jadeite and diamond necklace, which sold for HK$6,534,750 ($849,518; £588,128) in October. This season was also exciting for the watch department. Top pieces sell for serious prices, as was shown by the 'world-time' piece in October that made HK$2,354,750 ($306,117; £211,927). The spring sales included an impressive single-owner collection strong in jewelled watches, with 10 lots exceeding the US$100,000 (£70,000) mark.

A world auction record was set when this enigmatically smiling gilt-bronze Buddha, sold in October for HK$8,624,750 ($1,121,218: £776,228).

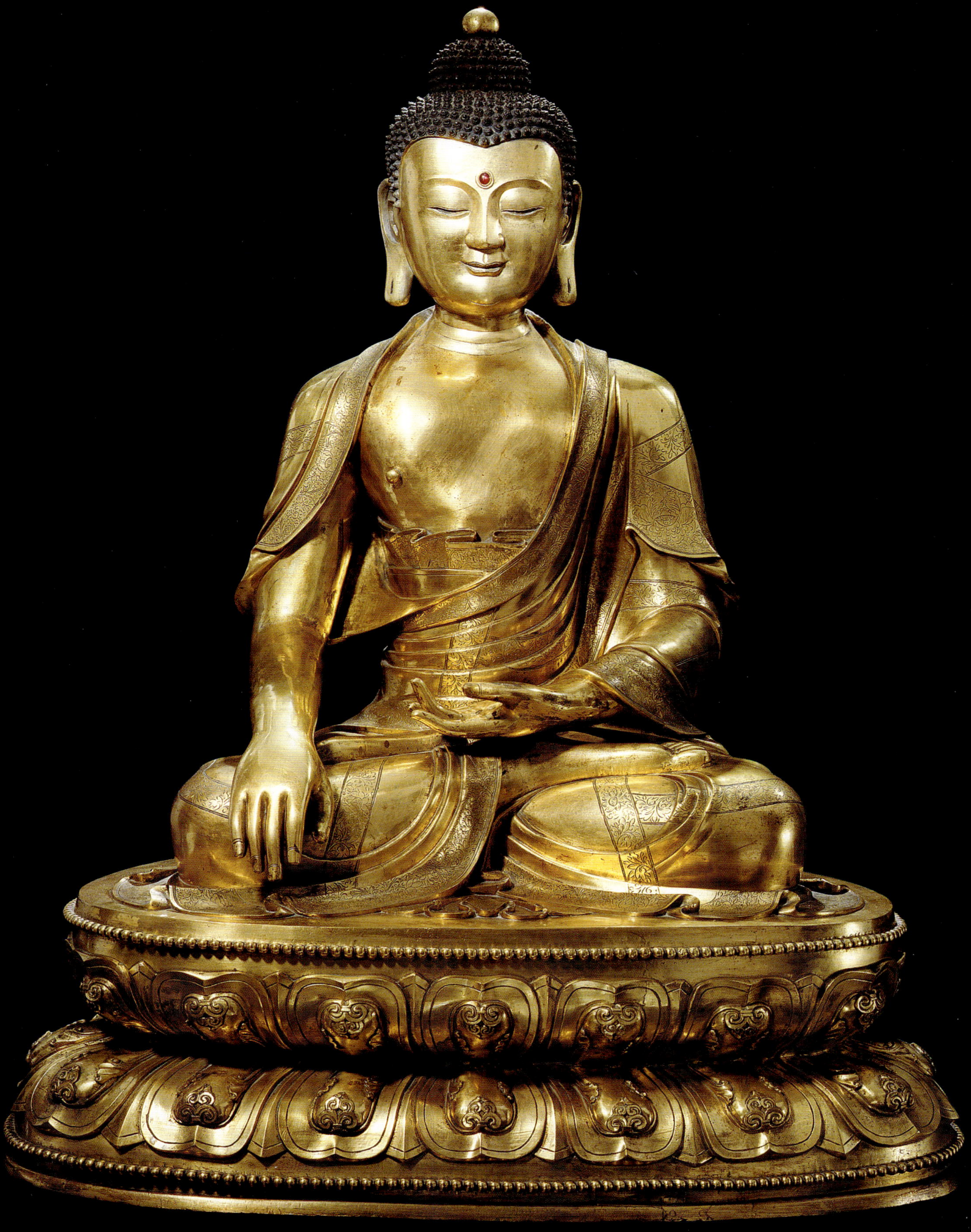

# Monet's *Meules, derniers rayons de soleil*

Richard
Aronowitz-Mercer

Over recent years Sotheby's summer season has brought with it a Monet masterpiece. The Impressionist and Modern Art evening sale on 26th June 2001 was no exception, with *Meules, derniers rayons de soleil* from 1890 achieving £10.1 ($14.2) million. Painted at the height of the artist's powers, the painting depicts two large *meules* or grainstacks with their peaked thatched 'roofs' typical of those found in Normandy. The slanting sunlight that suffuses the scene, filtering between the stacks and casting long shadows where they block its path, fills the composition with warmth, vitality and life.

The stacks upon which Monet lavished so much of his energy and vision between 1889 and 1891 were the stores for wheat and grain, and not for hay, as is the popular misconception. The notion of the stacks carrying the wealth of their owners finds a resonance in Monet's depiction of their surfaces and the volumetric play of their shapes: the stacks in *Meules, derniers rayons de soleil* are broad, full structures that suggest the great fertility and abundance of the Normandy landscape.

In choosing his subject, Monet continued a long tradition of depicting the French countryside seen in the paintings of such artists as Millet and those of the Barbizon school. However, Monet updates this tradition to striking effect: his grainstacks series contains virtually no anecdotal detail; no dogs or labourers, no figures walking through the fields or birds flying in the sky. The artist pares down his vision to focus solely on the grainstacks themselves, on the play of light or night on them, on the sky and the horizon.

The painting had never before appeared at auction, having been in the collection of only two French families since its purchase from the artist at the beginning of the 1890s. Furthermore, it had only ever been shown to the public twice, each time at the Durand-Ruel gallery in Paris during the 1890s, and it had remained hidden from public view throughout the 20th century. The opportunity to re-examine the painting confirmed spectacularly that in its elevation of the humble grainstack to a gentle icon of Impressionism it was one of the very greatest of the series remaining in private hands.

One of Claude Monet's 23 views of grainstacks, *Meules, derniers rayons de soleil* was unique in that it had not been seen in public since 1895. When it was exhibited in London in June it was also the first time it had ever left France.

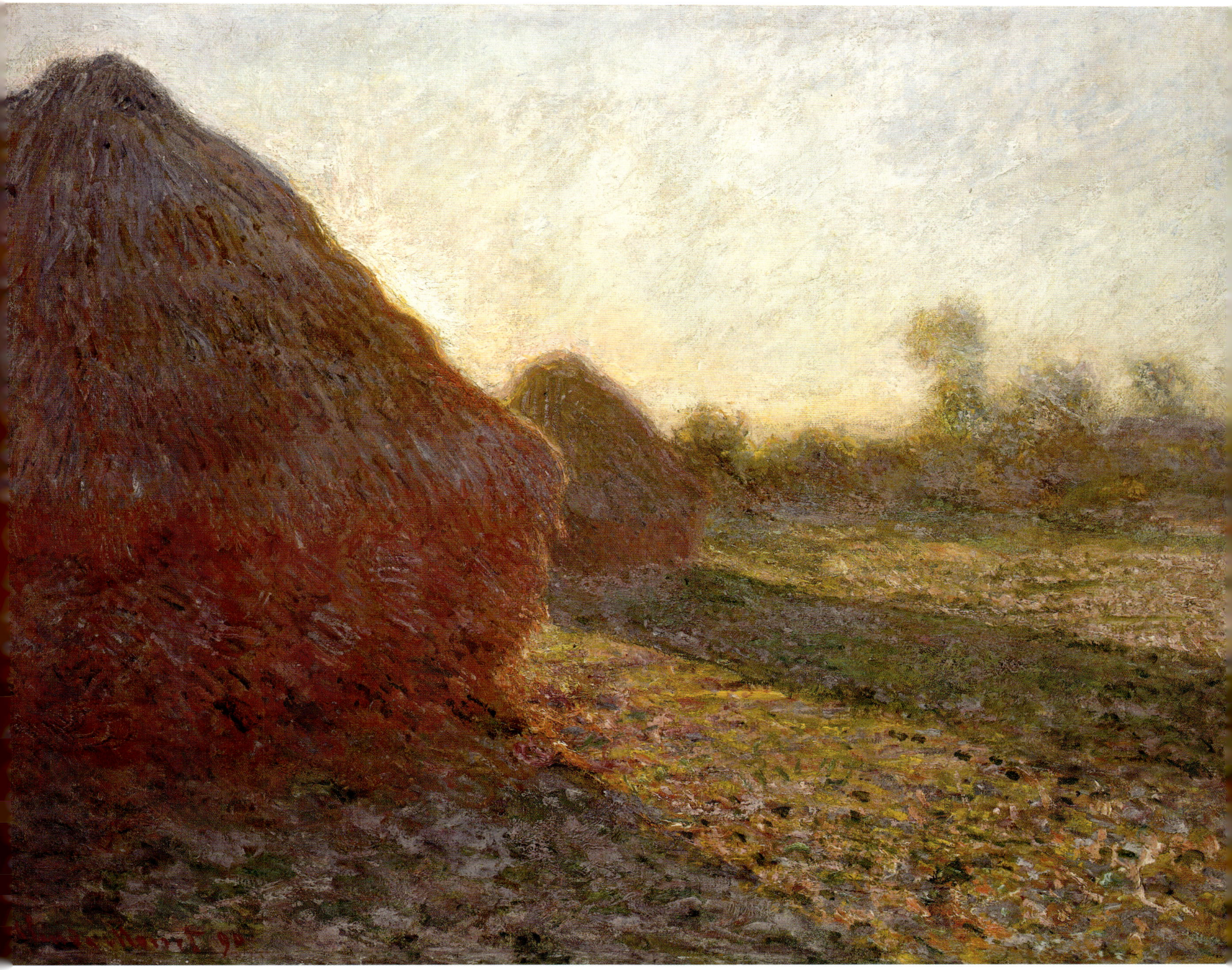

# Lewis Carroll's Alice

Catherine Porter

It was in September 2000 that Sotheby's was first approached by representatives of the Trustees of the Alice Settlement to look at some 'Alice in Wonderland' material at Christ Church, Oxford, that had belonged to Alice Liddell, for whom the stories were originally written. Some of these items had been loaned to Sotheby's for an exhibition in 1988, including the evocative albumen print of Alice Liddell as a beggar maid (opposite) and the extraordinary dedication copy of the 1886 facsimile edition of *Alice's Adventures Underground* (page 171).

The experts discovered a treasure trove of books, photographs, letters and personal effects, reinforcing the link between Lewis Carroll, known to his contemporaries as Charles Lutwidge Dodgson, and his muse, Alice, the young daughter of Henry Liddell, Dean of Christ Church. In the summer of 1862, on a memorable boat ride he told Alice the story of a young girl's adventures, which she insisted he write down, and in 1865 the tale was published as *Alice's Adventures in Wonderland*. All through the 1860s he photographed Alice and her sisters, but by the mid-1870s Lewis Carroll no longer featured prominently in their lives. In 1928 Alice decided to sell, through Sotheby's, the original manuscript of *Alice's Adventures Underground*, which became the most expensive modern literary manuscript to be sold at auction up to that time.

Alice, and her son Caryl Hargreaves, enthusiastically collected editions of the Alice stories. She signed many of these and after her death in 1934, Caryl added her signature, cut from her cheque stubs, to many others. At the time of Caryl's death in 1955 this collection comprised over 400 editions. The collection was bequeathed to Caryl's only child, his daughter Mary Jean, who eventually loaned it to Christ Church, where it was displayed until the Trustees engaged Sotheby's to handle the sale by auction.

The sale was a great success, with the majority of items finding homes all over the world, ranging from enthusiastic private collectors to institutions. A number of major items were purchased by an American private collector whose aim was to display them 'back where they belong' at Christ Church. Lewis Carroll's important album of photographs of his Oxford contemporaries and of Alice and her sisters, the dedication copy of *Alice's Adventures Underground*, and the coloured albumen print of Alice as a beggar maid will return for a while to their birthplace, surely a fitting repose for a wonderful, evocative collection.

Lewis Carroll's image of Alice Liddell dressed as 'The Beggar Maid' is not only a powerful memento of the relationship between Carroll and Alice but also, as with his other photographs, a pioneering work in what was then a painstaking art. It sold for £179,500 ($253,140), a record for a photograph by Carroll.

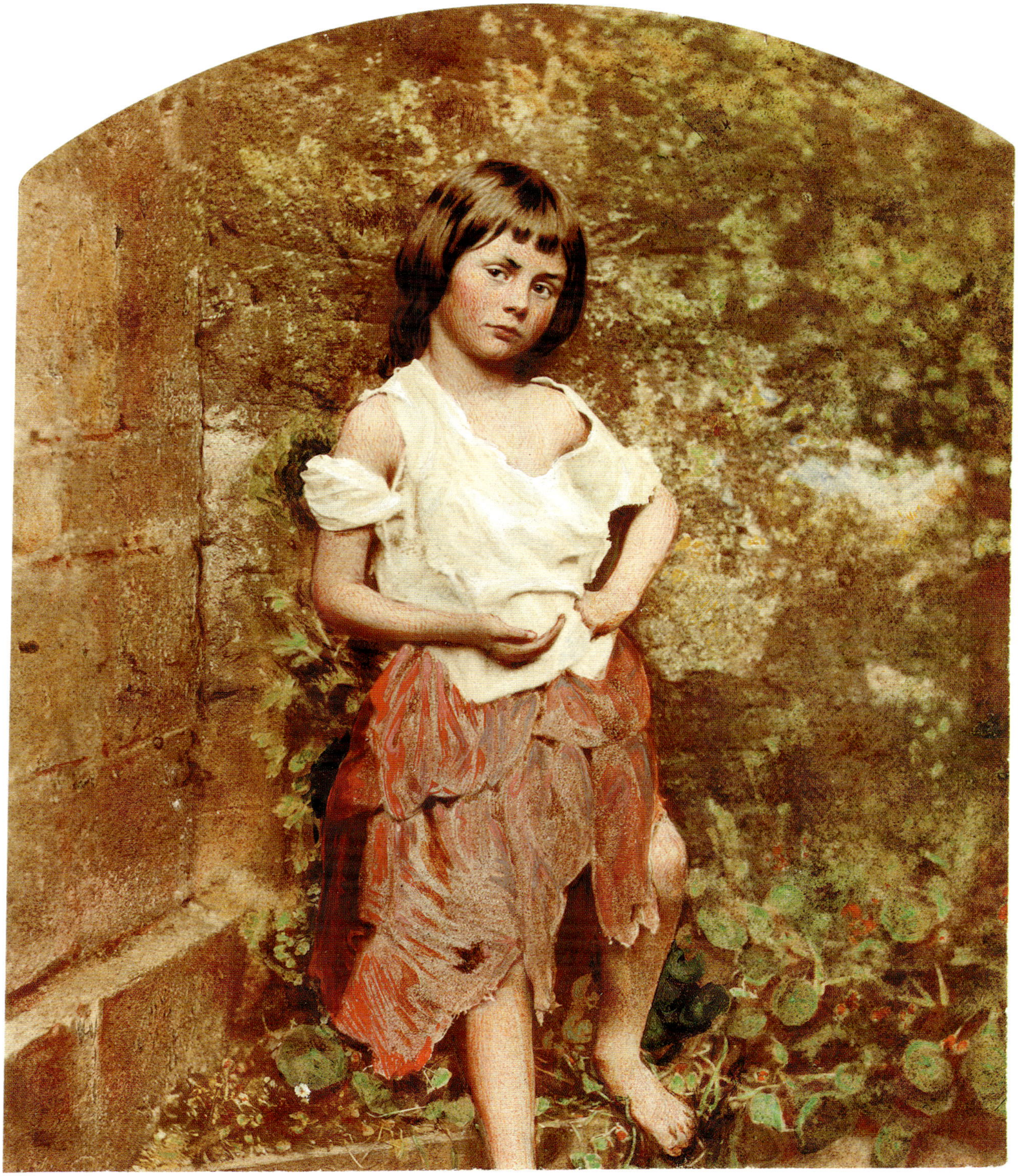

# The Eye of a Collector: Works from the Collection of Stanley J. Seeger

Tobias Meyer

A lover of beauty and human expression, Stanley J. Seeger began collecting art works while a student at Princeton University in the 1950s. His collection has been described as unusual, personal, tasteful and confident. Prior to the Sotheby's exhibitions in 2001, works from the Seeger collection had not been publicly shown since 1962. Mr Seeger trusted his own exceptional and instinctive sense of artistic strength and collected without surrendering to fluctuating markets and fashionable trends. Stanley Seeger collected what he believed in.

It was this same expression of trust and belief that allowed for the magnificent success of Sotheby's two-part single-owner sale. To quote the *Daily Telegraph* from 14th May, 'The quality was high, the estimates were modest, the buyers turned out in force and five records were broken in a £37 million triumph.' Having bought and sold through Sotheby's for many years, Stanley J. Seeger is an experienced participant in the auction market. He entrusted us with a free hand to offer works from his Modern and Contemporary Art collection in both New York and London, and this faith in our ability as a team of experts was the initial catalyst for the magic that unfolded in both salerooms.

The conservative estimates placed on this collection helped to inspire a number of veritable bidding wars, as prices for works by artists such as Francis Bacon, Max Beckmann, Joan Miró and Hans Hofmann were pushed to record levels. Joan Miró's *Nocturne* set a new record for the artist's works on paper at $5.6 million (£3.9 million). Max Beckmann's *Perseus'(Herkules') Letzte Aufgabe* also set a new record for the artist at $3.8 million (£2.7 million), broken the following night at Sotheby's Impressionist and Modern Art sale (see pages 24–5), and Hans Hofmann's *Towering Clouds* surpassed former highs to achieve a record for the artist at $797,750 (£558,425). In the London sale on 14th June, the Patrick Heron painting *Lux Eterna* soared past its pre-sale estimates of £25,000–35,000, before selling for £289,500 ($408,195).

The success of these sales was the product of a glorious and rare combination of beautiful objects along with the hard work afforded by a team effort. It has been both a great pleasure and an honour for Sotheby's to work with Stanley J. Seeger, an experience that I cherish as one of the highlights of my career.

Francis Bacon's triptych *Studies of the Human Body* is a powerful emotional work, addressing both his inner life and his obsession with Michelangelo: 'I am sure that I have been influenced by the fact that Michelangelo made the most voluptuous nudes in the plastic arts'. It set a world record for the artist at auction when it sold in New York for $8,585,750 (£6,010,025).

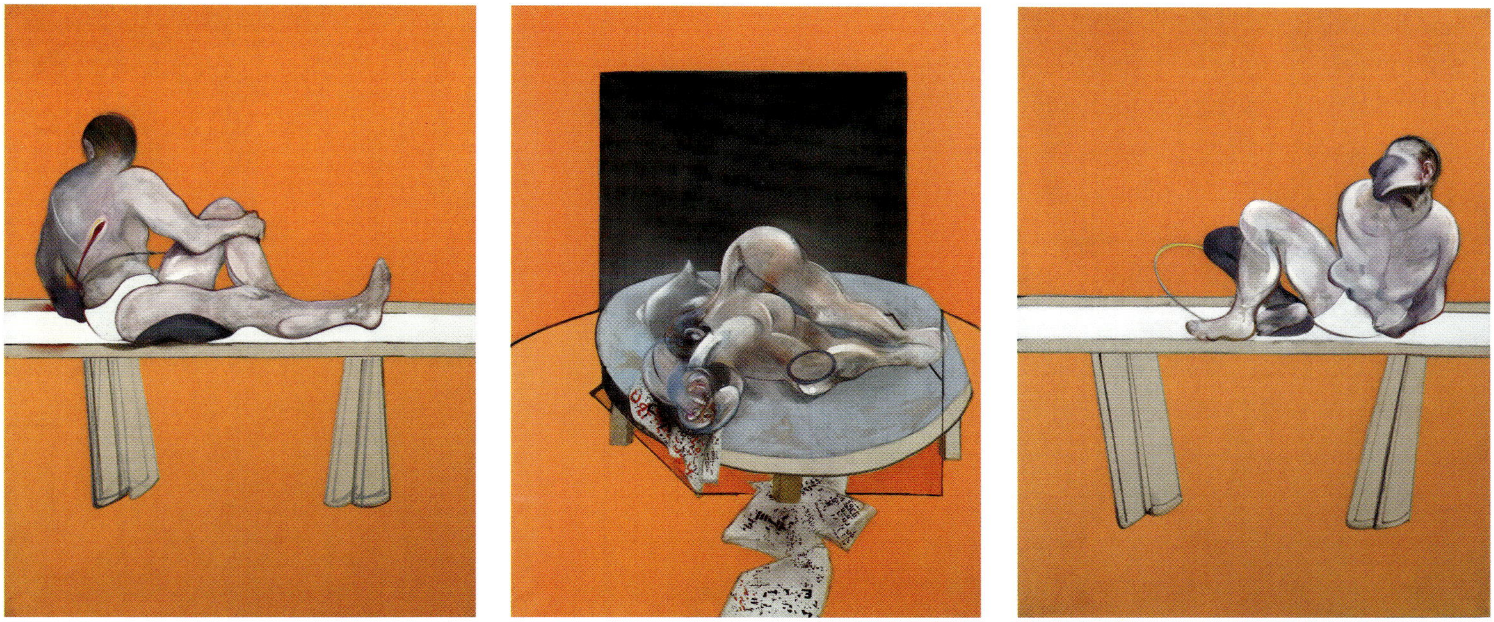

# Max Beckmann's *Self-portrait with Horn*

Stephane Cosman Connery

Painted in Amsterdam in 1938, while the artist was in exile from Nazi Germany, Max Beckmann's enigmatic, resonant and impenetrable *Self-portrait with Horn* became the most expensive German painting ever purchased at auction when it sold, after fierce bidding, for $22,555,750 (£15,789,025) on 10th May. Like Rembrandt, whom he greatly admired, Beckmann placed great importance on the self-portrait: of the 835 paintings he produced in his lifetime, 40 are self-portraits. Referring to *Self-portrait with Horn*, Robert Hughes writes of Beckmann's 'cannon-ball head'. This power is amplified by the slanting red bar to the right, which crops the pictorial space so dramatically.

While visiting Paris in 1938, Beckmann sold this painting to his great friend Stephan Lackner for FF1,665. Lackner owned *Self-portrait with Horn* for the rest of his life. Considering it his favourite among the 70 works by Beckmann in his collection, Lackner wrote most perceptively of the mood of the painting, which he owned for more than 50 years.

'In *Self-portrait with Horn*, a very lonely man stares out of the canvas. The painting is among the most melancholy, and perhaps the deepest, of Beckmann's many studies of his own persona. The man does not look at himself in the mirror, nor at the spectator before the canvas; his gaze follows the resonance of a horn call, which he has just sent out like a message. He seems to listen for a distant echo. But there is no response, only a great silence. Here is a man forsaken by his time. No furnishings, no amenities of civilization, just an empty frame remains behind him.'

The lives of Max Beckmann and Stephan Lackner were bound together by mutual admiration and boundless creativity. Having experienced the persecution of war-torn Europe, both men were steadfastly committed to artistic freedom and supported each other in their intellectual and artistic pursuits. Their friendship was founded upon a deeply rooted devotion to artistic individualism and Lackner's spectacular collection of Beckmann's masterpieces included *Portrait of Stephan Lackner*, a testament to the profound respect between the artist and the writer.

*Self-portrait with Horn* by Max Beckmann was purchased jointly by the Neue Galerie, New York and a private collector. It will now be on public display after remaining in private hands for over 60 years.

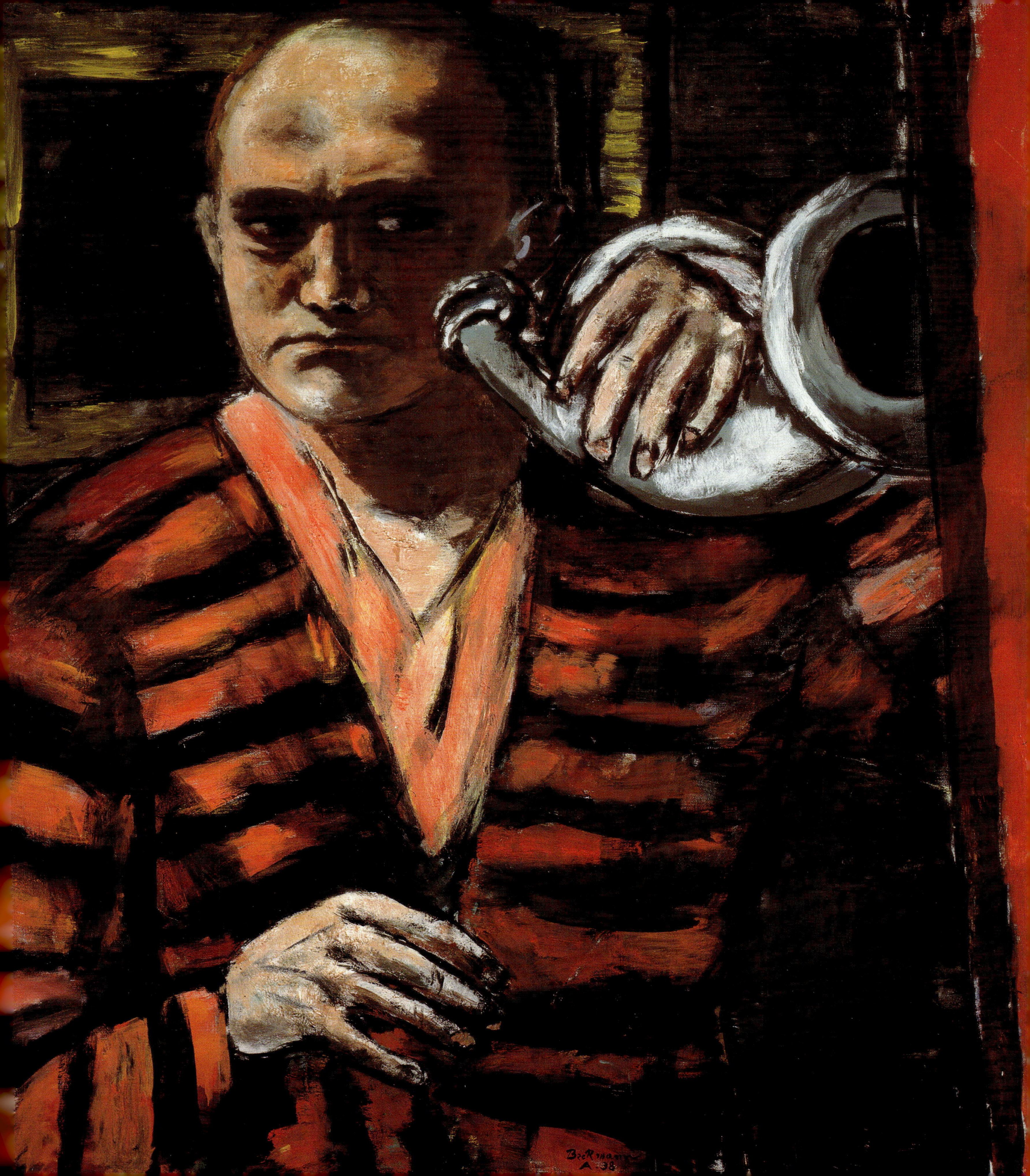

# The Year in Jewellery

Carlton C. Rochell, Jr.

For Sotheby's International Jewellery Division, 2000–2001 was an exciting and vibrant year. Among the many highlights of our European season was being entrusted with the sale in Geneva on 15th November of magnificent jewels from the Collection of H. H. Begum Sultan Mohamed Shah Aga Khan, the fourth and last wife of the late Aga Khan III. Each of the 19 pieces in the auction sold. With the makers including Bulgari, Harry Winston, Cartier, Chaumet and Sterlé, the majority of pieces achieved well over their pre-sale high estimates. As with other magnificent collections of jewellery sold by Sotheby's over the years – the Duchess of Windsor, Jacqueline Kennedy Onassis, Mrs Harry Winston and the Countess du Boisrouvray – the auction room was crowded with eager bidders, curious onlookers and a host of paparazzi.

Our London sales of antique jewellery were also outstanding, with a diamond bow brooch formerly among the French crown jewels selling for £1,433,500 – over 11 times its pre-sale low estimate. Commissioned by Napoleon III for the Empress Eugénie and created by the Parisian jeweller Kramer in 1855, the magnificent brooch was first sold at auction in Paris in 1887, purchased for Mrs William B. Astor.

A number of spectacular pieces of jewellery were sold at auction in Asia during this year, which is not surprising given the fact that Sotheby's is the only auction house to have continuously held sales of jewellery in Hong Kong since 1975. The largest Fancy Intense Purple-Pink diamond ring (page 109) and the largest strand of cultured pearls ever to be offered at auction brought HK$15,444,750 ($1,983,910; £1,235,580) and HK$5,324,750 ($683,980; £479,228) respectively. Magnificent jadeite jewellery also continues to attract a wide audience, as witnessed by the intense competition for the impressive jadeite and diamond necklace that brought HK3,344,750 ($429,365; £301,028).

The continued strength of our New York sales and the American market in general was demonstrated by the remarkable $4,405,750 (£3,039,967) paid for an extraordinary Fancy Vivid Blue, internally flawless, pear-shaped diamond weighing 11.23 carats – the highest price achieved worldwide in 2000 for a piece of jewellery by any auction house (page 104).

Selling in Geneva, this highly important diamond ring by Harry Winston, from the collection of H. H. Begum Sultan Mohamed Shah Aga Khan achieved the outstanding price of SF4,848,750 ($2,743,590).

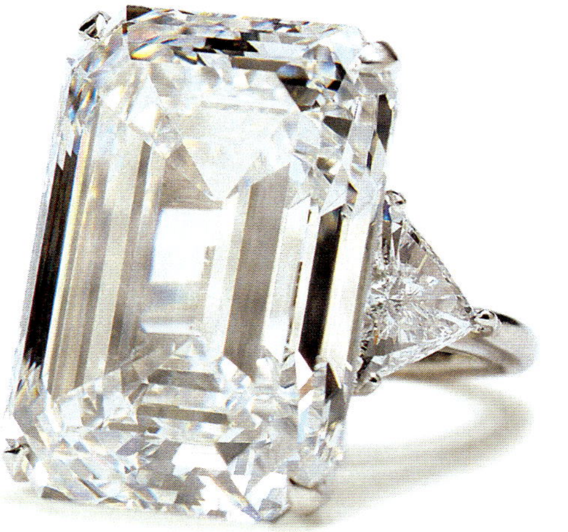

# Michelangelo's *Study of a Mourning Woman*

Gregory Rubinstein

'The discovery of a lifetime' is a greatly over-used phrase, but there is no other way to describe the finding of a very important and previously unknown drawing by Michelangelo. This powerfully drawn and profound *Study of a Mourning Woman* was discovered by my colleague Julien Stock during the course of a routine re-valuation of the contents of Castle Howard in Yorkshire. He was leafing through an album of drawings, which had come to light in the library, and as he neared the end of a long series of mediocre sketches and copies after the Old Masters, he suddenly came across it. He knew instantly what it was, but could hardly believe it. How could a major drawing by Michelangelo have been lying there, in one of England's greatest country houses, without anyone knowing about it? After lengthy research, however, Julien felt confident enough to present his discovery to the scholarly community, and his initial reaction to the drawing was vindicated. The leading experts in the field were unanimous in acclaiming the drawing as a major early work by the master, dating from *circa* 1495–1505, similar in style to the artist's earliest known drawings, in which he copied figures from masters such as Giotto and Masaccio, but providing an important link with his subsequent, independent creations.

The importance of this discovery cannot be overstated: in the past half century only a tiny handful of previously unknown drawings by Michelangelo have come to light, and as far as we know there are only three other significant works by the artist still in private hands. There is no record of how the drawing came to Castle Howard, but our research suggests that it was probably bought in 1747 when, as part of the famous collection of drawings belonging to Jonathan Richardson, Sr., it was auctioned in London. Richardson's collector's mark is visible in the bottom right-hand corner of the drawing.

As there was no satisfactory way to display or preserve the drawing at Castle Howard, the decision was made to sell it. After lengthy negotiations with the National Gallery of Scotland, who were extremely keen to buy the drawing but were ultimately unable to raise the necessary funds, it was offered for sale in London on 11th July, when it was sold for £5,943,500 ($8,392,222).

This previously unrecorded *Study of a Mourning Woman* by Michelangelo Buonarroti was discovered at Castle Howard, Yorkshire. It is shown here slightly smaller than its actual size of 26 by 16.4 cm. (10¼ by 6¾ in.).

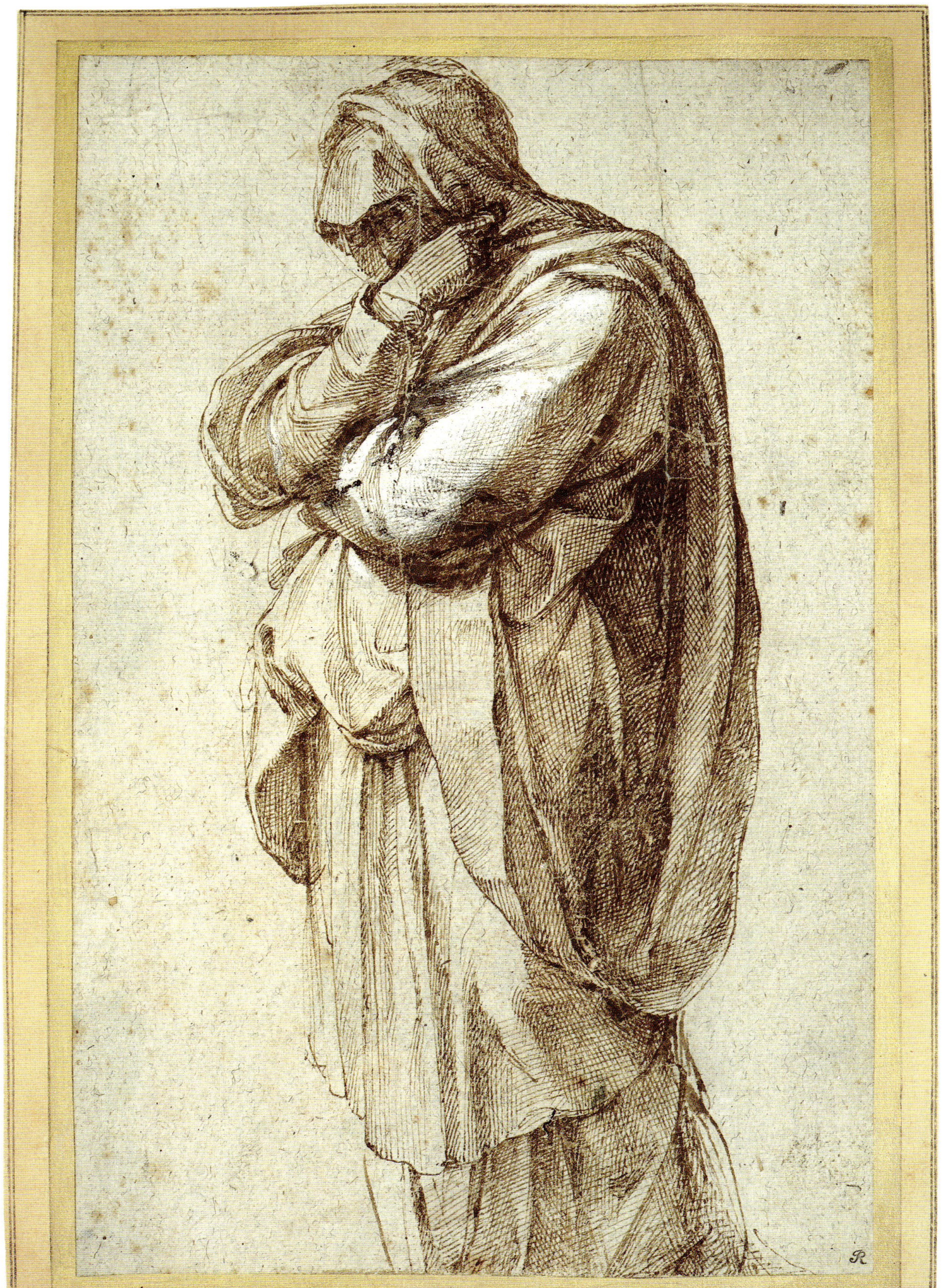

# Turner's *Heidelberg with a Rainbow*

Henry Wemyss

The British Sale in Bond Street in June witnessed a number of records, but none more spectacular than the price for Joseph Mallord William Turner's *Heidelberg with a Rainbow*, which sold for £2,038,500 ($2,874,285). This figure is nearly five times the previous record for a Turner watercolour, established at Sotheby's in March 1990 for Turner's *Hampton Court Palace*, and more than twice the record price for a British watercolour, again established at Sotheby's in 1996 for J. F. Lewis' *Lilium Auratum*.

Turner's *Heidelberg* was drawn in the early 1840s, when the artist was in his sixties. It captures the view from the north bank of the River Neckar looking towards the castle, the church of the Holy Ghost and the 18th-century bridge. In the foreground are women washing clothes, and students from the famous university smoking and talking. On the river itself are boats and two men watering their horses with their dog gambolling close by. One student standing by a slab of stone with a portfolio resting against it may, it has been suggested, be a representation of Raphael, corresponding to a similar figure in Turner's 1820 painting *Rome from the Vatican* in Tate Britain.

Turner drew this watercolour with the knowledge that an engraving would be made of it, which was duly executed by Thomas Abel Prior in 1846, one of the finest prints to be made from a Turner watercolour. The watercolour itself is based closely upon a 'colour beginning' in the Turner Bequest at Tate Britain, which is dated *March 10th 1841*.

Turner's *Heidelberg with a Rainbow* has had an exciting history on the auction block. Its first auction was 4th May 1872, when it was offered from the collection of the Birmingham steel magnate Joseph Gillott. It achieved the enormous price of £2,782.10s and was bought by the Earl of Dudley. It next appeared at auction in 1908, when the bidding started at 100 guineas and ended after a historic fight at £4,200, a record for a Turner watercolour, and it became one of the last purchases of Sir Donald Currie, the fabled ship owner. It was Sir Donald's descendants who offered it at Sotheby's in June, again re-writing the record books.

Turner's *Heidelberg with a Rainbow* has twice set the auction record for a watercolour by the artist, first in 1908 and again when, in 2001, it sold in London for nearly five times the previous record price for a Turner watercolour.

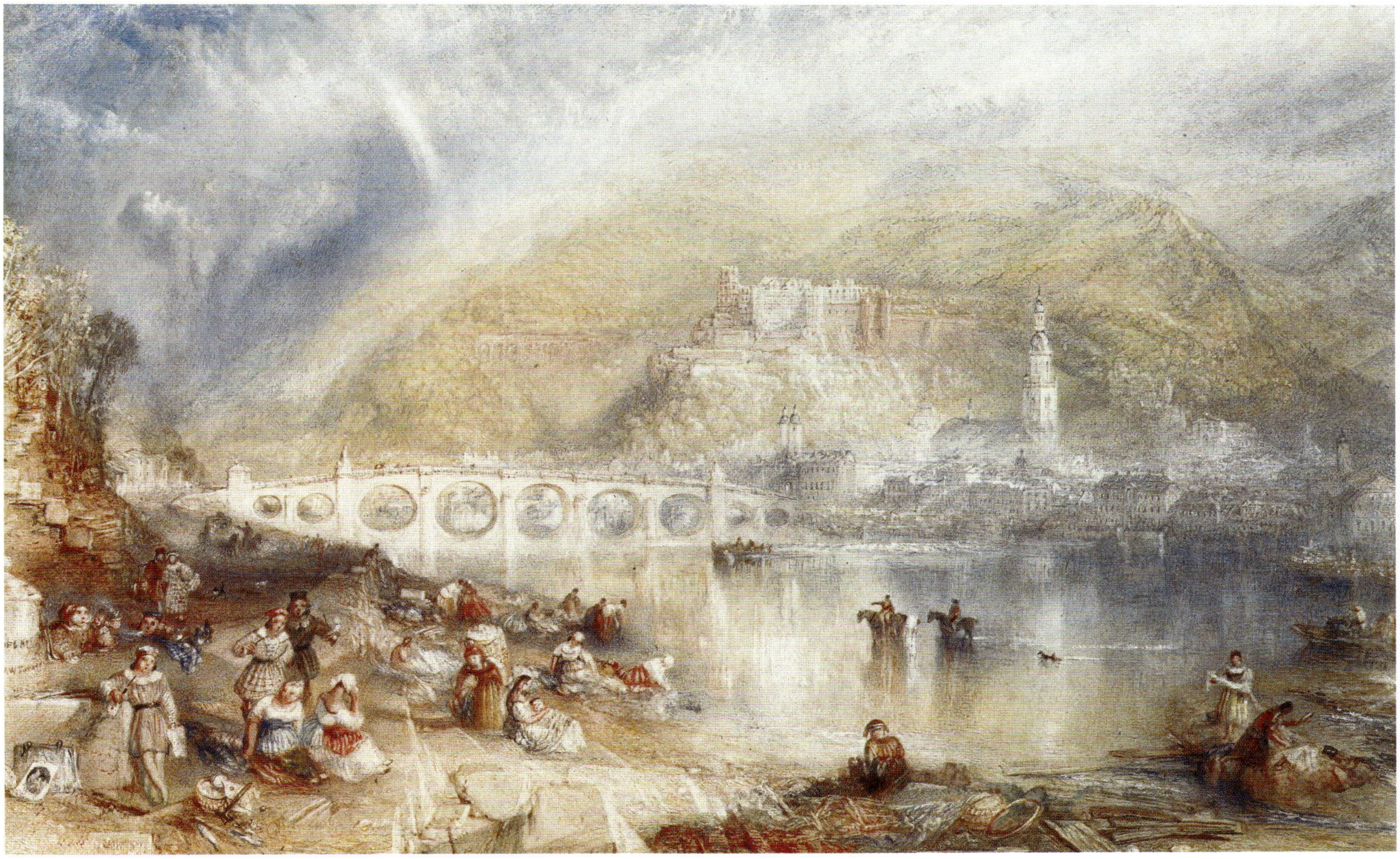

# The Collection of Gianni Versace

Phillips Hathaway

The world had certainly been aware of Gianni Versace's impact on the design community, but no one could ever have expected a residence graced with such scale and opulence. Each room in his Miami home, Casa Casuarina, opened on to a magnificent courtyard and was completely awash in colour from exotic murals, mosaic walls and floors to stained-glass windows that cast extraordinary patterns of light on every surface. Most surprising were the fantastic fabrics designed by Versace specifically for this residence. Their brilliant colours combined with whimsical subject matter exhibited his true genius. For the exhibition the Richard Gluckman-designed 10th-floor galleries at Sotheby's New York were transformed with spectacular colours inspired by Versace and enormous exotic palms banked with flowers.

On the evening of 5th April as the first session of the three-day auction began, Sotheby's main salesroom buzzed with a crowd of excited bidders and a multitude of press representatives. Over 600 people attended, with prices far exceeding their estimates. The first success of the evening was a superb Italian micromosaic from the 19th century by Francesco de Poletti (1779–1854), depicting *The Shield of Achilles*. There was spirited bidding both in the salesroom and on the telephone until it finally stopped at $154,250 (£107,250), against estimates of $20,000–30,000. This set the tone for the rest of Versace's extraordinary collection of over 30 micromosaics.

Gianni Versace's superb taste in 19th-century paintings was illustrated by Sophie Rude's (1797–1867) *The Death of Cenchirias, Son of Neptune*, which set a world record for the artist at auction and Antoine Dubost's (1769–1825) *Le Retour d' Hélène*, which also achieved a record price for the artist at $236,750 (£164,610). Another highlight of the evening session was a wonderful Charles X hardstone-mounted ormolu console from the dining-room at Casa Casuarina, that realized $192,750 (£134,020), and an exceptional set of six directoire mahogany *bergères à la reine*, *circa* 1800, from the drawing-room at Villa la Fontanelle. Interestingly Georges Jacob and Jean-Baptiste Sené, two craftsmen who were frequently in competition with one another, both signed these rare chairs. The celebrated chair-makers were, however, known to collaborate on commissions for the *Garde-Meuble* as well the *Menus-Plaisirs* for the Chateaux Versailles, Petit-Trianon, Fontainebleau, Saint Cloud and Rambouillet. Sold in pairs, the six chairs eventually realized a total $243,750 (£170,625).

The sale of the Collection of Gianni Versace, at Sotheby's New York, included the contents of his Miami residence, Casa Casuarina as well as selected pieces from his beautiful Villa on Lake Como, La Fontanelle, and his Renzo Mongiardino designed apartment in Milan. The auction totalled $10,177,340 (£7,093,605), against pre-sale estimates of $5,000,000–8,000,000.

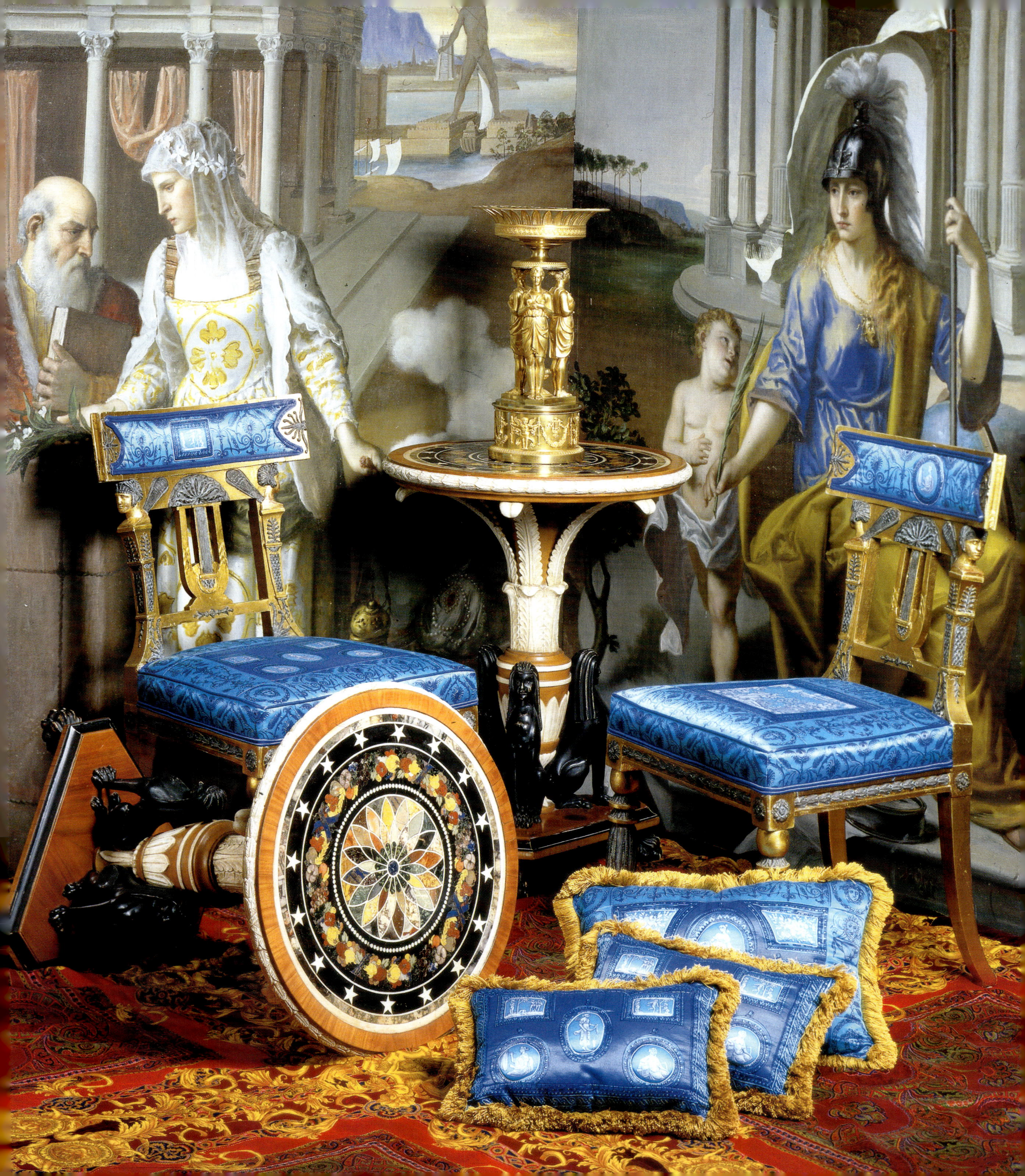

# Photographs from The Museum of Modern Art

Denise Bethel

The Museum of Modern Art, New York, was the first museum in America to establish a curatorial department devoted to photography as an art and, in April, Sotheby's auctioned a select group of photographs from this renowned collection, setting a new record for a single-owner sale of photographs in the United States. Proceeds from this $4,015,230 (£2,801,827) auction will be used by the Museum for photography acquisitions. High prices were realized for many artists whose careers were entwined with the Museum, an institution whose early entry into the world of photographs, in the 1930s, gave it outstanding collecting opportunities. Indeed, the April sale offered duplicates of photographs that in some cases are known to exist in quantities of only five or fewer.

One of the newest categories in the fine-art auction market, photographs have too often been characterized by an honest, if regrettable, lack of the kind of information that collectors of paintings, prints or sculpture have come to expect. The photographs sold by The Museum of Modern Art had, in almost every case, detailed provenance, exhibition and publication history, which, along with the Museum's imprimatur, boosted prices even for images that appear at auction on a regular basis. Especially important, and fascinating, were the Museum's ties to the photographers themselves, or the photographers' early patrons. The Man Ray photographs offered came to the Museum from James Thrall Soby, a prominent Museum board member who knew Man Ray and sponsored one of the earliest exhibitions of his work. The Imogen Cunninghams came to the Museum from Albert Bender, a West Coast supporter of both writers and artists. Many of the Edward Steichens were donated to the Museum by Steichen, himself a one-time director of the Museum's Department of Photography. Berenice Abbott's classic image *New York at Night*, which set a record for the artist at auction at $69,750 (£48,128), was acquired directly from her.

The highest price in the sale was achieved for a vintage print of *Penny Picture Display, Savannah*, 1936 (right), by Walker Evans, which was purchased from the artist in 1963 and exhibited several times in subsequent Museum shows. Not a landscape, not a portrait, neither nude or still-life study, the *Penny Picture Display* is a photograph about photography, its presence and its power. Like other images in the Walker Evans *American Photographs* series, the seemingly documentary nature of this work, carefully crafted by the photographer, signalled a new direction for American photography in the 20th century.

*Penny Picture Display, Savannah* by Walker Evans sold for $181,750 (£125,408), more than doubling the previous record at auction for a photographer whose talents were recognized and promoted early on by the Museum.

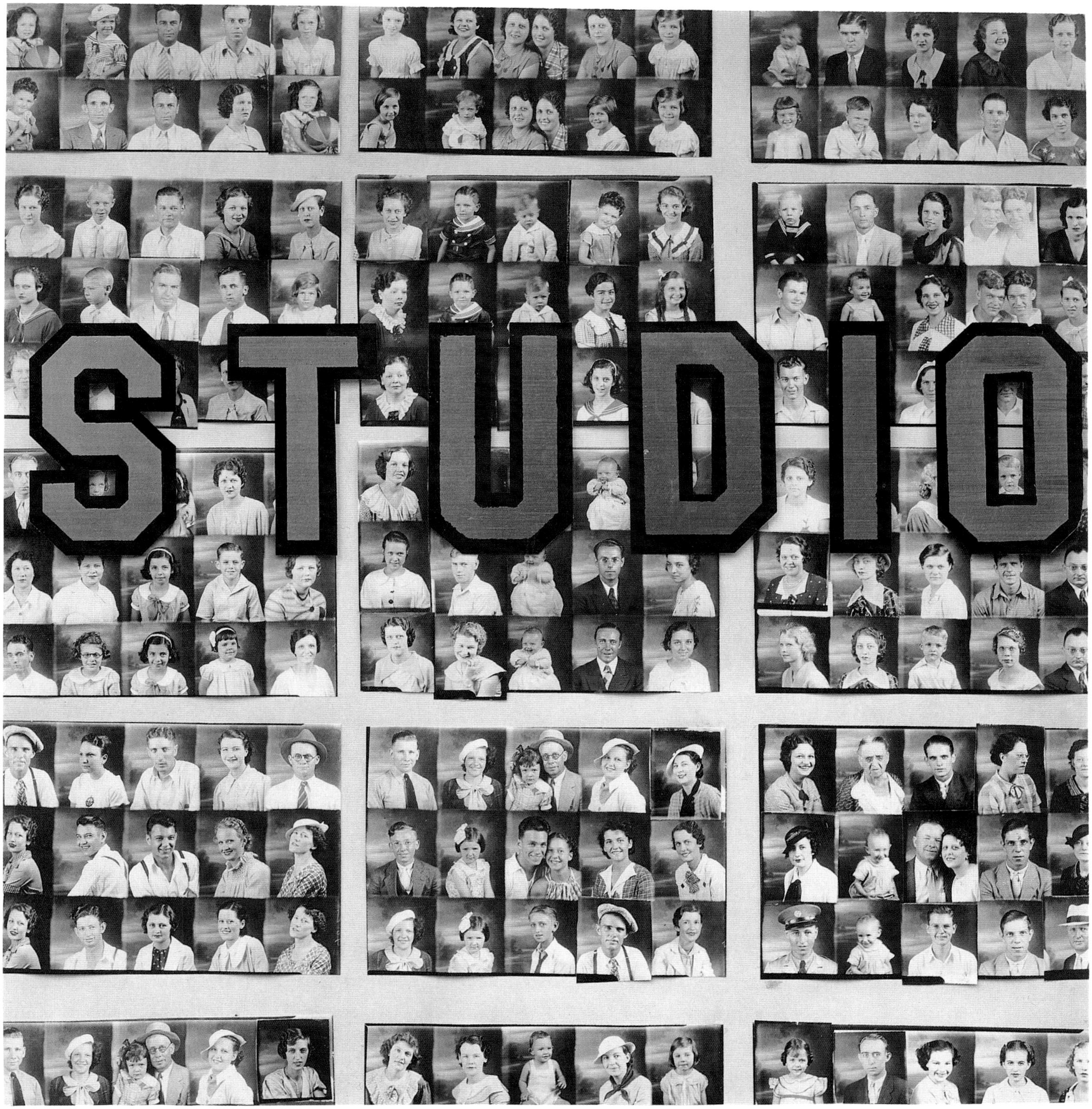
STUDIO

# The Leverhulme Collection

James Miller

For one glorious week in June the building and grounds of Thornton Manor on Merseyside buzzed with the excitement of a record-breaking English country house sale. The house was home to the industrialist and voracious art collector William Hesketh Lever, 1st Viscount Leverhulme (1851–1925), and its contents were sold following the death of the 3rd and final Viscount Leverhulme last year. During the four days of public viewing over 10,000 people thronged the property, and throughout the three-day sale the packed marquee witnessed sales totalling £9.6 million ($13.5 million).

In 1873, at the age of 22, the 1st Viscount Leverhulme founded Lever Brothers, and set about its rapid and multinational expansion. As a new centre for the company's operations he built Port Sunlight, near Thornton Manor, where he established both his factory and an airy model village to house his employees. Leverhulme was a man of astonishing vigour who slept upon a glass-covered, open-air platform and rose at 4.30 am to devote his energies to running his business empire, his philanthropic activities and art buying. From 1910 until his death in 1925, his purchasing of art, porcelain and furniture exceeded that of any museum in Britain. Thornton Manor became the sole family home, and repository of his private collection, after Leverhulme's death.

The sale at Thornton Manor reflected all of Leverhulme's diverse interests and the quality of the objects resulted in some outstanding prices. Symbolizing his love of fine English furniture, the oldest item in the sale also achieved the highest price: the James I walnut and inlaid chest, 1604 (page 140) sold for £350,000 ($493,500), creating a new auction record for 17th-century inlaid English furniture. On the second day Leverhulme's extensive collection of fine art produced some of the most exciting moments in the sale: the exceptional *Portrait of a Boy* by Dutch master Nicolaes Maes (1634–93) sold for £333,500 ($470,235) against a high estimate of £80,000 ($112,800). Frederick Walker's *The Wayfarers* achieved £91,500 and an oil study for *Flaming June* by Frederic, Lord Leighton, one of Leverhulme's favourite artists, was sold for £104,700 ($147,627) to dealers Hazlitt, Gooden and Fox, from whom Leverhulme bought it in 1916 for just over £25.

The excitement and success of this sale, and the enjoyment of the thousands who attended the viewing, were a testament to the zeal and energy of Lord Leverhulme, who leaves Port Sunlight, the Leverhulme Trust and the Lady Lever Art Gallery as an inspirational legacy.

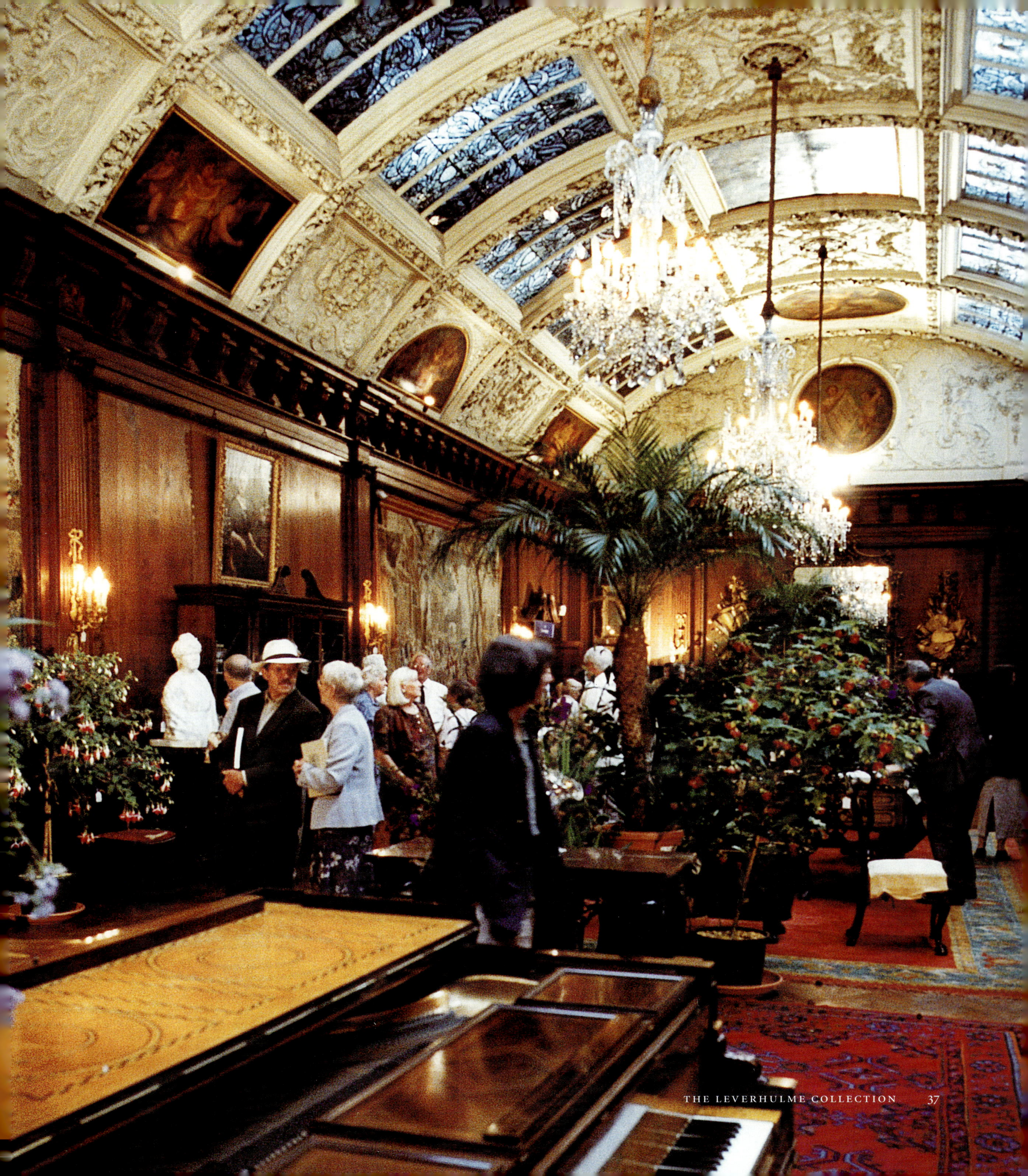

# The Scientific Library and Mineral Collection of Joseph A. Freilich

Selby Kiffer and
Justin Caldwell

The sales of Joseph A. Freilich's combined collections of rare books and important minerals contradicted one of the cardinal tenets of auction wisdom, but firmly upheld an even more important principle of collecting. Despite the relatively recent period during which the mineral cabinet and library were formed (no longer than a decade in either instance), both collections, particularly the books and manuscripts, were greeted with enthusiastic bidding. The basis for this reception was the high standard of condition that Mr Freilich maintained during his period of collecting.

While the library eclipsed the mineral specimens in size and significance, minerals were Mr Freilich's first passion. Constituting 550 museum-quality specimens, one of the most significant private cabinets of the entire 20th century, it was hard to believe that these minerals were neither cut nor polished, but remained exactly as they were naturally formed in the earth 10 to 20 million years ago.

The auction was handled by the Books and Manuscripts department in New York, whose reputation for versatility has been established with auctions of Russian space history and the *Tyrannosaurus rex* fossil, Sue. The Freilich mineral sale was another venture into uncharted territory, but the reputation of the Freilich collection ensured that mineral collectors, museums and dealers from around the world attended the sale. The great majority of the lots found buyers, and the total for the auction was more than $2.5 (£1.6) million.

The Freilich Library must be ranked as one of the great achievements in post-war American book collecting: a collection illustrating Western achievements in science and technology, natural history, cartography, medicine and a host of other subjects. Scanning the authors represented in the auction was akin to flipping through the *Dictionary of Scientific Biography*: among the innovators and inventors represented were Aristotle, Agricola, Linnaeus, Euclid, Locke, Curie, Erker, Descartes, Diderot, Kepler, Einstein, Lavoisier, Maxwell, Thomson, Pasteur, Buffon, Sowerby, Rutherford and Albertus Magnus.

The sale achieved an extraordinary $10,650,000 (£7,160,386), with three books selling for more than $500,000 (£330,000): the first edition of the works of Aristotle in Greek; a resplendent hand-coloured copy of *Locupletissimi rerum naturalium thesauri*, the catalogue of the natural history cabinet of Albertus Seba; and a wonderfully preserved first edition of Euclid's *Elementa in artem geometriae*, the first substantial mathematical work to be printed.

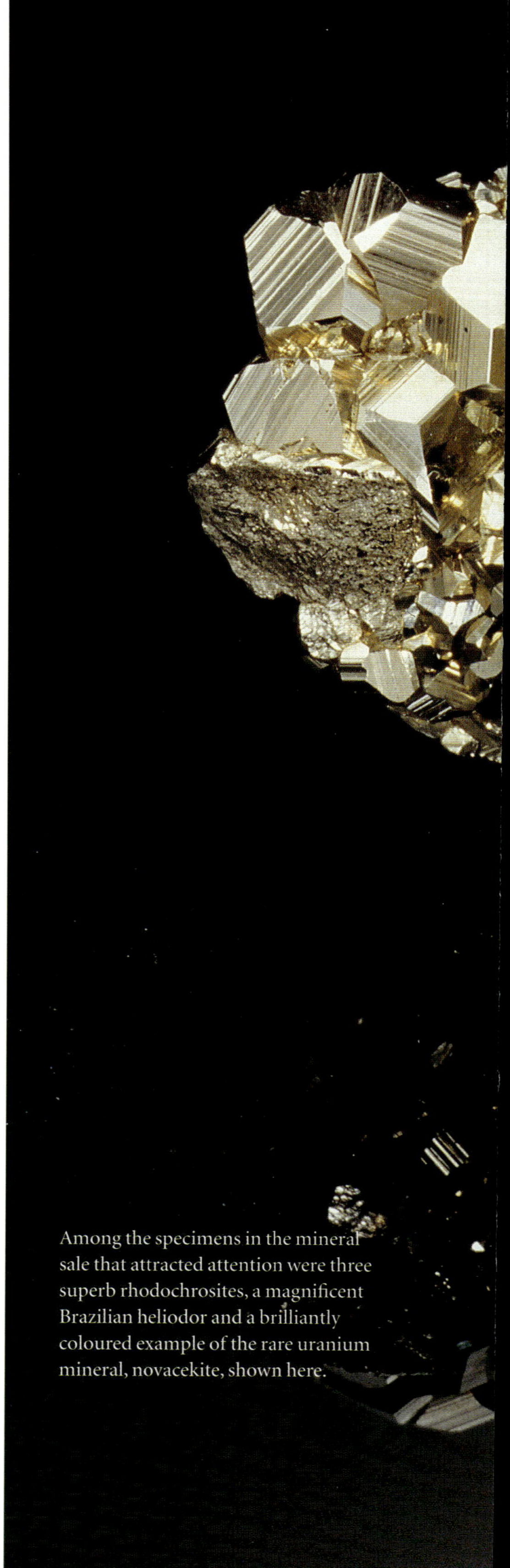

Among the specimens in the mineral sale that attracted attention were three superb rhodochrosites, a magnificent Brazilian heliodor and a brilliantly coloured example of the rare uranium mineral, novacekite, shown here.

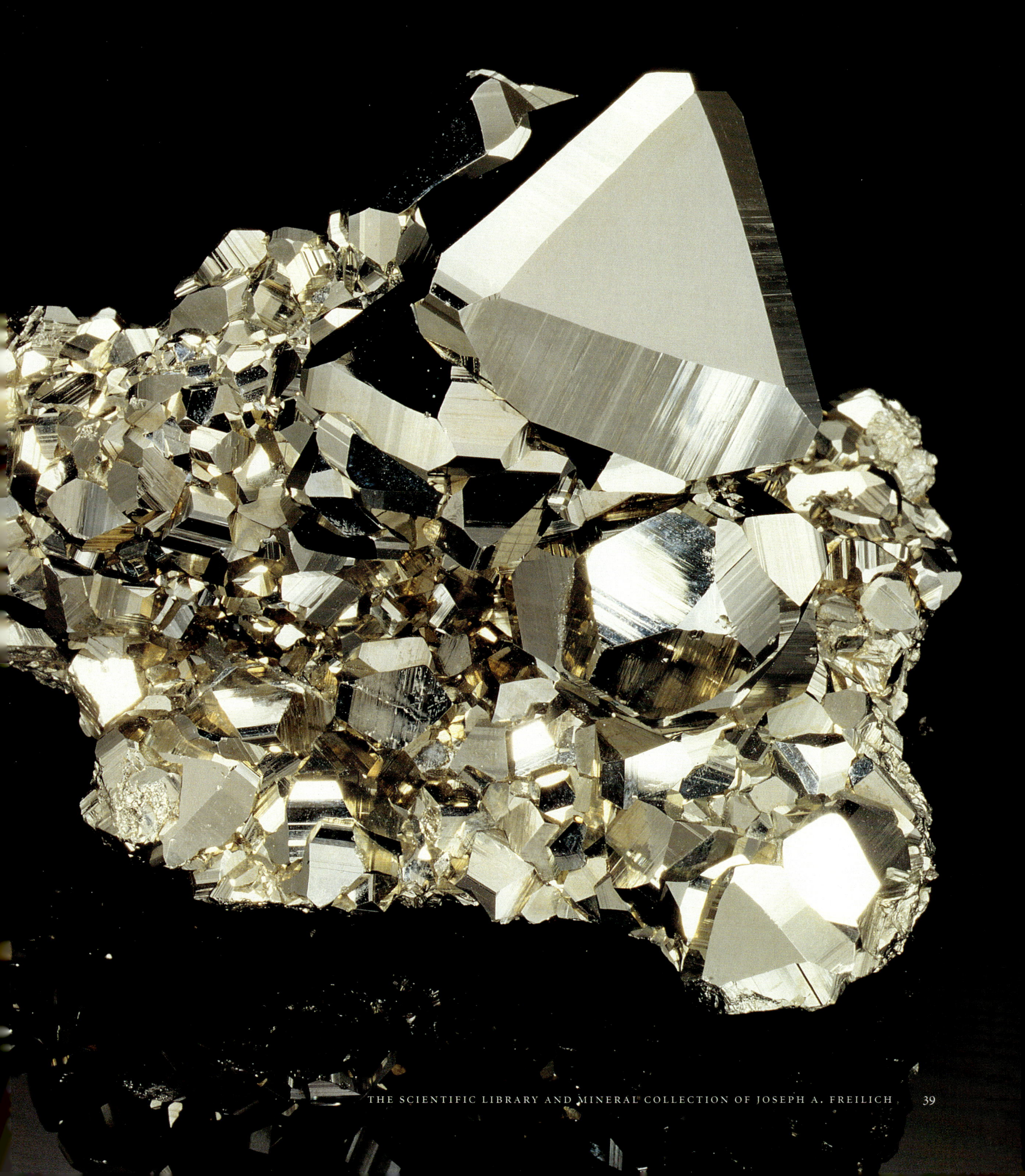

# The Year at Sotheby's Paris

Jean-Baptiste de Proyart

At the end of the auction season last summer Sotheby's France, in alliance with French auctioneers Poulain Le Fur, undertook the sale of two great collections: the 18th-century furniture and works of art of Luigi Anton Laura and the library of French books and manuscripts of Charles Hayoit. The success of the sales and the prices attained – the Laura Collection sold for FF64,143,230 ($8,455,585; £5,971,734) and the Library of Charles Hayoit, achieved FF26,245,000 ($3,408,572; £2,400,892) – in no way distracts from the beauty and quality of the objects.

There are three pieces from these sales that I regret not owning: the first was a *secrétaire à abbattant*, commissioned by the Duke of Choiseul, foreign secretary to Louis XV, which sold for FF4,142,000 ($546,010; £385,620). It was made by the *ébéniste* Jean-François Oeben and his brother in law, Roger Vandercruse, between 1761 and 1765, at a time when the Louis XV style was still popular. One of the first of its kind to be made in the Neoclassical style, it was inspired by the recent archaeological discoveries in Pompeii and Herculaneum. The second piece that caught my attention, a pair of gilt-bronze, mounted Sèvres *bleu nouveau* candelabra, *circa* 1770 by Dulac (one shown right), was also from the Laura Collection and exemplifies his attention to style and detail. The candelabra have a most prestigious provenance – first found in the Stroganoff Palace in St Petersburg, they only reappeared in 1931 during the Berlin sales of aristocratic property confiscated by the Soviets.

The sale of the Library of Charles Hayoit, which included the third outstanding item, was an equally stunning event. Book collecting is a sophisticated and discrete art in which the French excel and few were disappointed by this virtually unseen collection, Hayoit being one of the most private of 20th-century collectors. *Novembre,* one of only four Gustave Flaubert manuscripts still in private hands, took no more than five minutes to reach FF3,488,000 ($450,010; £319,082). This early work by one of France's greatest authors is the autobiographical, if slightly romanticized, account of his first experiences of love. It is covered in annotations, illustrating the phenomenal care and talent of the young Flaubert.

To witness the understanding and appreciation with which these two collections were assembled offers an insight into the importance of provenance and the eye for quality that connoisseurs of art must possess. That these sales took place in Paris was a great achievement and, undoubtedly, in 2002 Sotheby's France will continue to entice great collectors to experience the delights of French art.

This pair of Sèvres blue tripartite candelabra (one shown) from the collection of Mr and Mrs Luigi Anton Laura sold for FF6,867,000 ($905,230; £639,317).

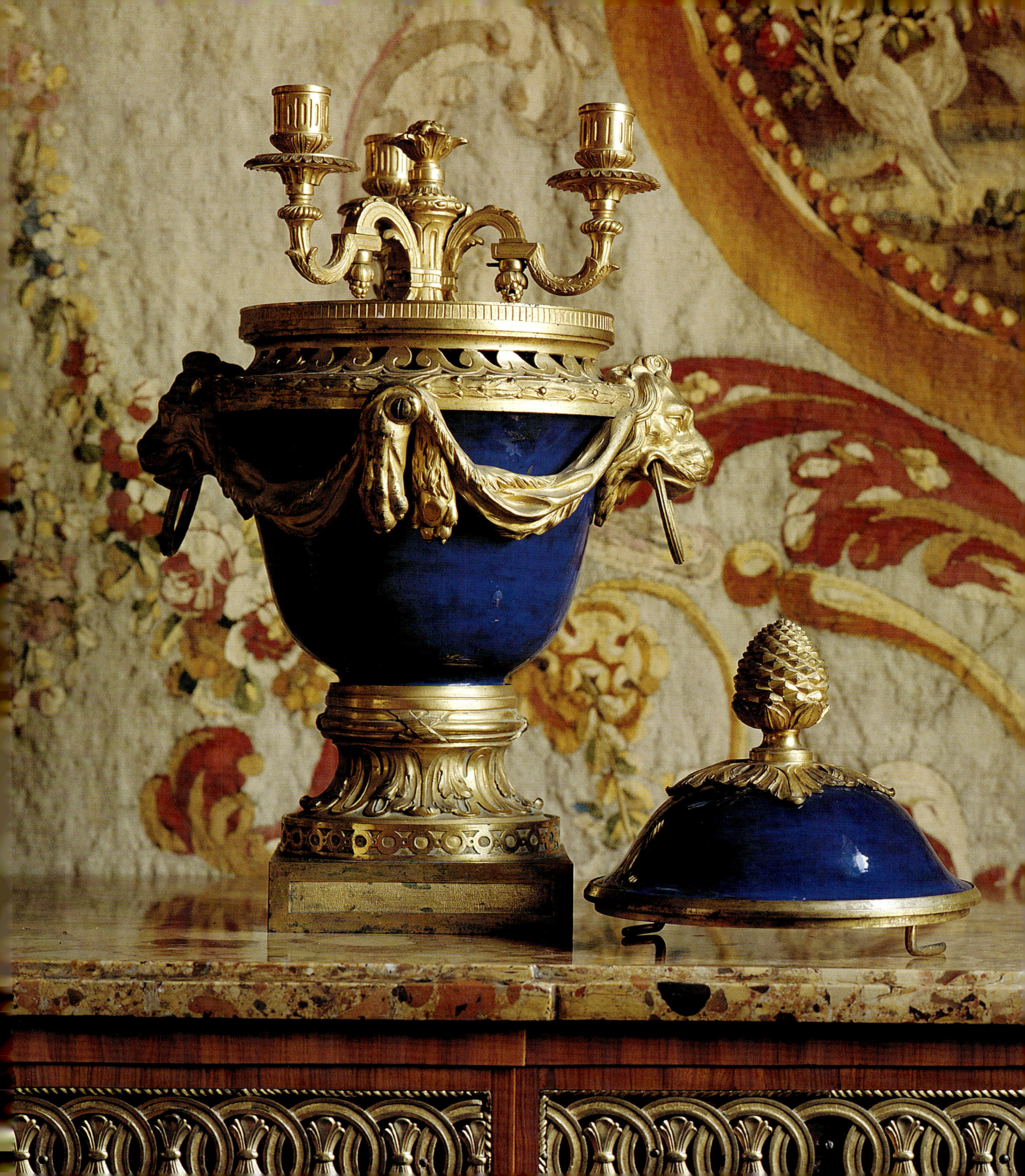

# The *Wucai* 'fish' Wine Jar

Julian Thompson

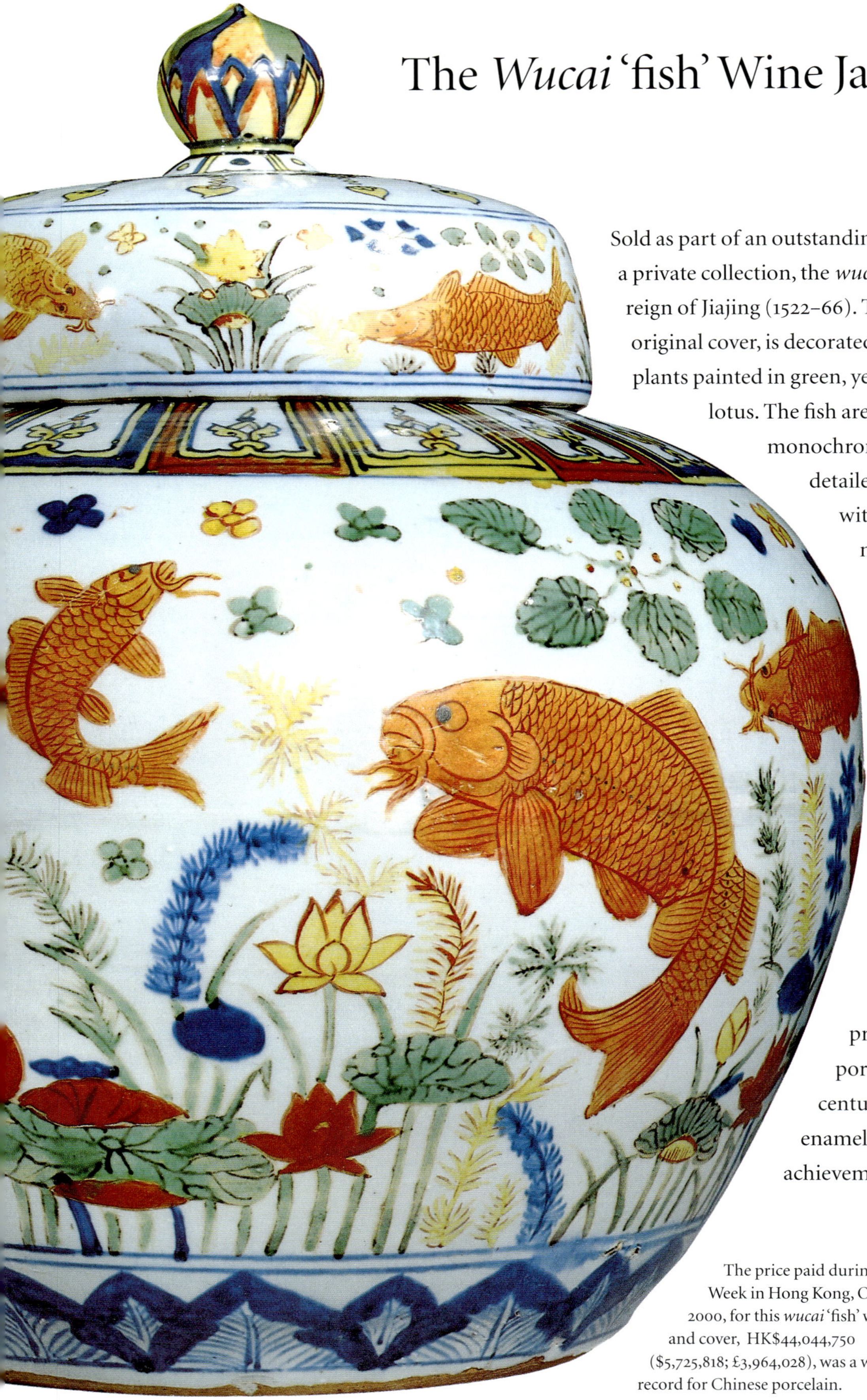

Sold as part of an outstanding group of Imperial Chinese porcelain from a private collection, the *wucai* 'fish' wine jar dates from the Ming dynasty reign of Jiajing (1522–66). This richly enamelled jar, complete with its original cover, is decorated with carp swimming among abundant pond plants painted in green, yellow and underglaze-blue, with red and yellow lotus. The fish are the 'Imperial' yellow colour familiar in Ming monochrome porcelain, with their features and scales detailed in vivid iron-red. The cover, also decorated with carp and water plants, is surmounted by a multi-coloured lotus-bud knop.

Like many Imperial porcelain designs, the subject of this jar is rich in symbolism, suggesting both wealth and plenty. The word for 'fish' in Chinese is a homophone of the word for 'surplus' and the lotus is a symbol of fertility, so when in use in the Imperial palace, the jar could be seen as conferring good fortune and prosperity to the Jiajing emperor and his court. The lotus bud, representing hands folded in prayer, is also associated with Buddhism where it is a symbol of purity.

The jar is in pristine condition and was probably part of the large collection of Ming porcelain preserved in the palace in the 18th century. Its large size and the brilliant colours of the enamels combine to make it one of the outstanding achievements of Chinese ceramic art.

The price paid during Asia Week in Hong Kong, October 2000, for this *wucai* 'fish' wine jar and cover, HK$44,044,750 ($5,725,818; £3,964,028), was a world record for Chinese porcelain.

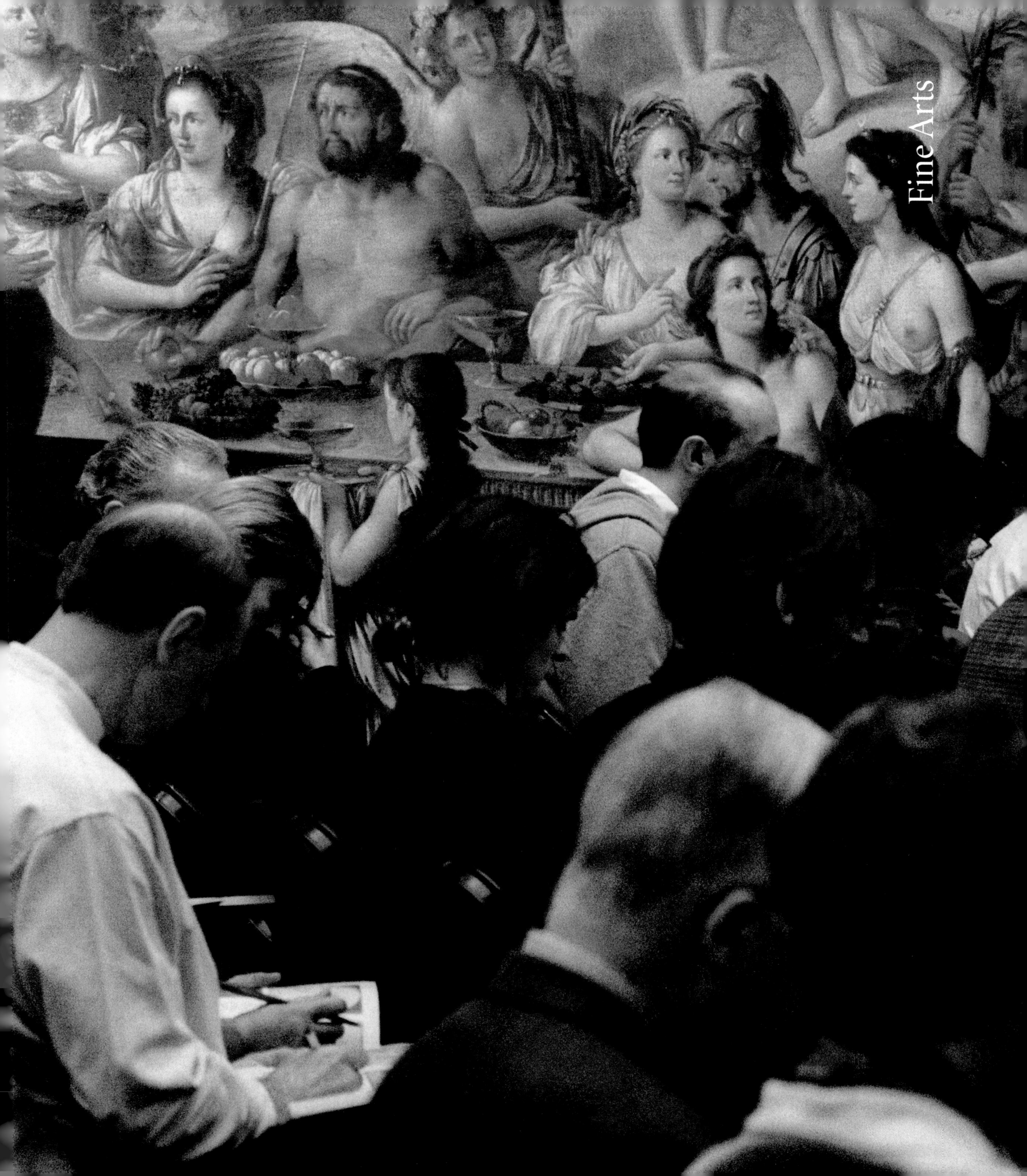

# Fine Arts

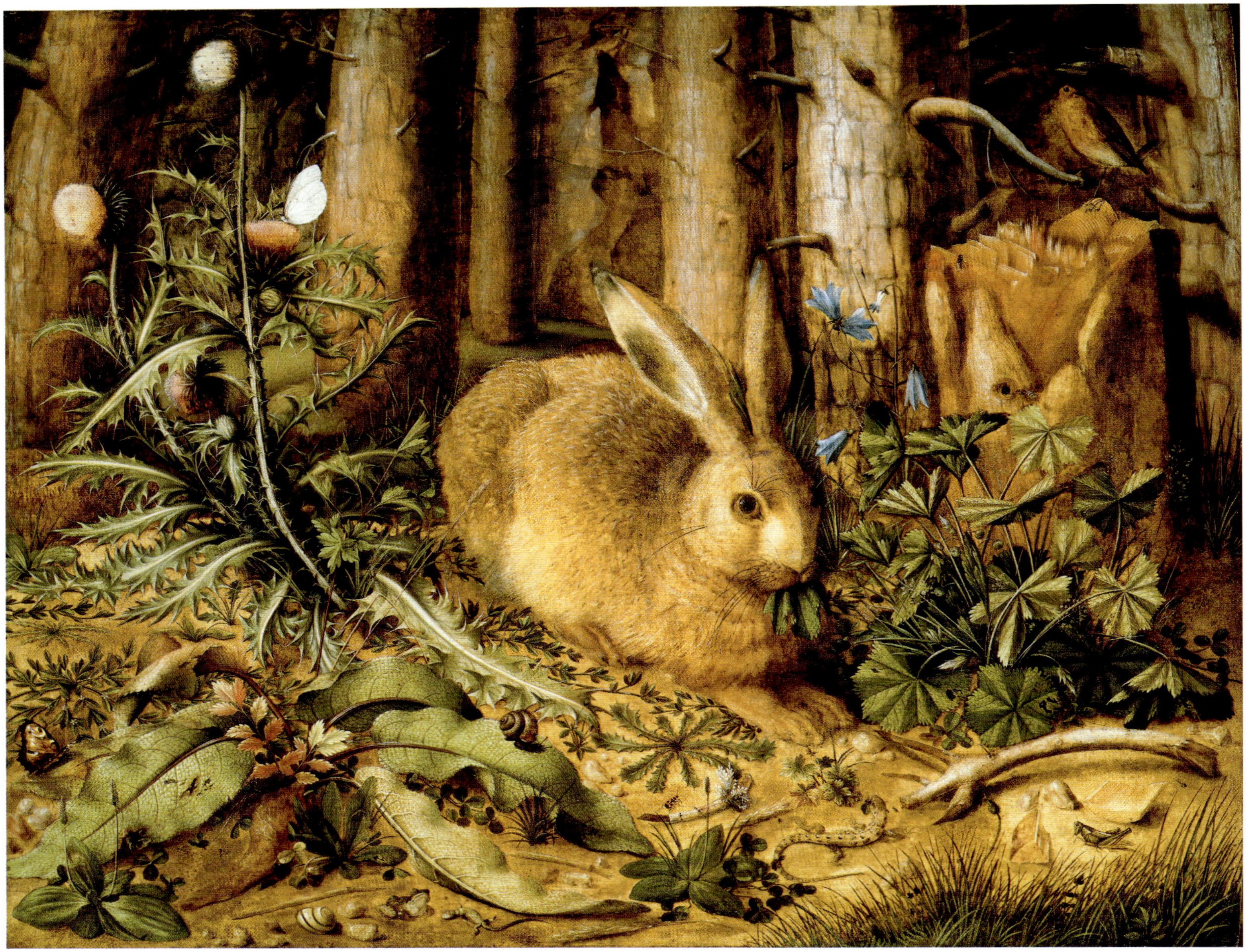

**Hans Hoffmann**
*A Hare in a Forest*
New York $2,645,750 (£1,799,110)
25.1.01

In this composition, Hoffman masterfully combines open-air still-life painting with a reinterpretation of Dürer's *Study of a Hare*. However, Hoffman places his hare among various exotic and commonplace plants, such as the African marigold and musk thistle. Oil on panel, 62.2 by 78.1 cm. (24½ by 30¾ in.).

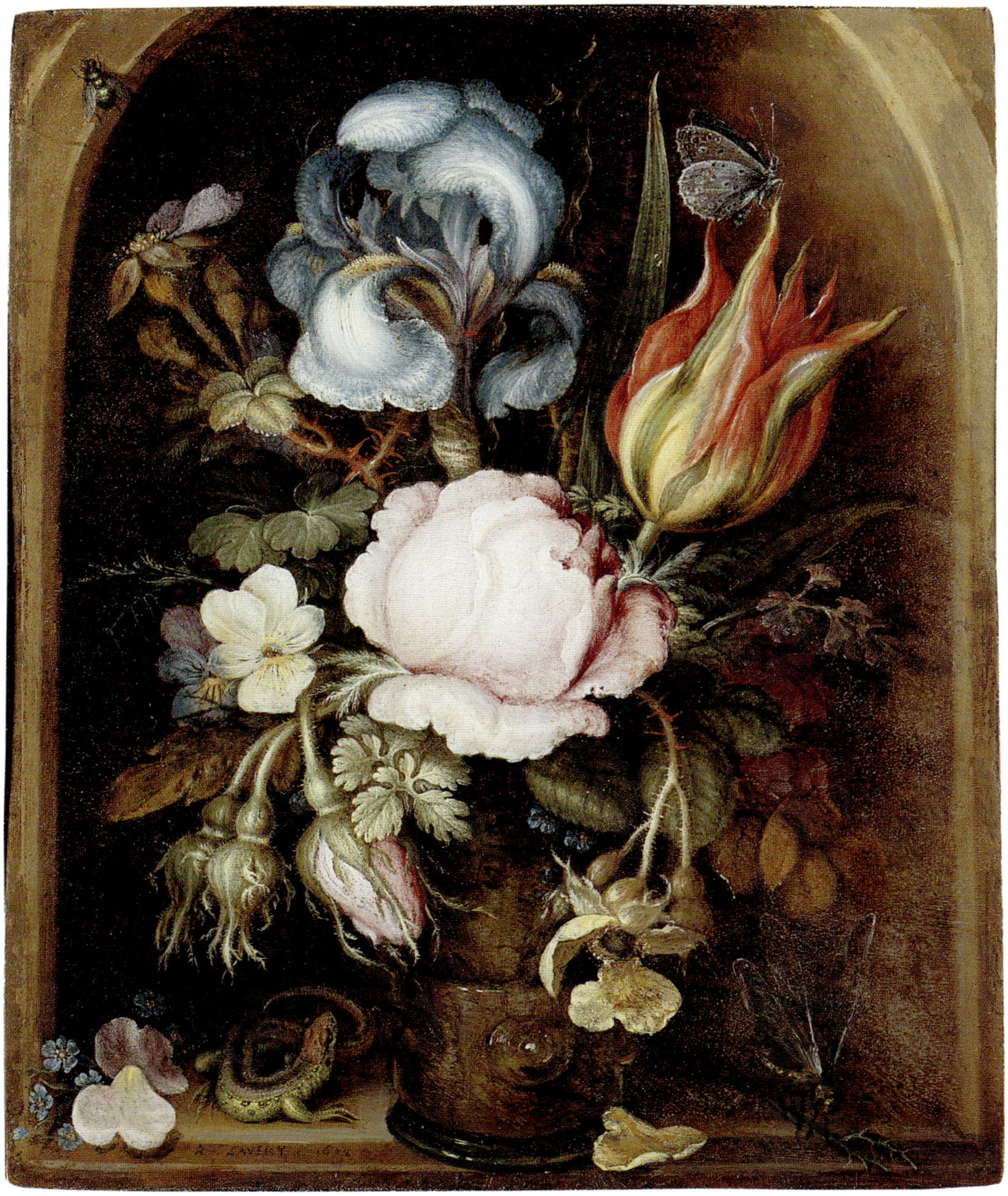

**Roelandt Savery**
*A Still Life of an Iris, a Tulip, a Rose, Moss-roses and Other Flowers and Plants in a Glass Vase*
London £1,763,500 ($2,468,900)
12.VII.01

Like Hans Hoffmann before him, Savery became court painter to Emperor Rudolf II in Prague from 1603 to 1612. Flower paintings by the artist are very rare, particularly from his early career. Signed and dated *r. savery. 1612*, oil on copper, 16.8 by 13.5 cm. (6¾ by 5¼ in.).

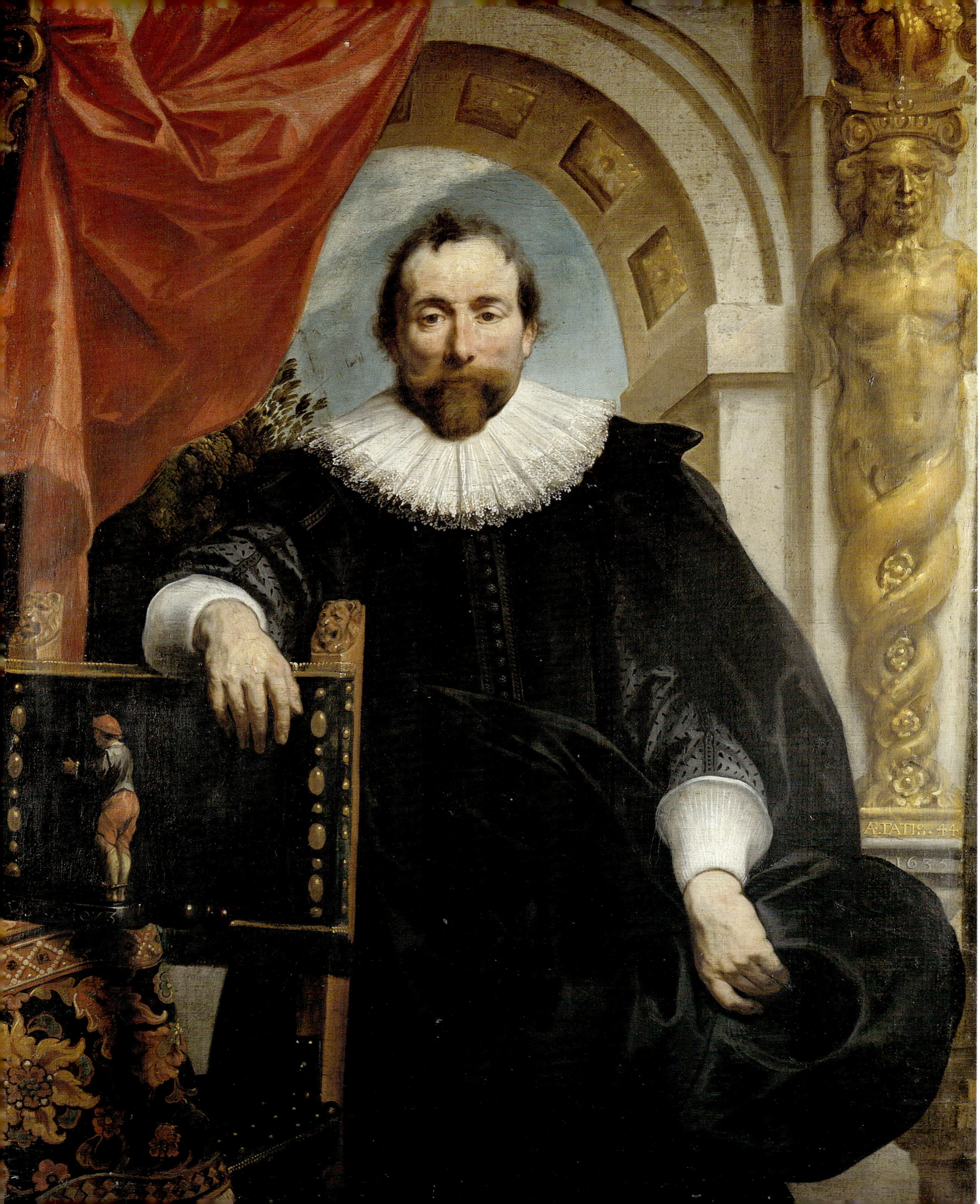
ÆTATIS. 44
1635

←

**Jacob Jordaens**
*A Portrait of Rogier le Witer at the age of 44*
London For the pair: £2,203,500 ($3,084,900) 12.VII.01

Sold as a pair with a portrait of Catharina Behagel, le Witer's wife, this painting is one of Jordaens' finest portraits. A deliberately low viewpoint is used, so the sitter gazes calmly down from this Baroque architectural setting.
Inscribed with the age of the sitter and the date *Aetatis.44/1635* and [A]ELEMOS[E], oil on canvas, 152 by 118.4 cm. (59¾ by 46¾ in.).

**(Giovanni) Ambrogio Figino**
*Portrait of Giovanni Angelo Dannona, Half Length, Holding Gloves and a Letter*
New York $1,435,750 (£976,310) 25.I.01

Figino (1548–1608), a prolific draughtsman and reputable painter, was considered an important artistic figure by the 16th-century Milanese nobility. This is his earliest dated work and only one of a handful of portraits by him that survive, although contemporary sources reveal that he was a renowned portraitist.
Signed and dated *AMBOSII./ FIGINI./OPUS./.1570*, oil on panel, 59.7 by 46.4 cm. (23½ by 18¼ in.).

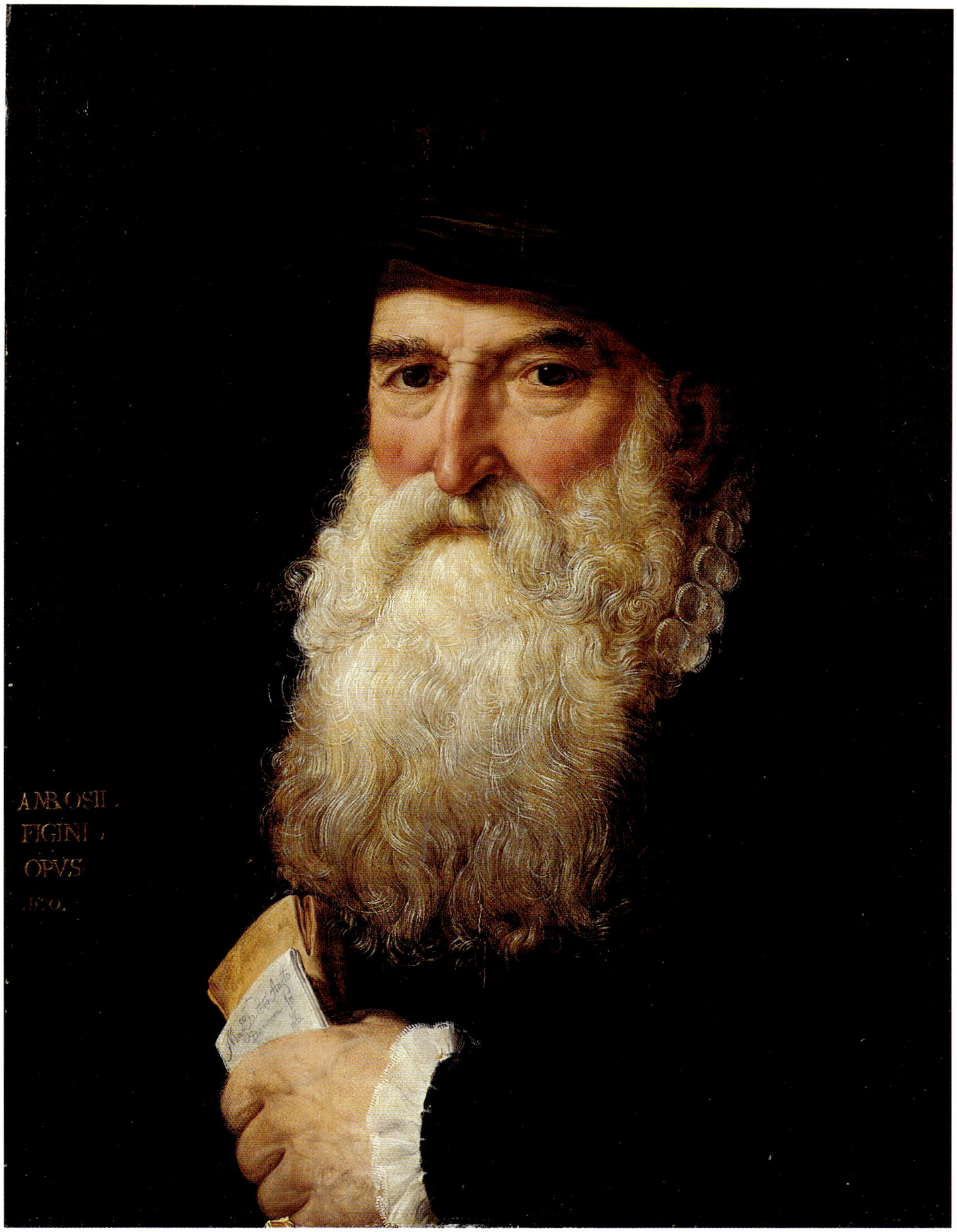

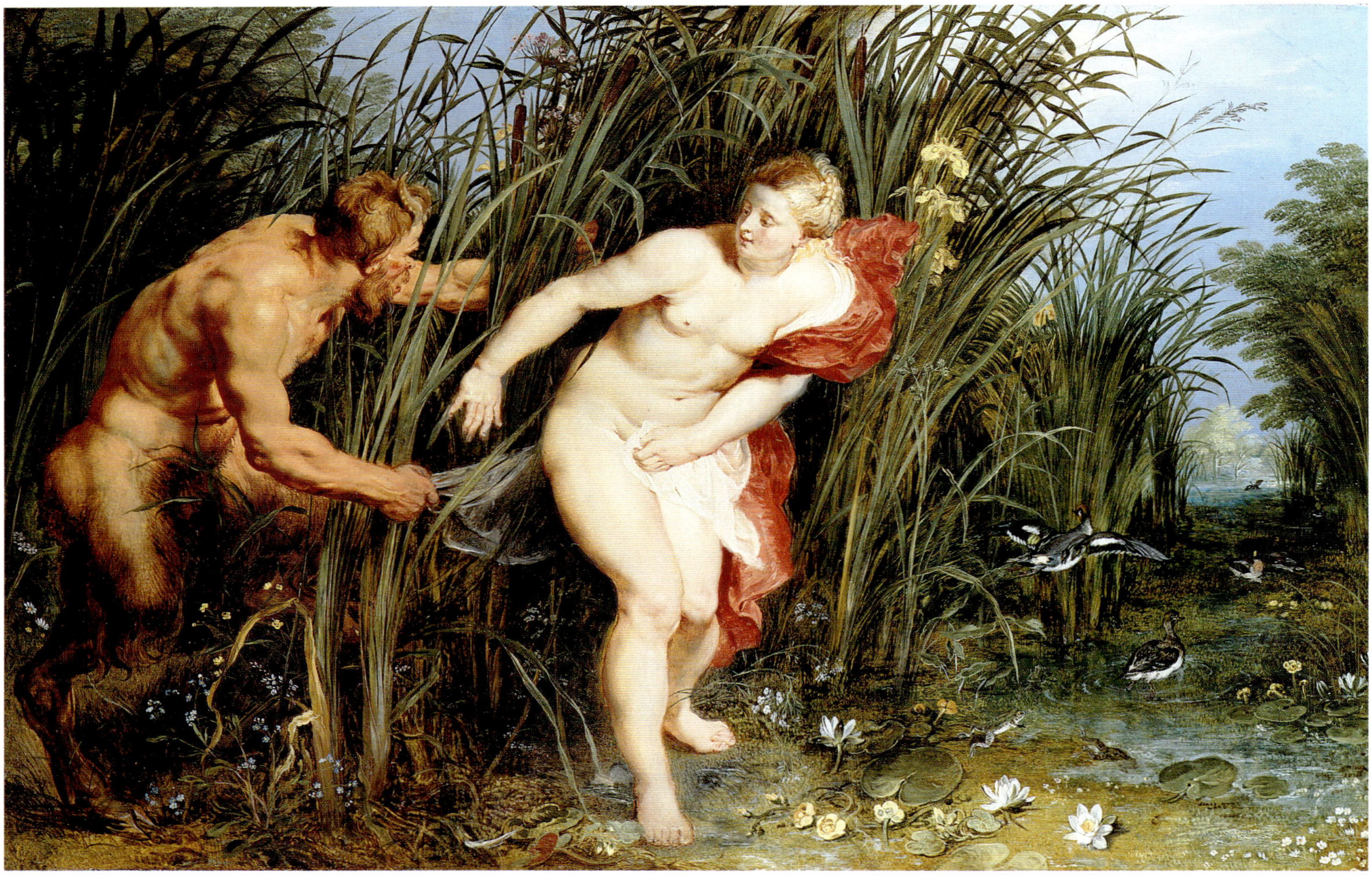

**Sir Peter Paul Rubens and**
**Jan Breughel the Younger**
*Pan and Syrinx*
London £2,203,500 ($3,084,900)
12.VII.01

In this collaborative work the landscape elements were long considered to be by Jan Breughel the Elder, although it is likely that the painting was completed by the younger Breughel shortly after his father's death. In the legend depicted, Pan pursued the wood nymph Syrinx who, unable to escape, was transformed into reeds, which were used by Pan to make his pipes.
Oil on oak panel, 40.3 by 61 cm.
(16 by 24 in.).

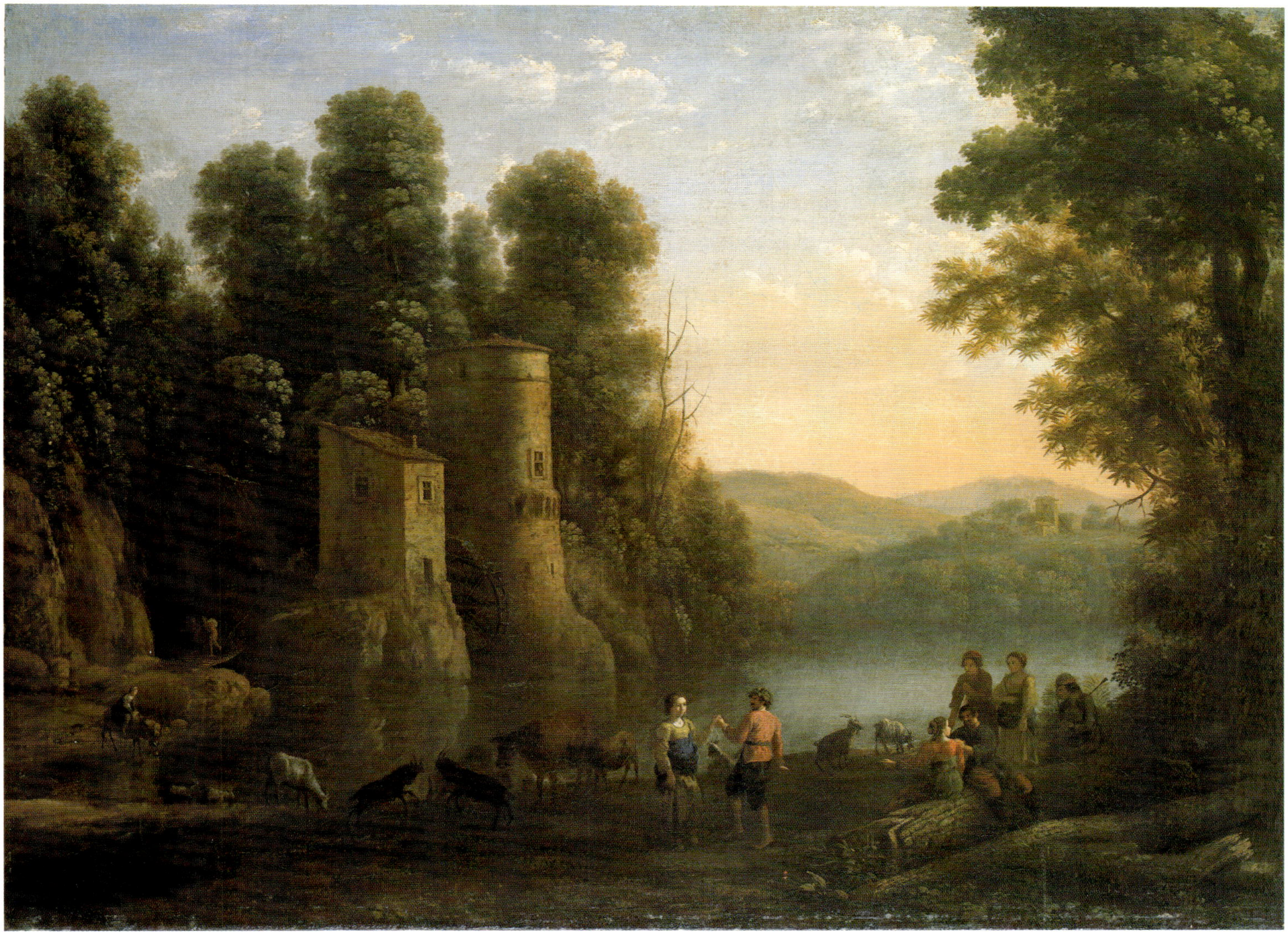

**Claude Gellé, called Claude Lorrain**
*Pastoral River Landscape with Figures by a Mill*
New York $2,095,750 (£1,425,110)
25.1.01

Although a native of Champagne, Claude moved to Rome at an early date where he was influenced by artists such as Paul Bril, Bartholomeus Breenbergh and Filippo Napoletano. Their guidance together with his genius led him to reinvent the genre of landscape with a use of light and tonality unlike any other artist of his generation.
Oil on canvas, 74.9 by 99.7 cm.
(29½ by 39¼ in.).

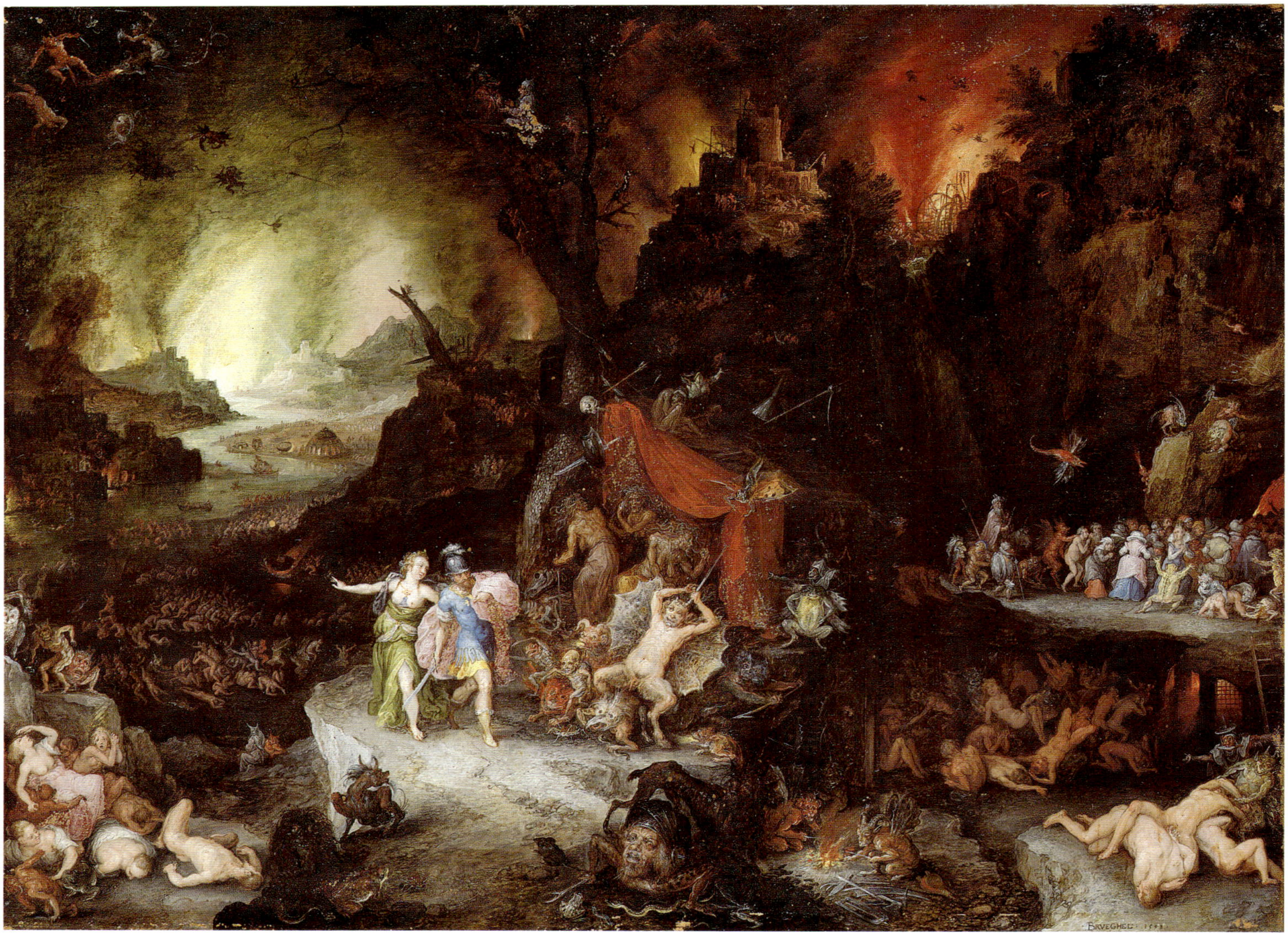

**Jan Brueghel the Elder**
*Aeneas and the Sibyl in the Underworld*
London £1,323,500 ($1,852,900)
12.VII.01

Hitherto unrecorded, this is the artist's earliest known treatment of this subject. It is an important addition to one of the most celebrated aspects of Brueghel 's oeuvre, and, until this work appeared at auction, was only known through a series of later replicas produced in the artist's workshop or by his son, Jan Brueghel the Younger. Signed and dated BRVEGHEL.*1598*, oil on copper, 26.4 by 35.3 cm. (10½ by 14 in.).

→

**Pieter Brueghel the Younger**
*A Village Kermesse* (detail)
London £3,853,500 ($5,394,900)
12.VII.01

While Pieter Brueghel the Younger usually drew inspiration from his father's compositions, here he has used a large woodcut engraving of 1539 by Hans Sebald Beham, whose prints were popular in Brueghel's time. The source was no doubt used as the subject matter perfectly suited his preferred genre.
Signed and dated P.BRVEGHEL *1616*, oil on oak panel, 99 by 167 cm. (39 by 65¾ in.).

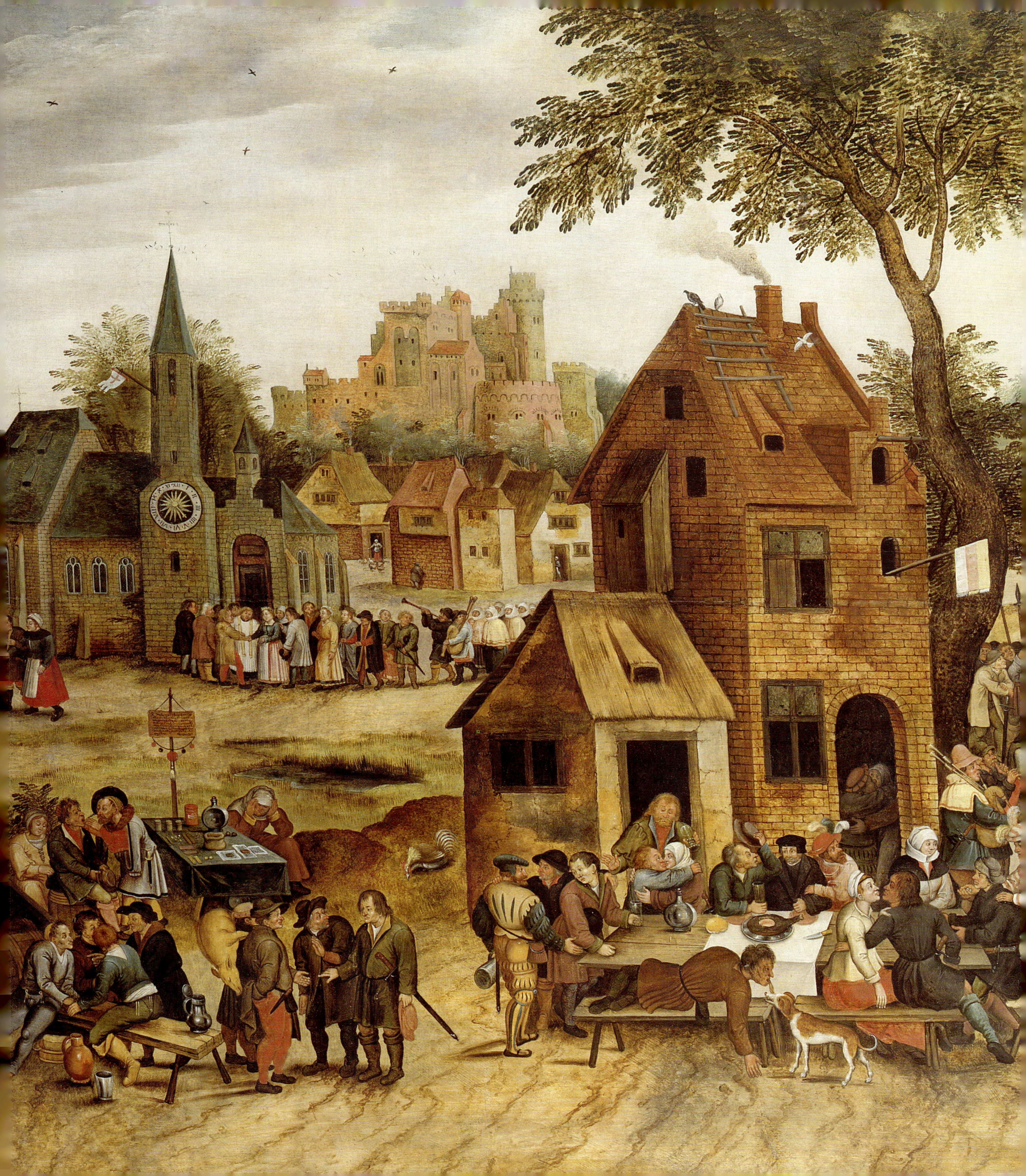

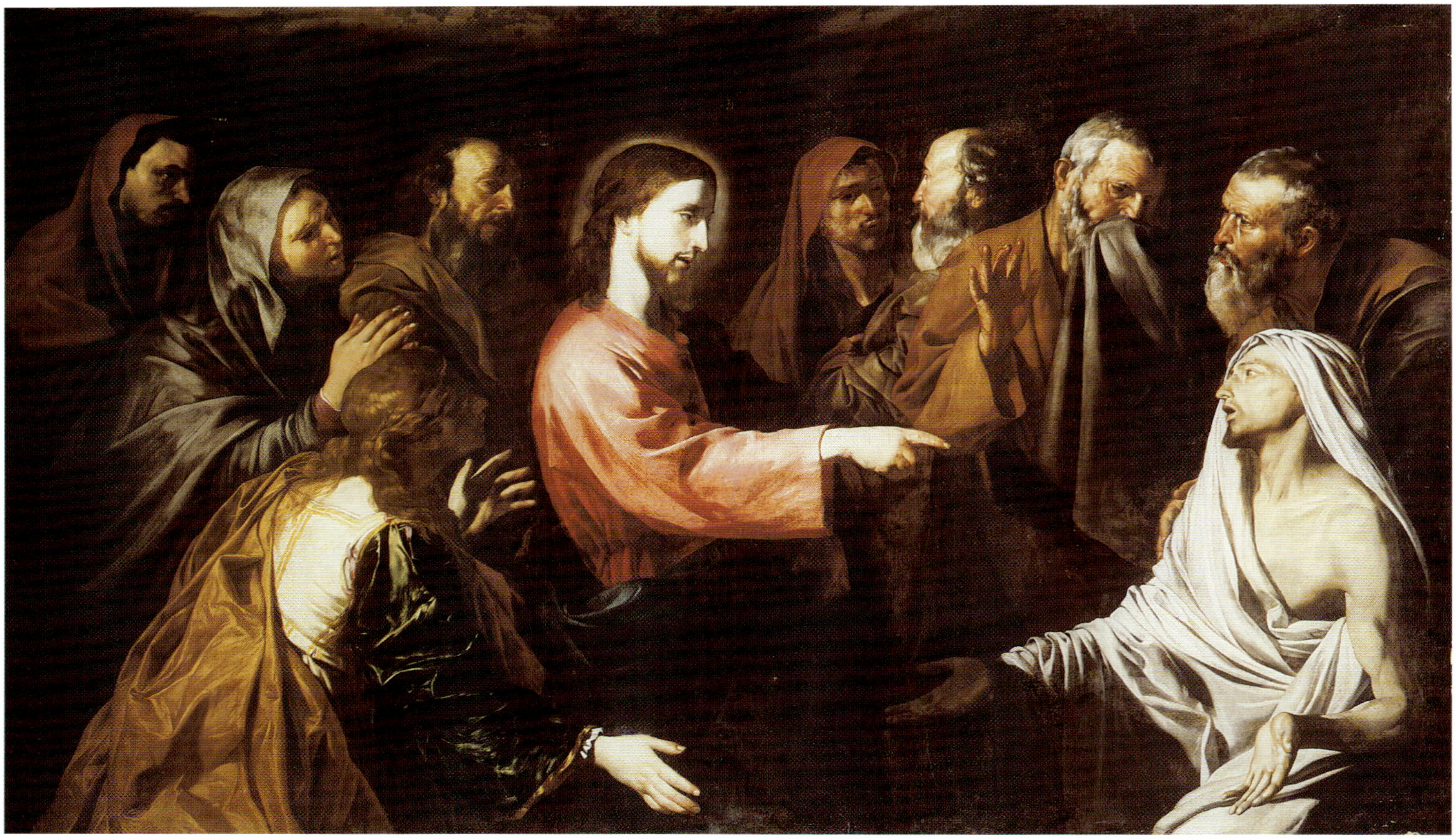

**Jusepe de Ribera,**
**called Lo Spagnoletto**
*The Raising of Lazarus*
New York $1,875,750 (£1,275,510)
25.I.01

An unpublished early work of *circa* 1613–15, this painting is an important addition to the artist's known oeuvre. The composition centres around four different planes in which primary, secondary and tertiary figures are densely packed into the picture space. It is a testament to the young Ribera's ingenuity; he was only in his early twenties when he painted this picture.
Oil on canvas, 170.8 by 288.9 cm.
(67¼ by 113¾ in.).

→

**The Master of the**
**Legend of St Lucy**
*The Virgin and Child Enthroned with Music-making Angels Before a Prospect of Bruges*
London £718,500 ($1,005,900)
12.VII.01

This anonymous artist is named after a 1480 panel representing the life of St Lucy, in St James' church, Bruges. This composition can be dated from the appearance of the belfry in the left-hand arch, whose roof was destroyed in a fire in 1493 and not replaced until 1499.
Oil on oak panel, 43 by 33.5 cm.
(17 by 13¼ in.).

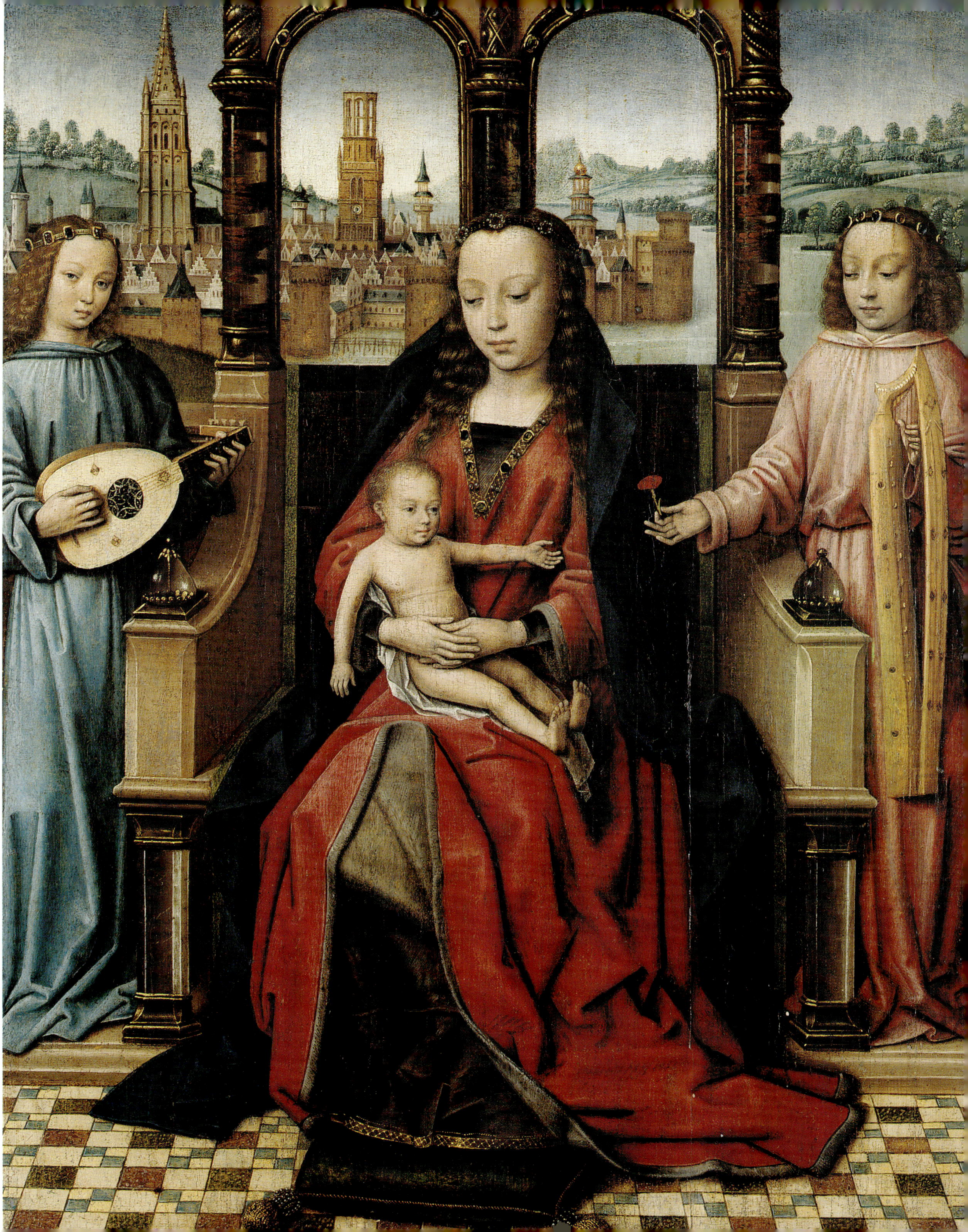

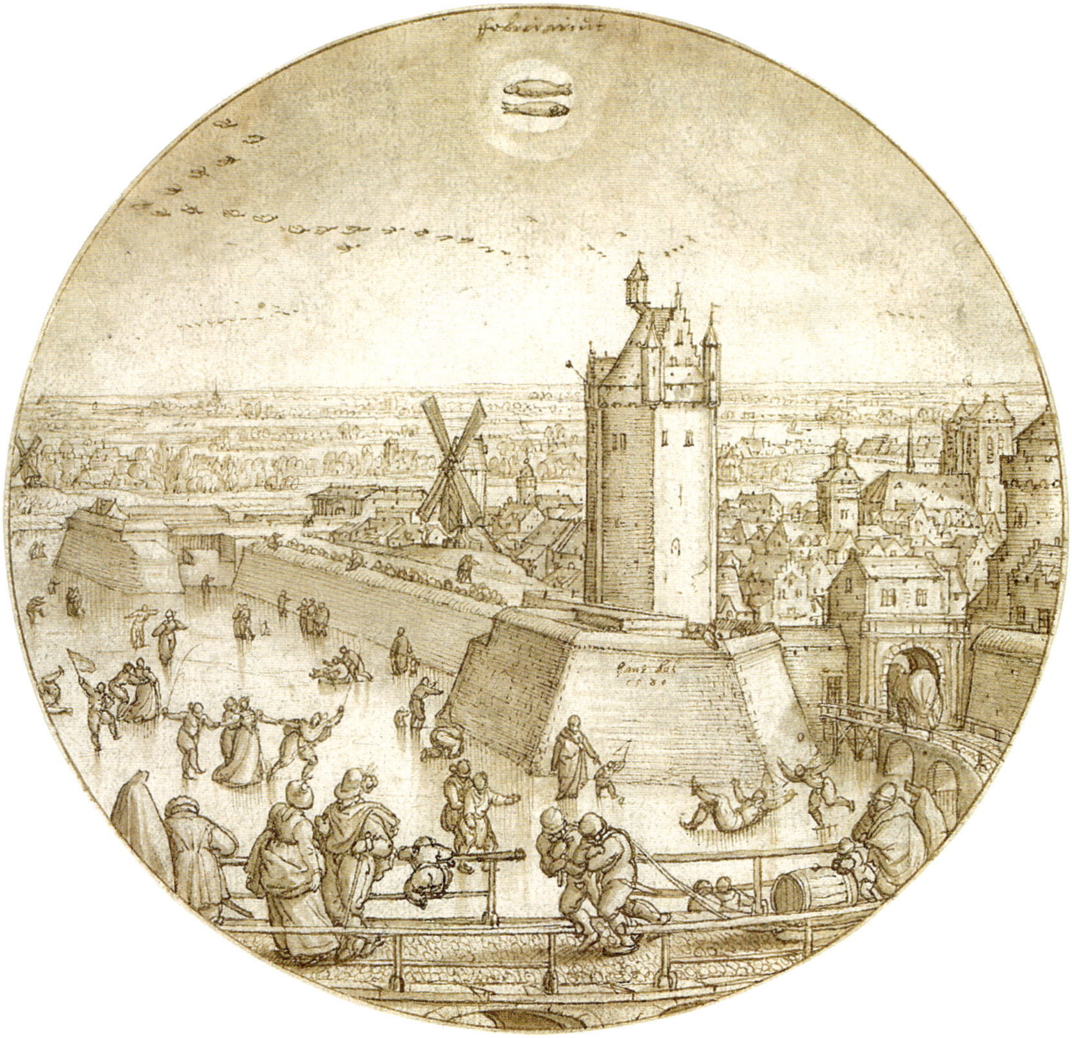

**Hans Bol**
*The Twelve Months*
New York $1,765,750 (£1,200,710)
23.1.01

This series of drawings from the Franz Koenigs collection achieved nearly four times its high estimate. Bol's compositions show the influence of Bruegel combined with a very different elegance of composition and handling. This drawing of February features ice skaters outside the walls of Antwerp. Pen and brown ink and wash, each: 14 cm. (5½ in.) diameter.

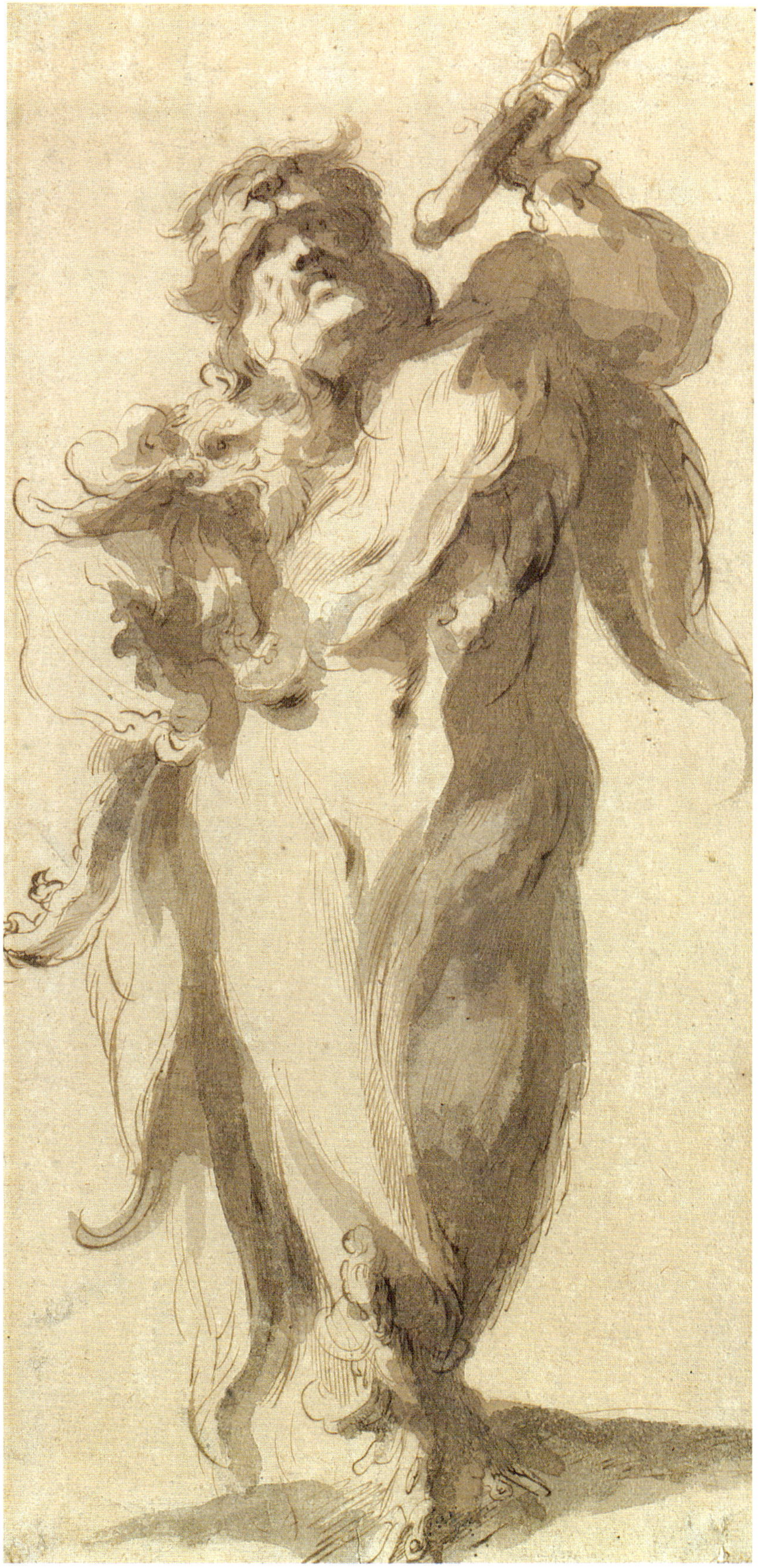

**Jacques Bellange**
*Hercules*
London £542,500 ($764,925)
11.VII.01

Drawings by this early-17th-century artist from Lorraine rarely appear on the market. Previously unrecorded, this study may have been: a design for a ballet costume; a study for one of Bellange's interior decoration projects; or a finished work in its own right. It sold for over ten times its low estimate. Pen and brown ink with grey and brown wash, 38.9 by 18.1 cm. (15⅜ by 7¼ in.).

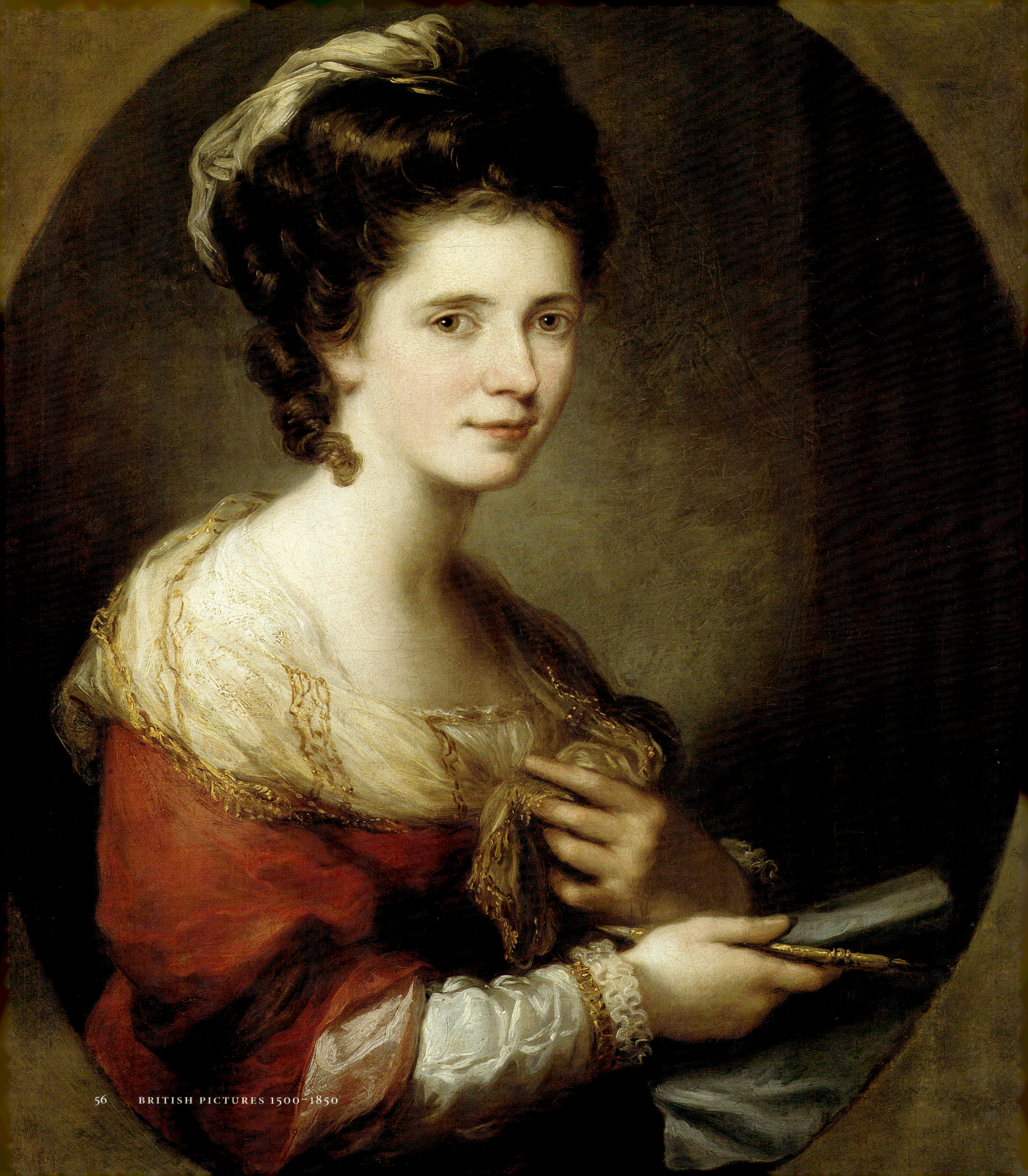

←

**Angelica Kauffmann, RA**
*Self-portrait*
London £421,500 ($586,429)
14.VI.01

Kauffmann was a child prodigy and accepted commissions before she was 15 and, in 1768, at the age of 27 she was made a founder member of the Royal Academy, one of only two women to be so honoured. This work set a new auction record for the artist.
*Circa* 1775–80, oil on canvas, 74 by 61 cm. (29 by 24 in.).

**George Stubbs ARA**
*Euston, a Dappled Grey Racehorse, the Property of William Wildman, with Jockey Up, in a River Landscape*
London £2,753,500 ($3,909,970)
30.XI.00

Executed for his friend and patron William Wildman, this portrait demonstrates anatomical excellence and a greatness in painting which has rewarded Stubbs with his unparalleled reputation.
Oil on panel, signed, 86.4 by 99.1 cm. (34 by 39 in.).

→ →

**Sir Thomas Lawrence PRA**
*Portrait of Andrew Reid*
London £795,500 ($1,121,655)
14.VI.01

Painted in 1799, the year that the young Andrew Reid left Harrow, this romantic portrait is the product of Lawrence's finest period and shows the exuberance of the self-taught artist who in 1792, at the age of 23, had succeeded Reynolds as painter to the King. This work set a new auction record for the artist.
Oil on canvas, 124.5 by 100 cm. (49 by 39⅜ in.).

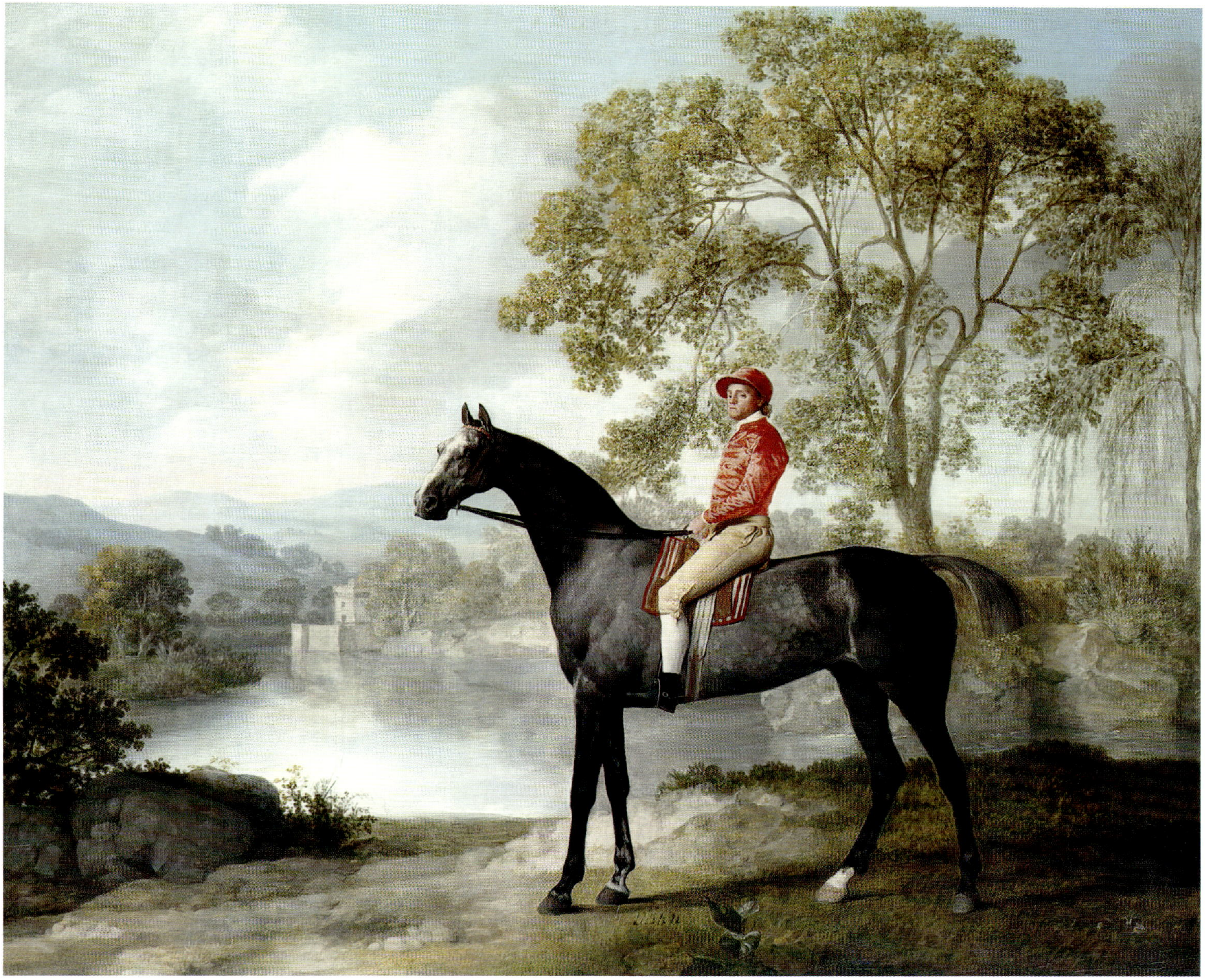

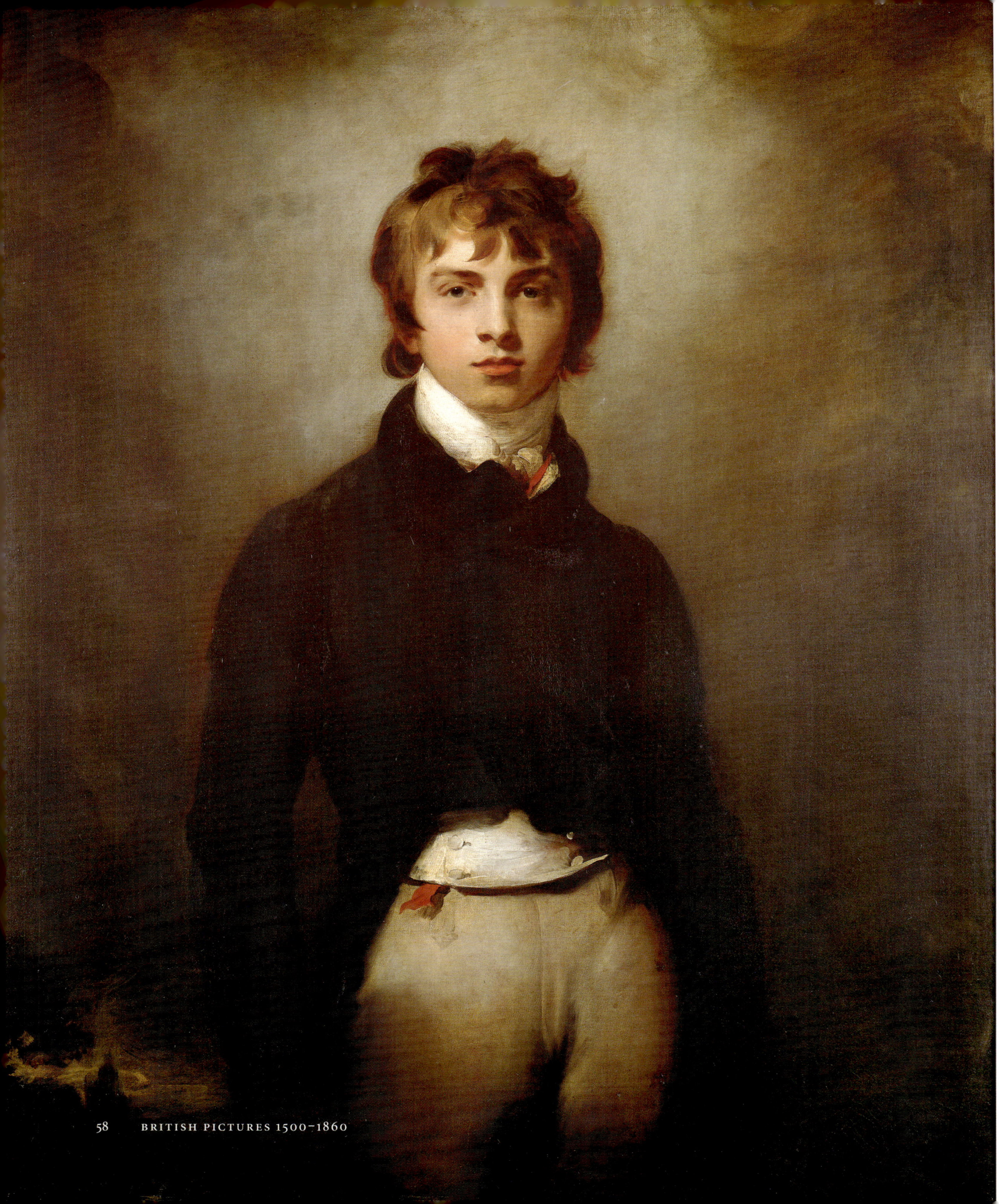

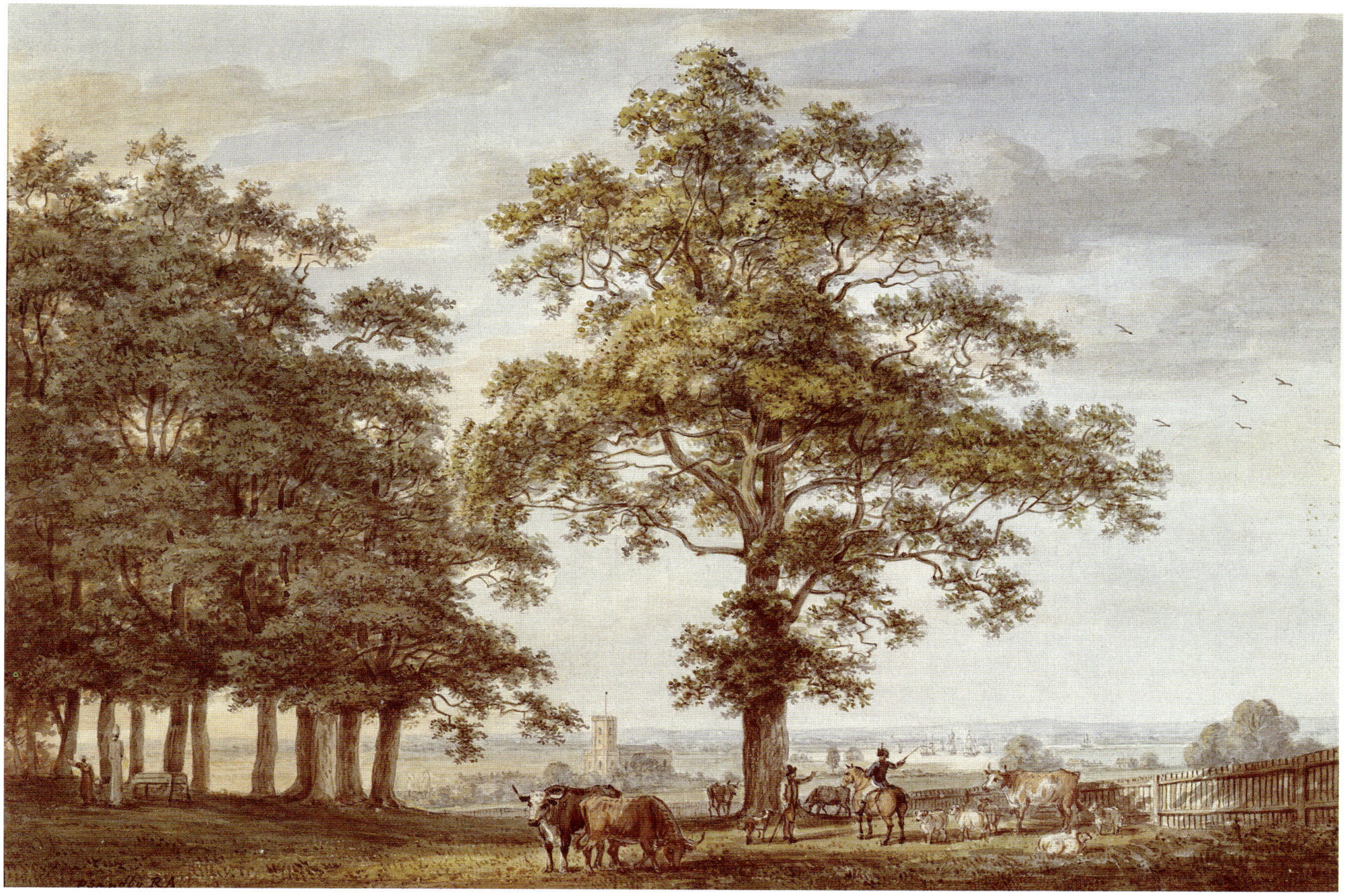

**Paul Sandby, RA**
*The Town of Woolwich from the Conduit Hill, The River Thames in the Distance*
London £40,750 ($57,865) 30.XI.00

As part of his employment as Drawing Master at the Royal Military Academy at Woolwich Paul Sandby used his views of Woolwich to encourage students to look properly at nature. Signed *P Sandby RA* and inscribed *N12 Town of Woolwich from the Conduit hill the River Thames in the distance*, watercolour over pencil heightened with bodycolour on laid paper, 31.5 by 47 cm. (12½ by 18½ in.).

→ →

**Joseph Wright of Derby, ARA**
*Study of a Boy Reading* (detail)
London £234,500 ($332,990) 30.XI.00

This delicate work in chalk shows the concentration of a young boy reading, which is emphasized by the direct light outlining the contours of his face. The boy is the same model as used by Wright of Derby in 1766 in his first scientific painting *A Philosopher Giving the Lecture on the Orrery in which the Lamp Is Put in Place of the Sun.* Inscribed by William Bemrose on the reverse of the mount *Drawn by / 'Wright of Derby'/Wbemrose/N.B.*, black and white chalk on laid paper, 42 by 28 cm. (16½ by 11 in.).

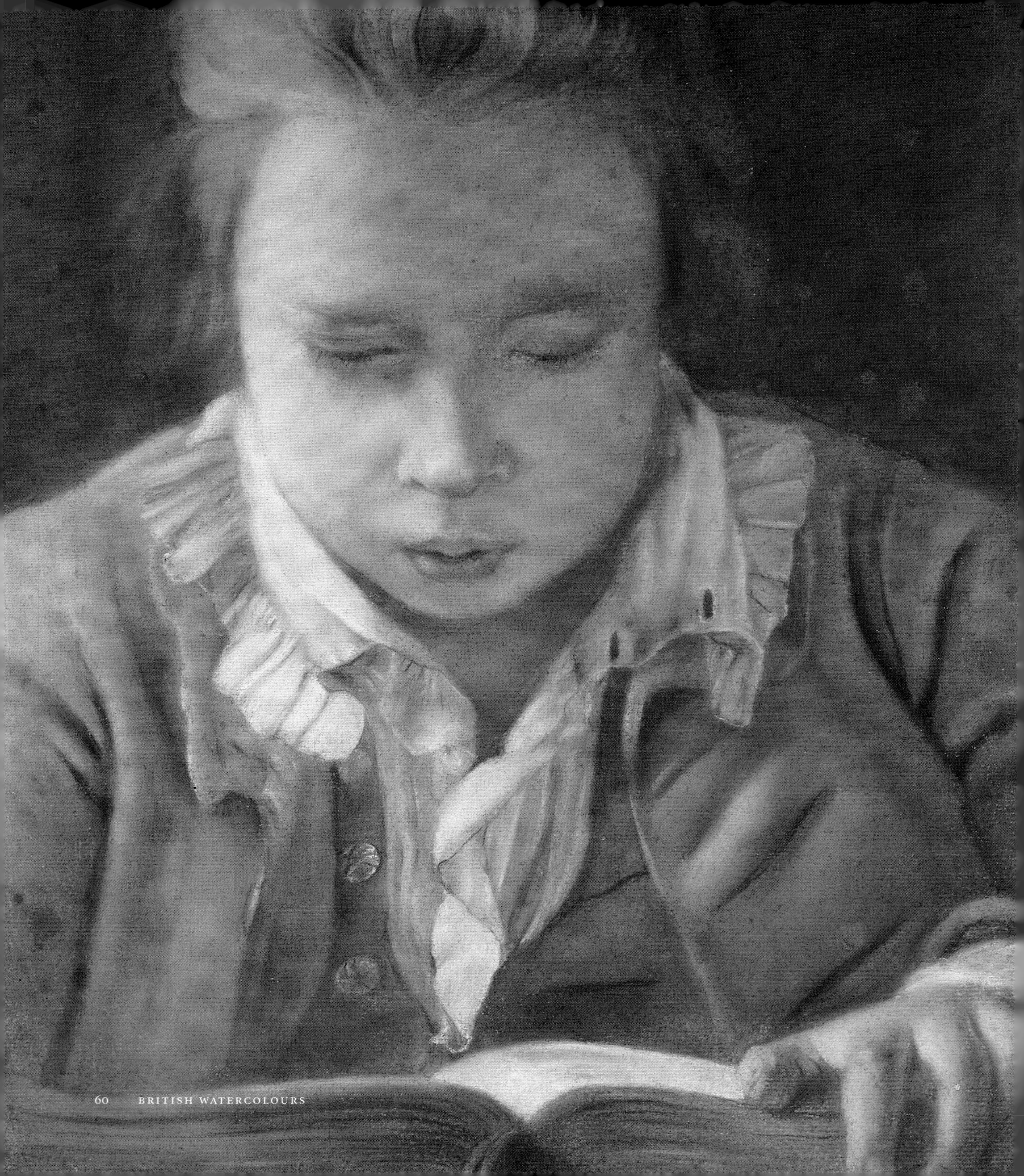

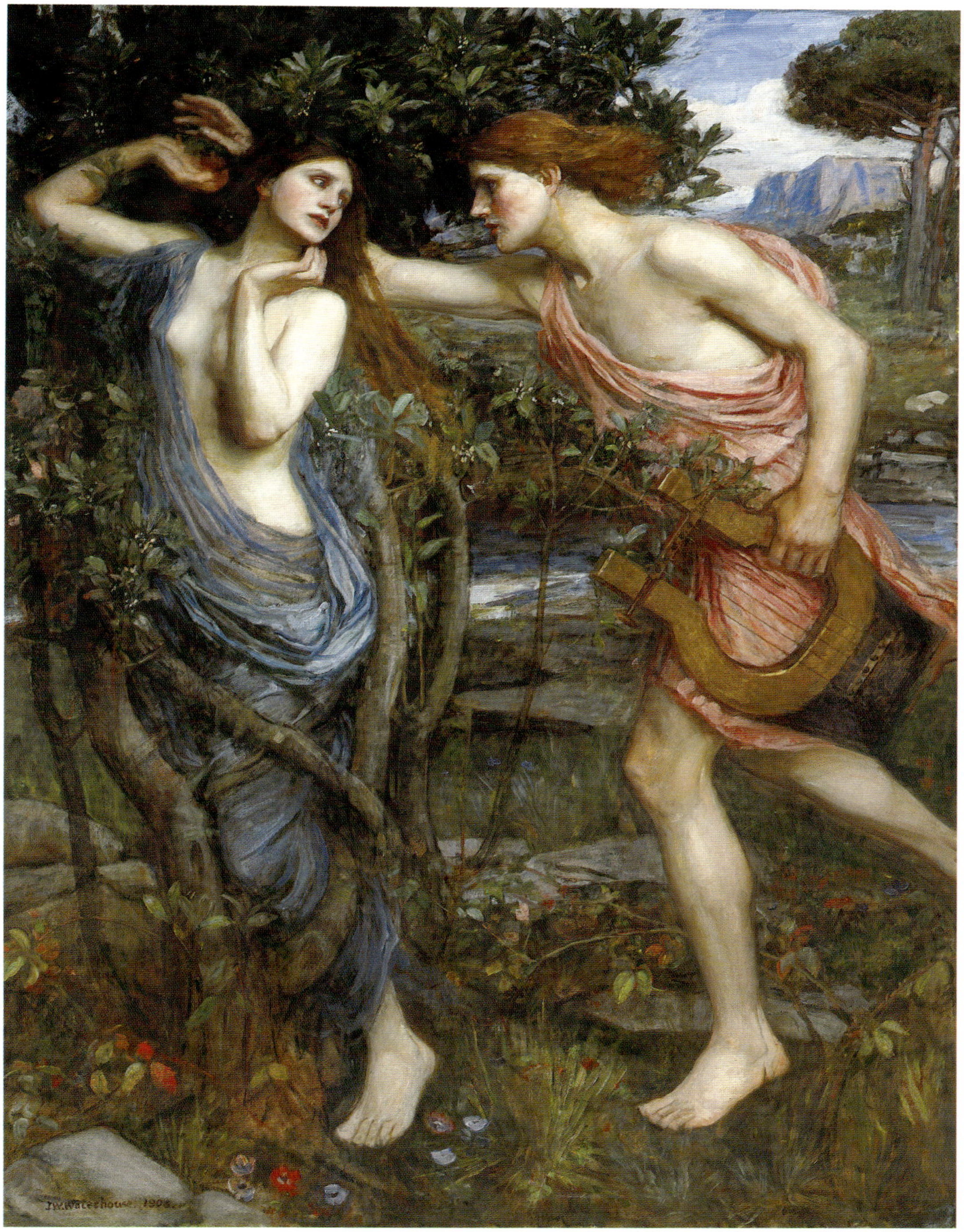

**John William Waterhouse, RA, RI**
*Apollo and Daphne*
London £1,103,500 ($1,555,935)
14.VI.01

Waterhouse, by this time established as one of the leading artists of his day, favoured moments of confrontation from Greek and Roman legend. Here Daphne is turned by her father, the river-god Peneus, into a bay tree to save her from Apollo's pursuit. Signed and dated *1908*, oil on canvas, 145 by 112 cm. (57 by 44 in.).

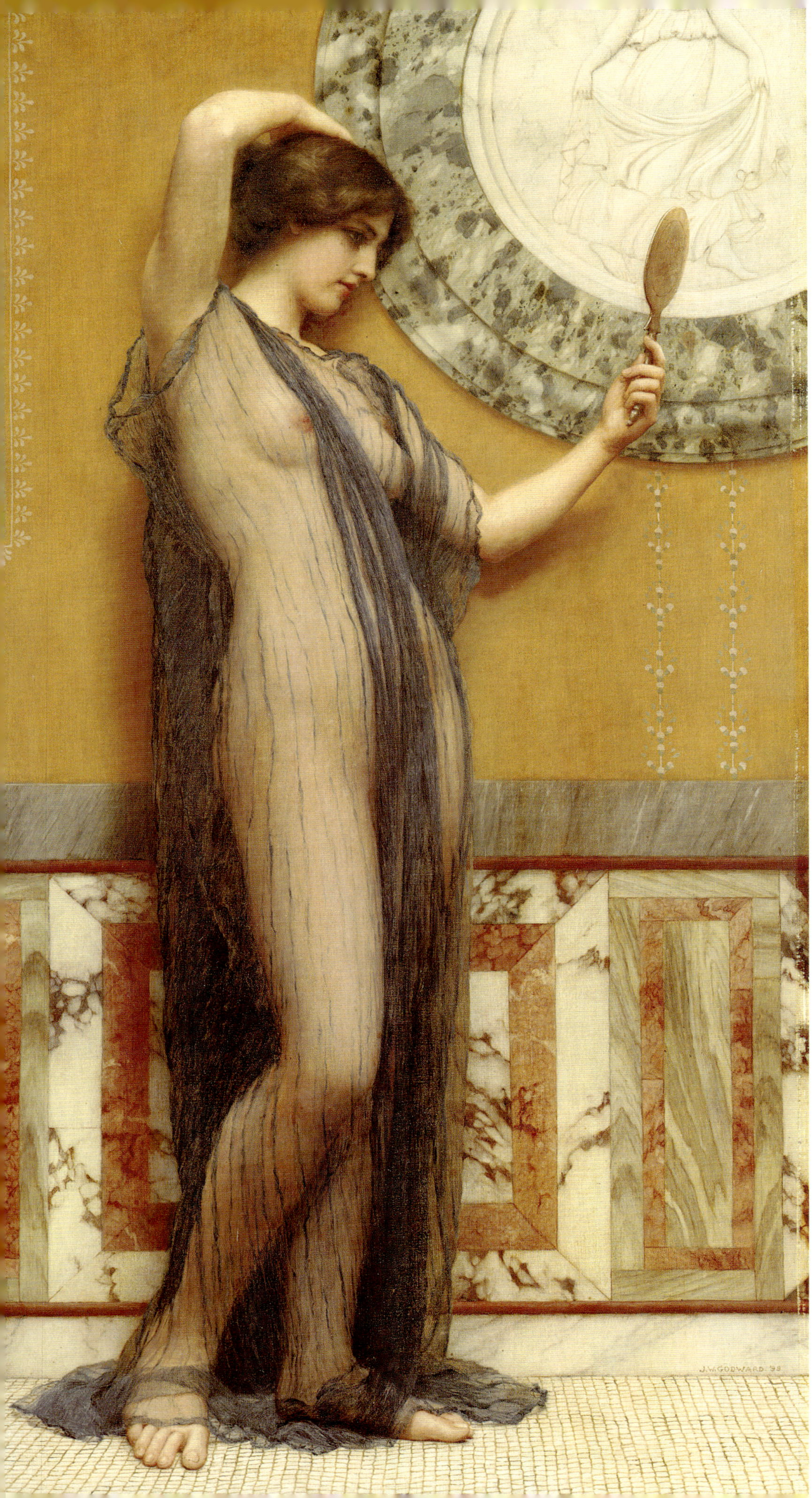

**John William Godward, RBA**
*A Fair Reflection*
London £300,500 ($423,705)
14.VI.01

Lost since its sale by Godward's dealer Thomas McLean in 1899, of Godward's four 'mirror' paintings this is the most famous, made popular by the publication of McLean's photogravure in 1907. Signed and dated '99, oil on canvas, 76 by 40.5 cm. (30 by 16 in.).

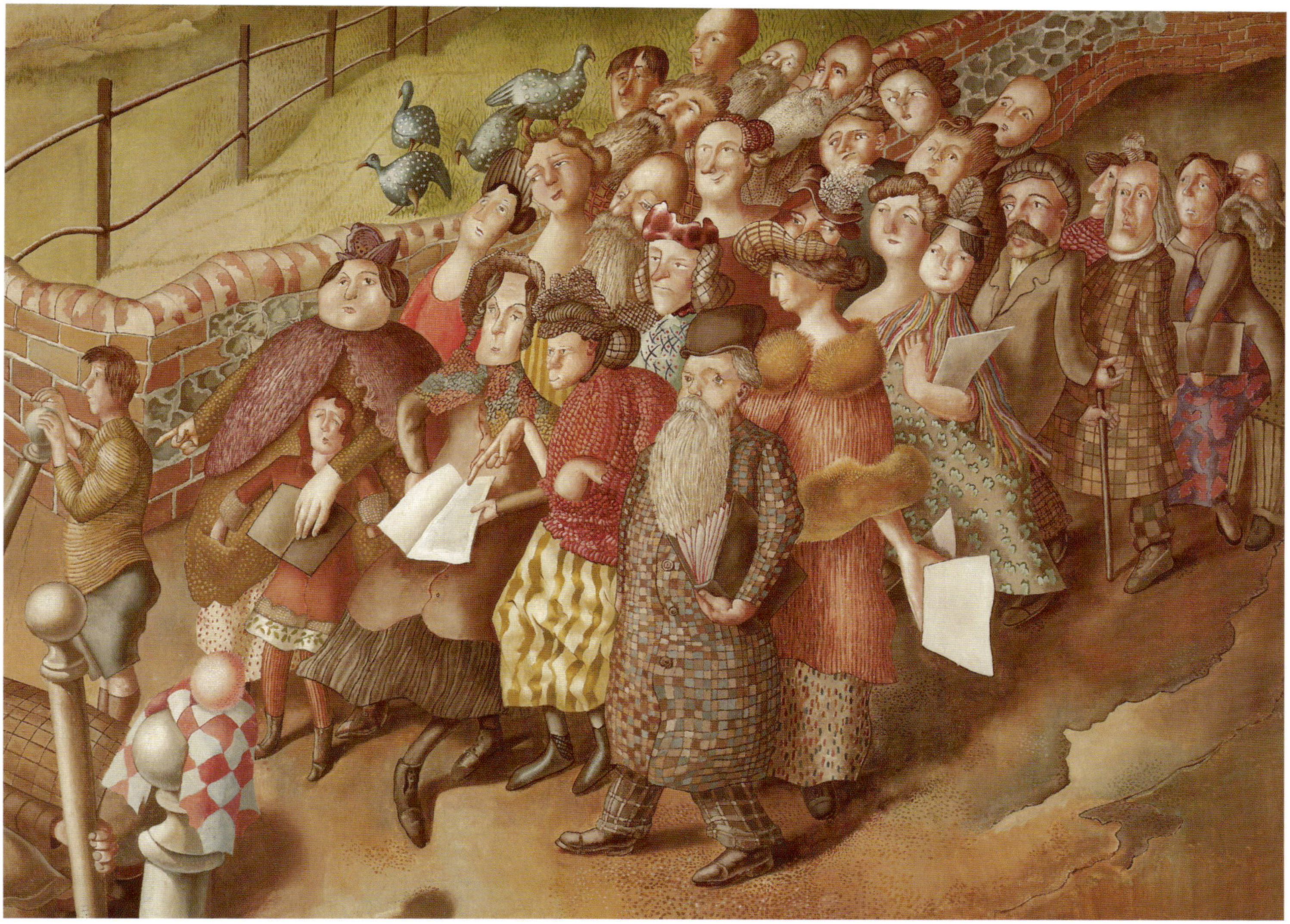

**Sir Stanley Spencer**
*From Up the Rise*
London £1,290,500 ($1,819,605)
14.VI.01

This painting belongs to a remarkable body of work known as Church House, a project that was never realized but which was of crucial importance to the development of Spencer's work.
Oil on canvas, 80 by 107 cm.
(31½ by 42 in.).

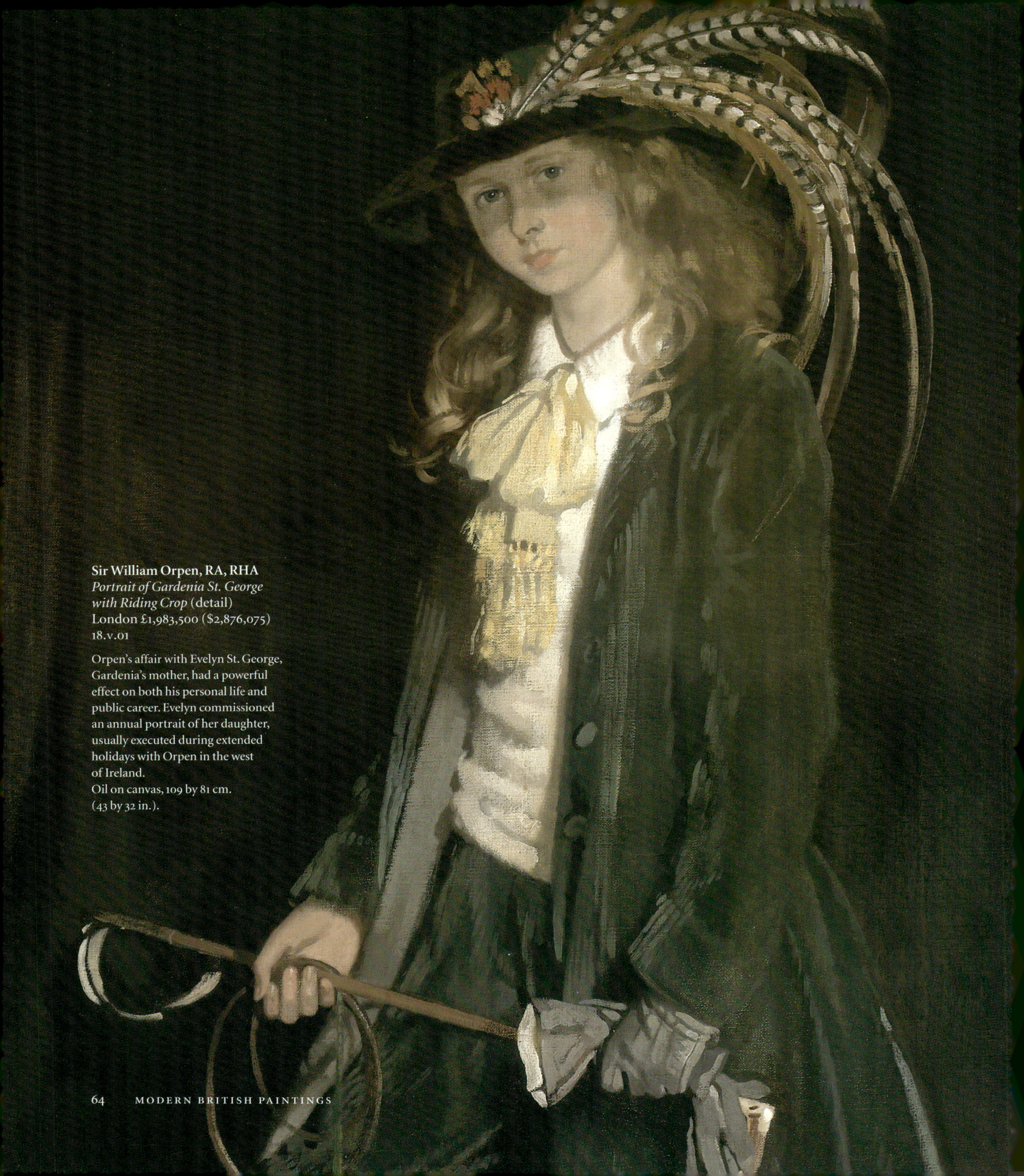

**Sir William Orpen, RA, RHA**
*Portrait of Gardenia St. George with Riding Crop* (detail)
London £1,983,500 ($2,876,075)
18.v.01

Orpen's affair with Evelyn St. George, Gardenia's mother, had a powerful effect on both his personal life and public career. Evelyn commissioned an annual portrait of her daughter, usually executed during extended holidays with Orpen in the west of Ireland.
Oil on canvas, 109 by 81 cm. (43 by 32 in.).

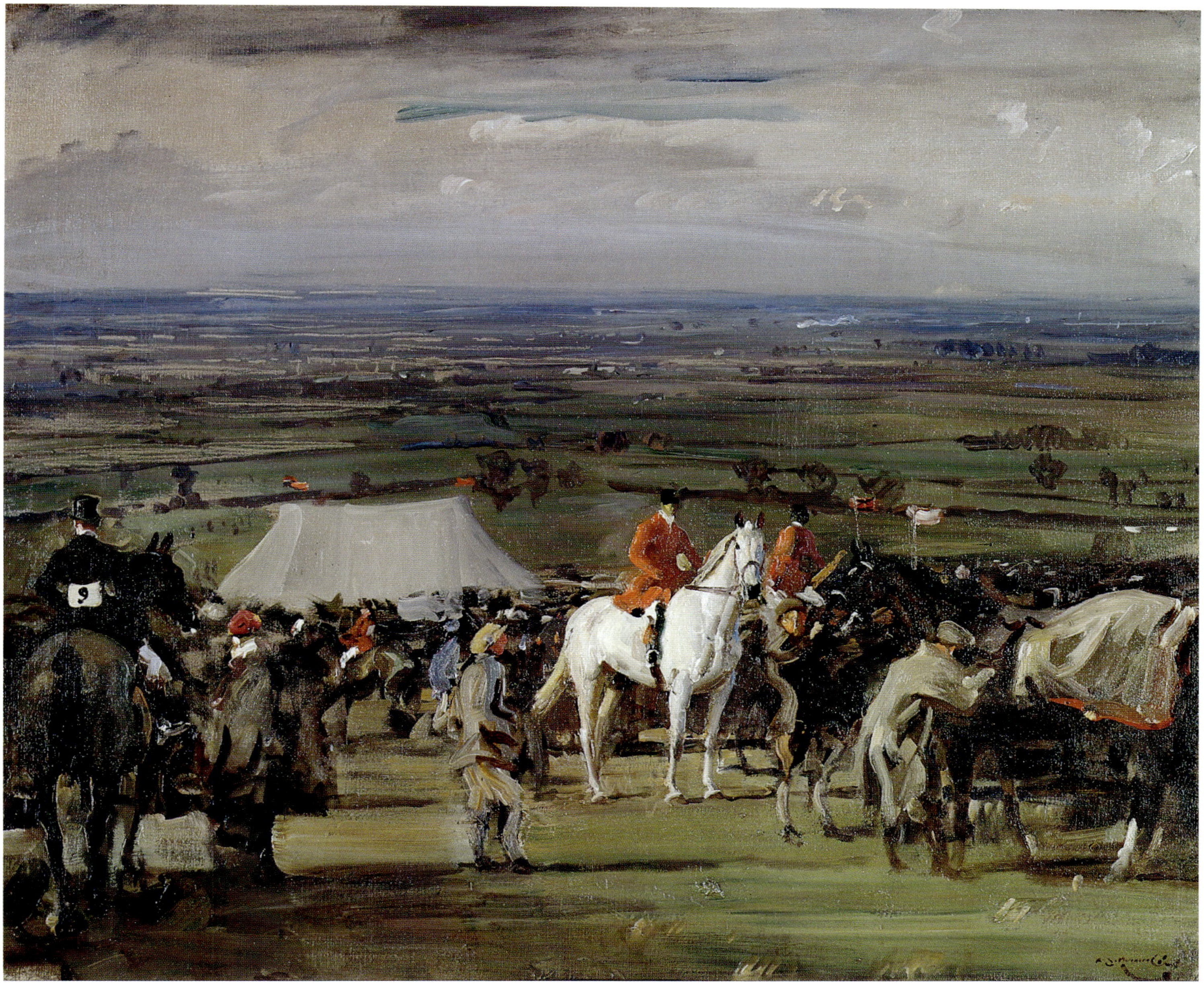

**Alfred Munnings**
*Impression – The Belvoir*
*Point-to-point on Barrowby Hill*
New York $577,750 (£410,202)
6.VI.01

This is one of a series of paintings commissioned by Major Tommy Bouch, Master of the Duke of Rutland's Hounds, in 1920–21, which captured both the public imagination and widespread critical acclaim.
Signed, oil on canvas, 63.5 by 76.2 cm. (25 by 30 in.).

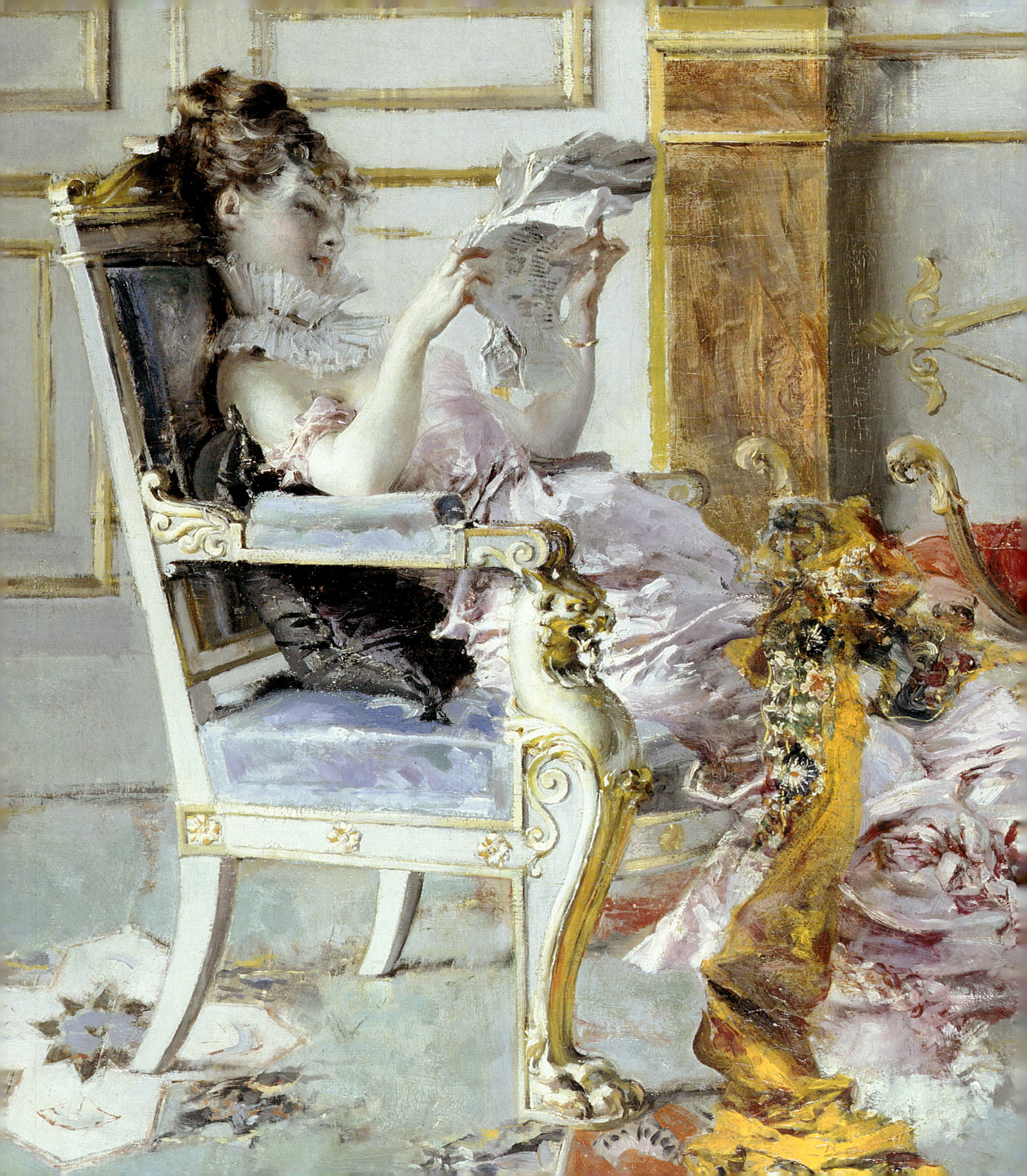

←

**Giovanni Boldini**
*Liseuse dans un salon* (detail)
New York $731,750 (£504,907)
1.v.01

This portrait beautifully illustrates how Boldini, one of the most highly regarded and sought-after painters, captured the elegance of women in 19th-century Paris. Boldini's masterful layering of contrasting fabrics and textures, while maintaining the integrity of each distinct article, is an incredible technical achievement. Signed *Boldini/76*, oil on canvas, 73 by 57.2 cm. (28¾ by 22½ in.).

**Gustave Moreau**
*Eve*
London £619,500 ($873,495)
23.xi.00

Executed between 1880 and 1885, and notable for its vibrant, sumptuous colours, this is the culmination of Moreau's watercolour series of landscapes with female nudes and temptors. Signed, watercolour and gouache on paper, 33 by 19.5 cm. (13 by 7⅝ in.).

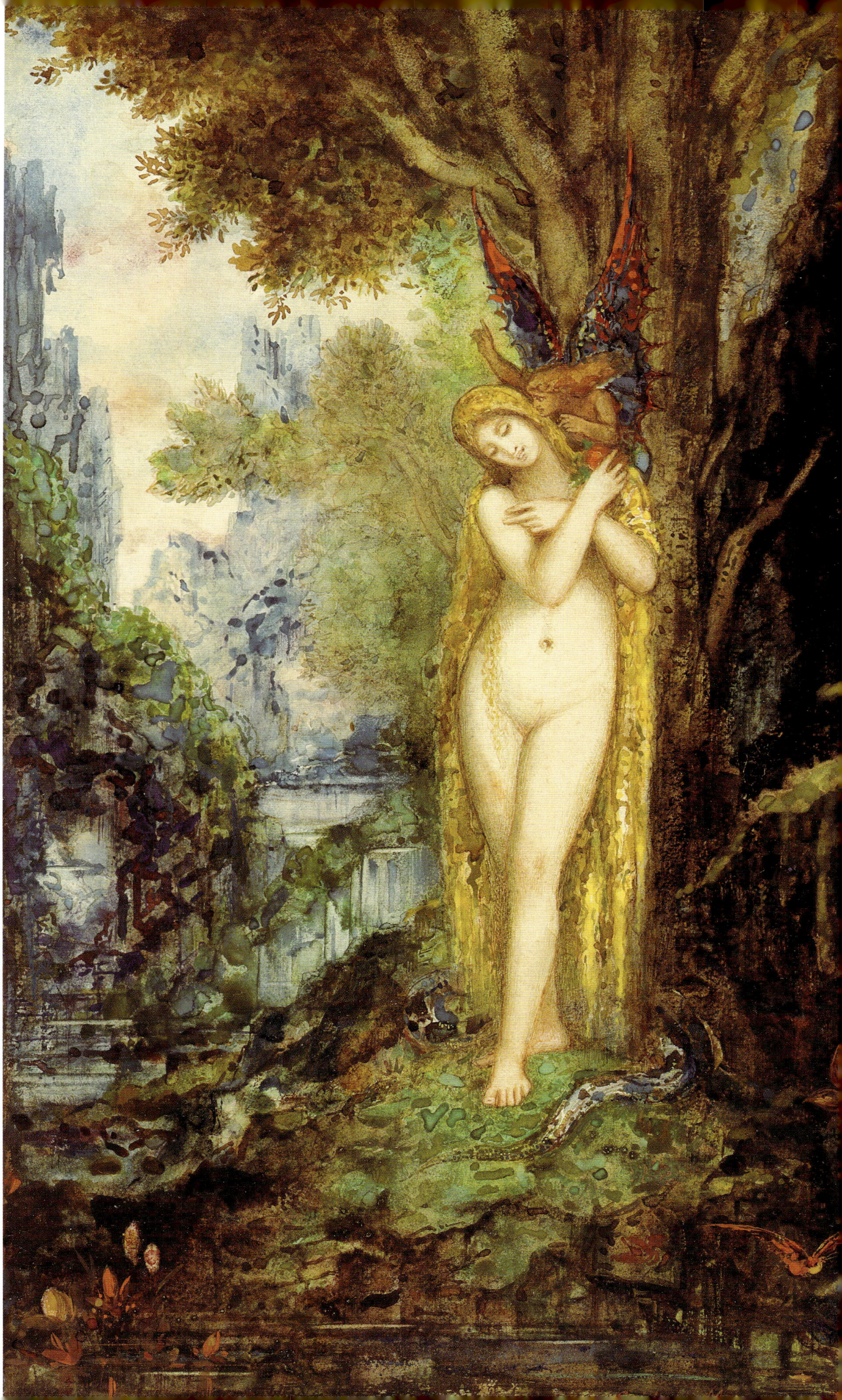

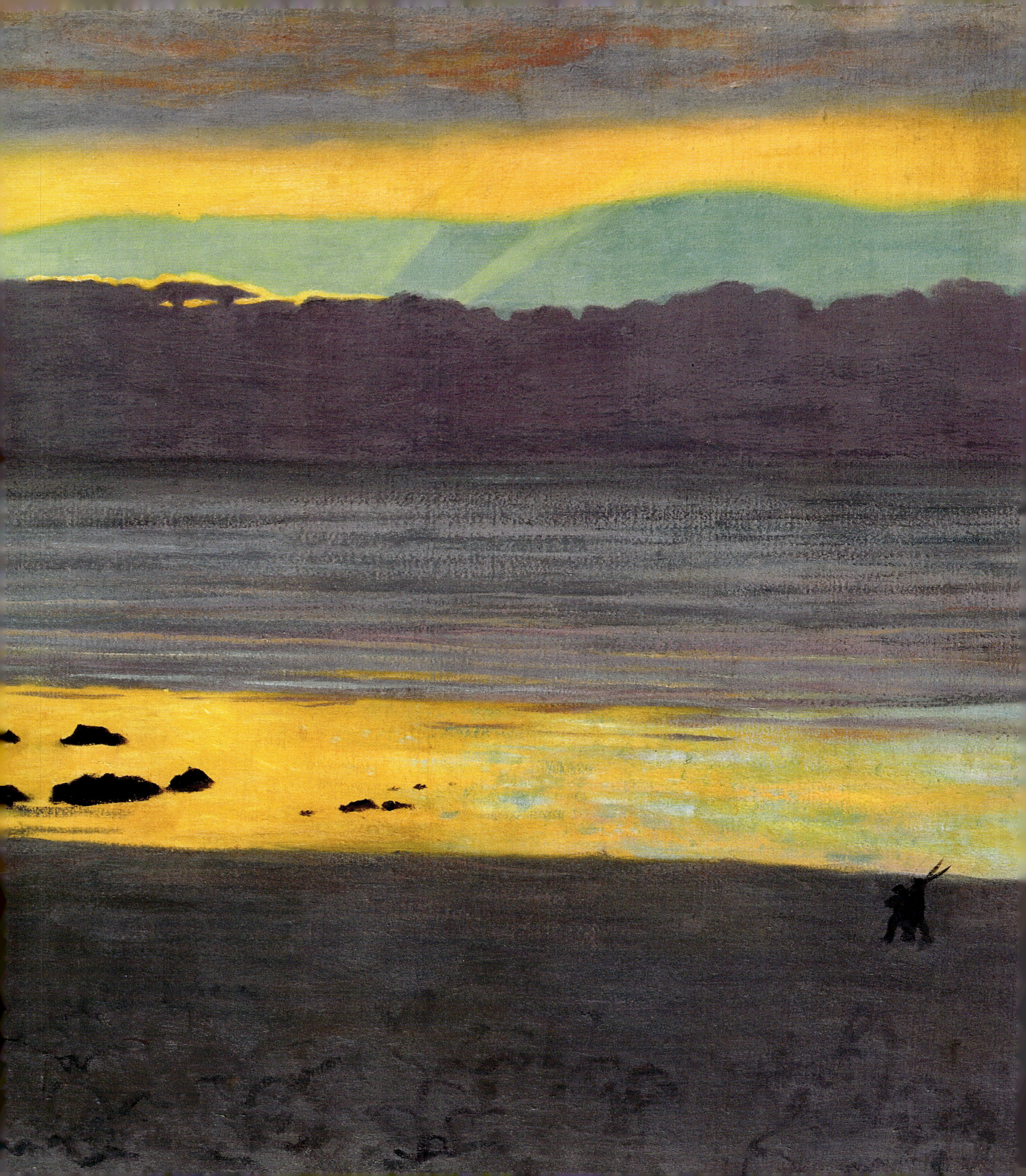

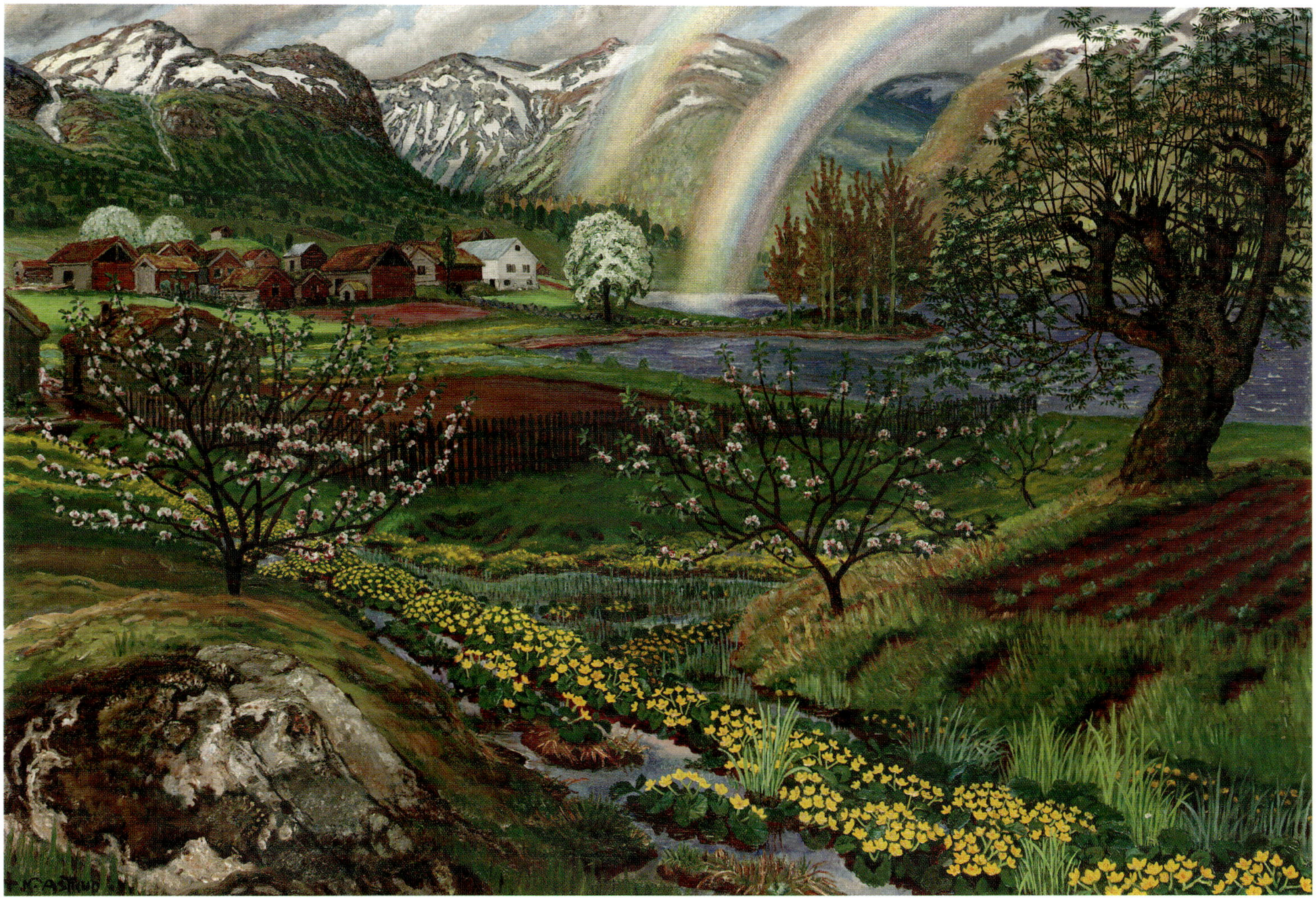

←

**Félix Vallotton**
*Coucher de soleil jaune et vert (Sunset in Yellow and Green)* (detail)
Zurich SF1,652,000 ($958,160; £660,800) 7.XII.00

Vallotton's breathtaking sunset shows his characteristic combination of naturalism with simplified form, the latter inspired by his love of Japanese prints.
Signed and dated *'11*, oil on canvas, 54 by 81 cm. (21¼ by 31⅞ in.).

**Nikolai Astrup**
*Soleier og regnbue (Buttercups and Rainbow)*
London £410,500 ($578,805) 6.VI.01

This work is Astrup's most ambitious and majestic celebration of his beloved Alhus in Norway, combining the two themes that he was preoccupied with: his local community and the forces of the natural world.
Signed, oil on canvas, 72 by 98 cm. (28½ by 38½ in.).

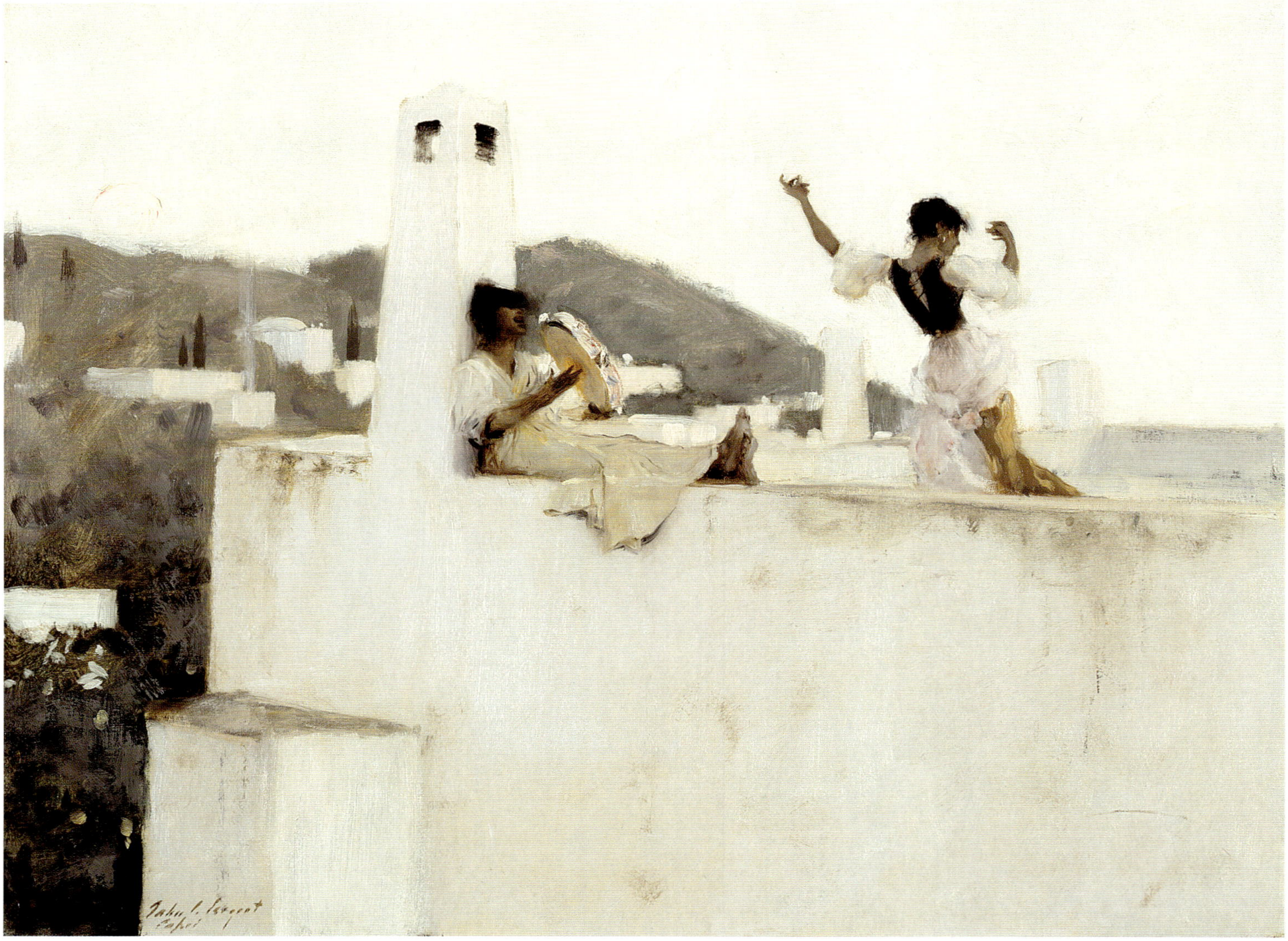

**John Singer Sargent**
*Rosina – Capri*
New York $5,395,750 (£3,777,025)
24.V.01

In 1878, John Singer Sargent travelled to the Mediterranean island of Capri in search of subject matter that would appeal to the contemporary public and satisfy his own fascination with foreign cultures. Rosina Ferrara, the Anacapriote woman who appears in the present painting, personified the seductive beauty and exotic culture of Capri.
Signed, oil on canvas, 50.2 by 64.8 cm. (19¾ by 25½ in.).

→
**Thomas Moran**
*Mount Moran, Teton Range*
New York $2,975,750 (£2,083,025)
30.XI.00

*Mount Moran, Teton Range* is a beautiful and quintessential example of Thomas Moran's grandly romantic vision of the American West. Moran's paintings of the dramatic western panorama captured the imagination of turn-of-the-century America and inspired the creation of the National Park system.
Signed and dated *1903*, oil on canvas, 101.6 by 76.2 cm. (40 by 30 in.).

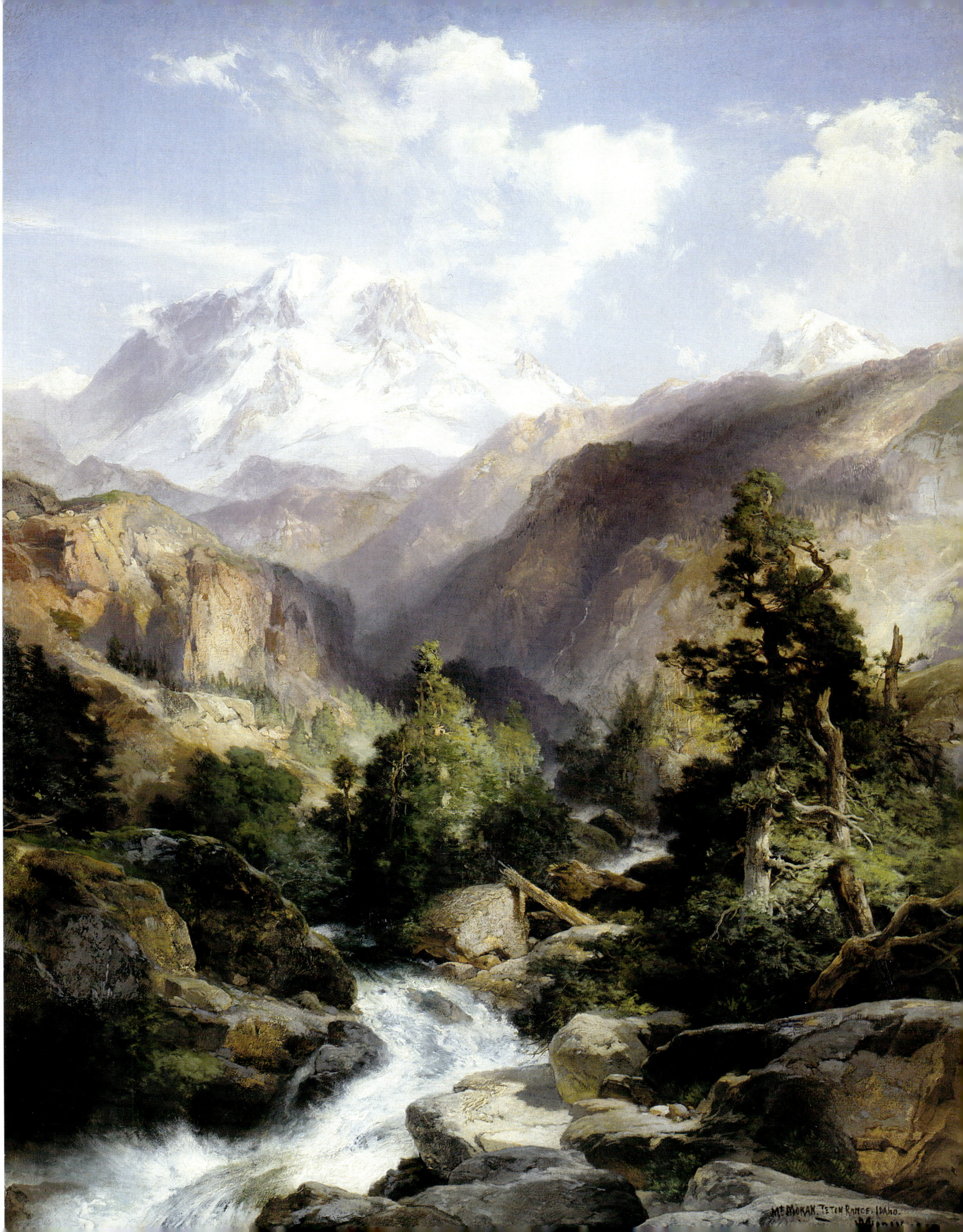
M^t MORAN. TETON RANGE, IDAHO.

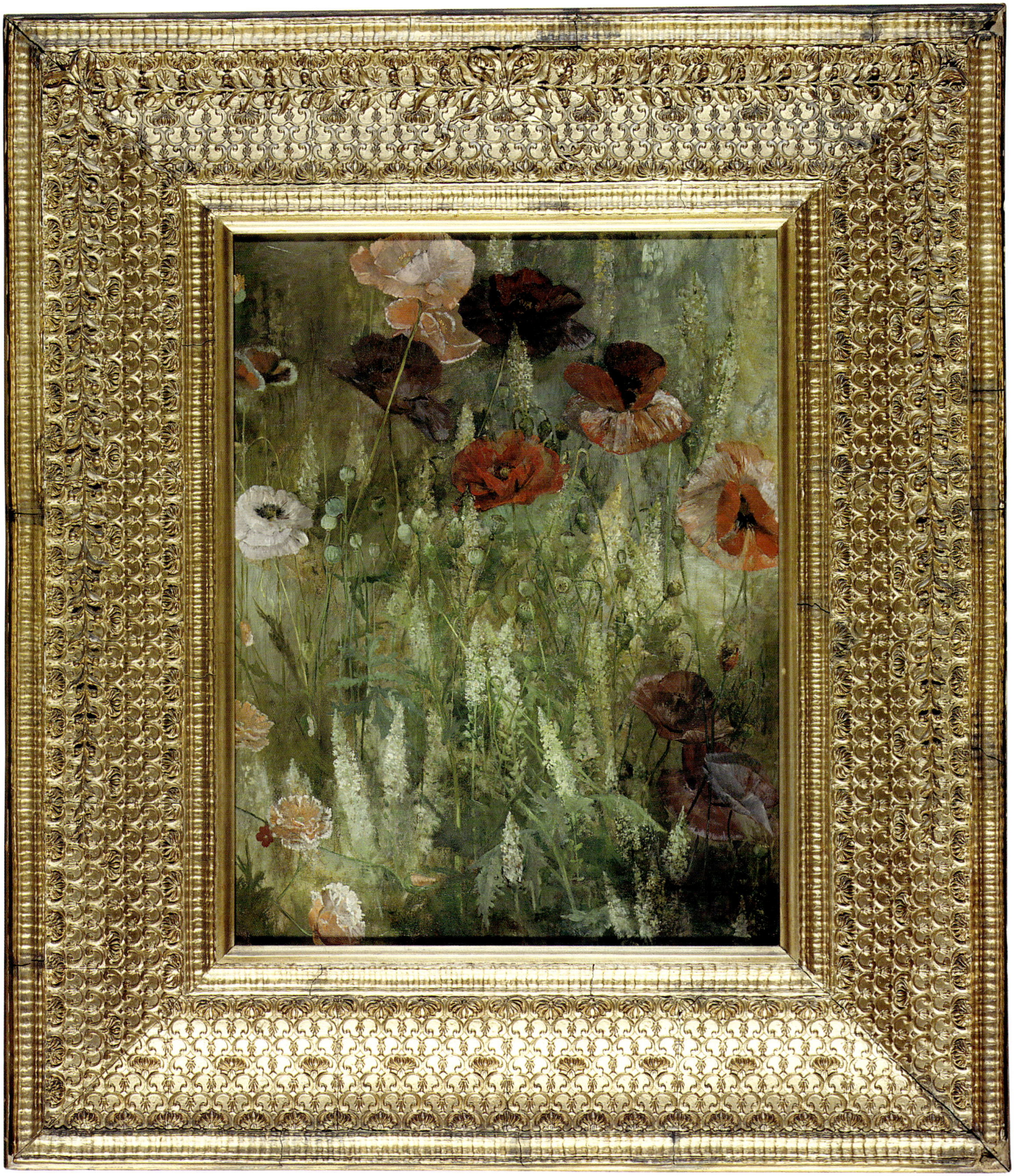

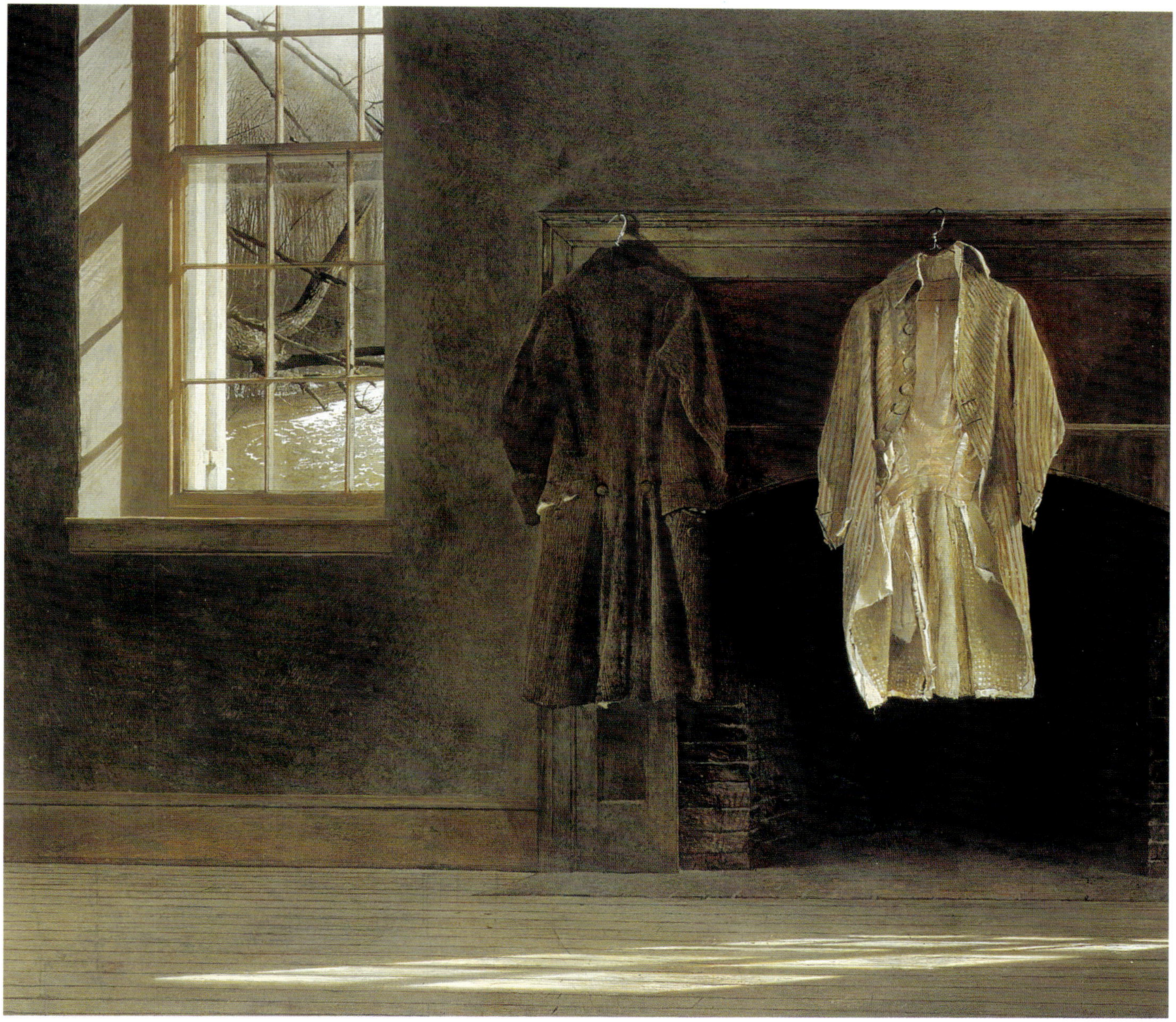

←

**Maria Oakey Dewing**
*Poppies and Italian Mignonette*
New York $2,535,750 (£1,775,025)
30.XI.00

One of only two paintings of poppies executed by Maria Oakey Dewing, *Poppies and Italian Mignonette* is a charming example of the artist's unique talent for flower painting, which was widely recognized during her lifetime.
Signed and dated *1891*, oil on canvas, 58.4 by 43.2 cm. (23 by 17 in.).

**Andrew Wyeth**
*The Quaker*
New York $2,535,750 (£1,775,025)
30.XI.00

Andrew Wyeth inherited his father N.C.'s fascination with story characters and costumes, which had been instilled in the elder Wyeth by his teacher Howard Pyle, to whom this Quaker coat and fop's costume originally belonged.
Signed, tempera on panel, 93.3 by 102.9 cm. (36¾ by 40½ in.).

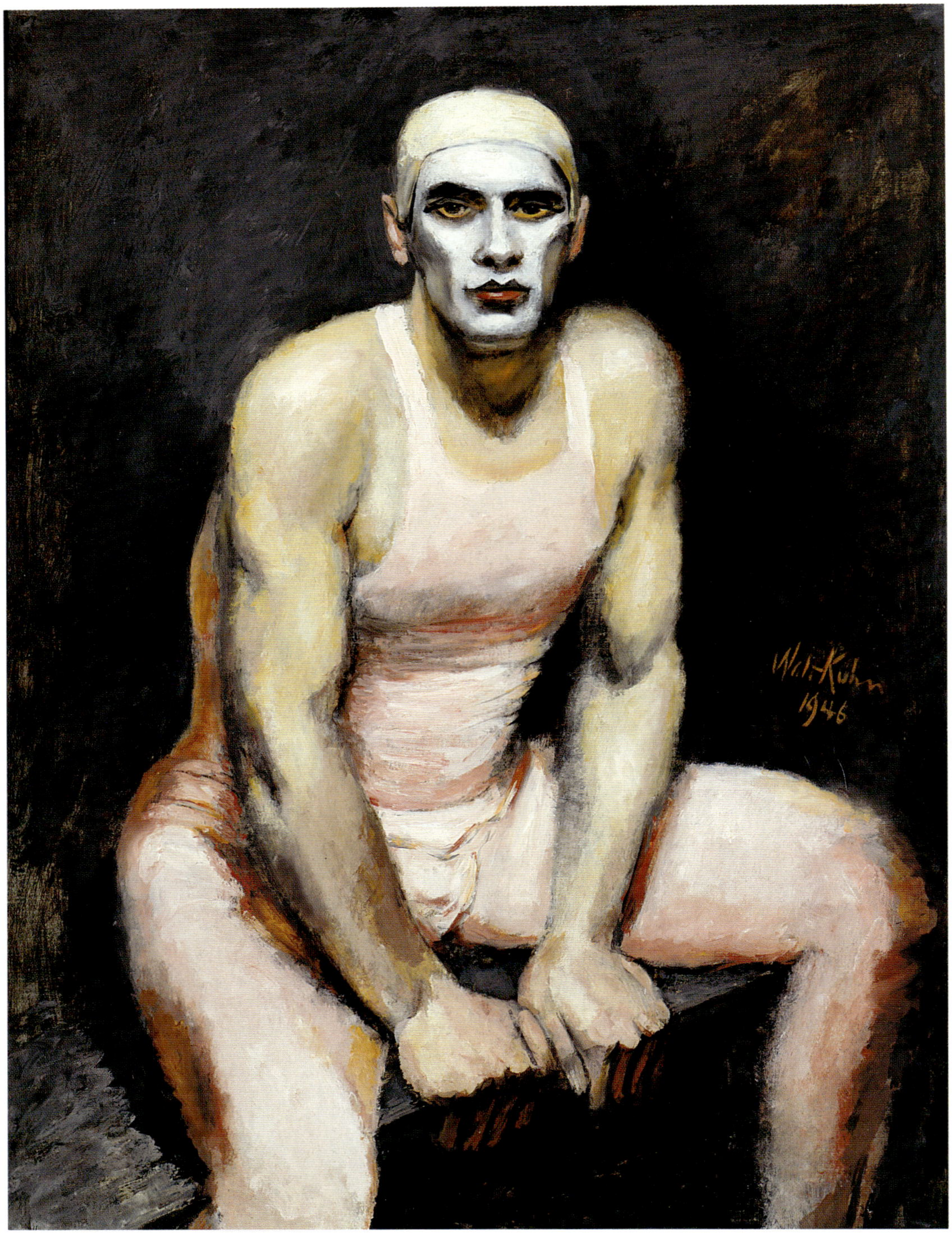


**Walt Kuhn**
*Roberto*
New York $1,105,750 (£774,025)
24.V.01

In his paintings of clowns and circus performers Walt Kuhn strove to capture the human character beneath the show personalities. At its first exhibition in 1946 *Roberto* was highly praised by critics, who described it as 'one of the most vital and arresting portraits the artist has ever done'. Signed and dated *1946*, oil on canvas, 101.6 by 76.2 cm. (40 by 30 in.).

→
**Marsden Hartley**
*Abstraction*
New York $2,205,750 (£1,544,025)
30.XI.00

Painted in 1913, *Abstraction* belongs to a distinctive body of Hartley's early work that was influenced by the artist's encounters with contemporary European art. It exemplifies Hartley's non-representational work at its most essential, rejecting all figurative images in favour of completely abstract forms. Oil on canvas, 119.4 by 100.3 cm. (47 by 39½ in.).

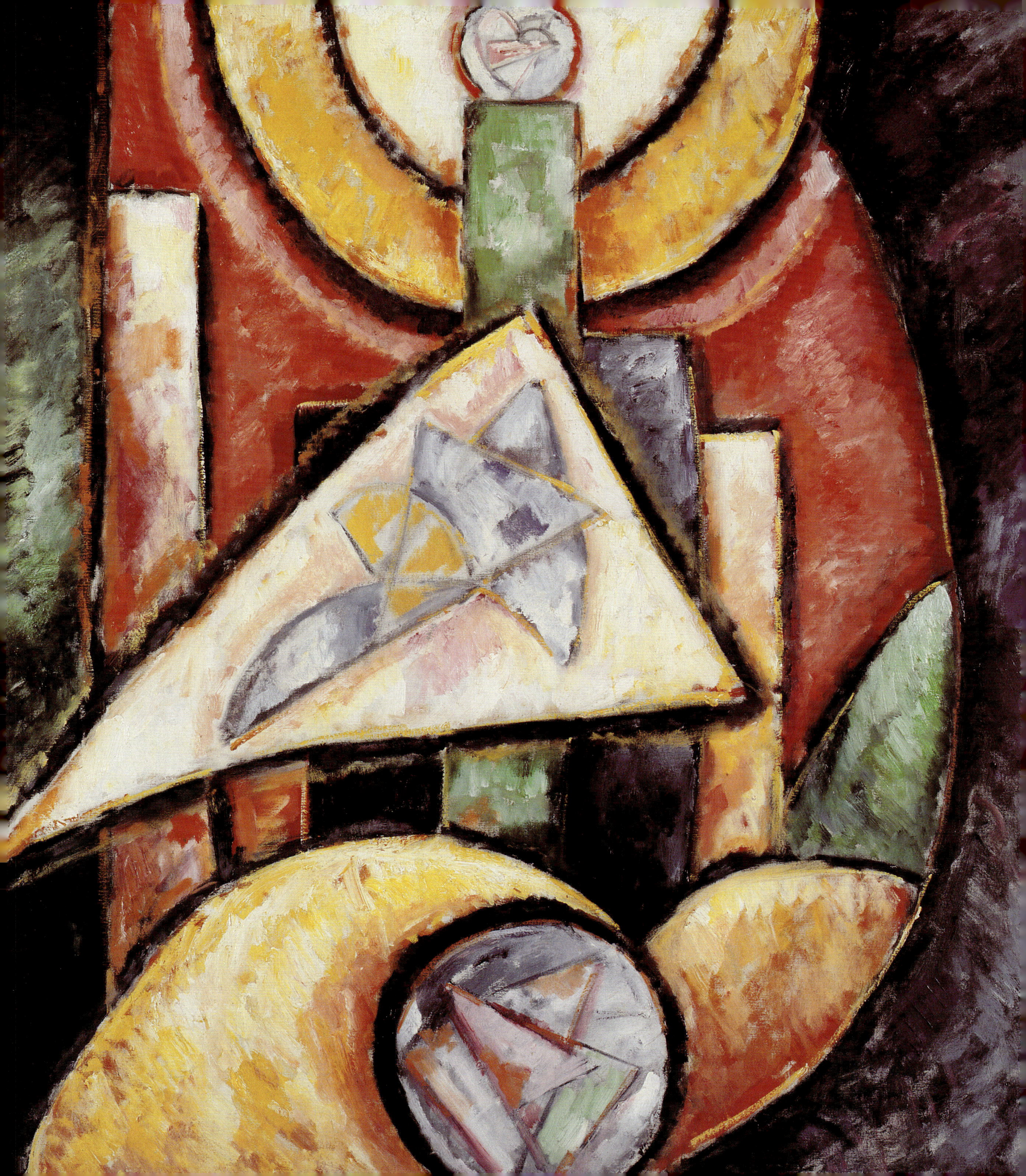

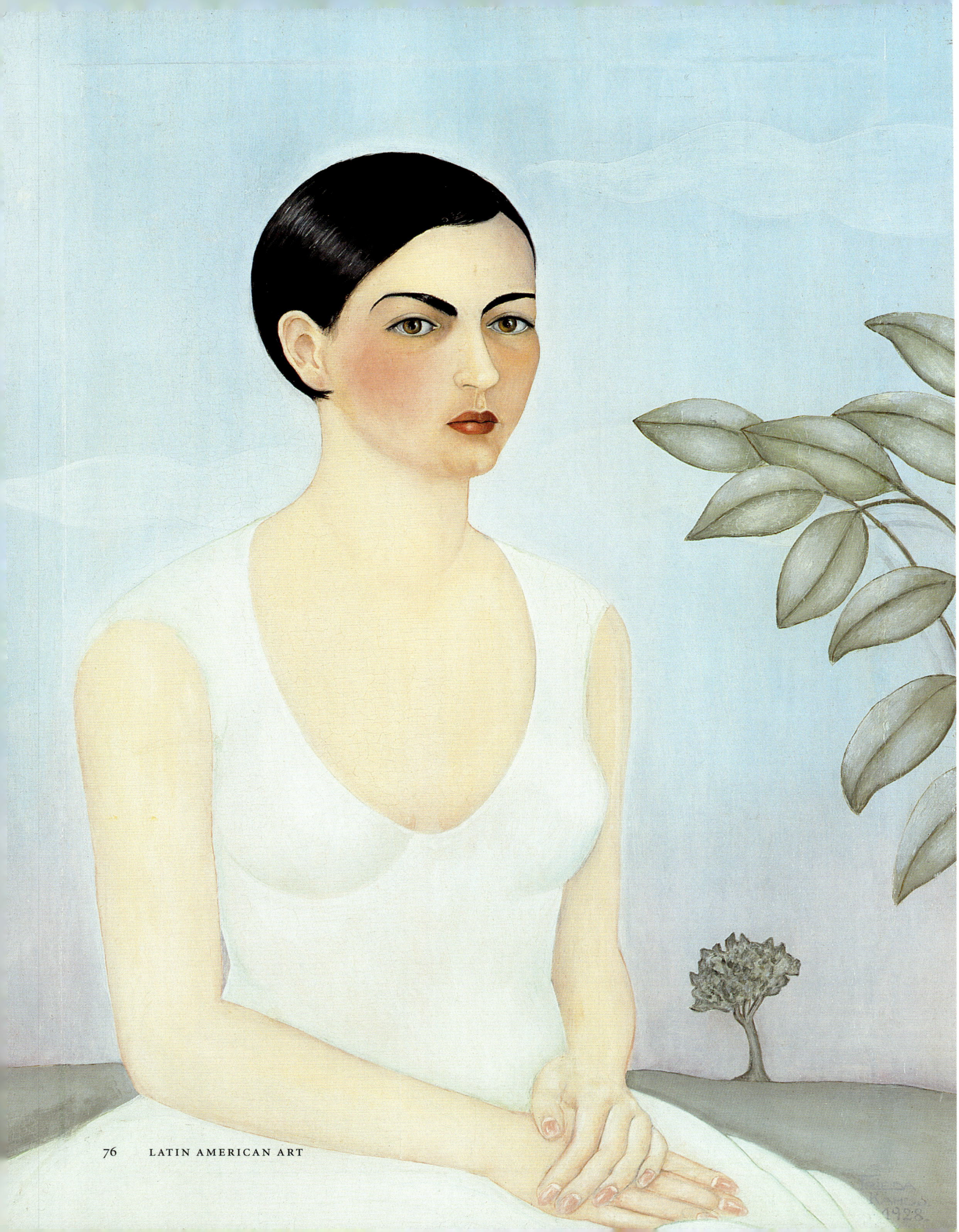

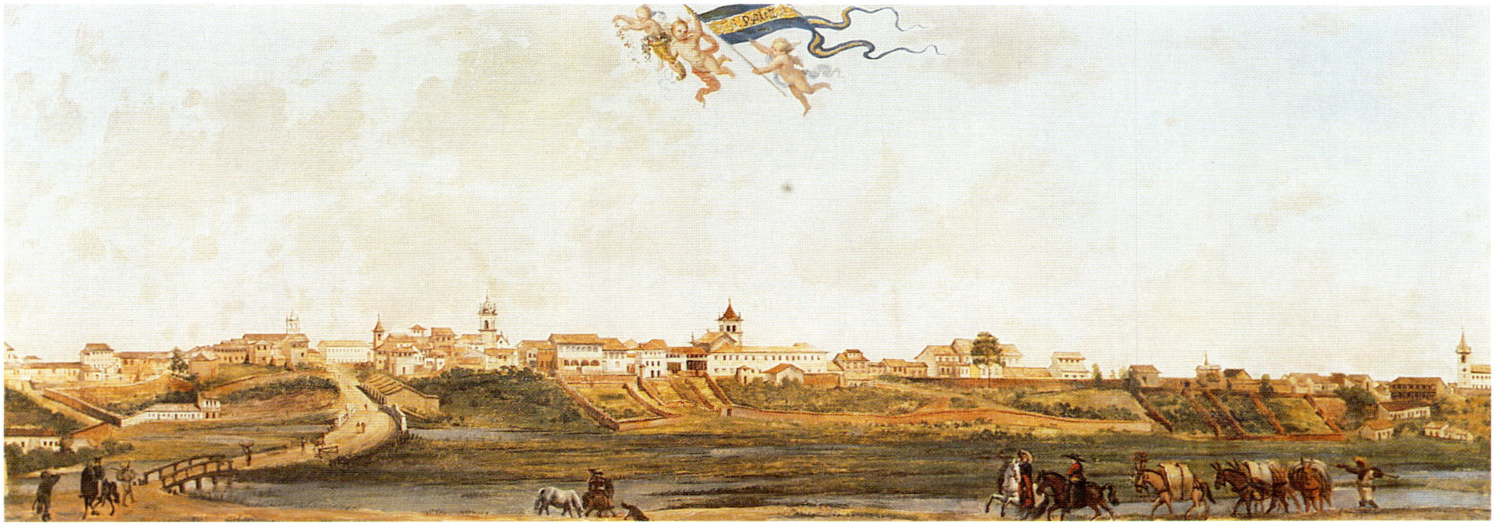

←

**Frida Kahlo**
*Portrait of Cristina, My Sister*
New York $1,655,750 (£1,159,025)
31.V.01

The youngest of four sisters, Cristina was Frida's dearest friend. Frida's love for her sister is evident through this sensitive depiction, as well as through Frida's ability to forgive her for the affair she had with Frida's husband, the artist Diego Rivera.
Signed and dated *1928*, oil on panel, 79 by 60 cm. (31⅛ by 23⅝ in.).

**Arnaud Julien Pallière**
*Panorama of the City of São Paulo*
New York $830,750 (£581,525)
20.XI.00

This panorama, painted in 1821, is the earliest known view of São Paulo in Brazil. It disappeared in the 19th century until it was discovered in 1999 in the home of a prominent family from Rio de Janeiro.
Oil on canvas, 36.5 by 96.8 cm. (14⅜ by 38⅛ in.).

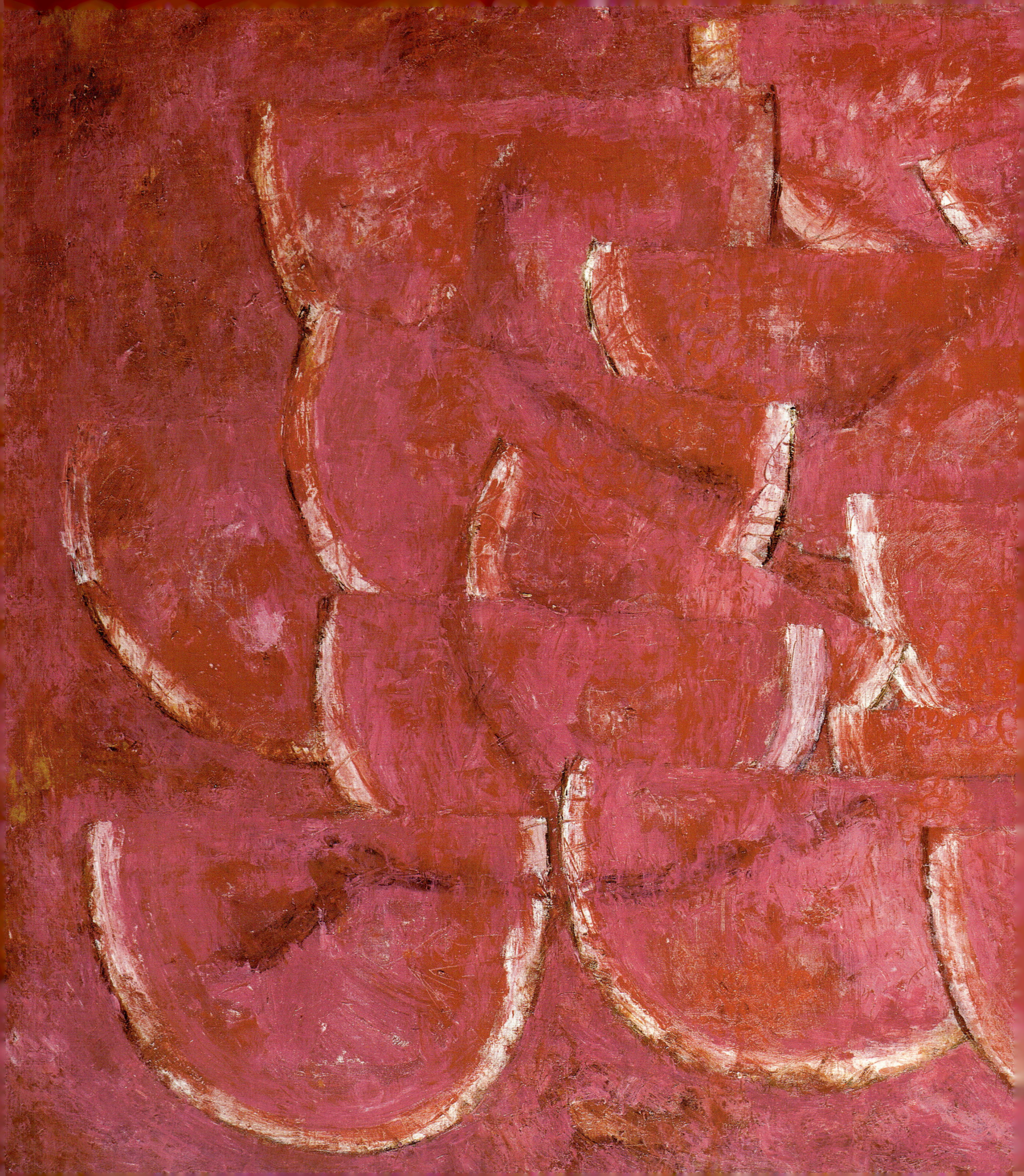

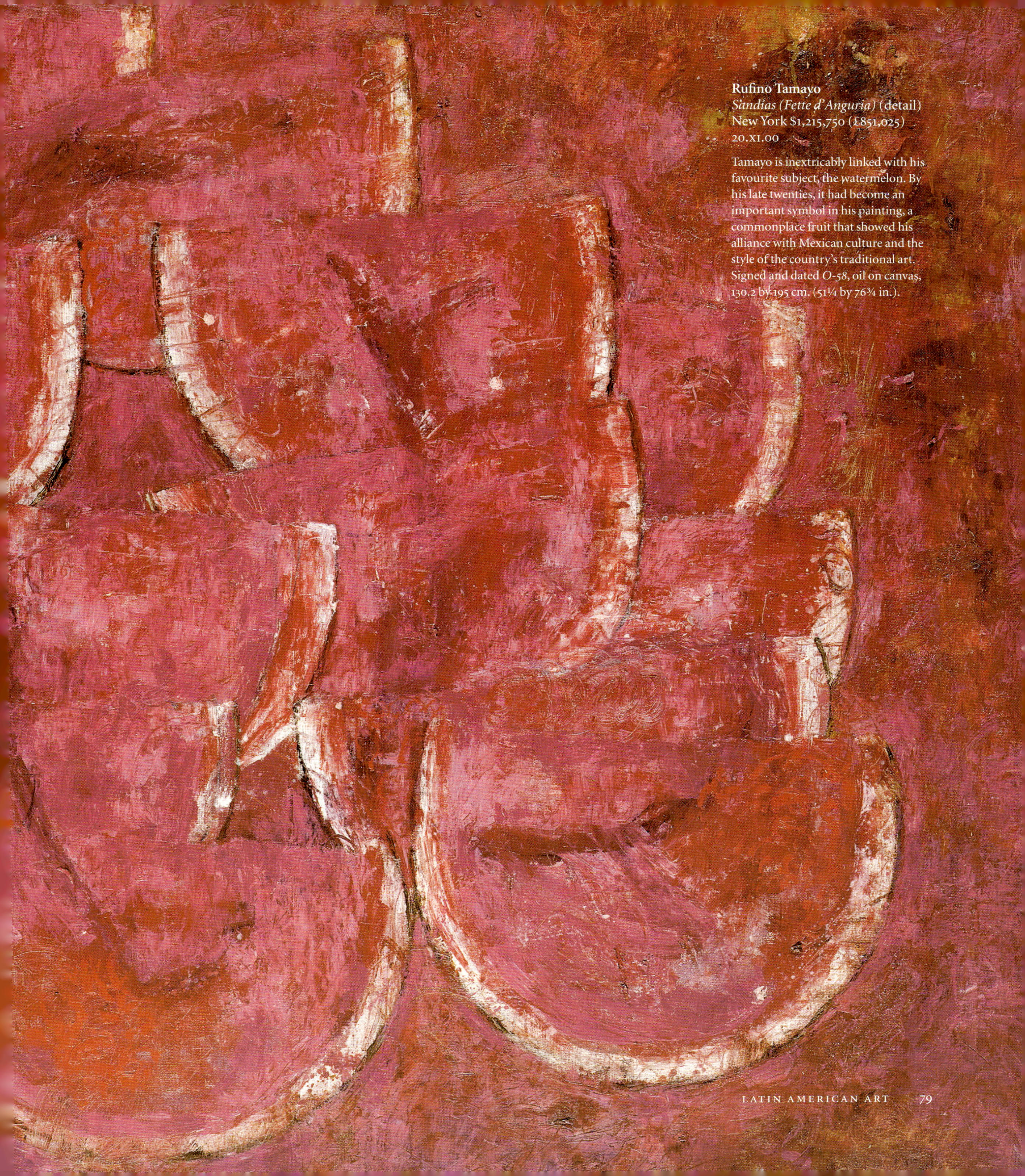

**Rufino Tamayo**
*Sandías (Fette d'Anguria)* (detail)
New York $1,215,750 (£851,025)
20.XI.00

Tamayo is inextricably linked with his favourite subject, the watermelon. By his late twenties, it had become an important symbol in his painting, a commonplace fruit that showed his alliance with Mexican culture and the style of the country's traditional art. Signed and dated *O-58*, oil on canvas, 130.2 by 195 cm. (51¼ by 76¾ in.).

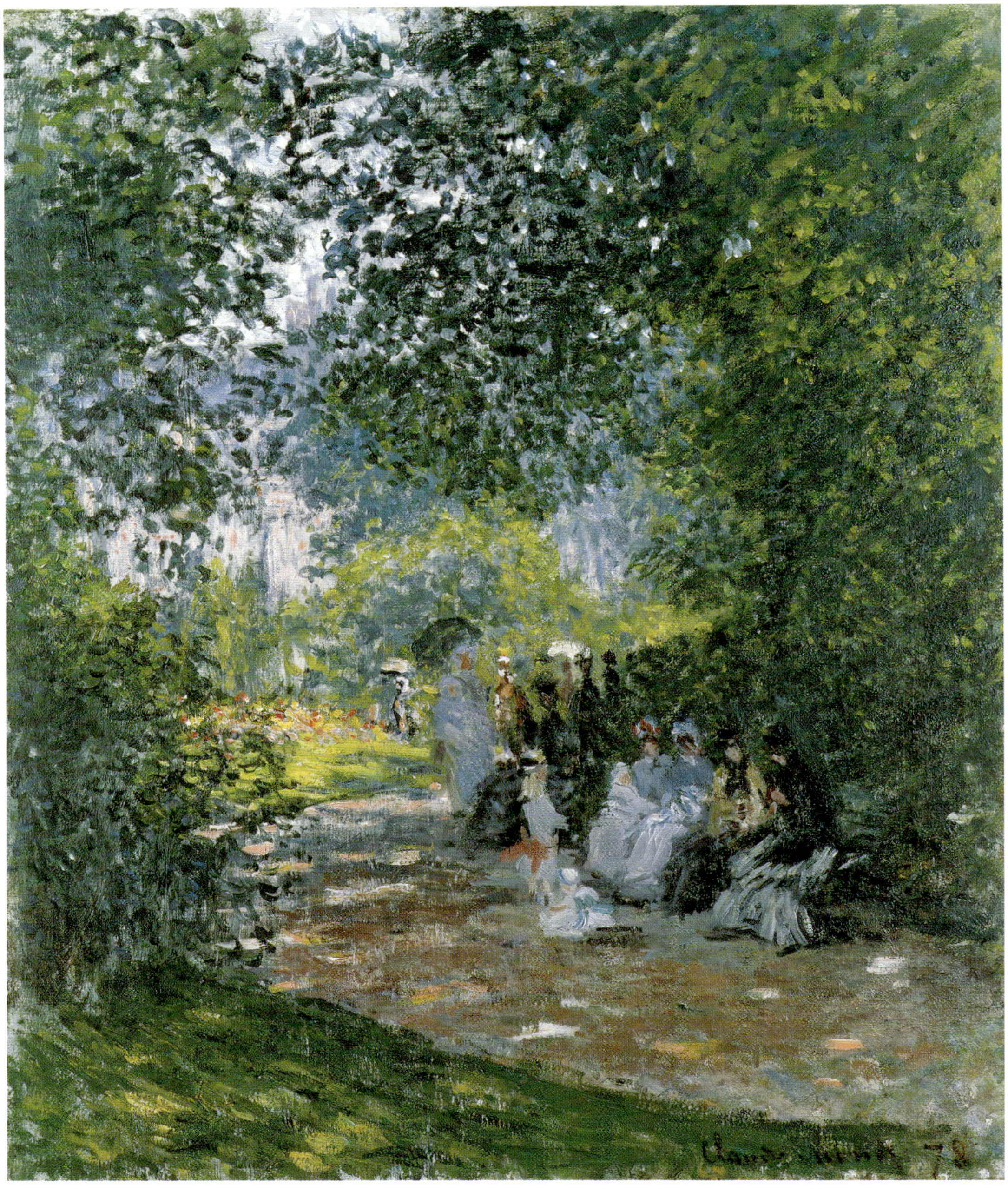

**Claude Monet**
*Au Parc Monceau*
London £3,743,500 ($5,278,335)
26.VI.01

Monet left Argenteuil at the beginning of 1878, moving to Paris where Camille gave birth to their second son, Michel. Monet spent days roaming the city for inspiration, and found the perfect subject in the parks of Paris.
Signed and dated *78*, oil on canvas, 65.5 by 54.5 cm. (25¾ by 21½ in.).

→
**Claude Monet**
*Le Parlement, soleil couchant*
(detail)
New York $14,580,750 (£10,206,525)
10.V.01

Monet's series of paintings of the Houses of Parliament are the most unified of his London series. He is reported to have followed the same painting routine in each of his visits to London: Waterloo Bridge in the early morning, Charing Cross Bridge midday and afternoon, and the Houses of Parliament at sunset.
Signed and dated *1902*,
oil on canvas, 81.6 by 93 cm.
(32⅛ by 36⅝ in.).

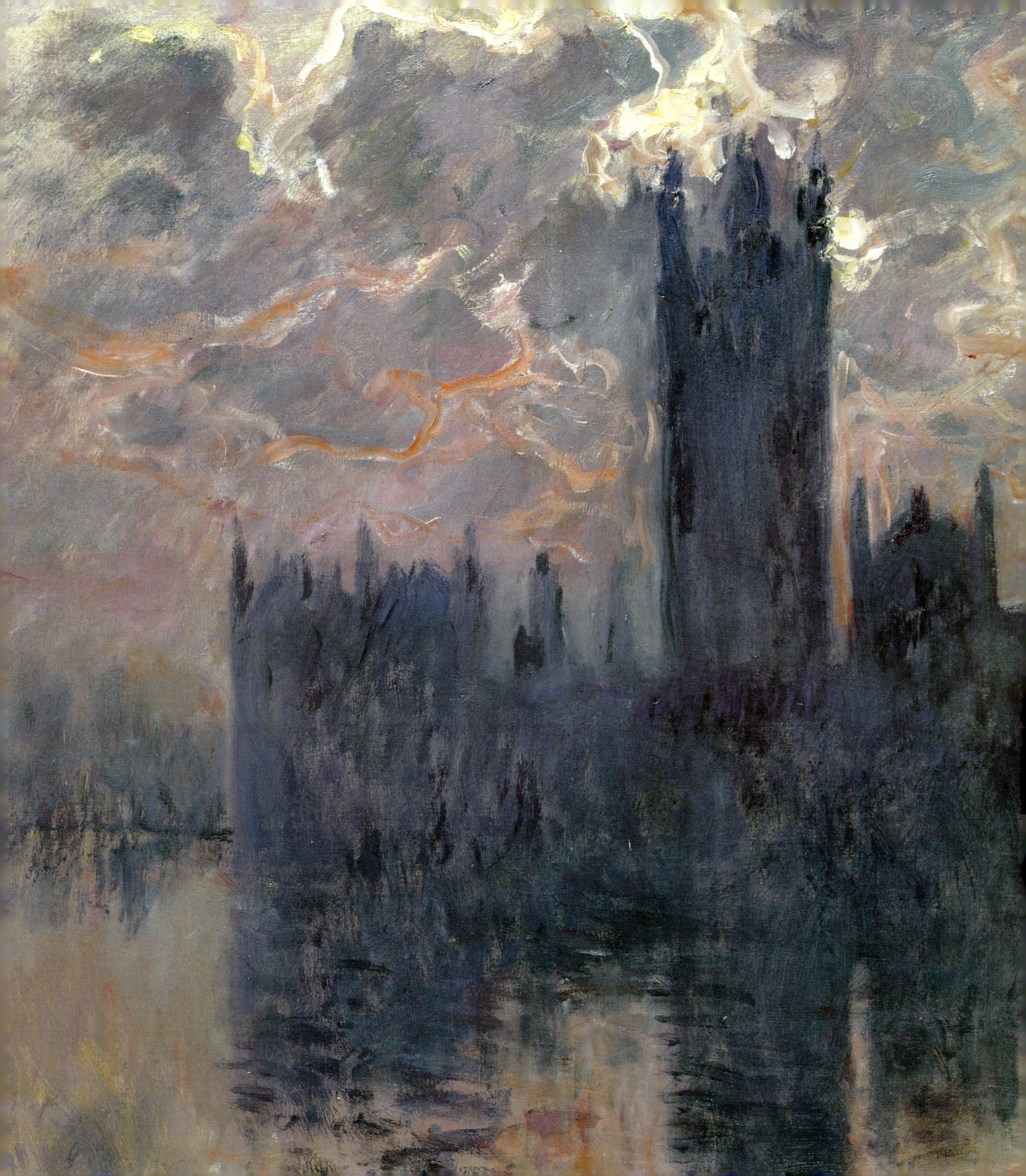

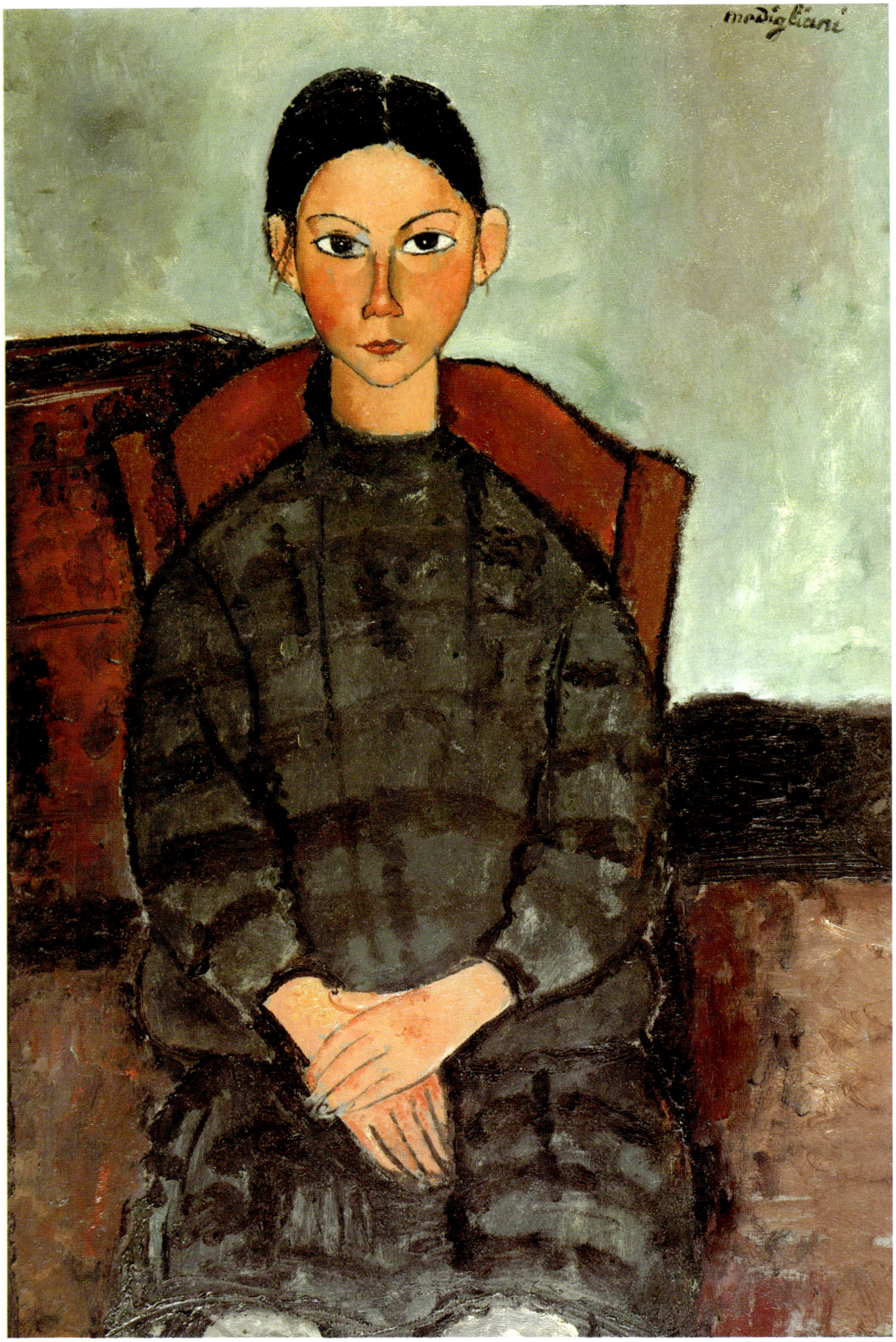


**Amedeo Modigliani**
*Fillette assise en robe*
New York $15,625,750 (£11,094,282) 9.XI.00

In 1918 Modigliani left Paris and his bohemian circle of friends for the south of France, where he painted local people and children in sensitive forthright poses that differed dramatically from his mannered portraits of Parisian artists, models and notables.
Signed, oil on canvas, 93 by 61 cm. (36½ by 23⅞ in.).

→
**Edouard Manet**
*Jeune fille dans un jardin*
New York $20,905,750 (£14,843,082) 9.XI.00

This portrait was painted in the garden of the house in the suburb of Bellevue, near Paris, that Manet rented during the summer of 1880. This is one of two paintings of Marguerite, an American who was the sister-in-law of Manet's friend Jules Guillemet.
Oil on canvas, 153.7 by 116.8 cm. (60½ by 46 in.).

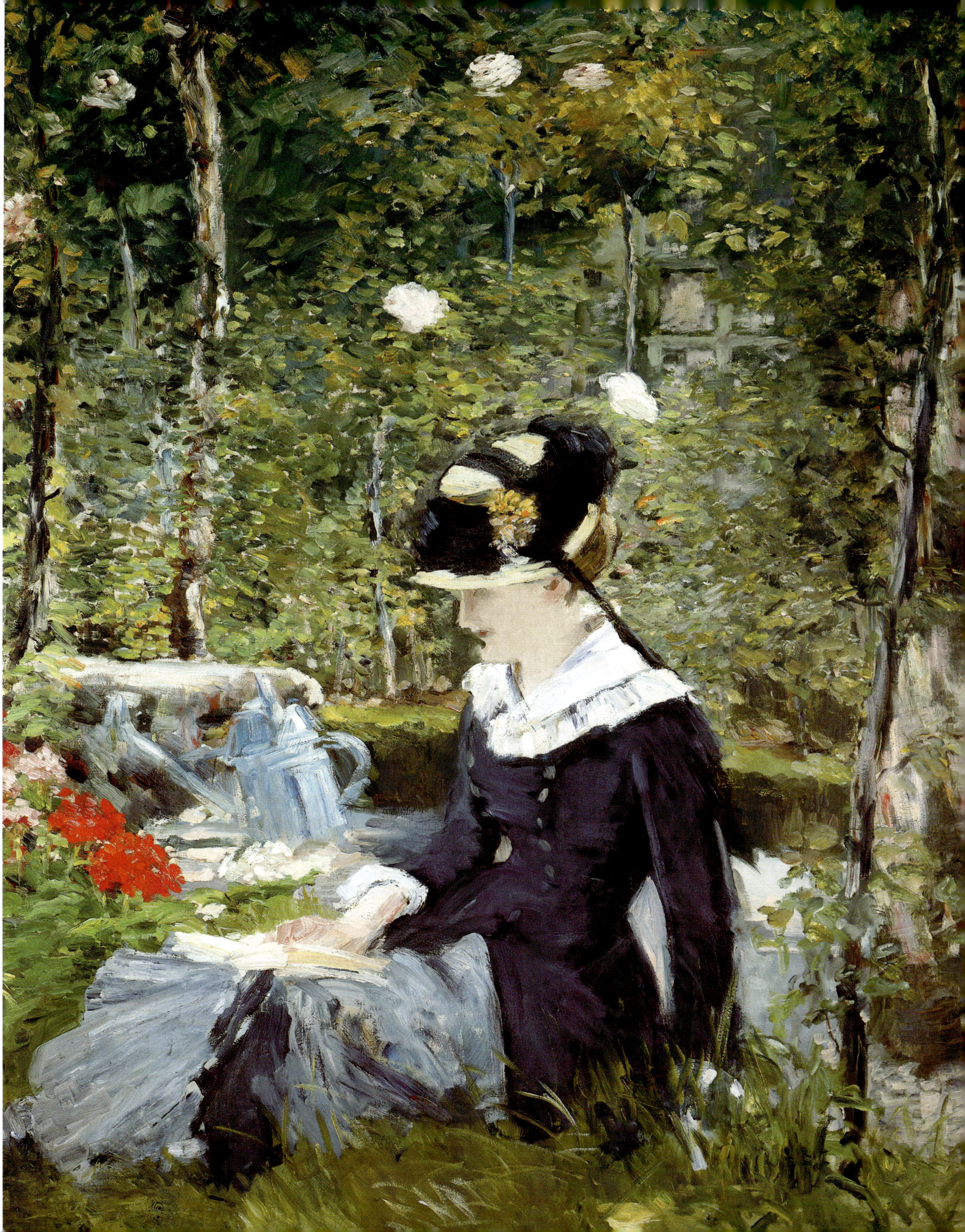

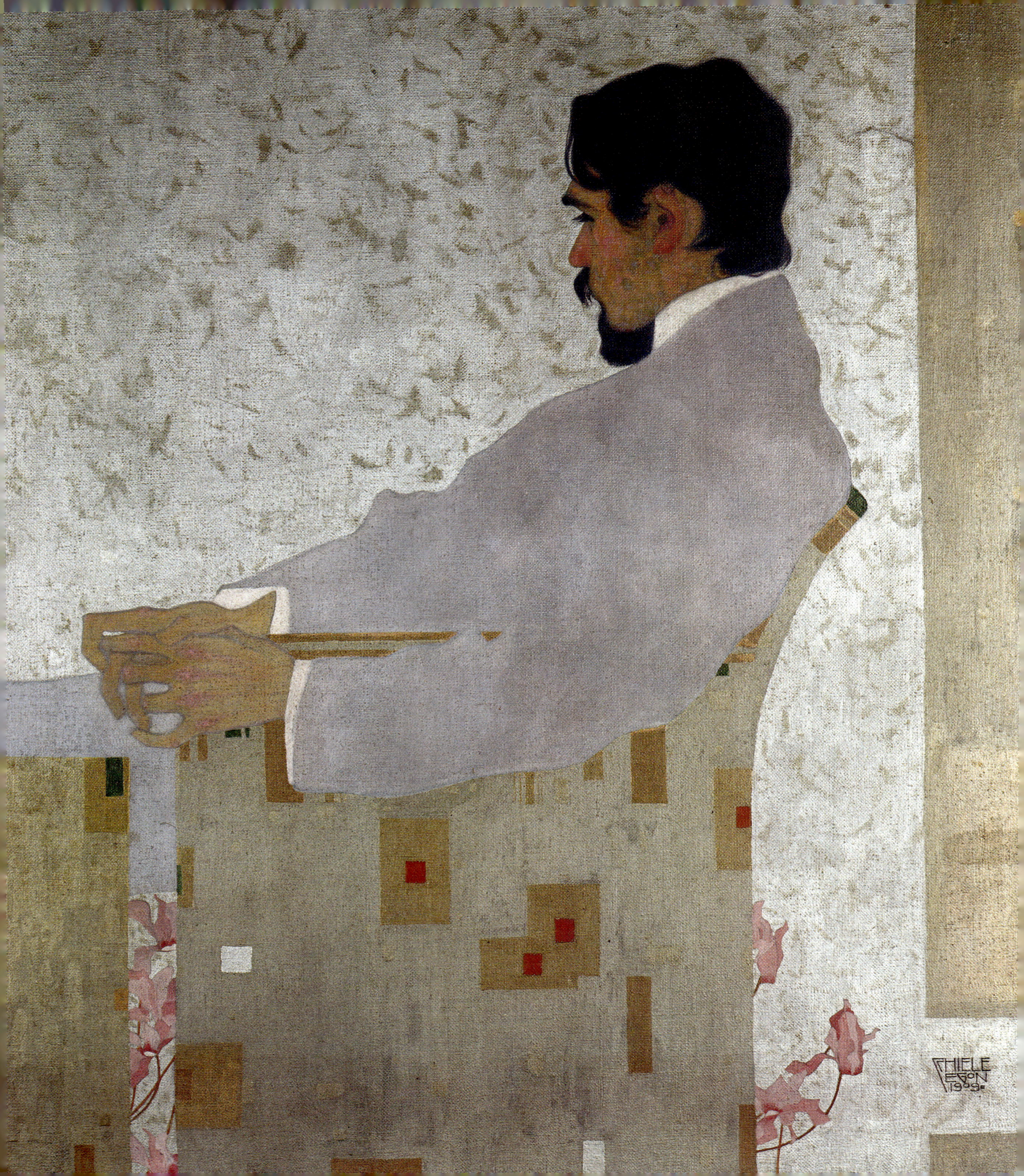
SCHIELE
EGON
1909

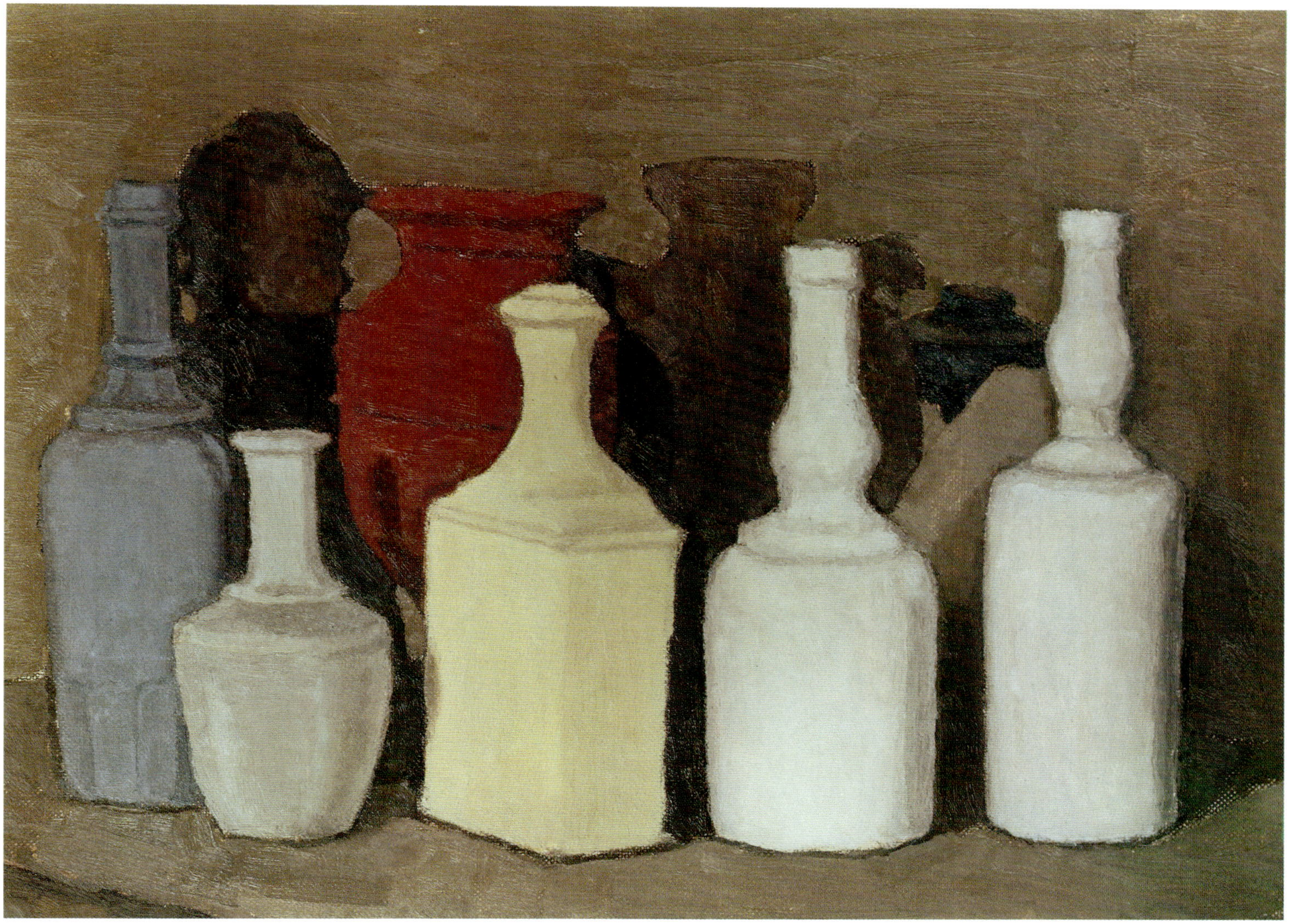

←

**Egon Schiele**
*Porträt des Malers Anton Peschka (Portrait of the Painter Anton Peschka)* (detail)
London £7,703,500 ($11,324,45)
5.II.01

Painted in 1909, this monumental portrait is one of the artist's greatest early masterpieces. Anton Peschka was Schiele's classmate at the Academy of Fine Arts in Vienna, and later married the artist's sister Gertrude. The sale of this painting in February established a world auction record for an oil by Schiele.
Signed and dated *1909*, oil, silver and gold bronze paint on canvas, 110 by 100 cm. (43¼ by 39⅜ in.).

**Giorgio Morandi**
*Natura morta*
London £839,500 ($1,217,275)
25.X.00

Painted in 1938, this early still life sold in London in October's Italian Sale. It achieved a record price for the artist, reaching double its low estimate.
Oil on canvas, 30 by 42 cm. (11⅜ by 16½ in.).

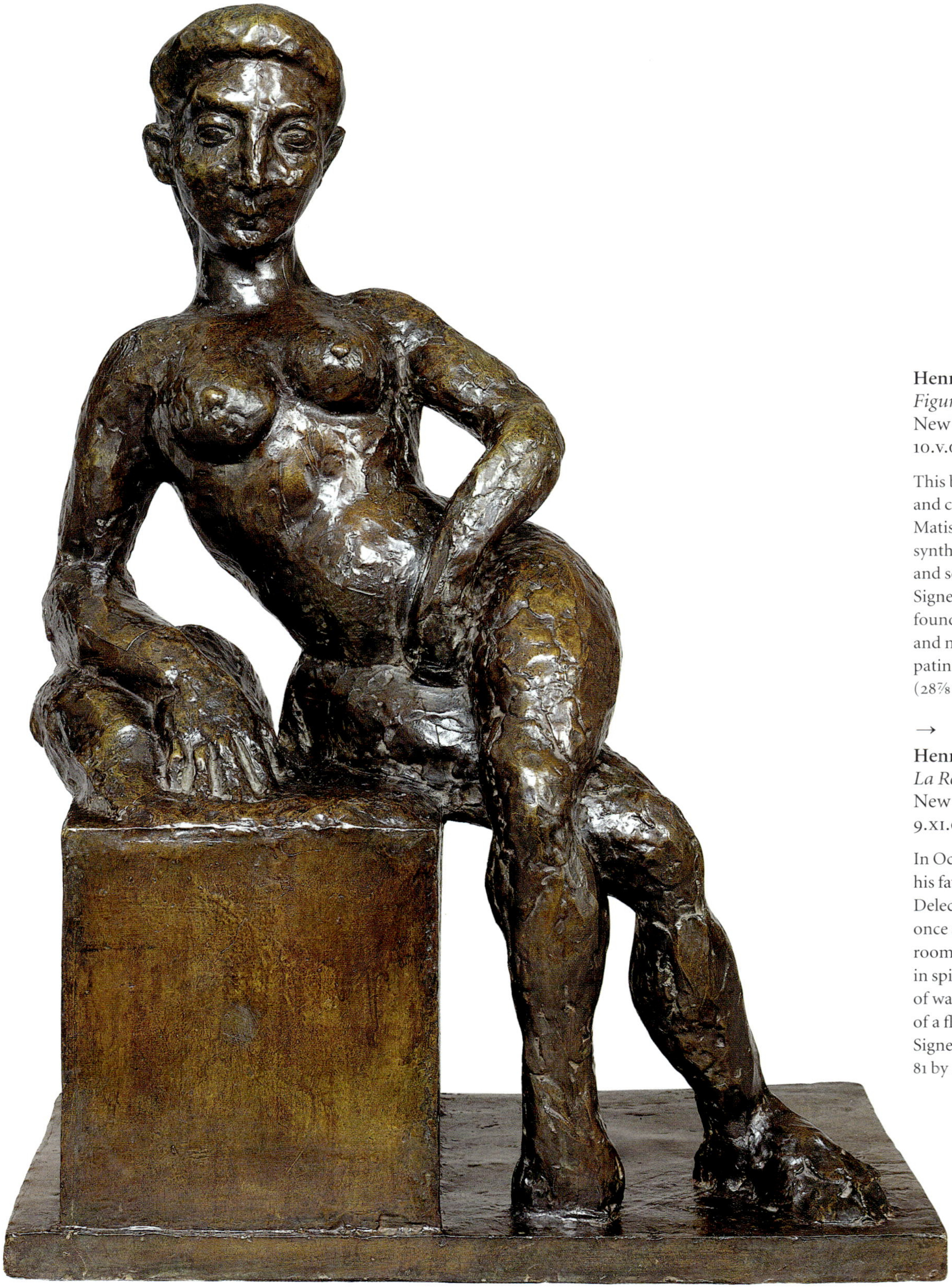

**Henri Matisse**
*Figure decorative*
New York $12,655,750 (£8,859,025)
10.V.01

This bronze was conceived in 1908 and cast in 1952. With this sculpture, Matisse achieved a remarkable synthesis of formal rigour and sensuousness.
Signed *H.M.*, stamped with the foundry mark *C. Valsuani cire perdue*, and numbered *8*, bronze, rich brown patina with gold highlights, 73.3 cm. (28⅞ in.) high.

→

**Henri Matisse**
*La Robe Persane*
New York $17,055,750 (£12,109,582)
9.XI.00

In October 1939 Matisse and his favourite model Lydia Delectorskaya returned to Nice, once again taking over the grand rooms at the Hotel Régina where, in spite of the troubles and uncertainty of war, he continued to paint canvases of a fluid, joyous quality.
Signed and dated *40*, oil on canvas, 81 by 65 cm. (32 by 25⅝ in.).

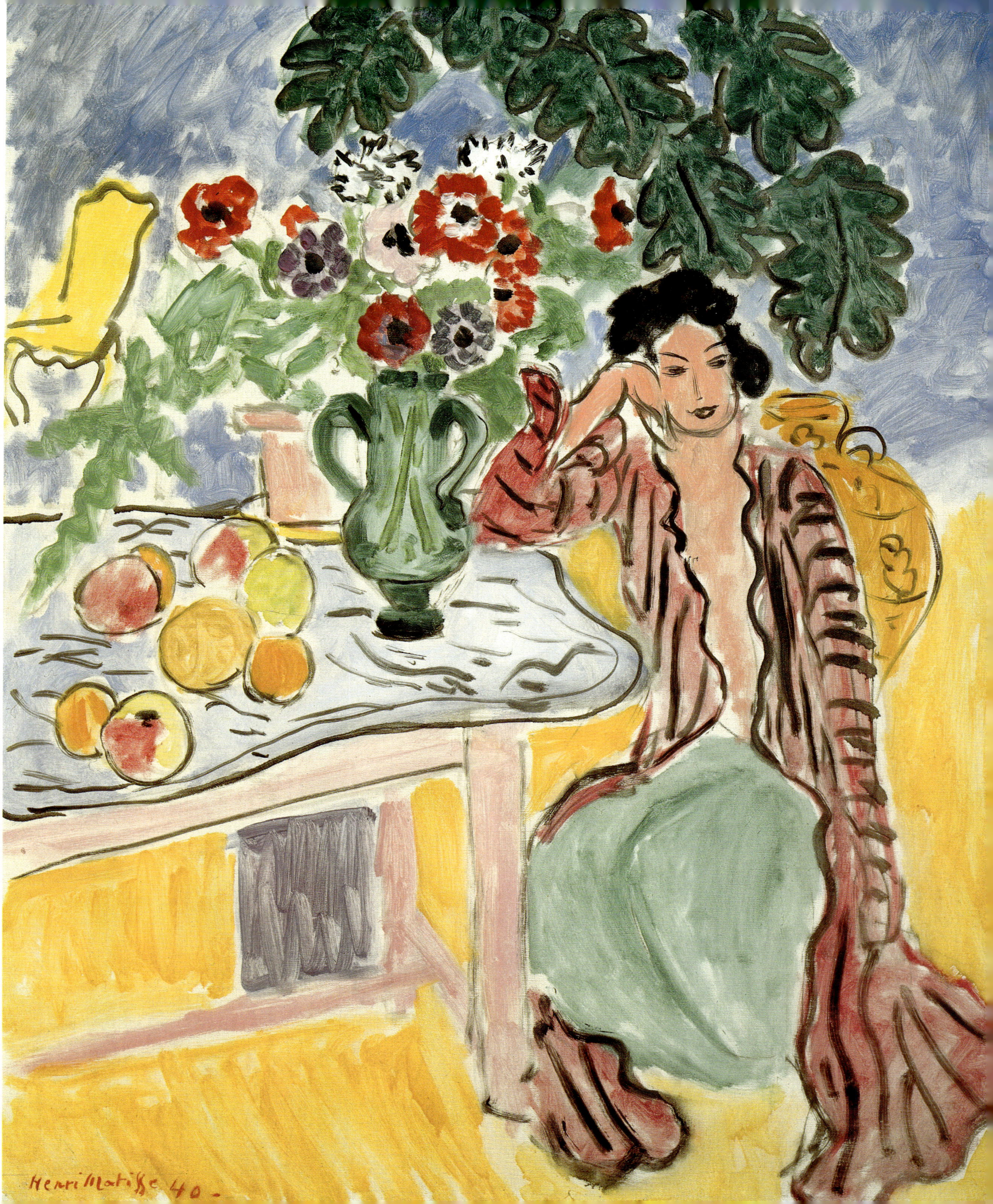
Henri Matisse 40

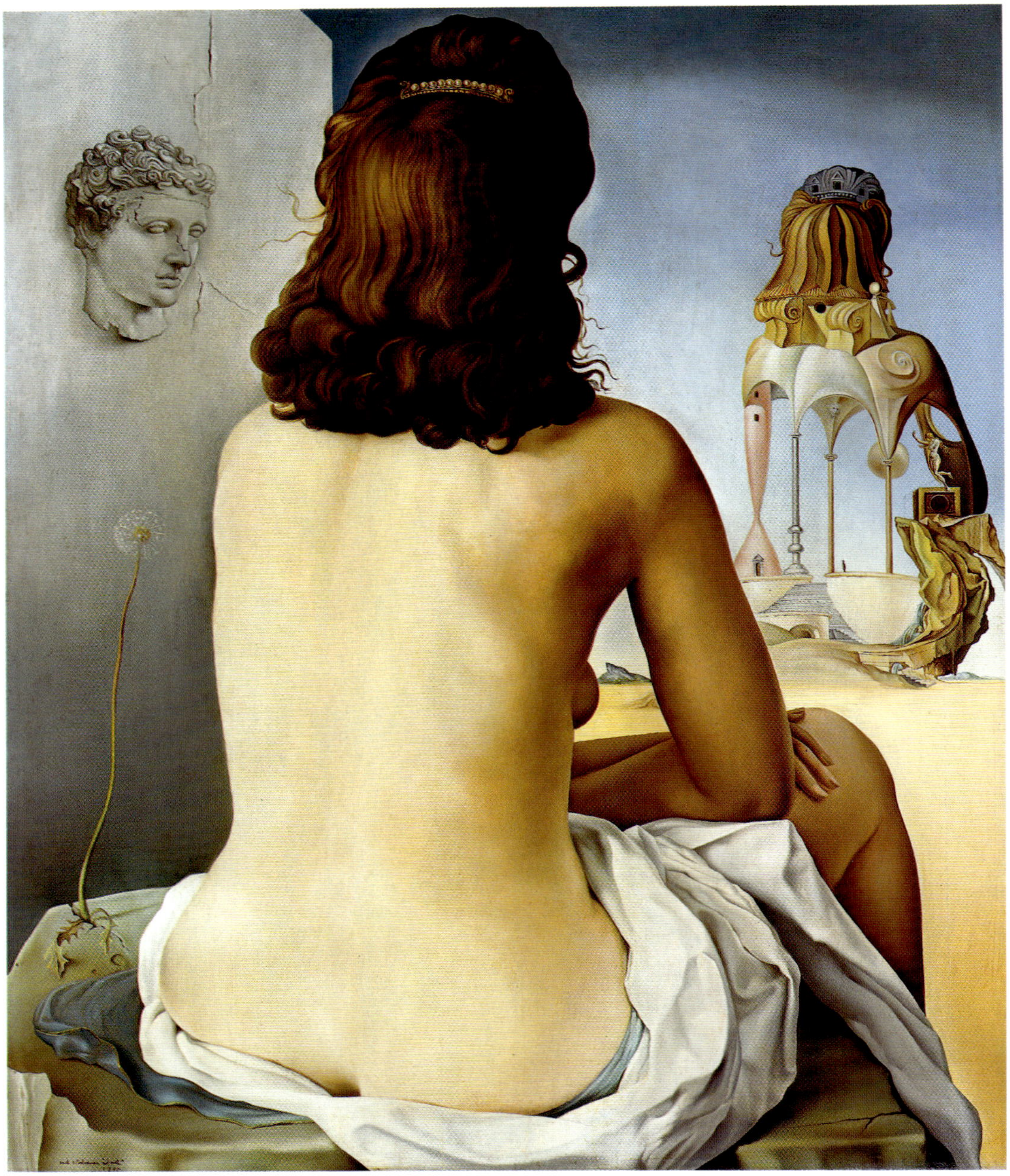

**Salvador Dalí**
*Ma Femme nue regardant son propre corps devenir marches, trois vertebres d'une colonne, ciel et architecture*
London 2,863,500 ($4,123,440)
4.XII.00

This work, painted in New York in 1945 of the artist's wife Gala, set a world auction record for a work by Dalí. A dandelion placed beneath a classical head symbolizes Dalí's love for Gala. In the distance a fantastical architectural structure echoes the shape of Gala's body.
Signed *Gala Salvador Dalí* and dated *1945*, oil on panel, 60.6 by 51 cm. (23⅞ by 20⅛ in.).

→
**Man Ray**
*Vénus restaurée*
London £163,000 ($234,720)
4.XII.00

Man Ray assembled everyday objects either 'found' or 'readymade' and invented and assigned titles to these works to express a concept, a play on words or a mystery. These inventions he called 'Objects of my Affection'. Many, such as this work, which achieved a record price for an object by Man Ray, have become Surrealist icons.
Inscribed, titled and dated on a metal plaque affixed to the base, plaster and rope assemblage, 71 cm. (28 in.) high.

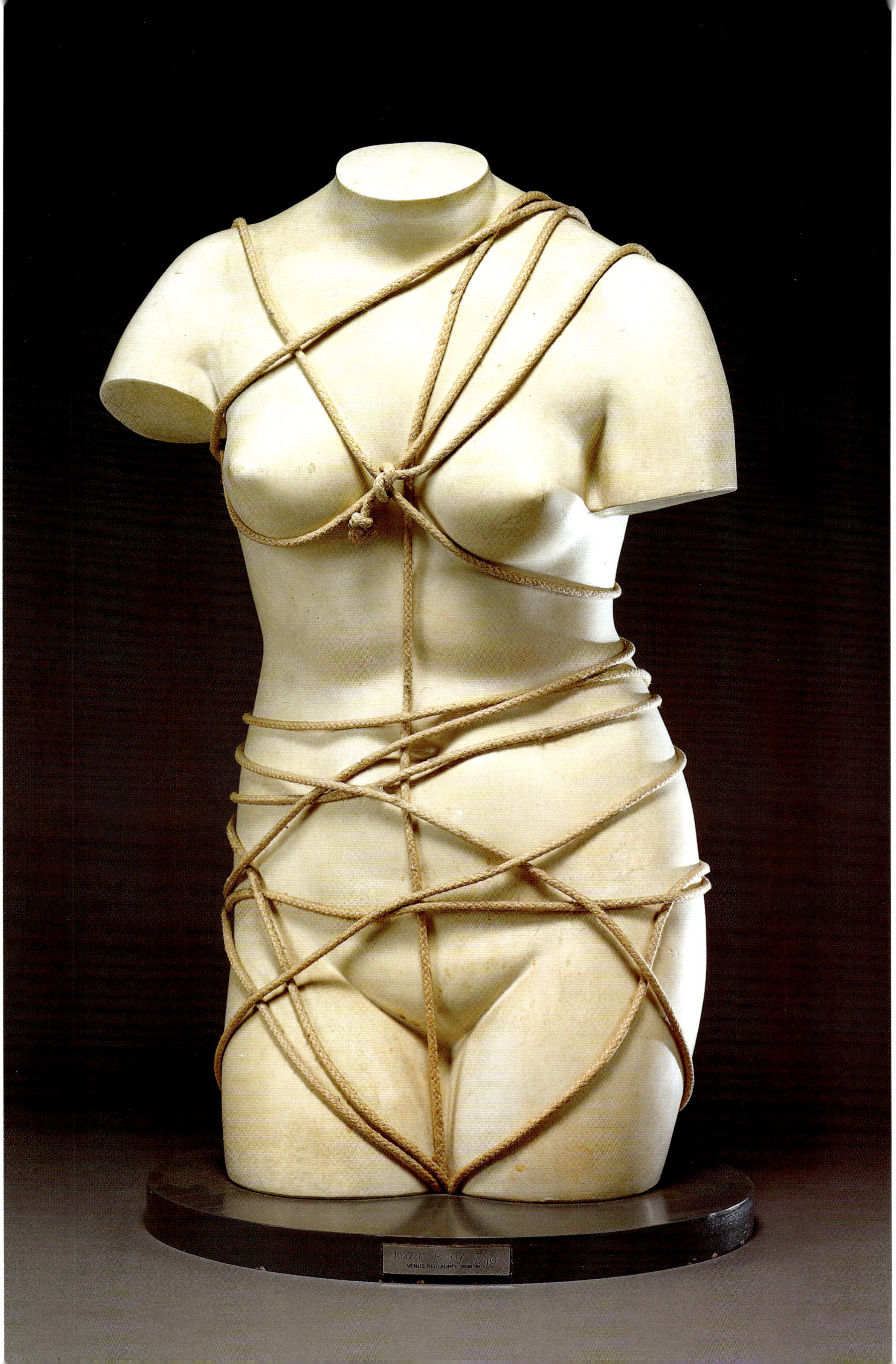
man Ray 7/10
VENUS RESTAUREE, 1936-1971

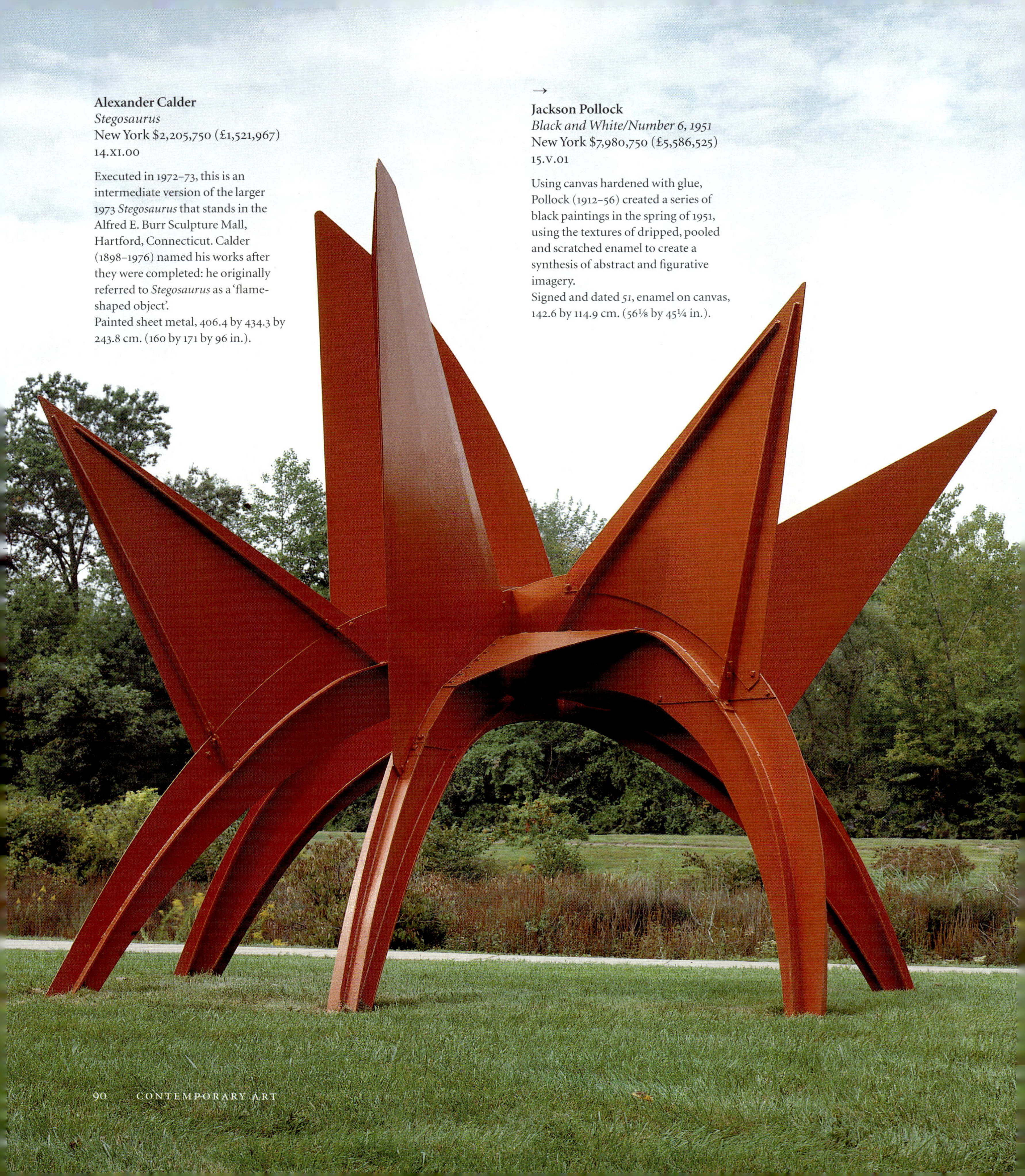

**Alexander Calder**
*Stegosaurus*
New York $2,205,750 (£1,521,967)
14.XI.00

Executed in 1972–73, this is an intermediate version of the larger 1973 *Stegosaurus* that stands in the Alfred E. Burr Sculpture Mall, Hartford, Connecticut. Calder (1898–1976) named his works after they were completed: he originally referred to *Stegosaurus* as a 'flame-shaped object'.
Painted sheet metal, 406.4 by 434.3 by 243.8 cm. (160 by 171 by 96 in.).

→
**Jackson Pollock**
*Black and White/Number 6, 1951*
New York $7,980,750 (£5,586,525)
15.V.01

Using canvas hardened with glue, Pollock (1912–56) created a series of black paintings in the spring of 1951, using the textures of dripped, pooled and scratched enamel to create a synthesis of abstract and figurative imagery.
Signed and dated *51*, enamel on canvas, 142.6 by 114.9 cm. (56⅛ by 45¼ in.).

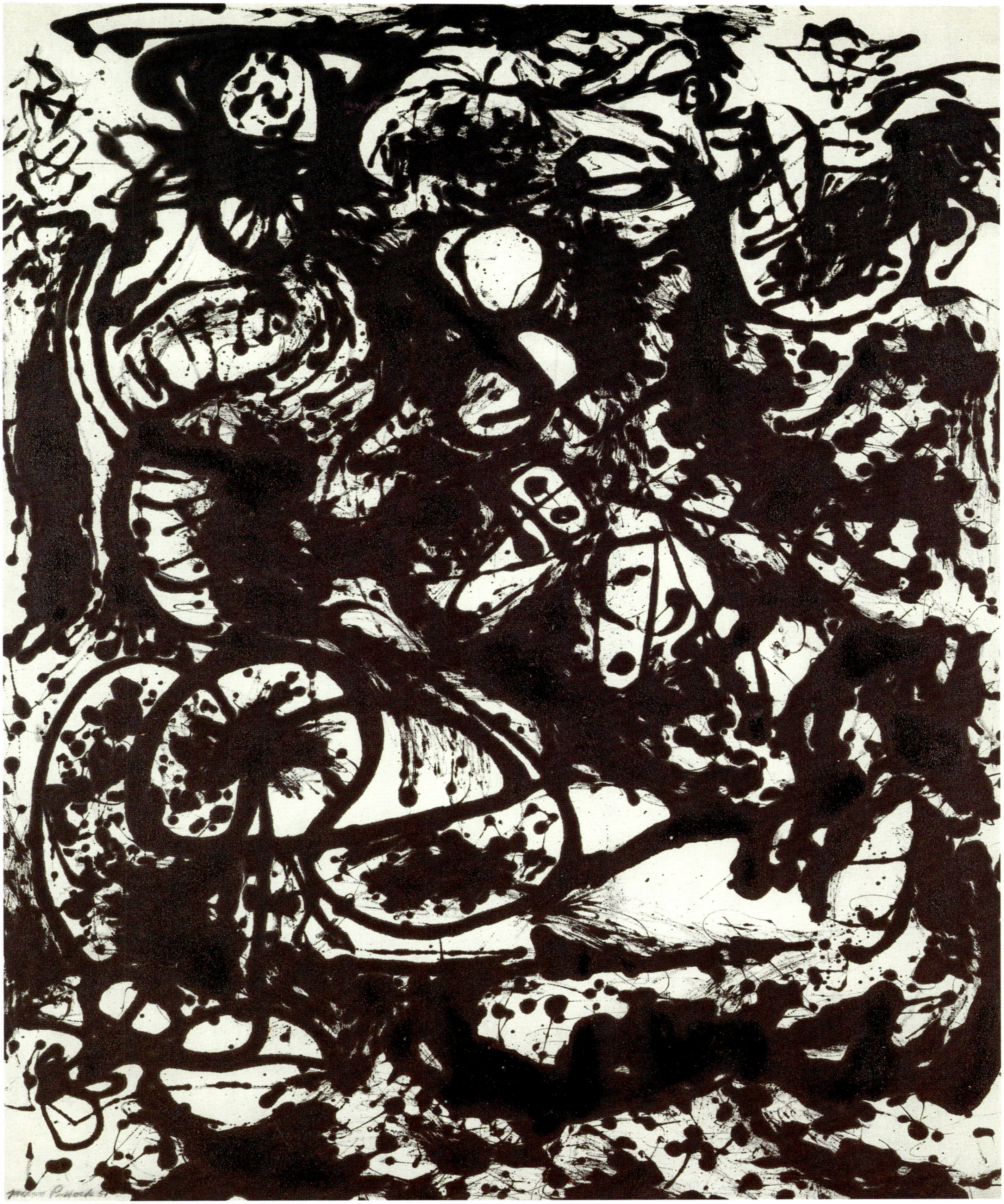

**Gerhard Richter**
*Drei Kerzen*
New York $5,395,750 (£3,777,025)
15.V.01

One of a series of 32 *Photo-paintings* executed between 1982 and 1983 depicting skulls and candles, *Drei Kerzen* is an exploration of the role of light in painting, produced with a stunning refinement of technique. Signed, numbered *513–1* and dated *1982*, oil on canvas, 125.1 by 151.1 cm. (49¼ by 59½ in.).

→

**Mark Rothko**
*No. 2 (Blue, Red and Green)*
New York $11,005,750 (£7,646,800)
14.XI.00

Rothko's experimentation in the balance of colour, texture and composition in the 1950s resulted in a series of sensual and enigmatic masterpieces, of which this is one. Despite the vibrant and apparently joyful colours, Rothko claimed that he was representing tragedy. Signed and dated *1953*, oil on canvas, 205.7 by 170.5.cm. (81 by 67⅛ in.).

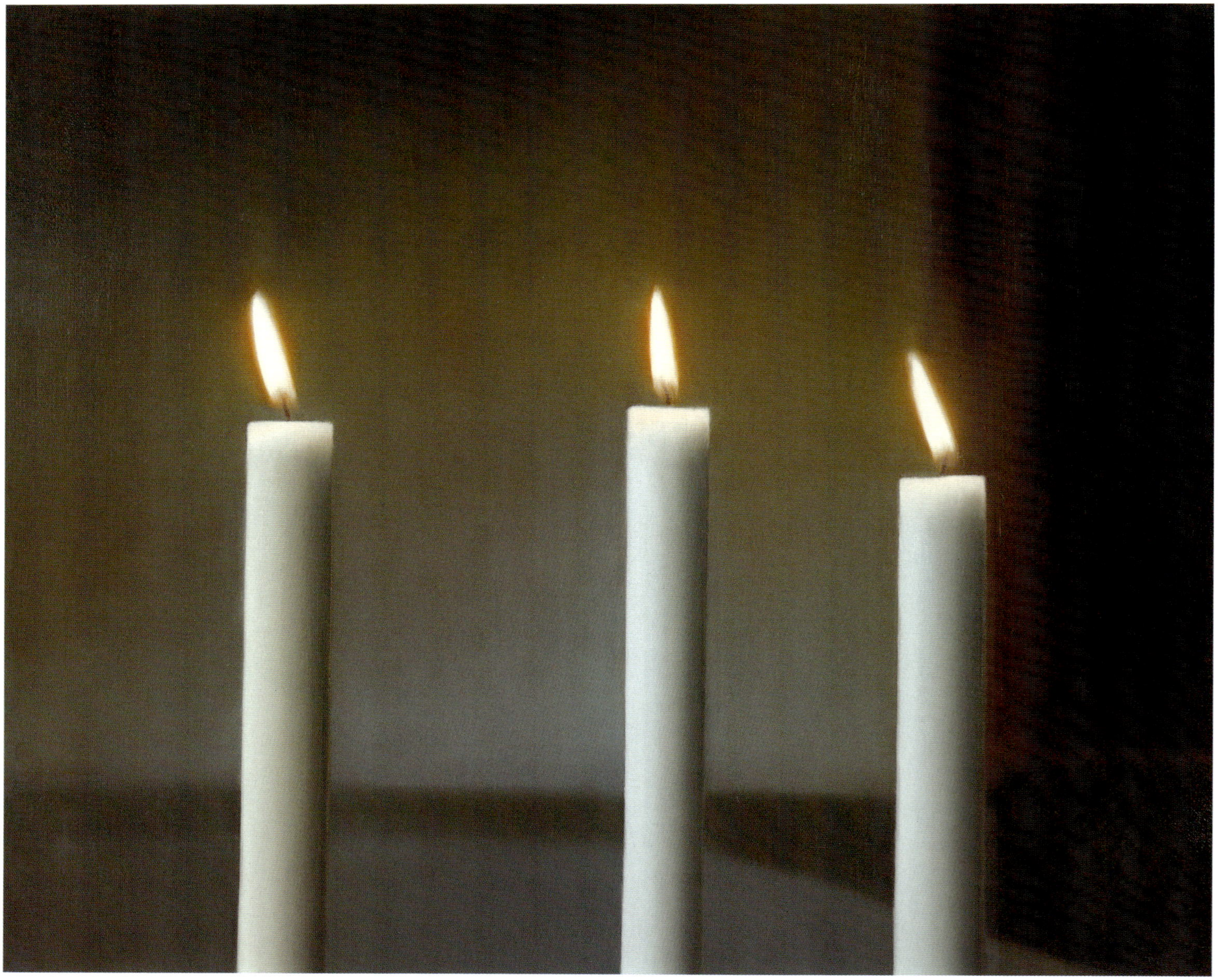

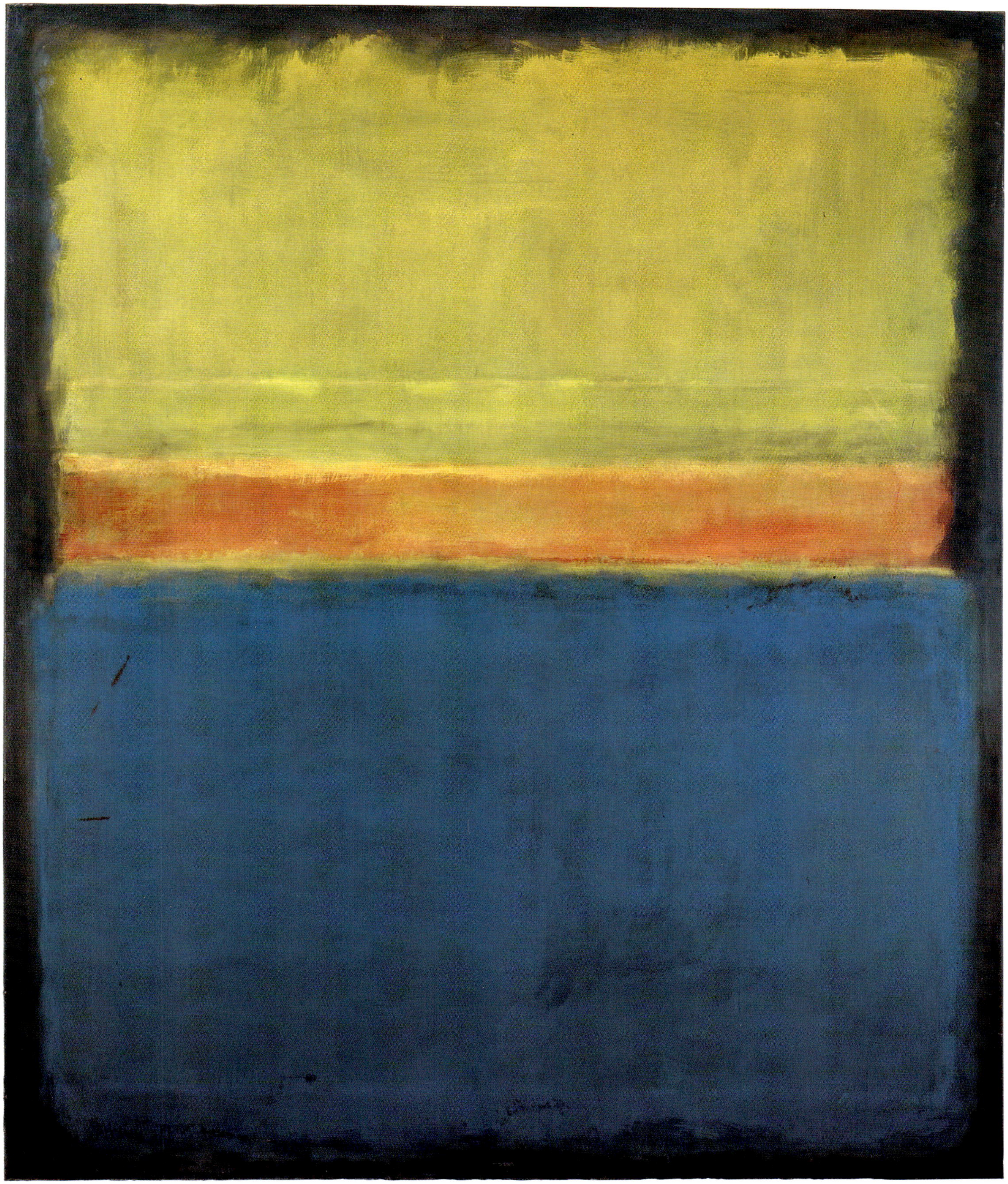

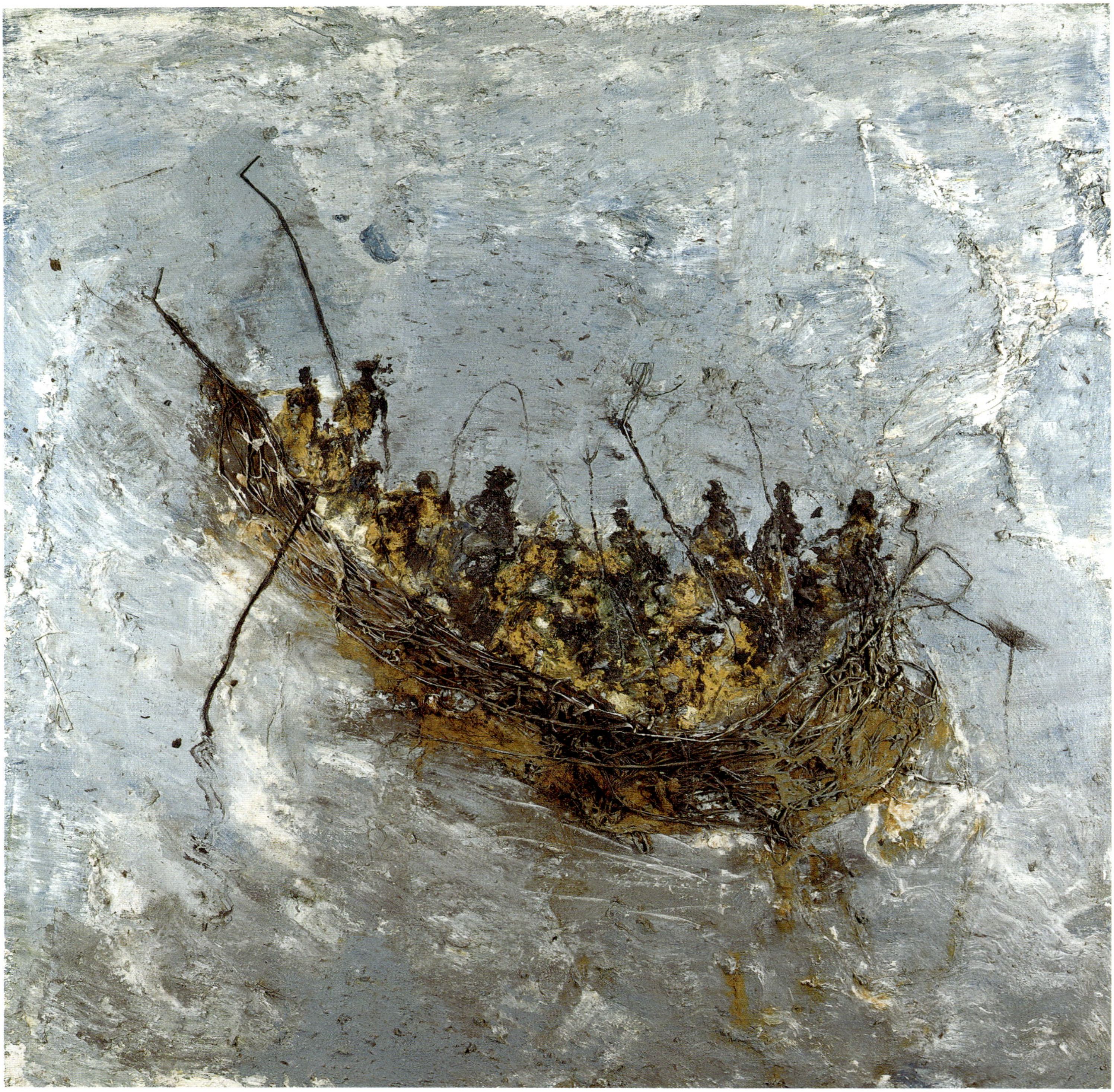

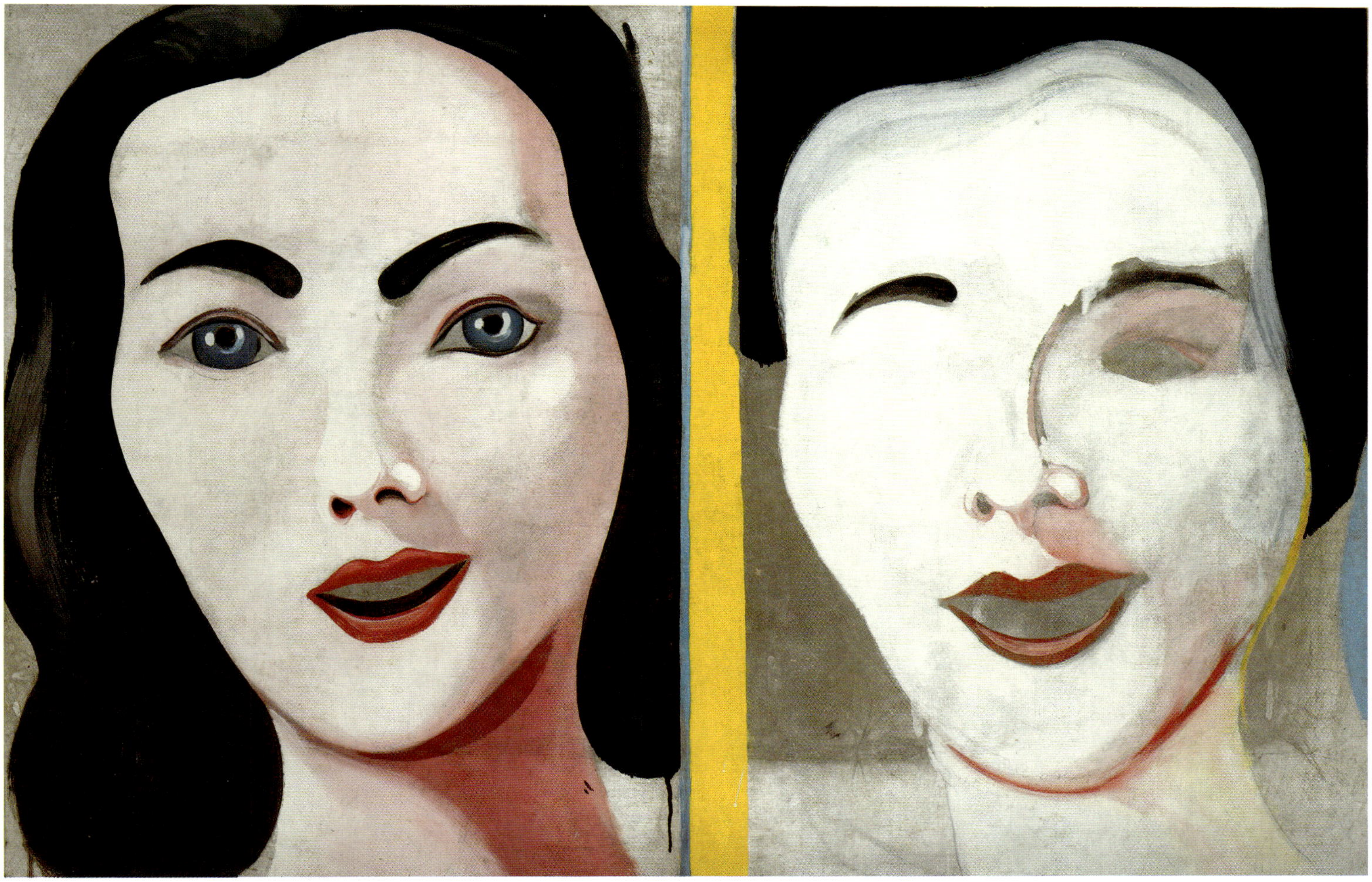

←

**Miquel Barceló**
*Kulu Be Ba Kan*
London £718,500 ($1,013,085)
27.VI.01

One of only six canvases inspired by the gigantic canoes that navigate the River Niger, *Kulu Be Ba Kan* conveys the epic dimension of human adventure, as the boat's passengers struggle to catch their evening meal.
Signed and dated *VII 1991*, mixed media on canvas, 200 by 200 cm. (78¾ by 78¾ in.).

**Sigmar Polke**
*Untitled (Doppelporträt)*
London £1,158,500 ($1,691,410)
7.II.01

Polke's 1963–4 *Doppelporträt*, which achieved a record at auction for the artist, is one of his most important early works. A muse on the subject of idealized beauty, it also refers to Pop Art, the processes of painting and of transformation, and the notion of self and other.
Signed, lacquer on canvas, 128 by 194 cm. (50⅜ by 76⅜ in.).

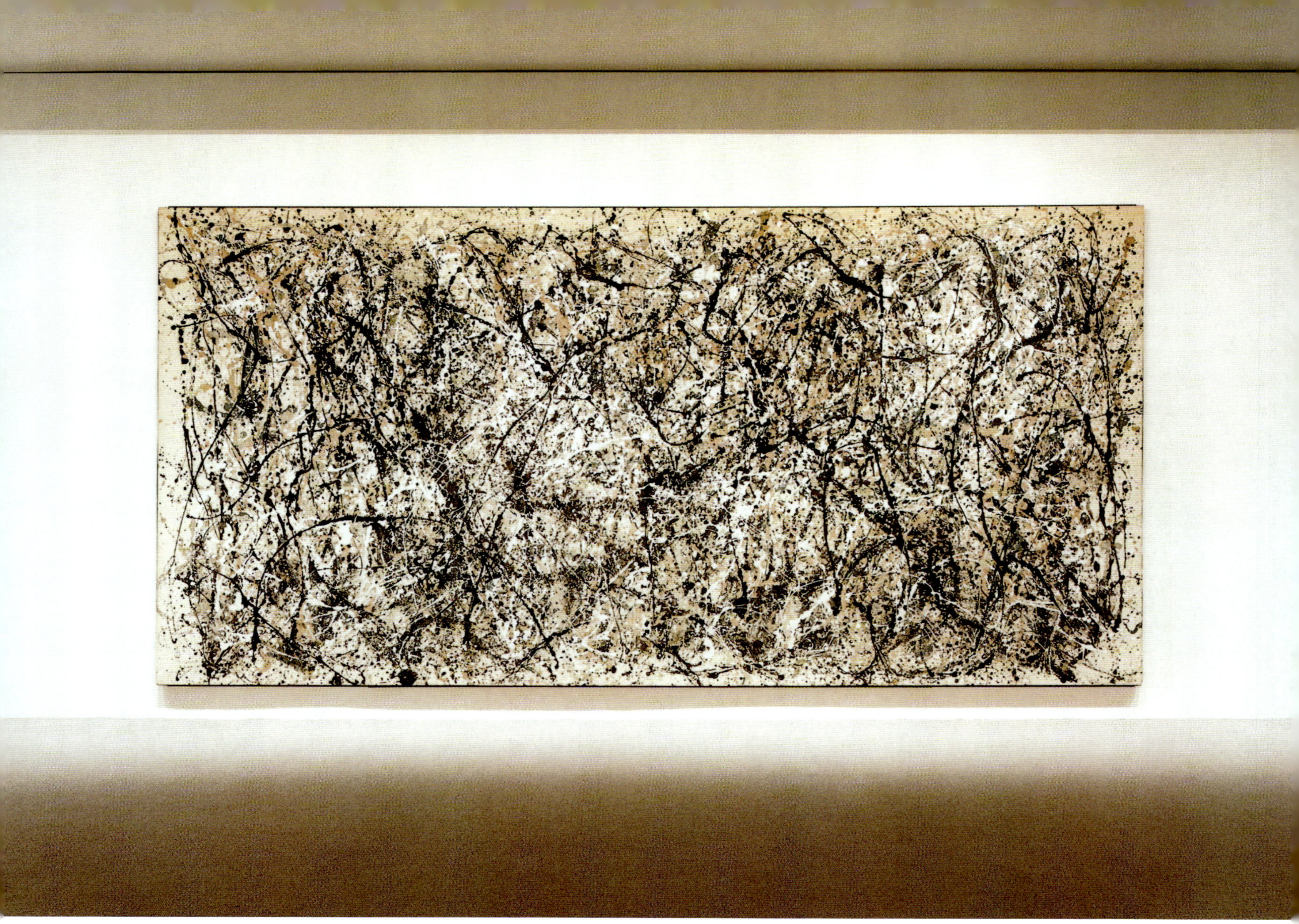

**Andreas Gursky**
*OT VI*
London £212,500 ($310,250) 7.11.01

Gursky's photograph, the most expensive ever sold at auction, is described in the Wolfsburg exhibition catalogue as presenting 'a shrine for an ornament'. It shows Jackson Pollock's 1950 work *One: Number 31* hanging in an exhibition space, uninterrupted by gallery visitors.
Signed, titled and dated *97*, and numbered *3/6*, cibachrome print, 186 by 239 cm. (73¼ by 94⅛ in.).

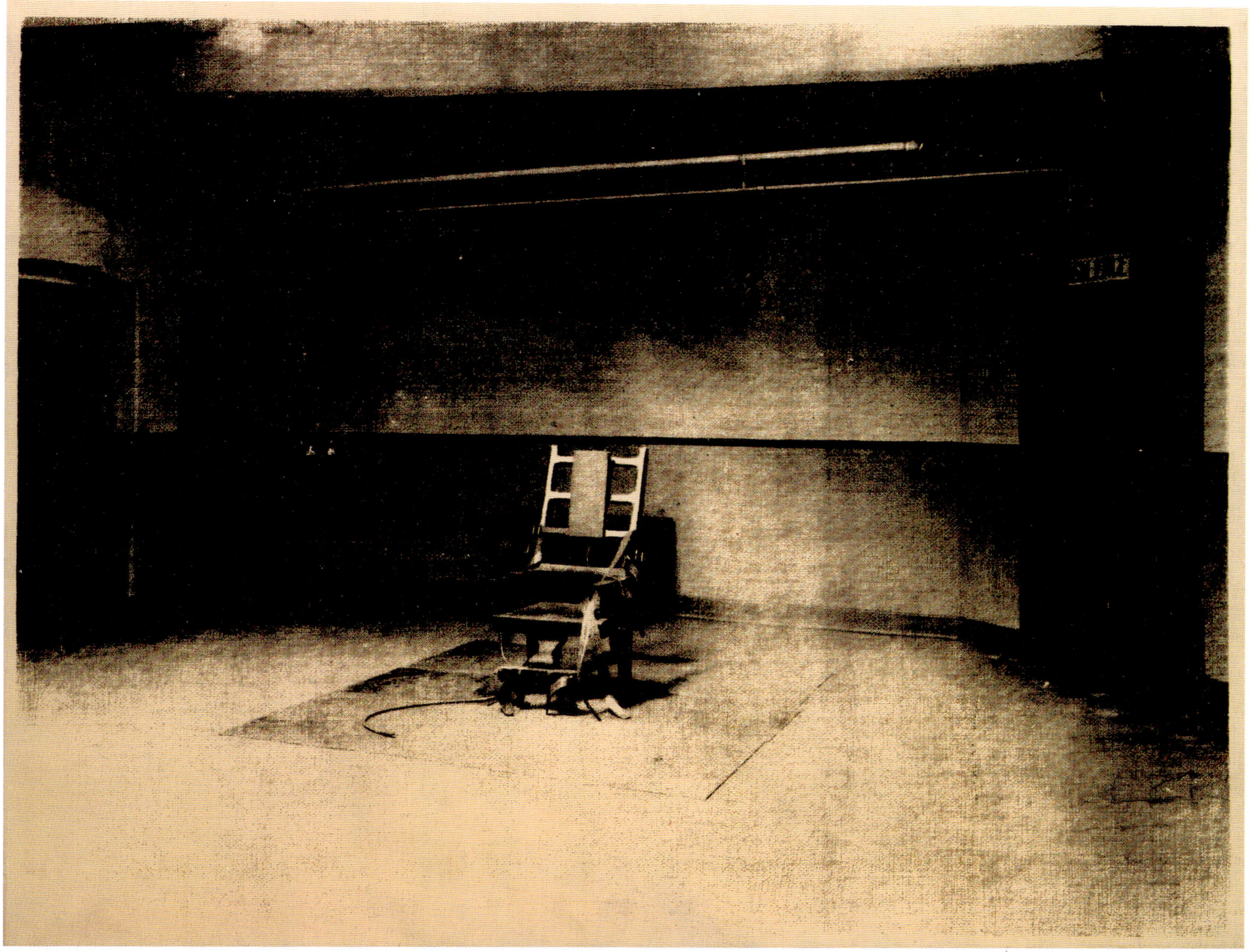

**Andy Warhol**
*Little Electric Chair*
London £1,653,500 ($2,331,435)
27.VI.01

Created during a time when Warhol was devoting himself to producing images of unremitting morbidity, including silkscreens of suicides and car crashes, *Little Electric Chair* presents the paradox of an instrument of death against a fresh and vibrant pink background. Signed and dated *64*, acrylic and silkscreen ink on canvas, 61 by 71.2 cm. (24 by 28 in.).

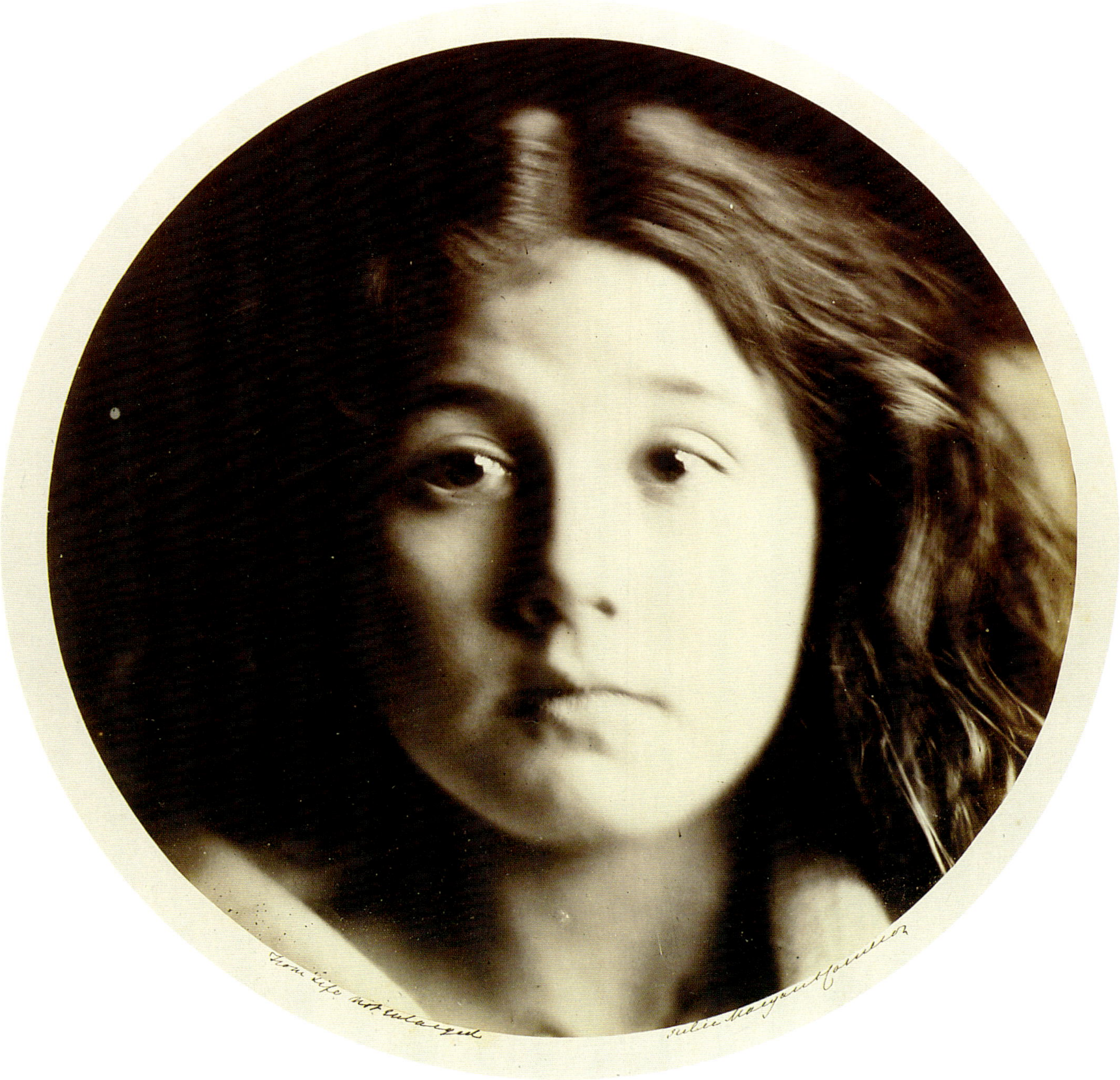

**Julia Margaret Cameron**
*Kate Keown*
London £174,000($248,820)
10.v.01

Part of the Paul F. Walter collection, Julia Margaret Cameron's portrait of Kate Keown sold for over four times its low estimate and established a new world record for a work by the photographer.
Signed and inscribed *from Life not enlarged, 1866,* albumen print, 29.2 by 29 cm. (11½ by 11⅜ in.).

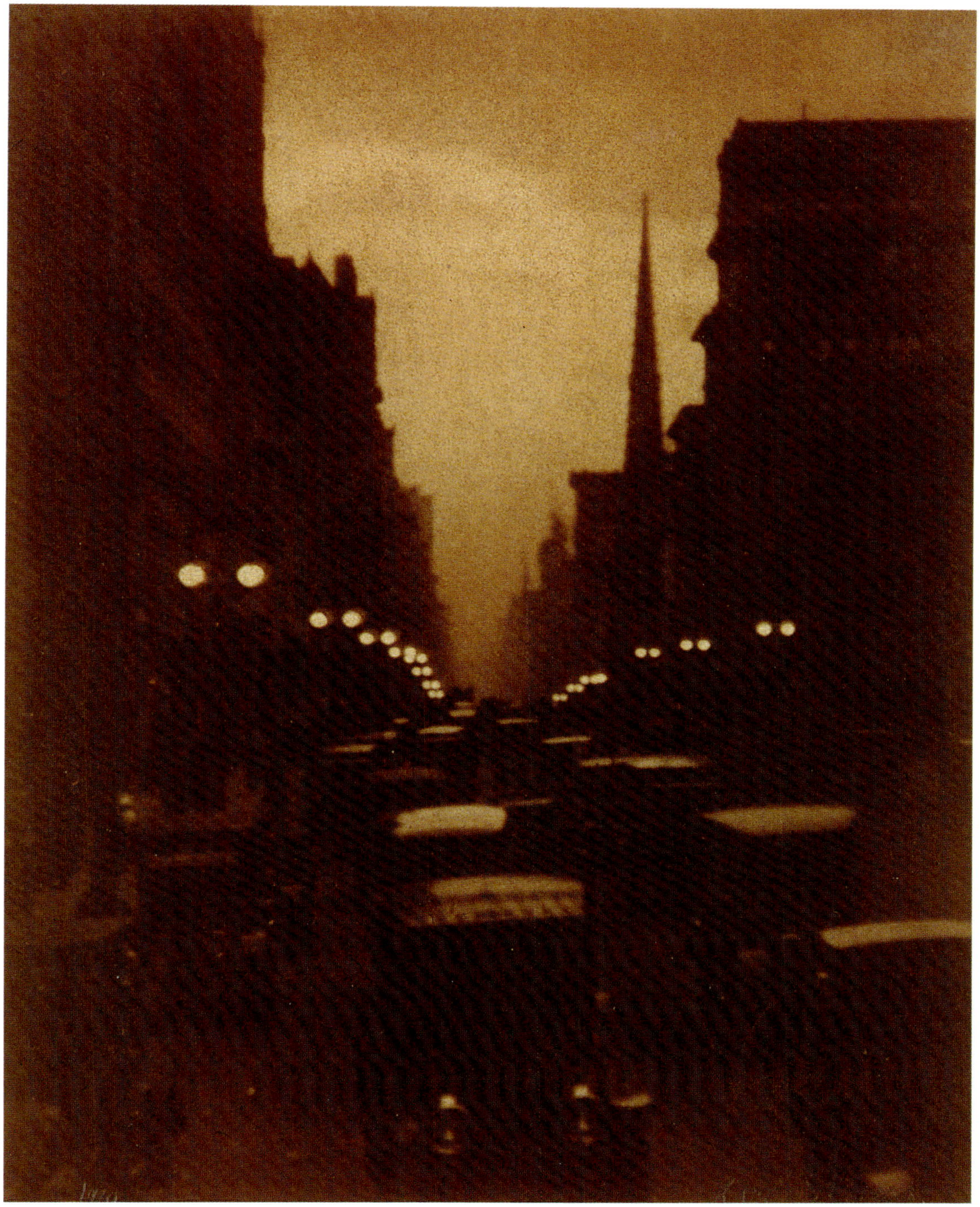

**Karl Struss**
*Fifth Ave. – Twilight, 1910*
New York $170,750 (£116,790)
12.X.00

Karl Struss captured this study of New York City at twilight from the top of a double-decker bus. One of three large-format exhibition prints of the image extant, this photograph set a new record for Struss at auction. Signed and dated by the photographer in pencil on the image, gum platinum print, 30.5 by 23.8 cm. (12 by 9⅜ in.).

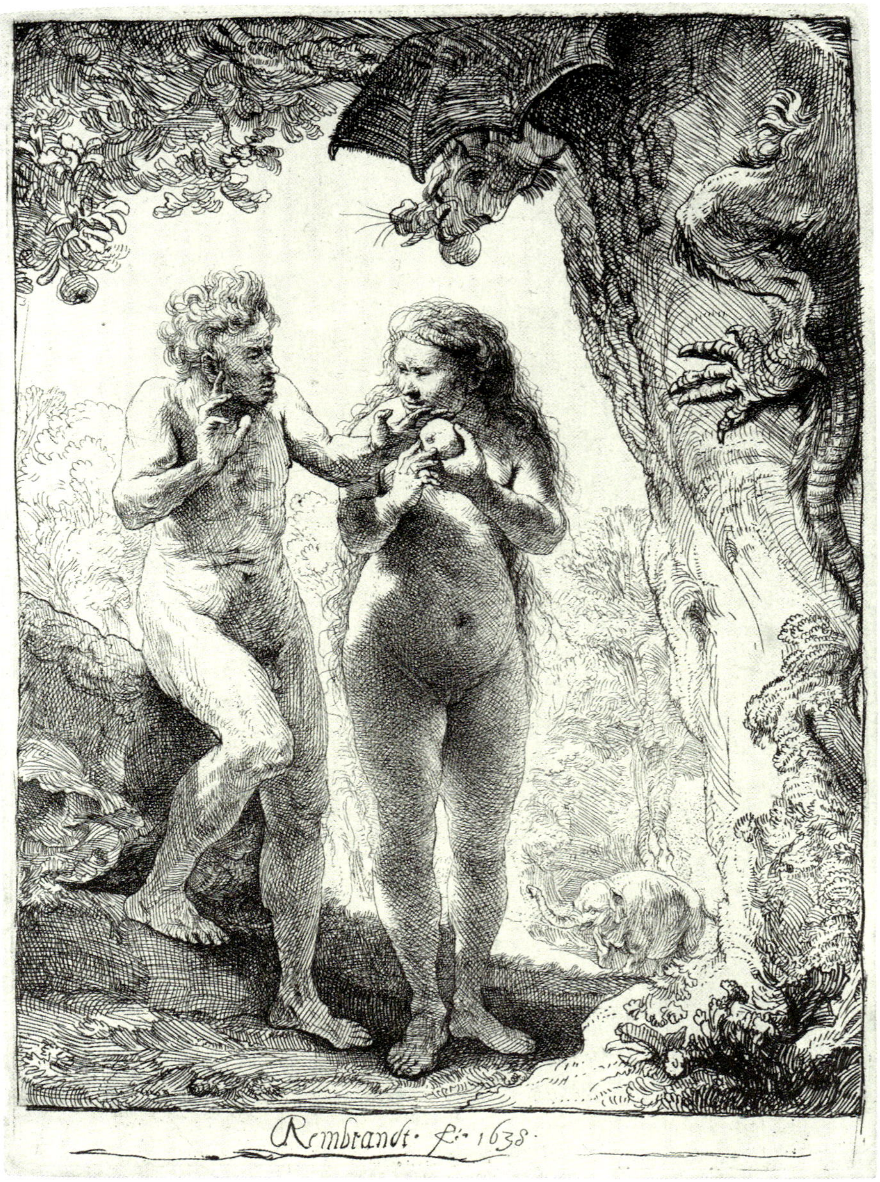


**Rembrandt Harmensz. Van Rijn**
*Adam and Eve*
London £44,200 ($63,405)
6.XII.00

This etching, which is signed and dated *1638*, shows the moment when Adam receives the apple from Eve, provoking the Fall of Man. It is a very fine impression of the second state.
16.5 by 11.8 cm. (6½ by 4½ in.).

→

**Pablo Picasso**
*Le Chef d'oeuvre inconnu*
by Honoré de Balzac,
£63,750 ($89,887) London 6.VI.01

Picasso's set of 12 etchings explores the relationship between the artist and his model as captured in Balzac's major work. As his love for his model grows, the artist's canvas becomes 'a confused mass of colours'.
52.5 by 40.6 cm. (20⅝ by 16¾ in.).

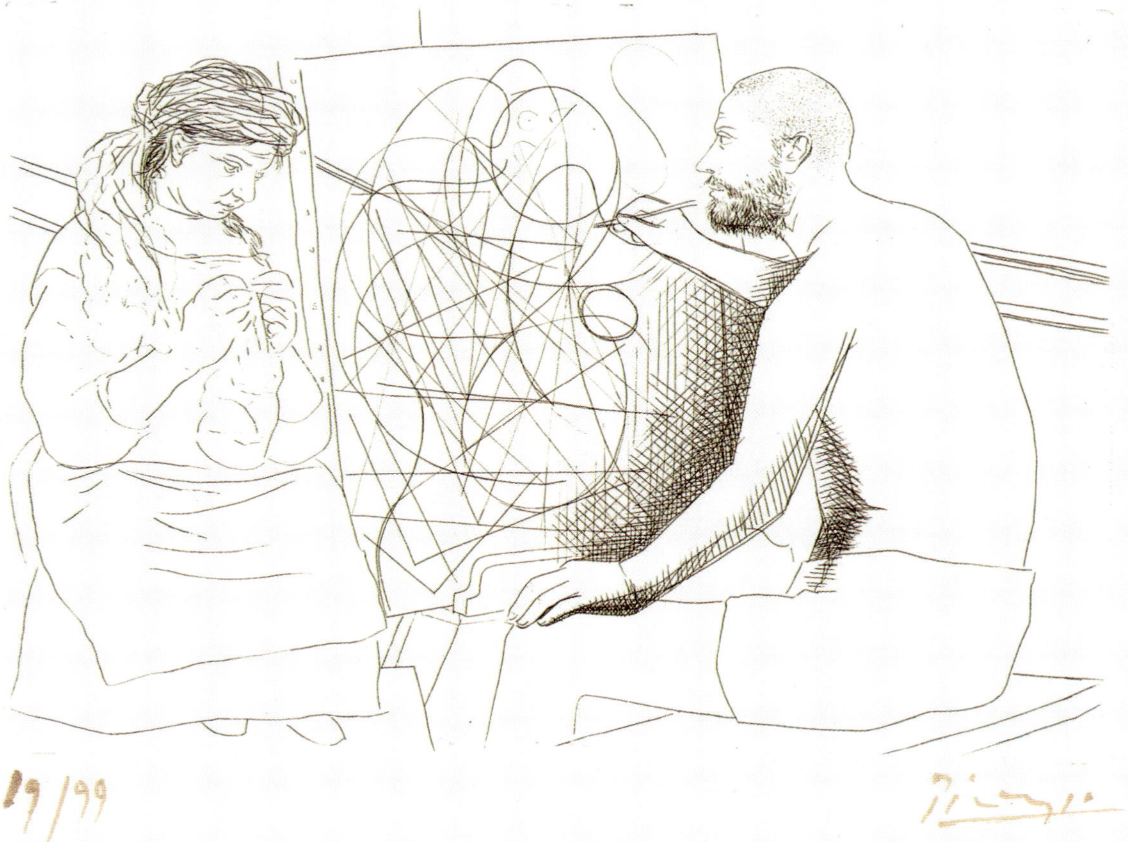
19/99

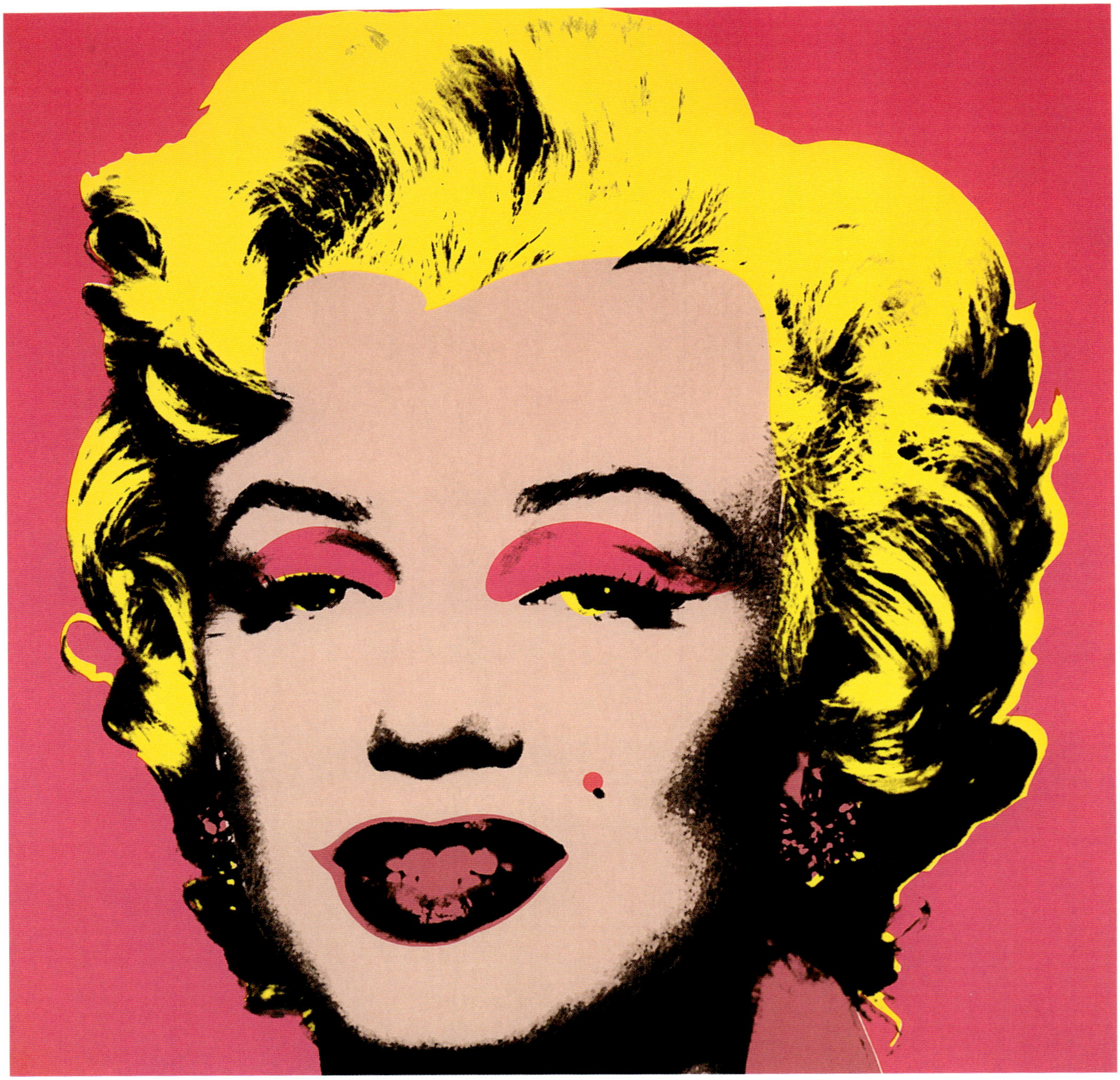

**Andy Warhol**
*Marilyn*
New York $346,750 (£239,257)
5.V.01

This is one of 26 lettered artist's proof sets, aside from the stamp-numbered edition of 250, published by Factory Additions, New York, 1967, in the original cardboard box.
Signed, 10 screenprints in colours, each sheet *circa* 91.4 by 91.4 cm. (36 by 36 in.).

# Precious Objects

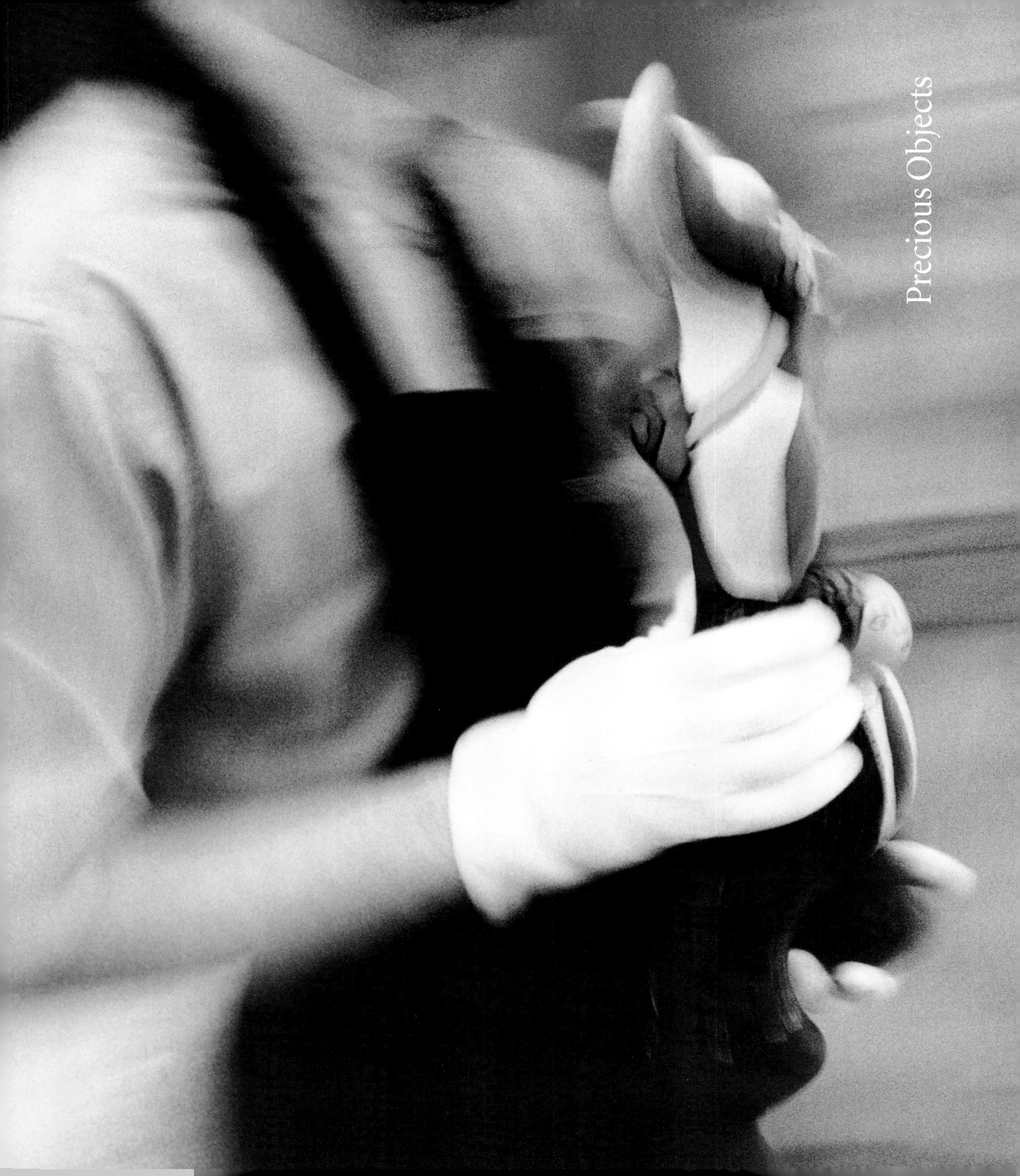

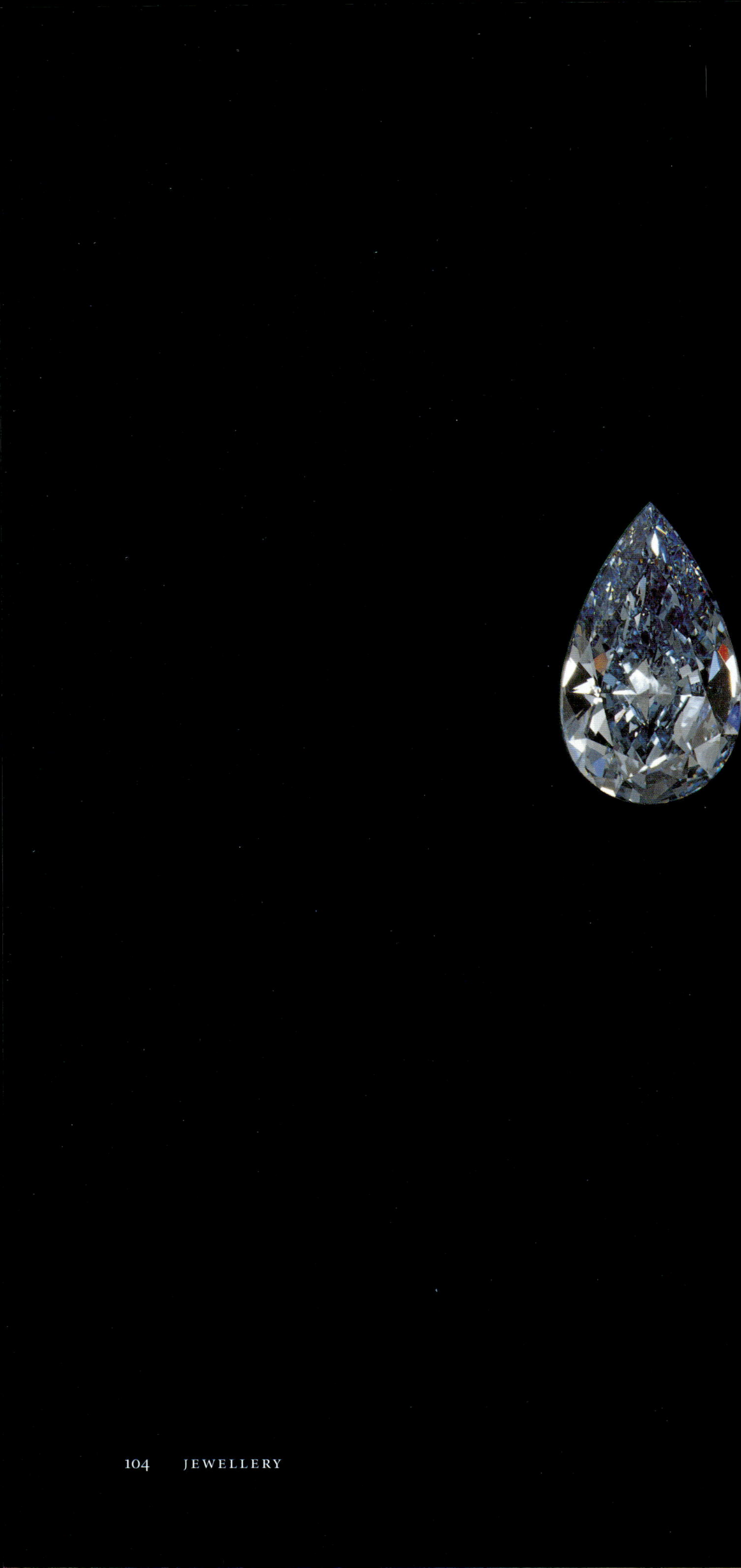

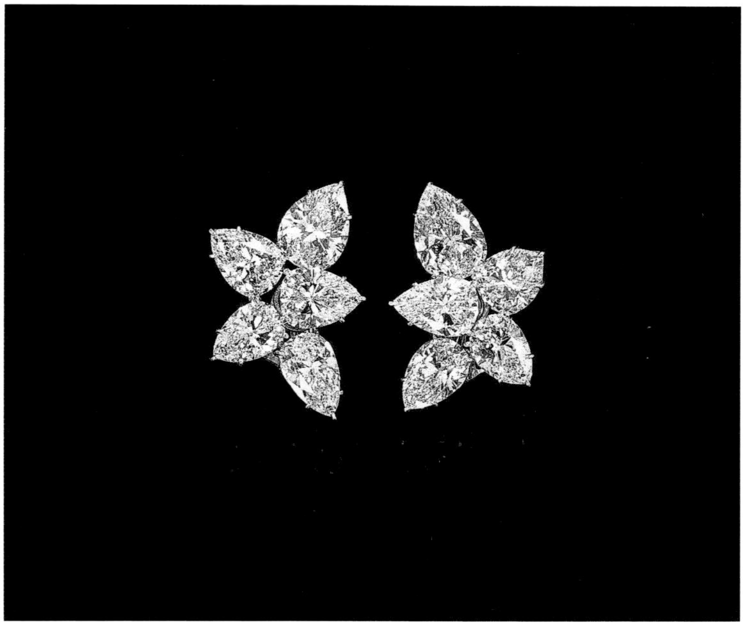

**A Pair of Diamond Cluster Earclips, Harry Winston**
New York $775,750 (£527,510)
24.x.00

One of Harry Winston's most brilliant ideas is said to have originated from observing a cluster of fir boughs in a Christmas wreath on the door of his home. What evolved were so-called 'cluster' mountings, which allowed the stones to sparkle from every angle. This pair of earclips is one of the most spectacular ever made in the design. 37.13 carats in total.

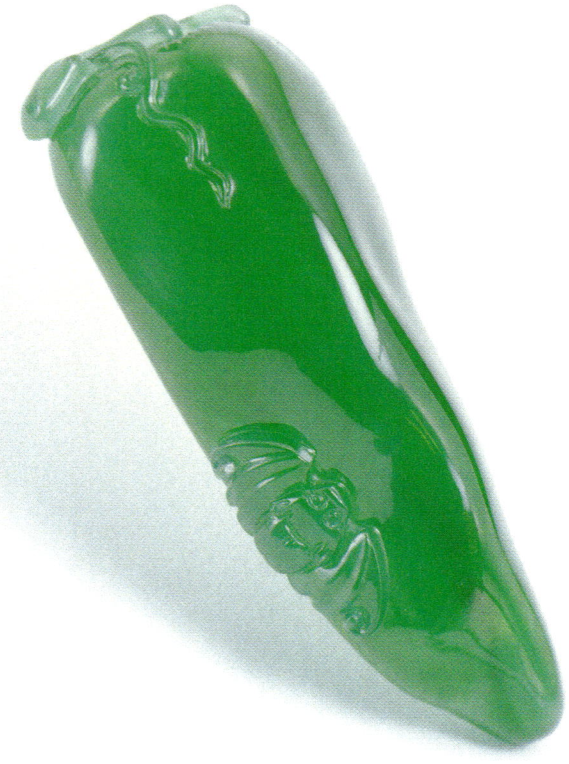

**A Jadeite Pepper Pendant**
Hong Kong HK$5,544,750
($665,370; £443,580) 9.IV.01

The pepper was a symbol of plenty during the Song period (960–1279), when a fascination, among artists, with the natural world led to a golden age of natural themes in art, especially in painting and sculpture.
Approximately 5.774 by 2.213 by 1.636 cm. (2¼ by ⅞ by ⅝ in.).

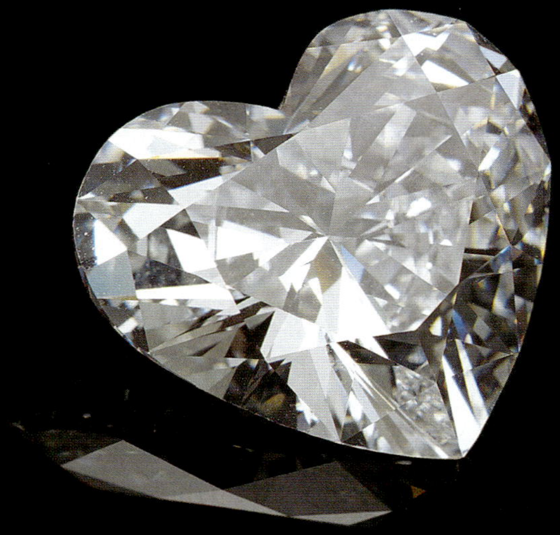

**A Diamond Pendant**
Geneva SF2,758,750 ($1,600,075; £1,103,500) 16.v.01

This vary rare type IIa diamond is chemically pure and, therefore, colourless. It possesses a near perfect outline, unusual in a heart shape, as well as the coveted D colour and Internally Flawless clarity, making it one of the finest of its kind to appear at auction. 28.03 carats.

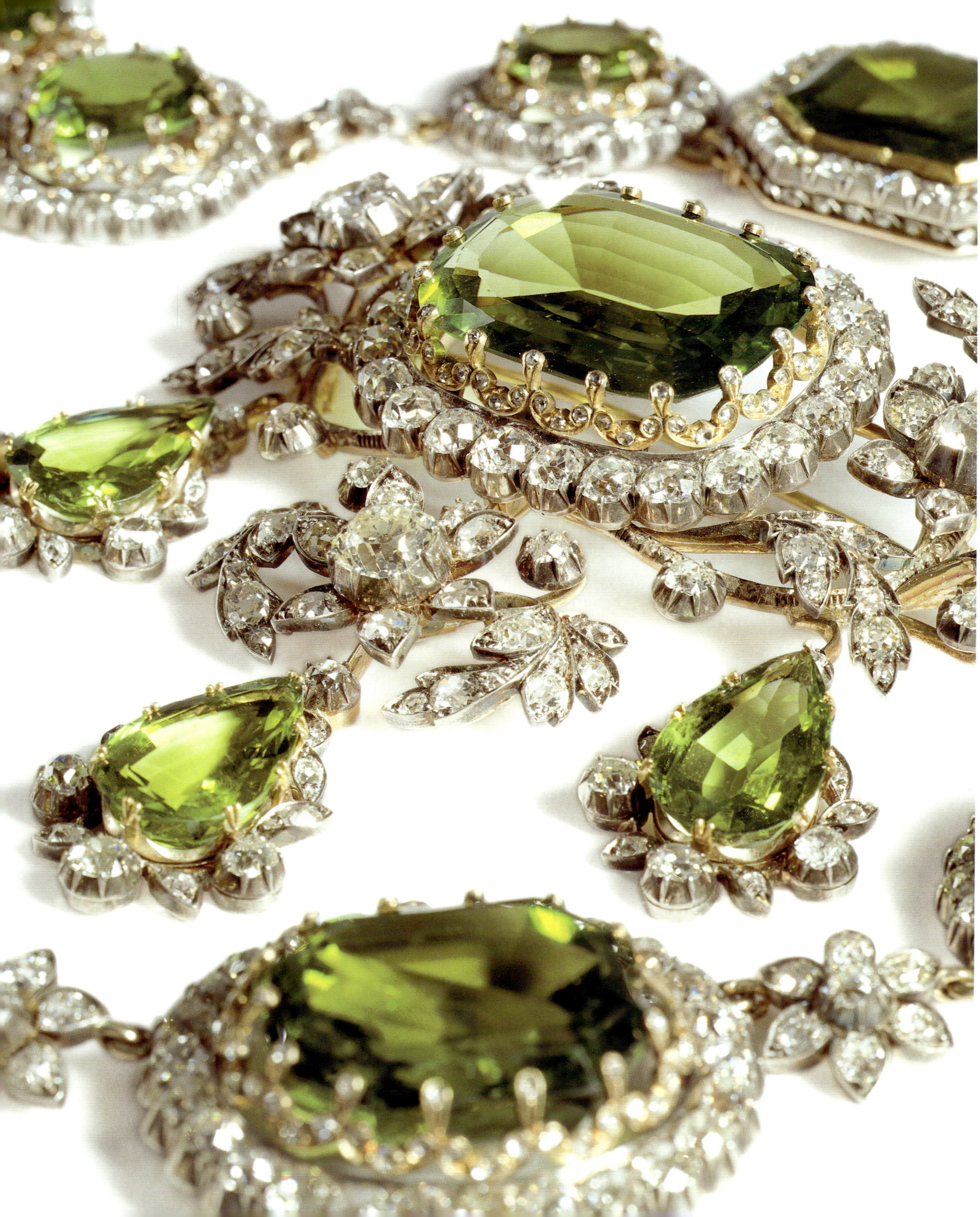

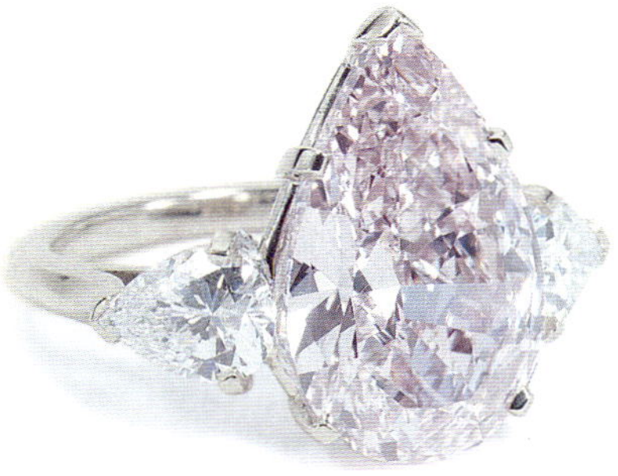

←

**A Peridot and Diamond Parure, *circa* 1825**
London £256,500 ($359,100)
20.VI.01

It is extremely rare to find parures of such importance still complete in all their parts. The grand scale of the design, the sheer size of the jewels and the lavish abundance of gemstones make this parure a truly unique example.
Property from the Estate of Countess Marina Coudenhove-Kalergi.

**A Fancy Intense Purple-Pink Diamond Ring**
Hong Kong HK$15,444,750 ($1,983,910; £1,235,580) 31.X.00

It is estimated that for every 10,000 colourless diamonds discovered, one of fancy colour may be found. This Internally Flawless diamond is of unusual size and clarity, with the colour evenly distributed throughout the stone.
8.82 carats.

**A Burmese Ruby and Diamond Ring**
Geneva SF5,838,750 ($3,280,196; £2,298,720) 15.XI.00

During the 1990s and late 1980s, Sotheby's sold the five most important rubies to come to auction. The finest examples of one of the world's most highly prized gems, the ruby, are found in Mogok, in the north of Myanmar, formerly Burma.

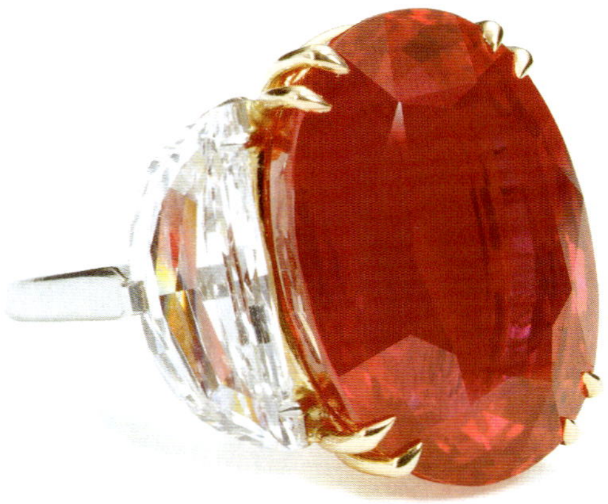

**A Diamond Bracelet by Harry Winston**
St Moritz SF173,750 ($104,042; £72,095) 24.11.01

Annually, Sotheby's brings the excitement of the jewellery auction world to the glamour of St Moritz. This elegant Harry Winston creation from the sale this year is composed of a diamond baguette ribbon woven around fine-cut stones.
19 cm. (7½ in.) long.

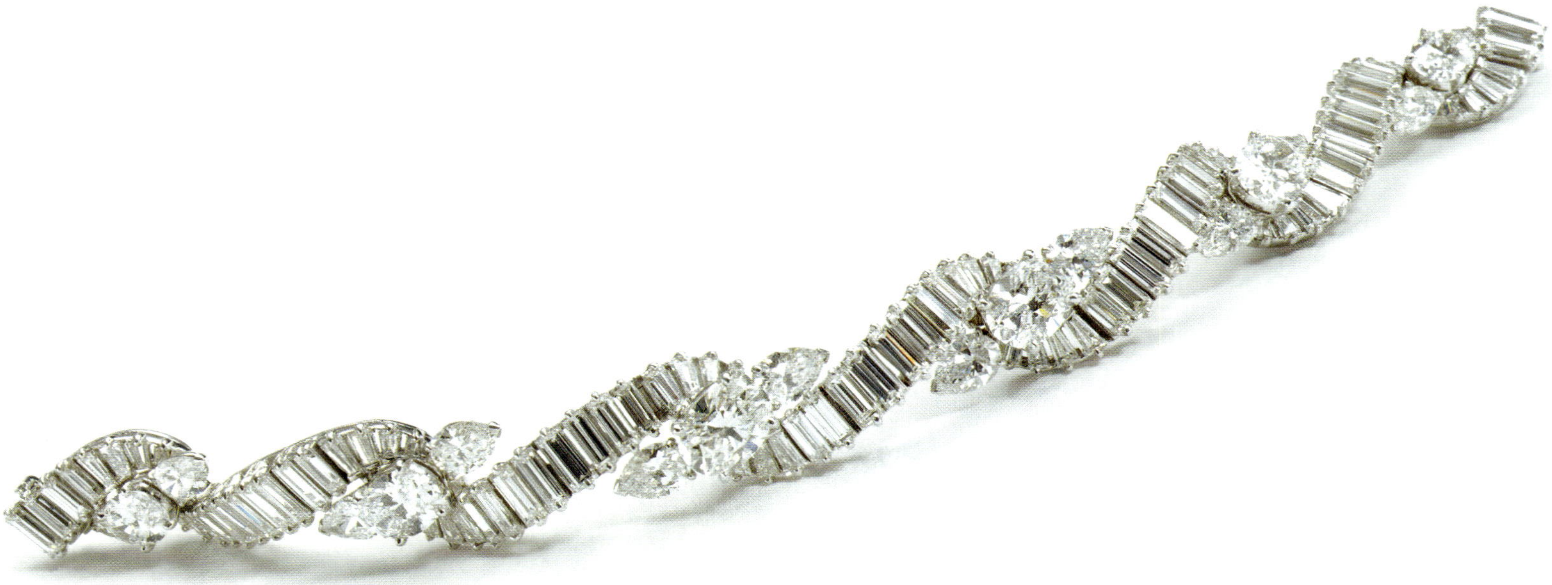

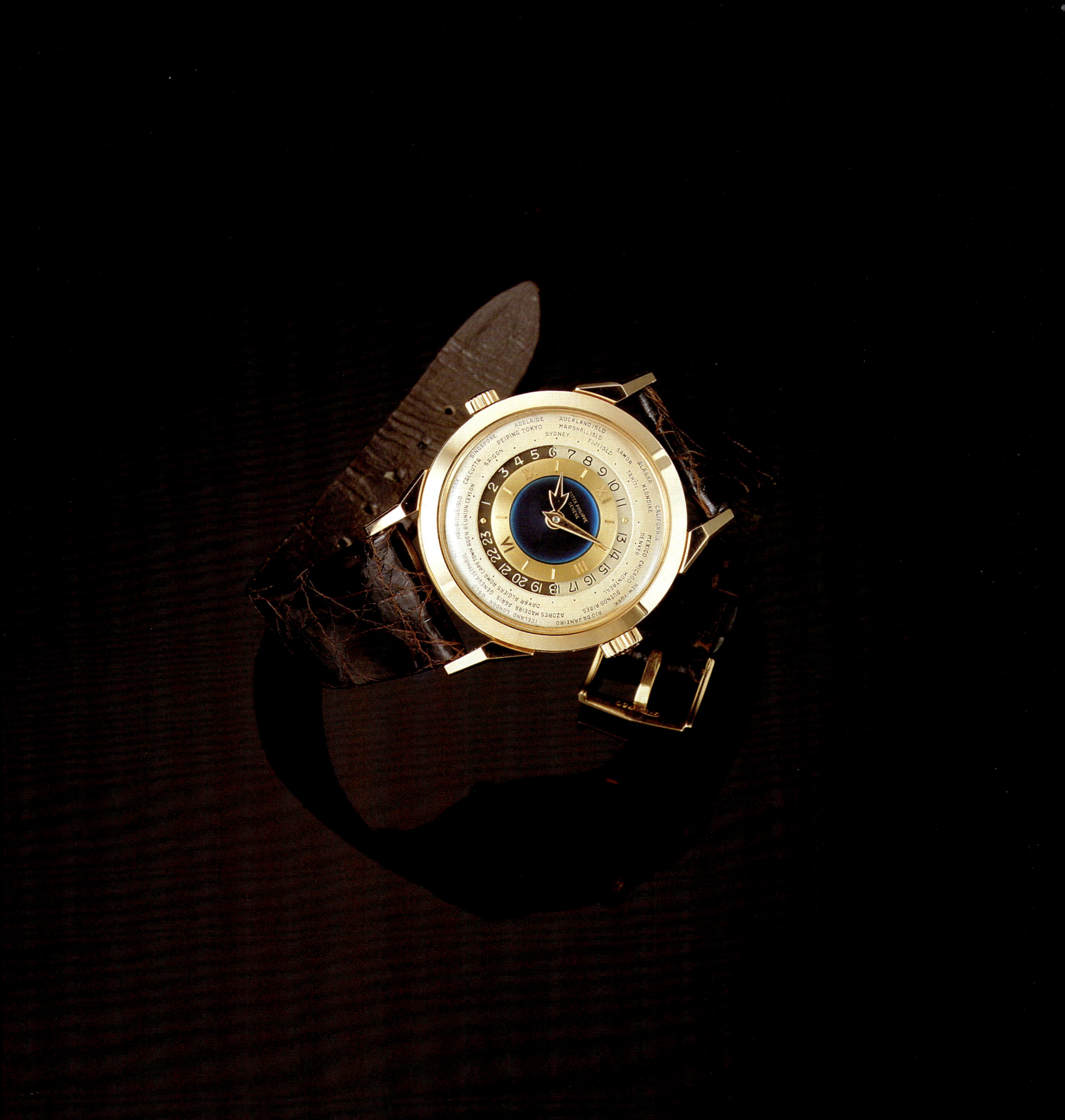

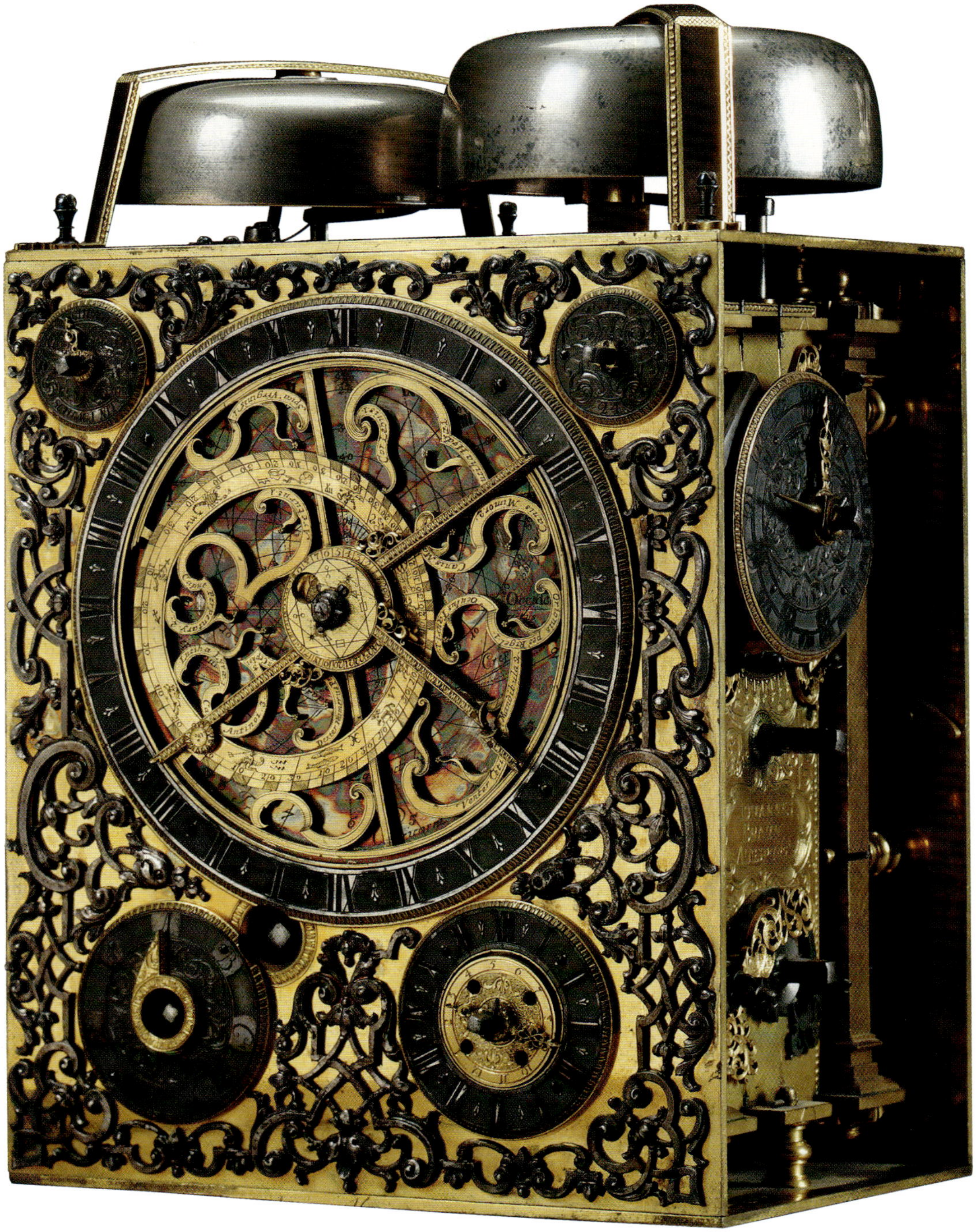

**A Silver-mounted Gilt-brass Astronomical Quarter-striking and Alarm Masterpiece Clock**
London £60,300 ($88,641)
19.XII.00

This clock, made by Johannes Braun in *circa* 1714, owes its old-fashioned appearance to the fact that Braun used it as his 'masterpiece'. To enter the Clockmakers' Guild it was necessary to make a masterpiece clock according to guidelines laid down in 1558.

←

**A Patek Philippe & Co. Pink Gold Dual-crown World-time Wristwatch with Enamel Dial**
New York $1,050,750 (£725,017)
21.II.01

Incorporating the two-crown world-time mechanism invented and produced by the Geneva watchmaker Louis Cottier, this wristwatch has an outer silver ring enamelled with 40 world locations. It is possibly the only known example executed in pink gold.
Geneva *circa* 1953, no. 722714, ref. 2523.

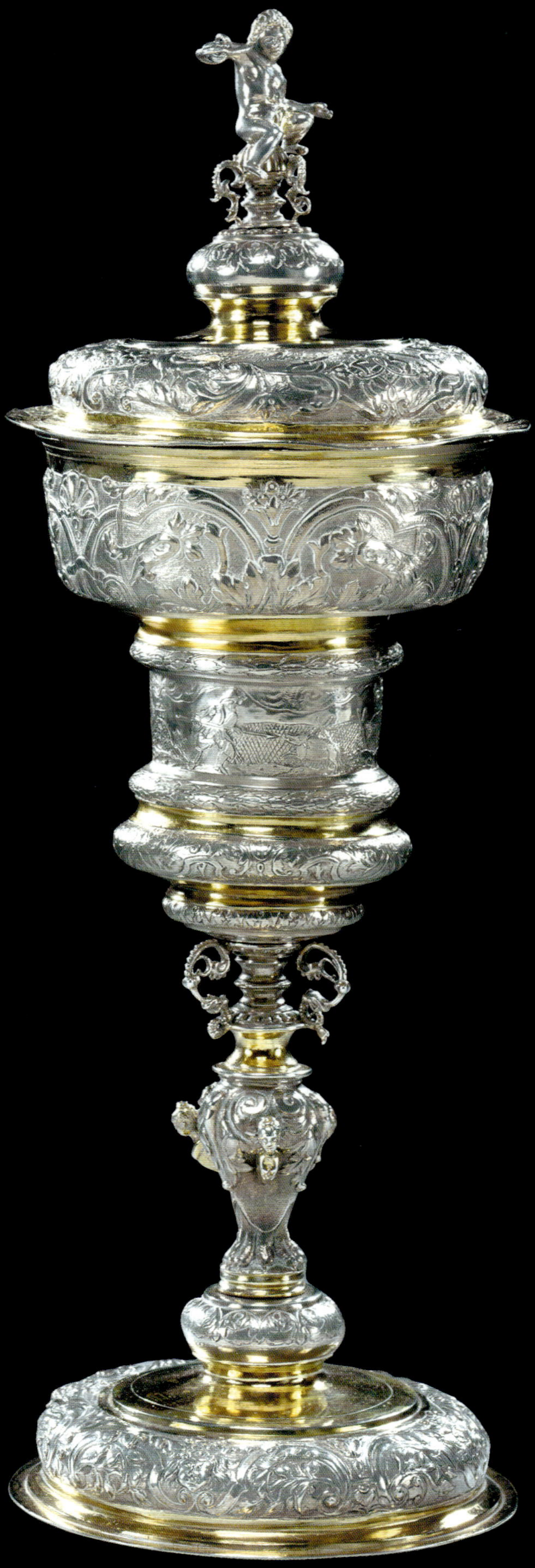

**A Norwegian Parcel-gilt Silver Cup and Cover by Christian Berger**
London £25,800 ($36,636) 9.XI.00

This silver cup was made in Bragernes in 1724, the year that Christian Berger became a master. It is decorated in the Régence style with exotic birds, masks, fruit and hunting scenes, and the cover is inset with a disc engraved with Cupid carrying arrows and Summer holding a basket of fruit, while the finial features a baby Hercules.
36 cm. (14 in.) high.

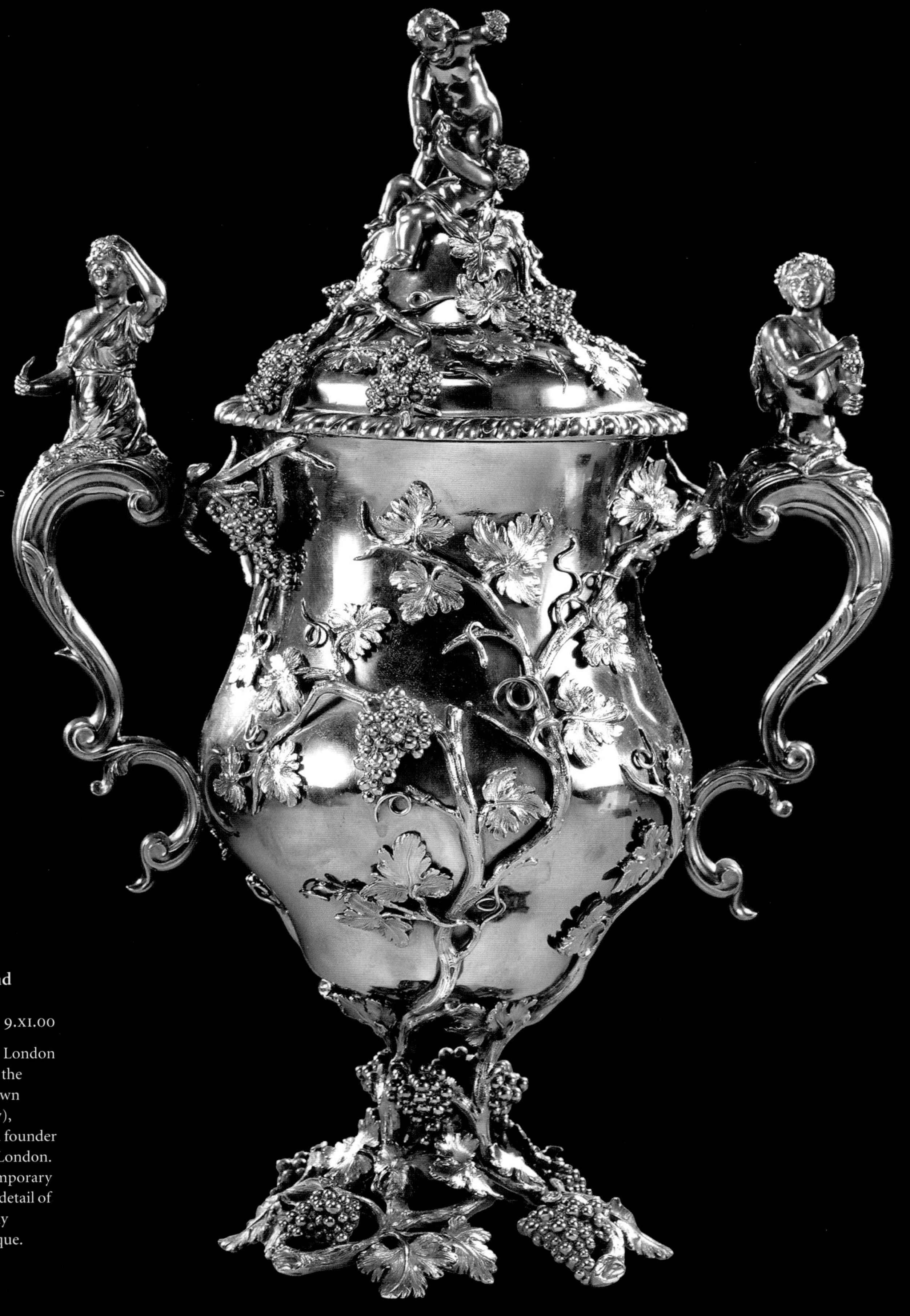

**A George III Silver Cup and Cover, Samuel Courtauld**
London £46,500 ($66,030) 9.XI.00

This Rococo cup was made in London in 1764 by Samuel Courtauld, the grandfather of the better-known Samuel Courtauld (1876–1947), industrialist, art collector and founder of the Courtauld Institute in London. The form originates in contemporary French designs, although the detail of the openwork foot is especially inventive and apparently unique. 46 cm. (18 in.) high.

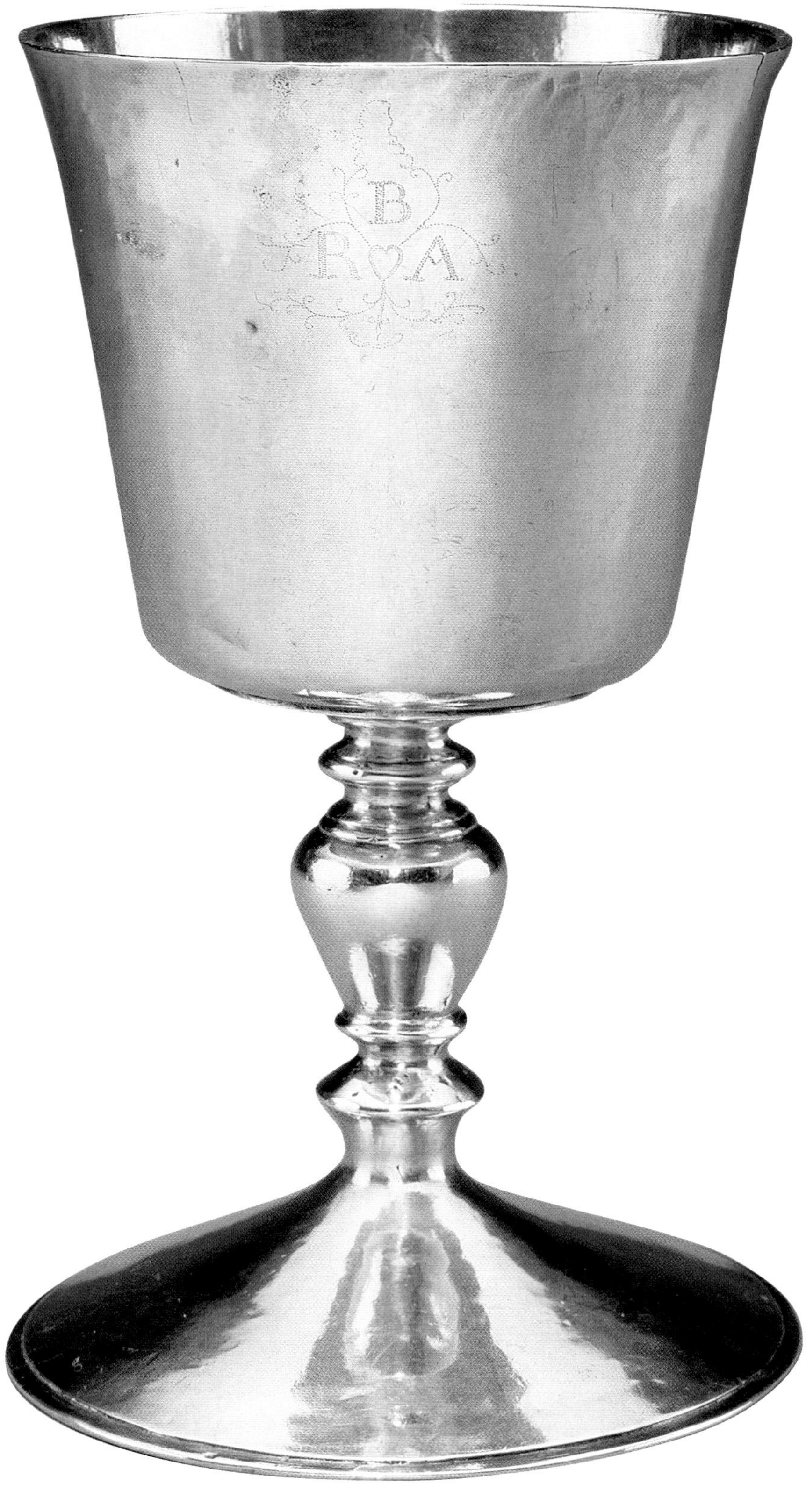

**The Richard and Alice Brackett Cup, John Hull and Robert Sanderson, Sr.**
New York $775,750 (£527,510)
19.I.01

The Quincy church silver encompassed the entire history of the craft of silversmithing in colonial Boston. This cup, made in Boston, *circa* 1660, set a new world record for any piece of American silver at auction. 17.5 cm. (6 in.) high.

→

**A French Silver-gilt and Enamel 'Japanese Style' Inkstand, Boucheron**
New York $247,750 (£170,948)
24.X.00

After Admiral Perry opened Japan to Western markets in the mid-19th century, the outpouring of ceramics, textiles and bronzes caused a sensation throughout Europe and America. In Paris, Frédéric Boucheron applied this new aesthetic to *objets de fantasie* for his wealthy clientele.
Attributed to his designer Paul Legrand *circa* 1876, Paris, 33.6 cm. (13 in.) long.

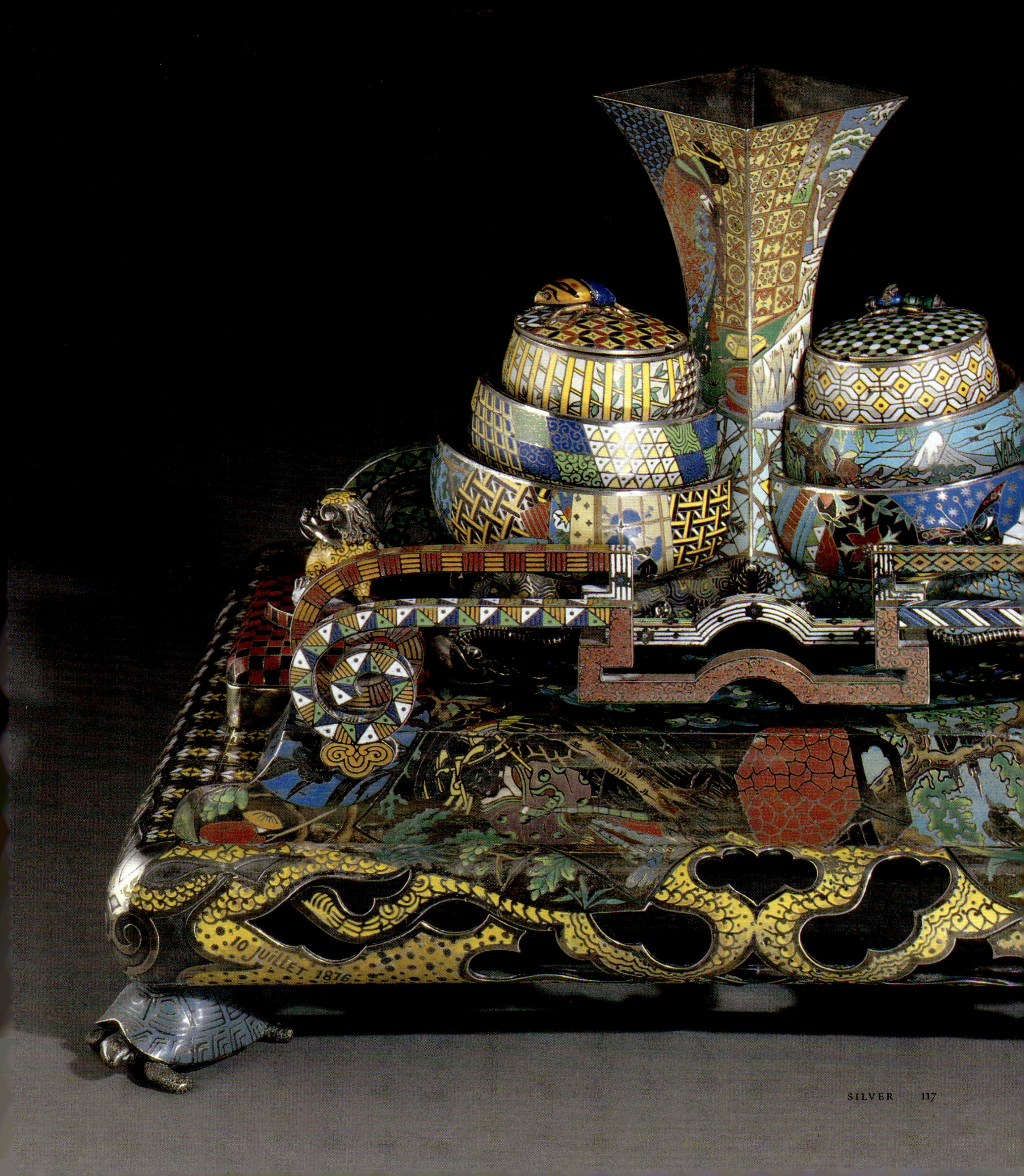
10 JUILLET 1876

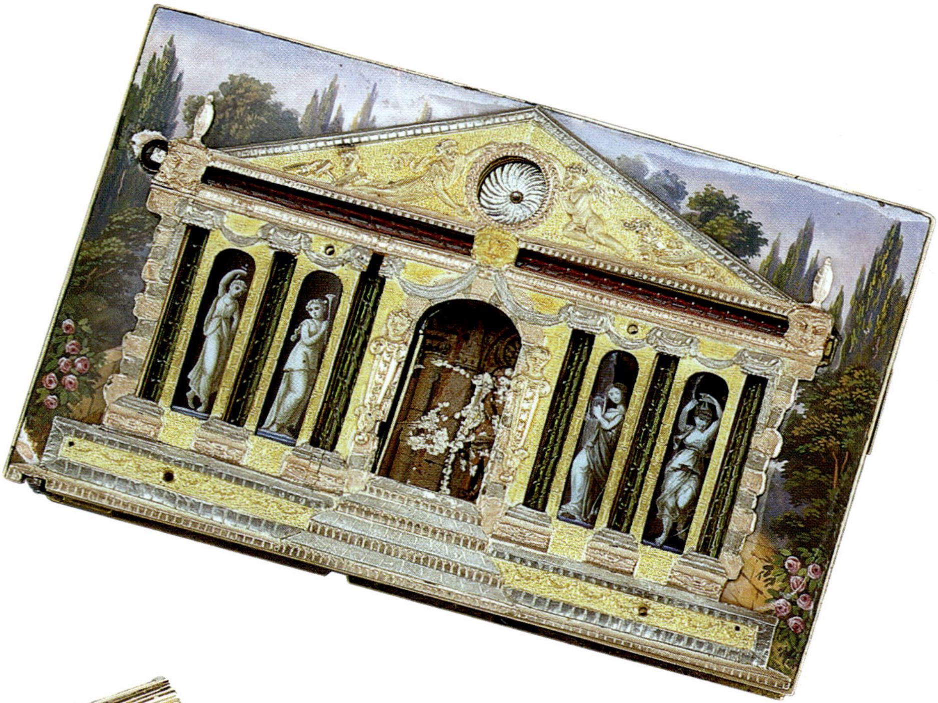

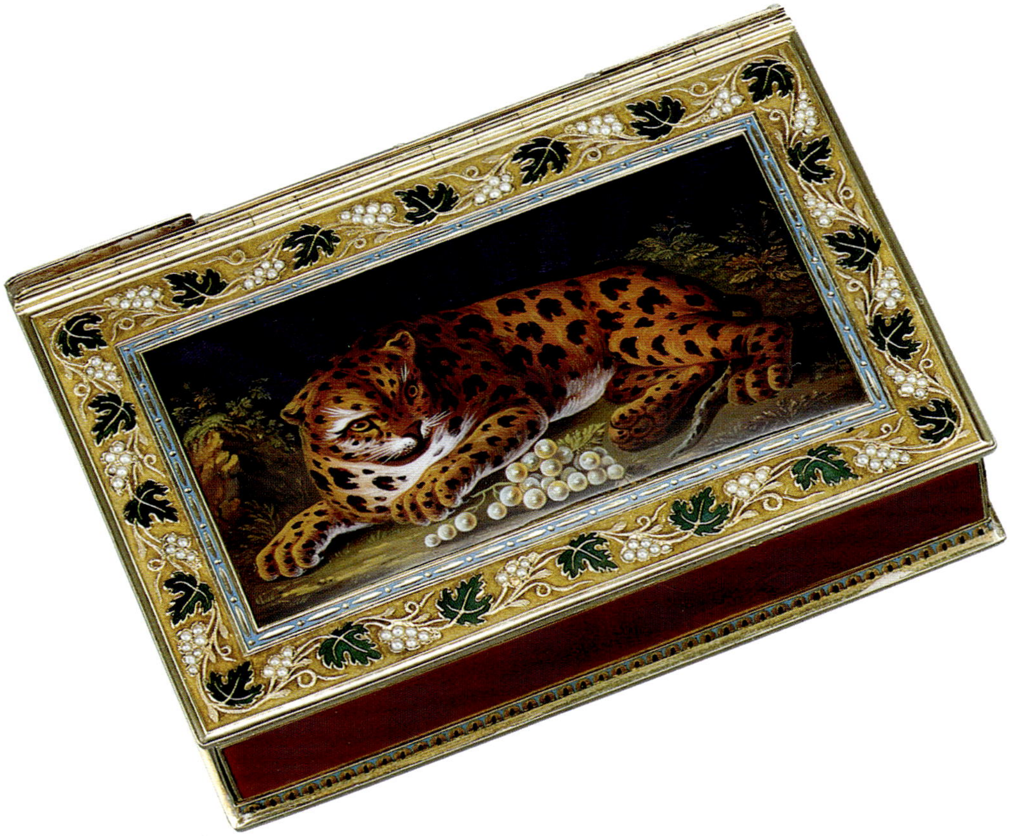

**A Musical Automaton Snuffbox with Watch and Vinaigrette**
London £641,500 ($910,930)
9.XI.00

This snuffbox set with pearls made in Geneva *circa* 1805–8, is designed to look like a book. The front cover with its leopard lifts to expose a theatrical temple dedicated to Music. As the music plays the glass columns revolve and change colour, and the central doors open to show an articulated dancer and musician. Behind them is an inner sanctuary with a flaming altar to Love.
The case with makers' mark *Sené & Neiser*, 8.4 cm. (3¼ in.) wide.

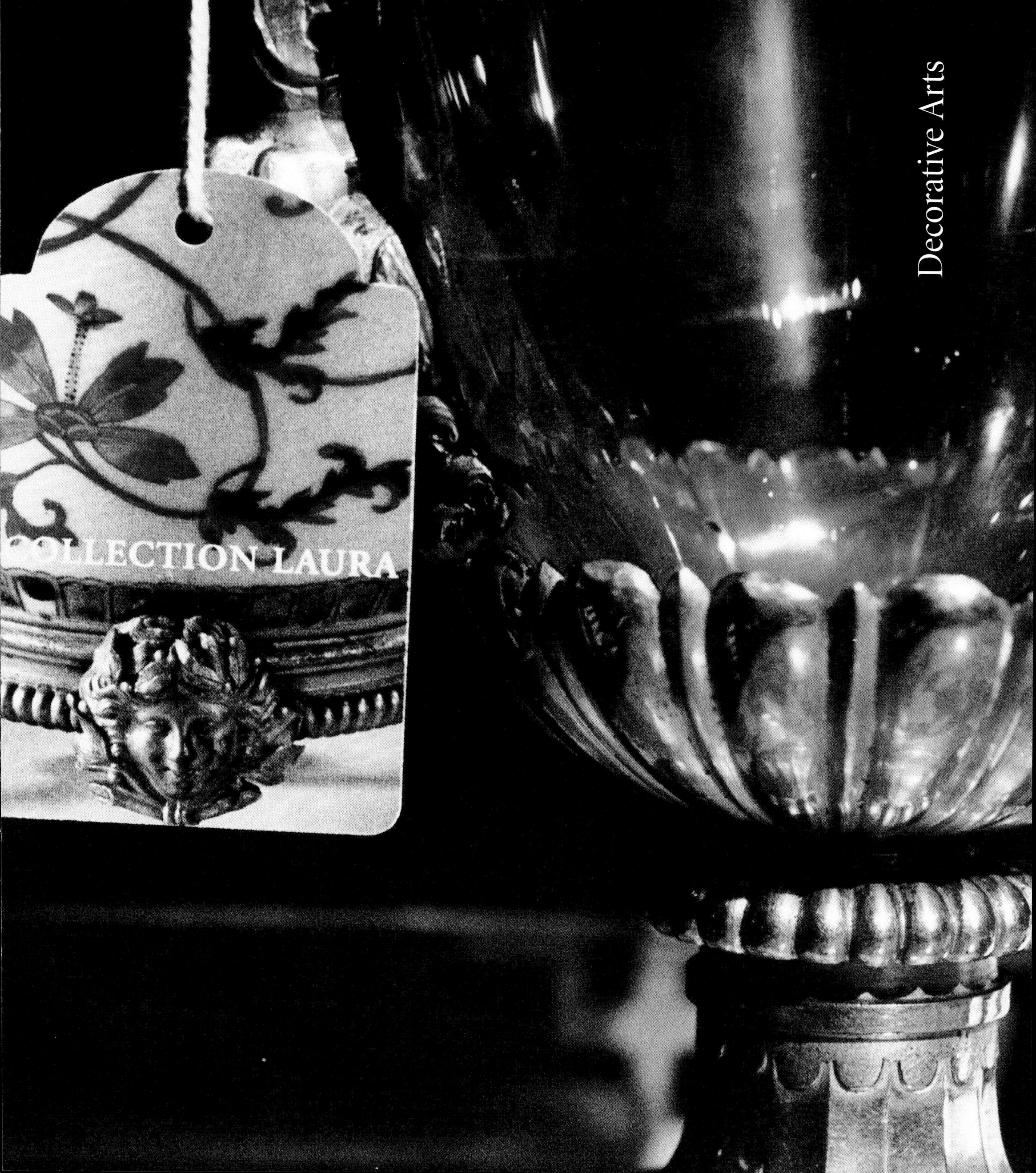


# Decorative Arts

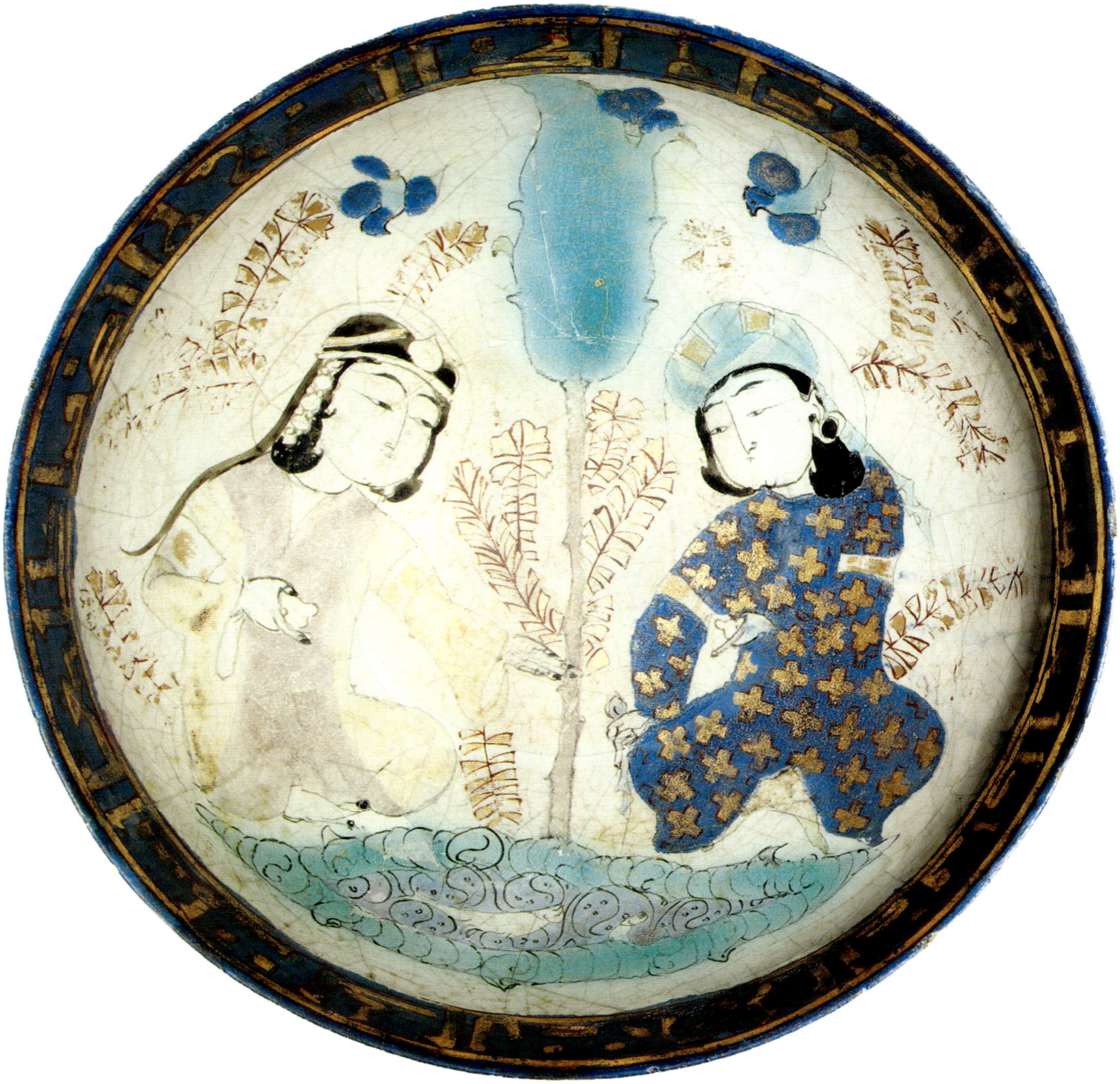

**A Mina'i Pottery Bowl**
London £95,900 ($138,096) 3.v.01

The artistic, stylistic and thematic evidence suggest that this medieval bowl, illustrated with an image of a courting couple, is a product of the atelier of master potter Abu Zaid, who was active around the late 12th century.
Persia, late 12th/early 13th century, 20.5 cm. (8 in.) diameter.

→
***A Man Walking Through a Landscape with his Saluki Hound***
London £344,500 ($502,970) 12.x.00

Shaykh Muhammad, to whom this painting can be attributed, has been described as 'one of the most versatile and imaginative artists of the Safavid era', and was a renowned calligrapher as well as a painter.
Persian, Safavid, *circa* 1555, gouache with gold on cotton, 18.3 by 13.6 cm. (17¼ by 5⅜ in.).

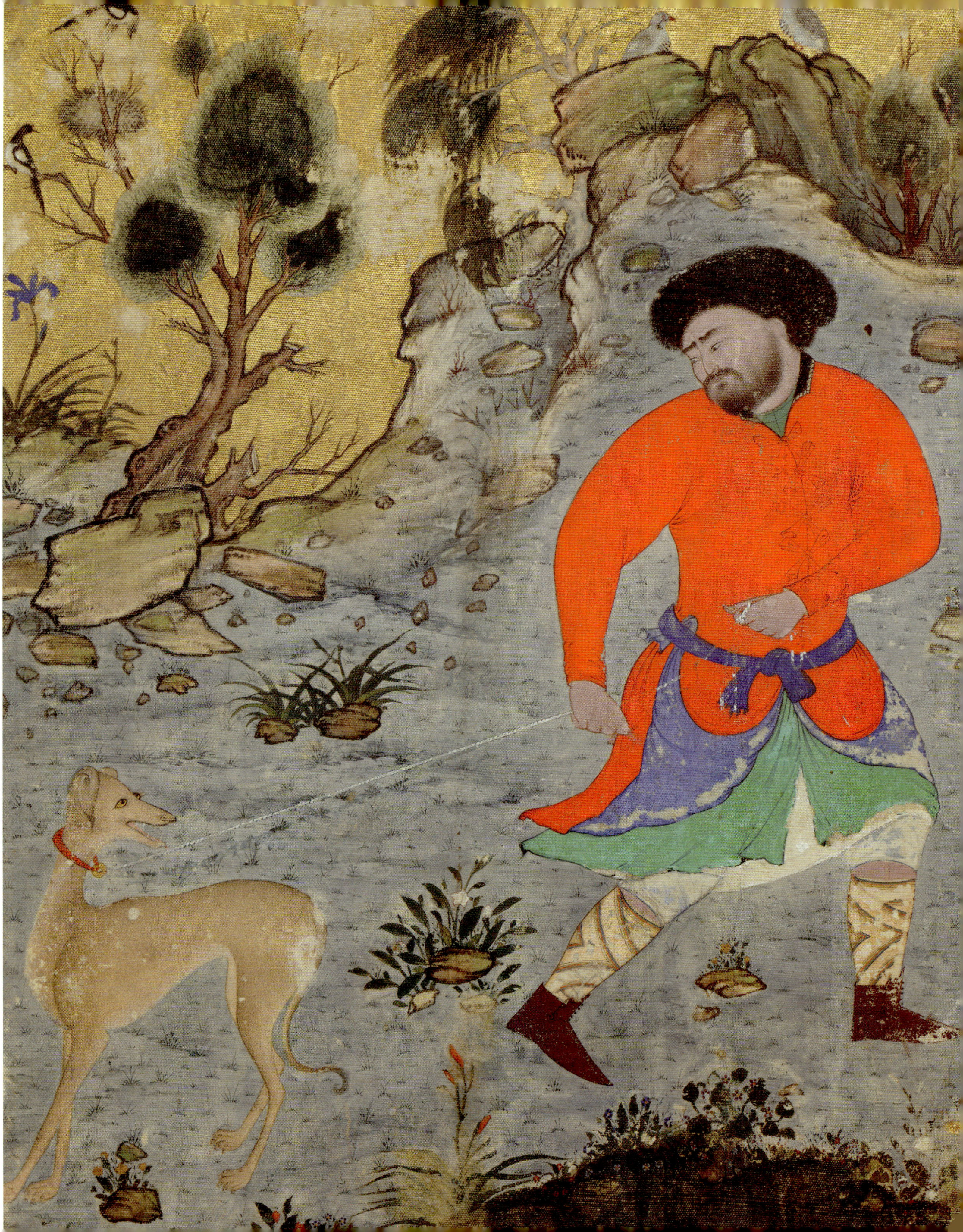

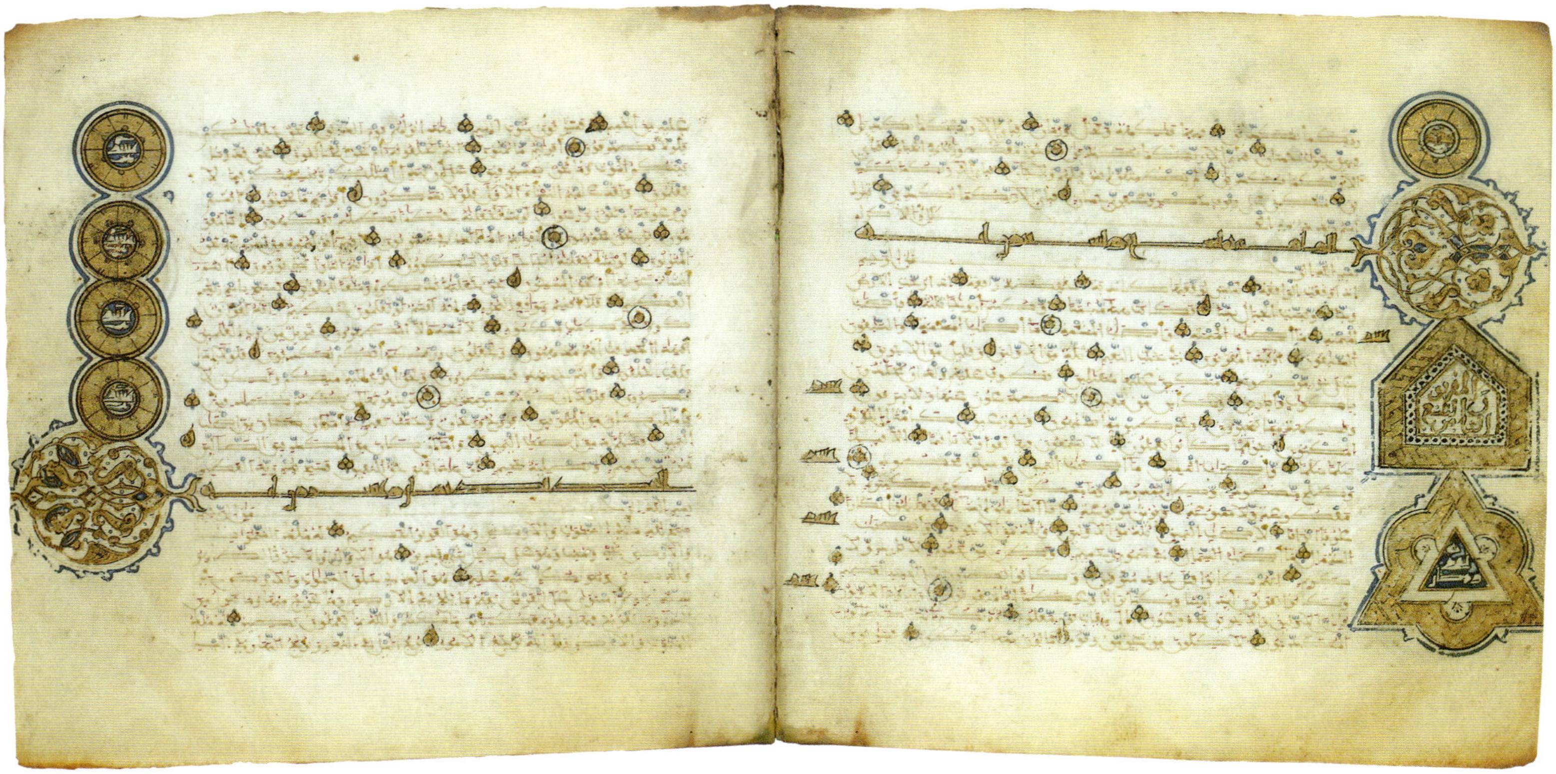

**Qur'an**
London £174,000 ($254,040)
12.X.00

This *Qur'an* has 129 leaves written in brown ink on vellum with illuminated palmettes in the margins. The manuscript was almost certainly written in southern Spain in the late 12th century, and can confidently be linked with a group of six Valencian *Qur'ans*.
Probably southern Spain, late 12th century, 11.3 by 11.3 cm. (4½ by 4½ in.).

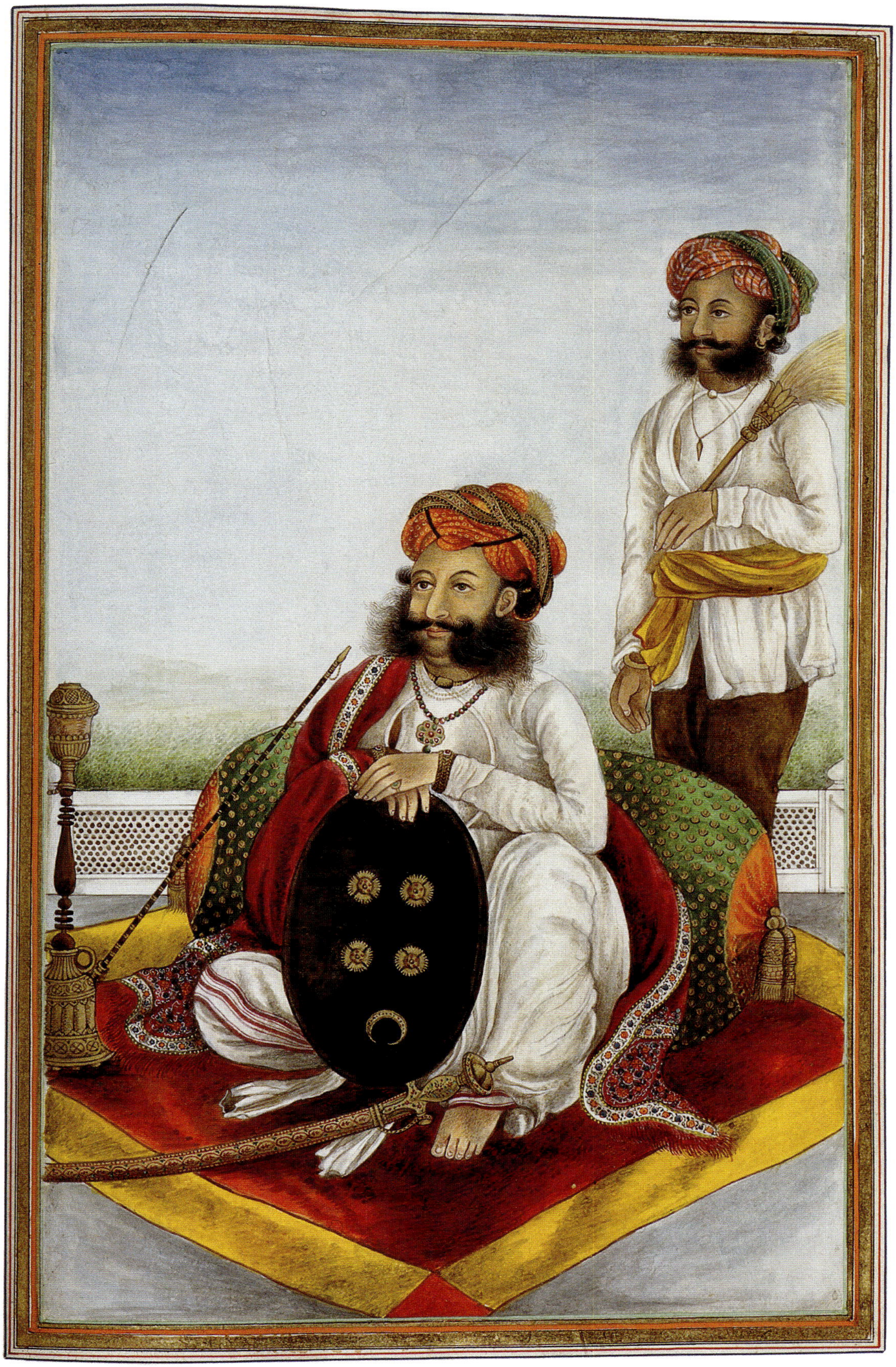

***Tashrih ul Akwam (Concise Account of the People)***
New York $98,500 (£67,965) 20.IV.01

This bound manuscript includes 122 illustrations that consist of noble portraits and images of the various castes of the Indian sub-continent at work. They are complemented by fine Persian script written by Colonel James Skinner.
Colours and gold on paper, Delhi, *circa* 1825, leaves: 31.7 by 21 cm. (12½ by 8¼ in.), images: 17.8 by 11.4 cm. (7 by 4½ in.).

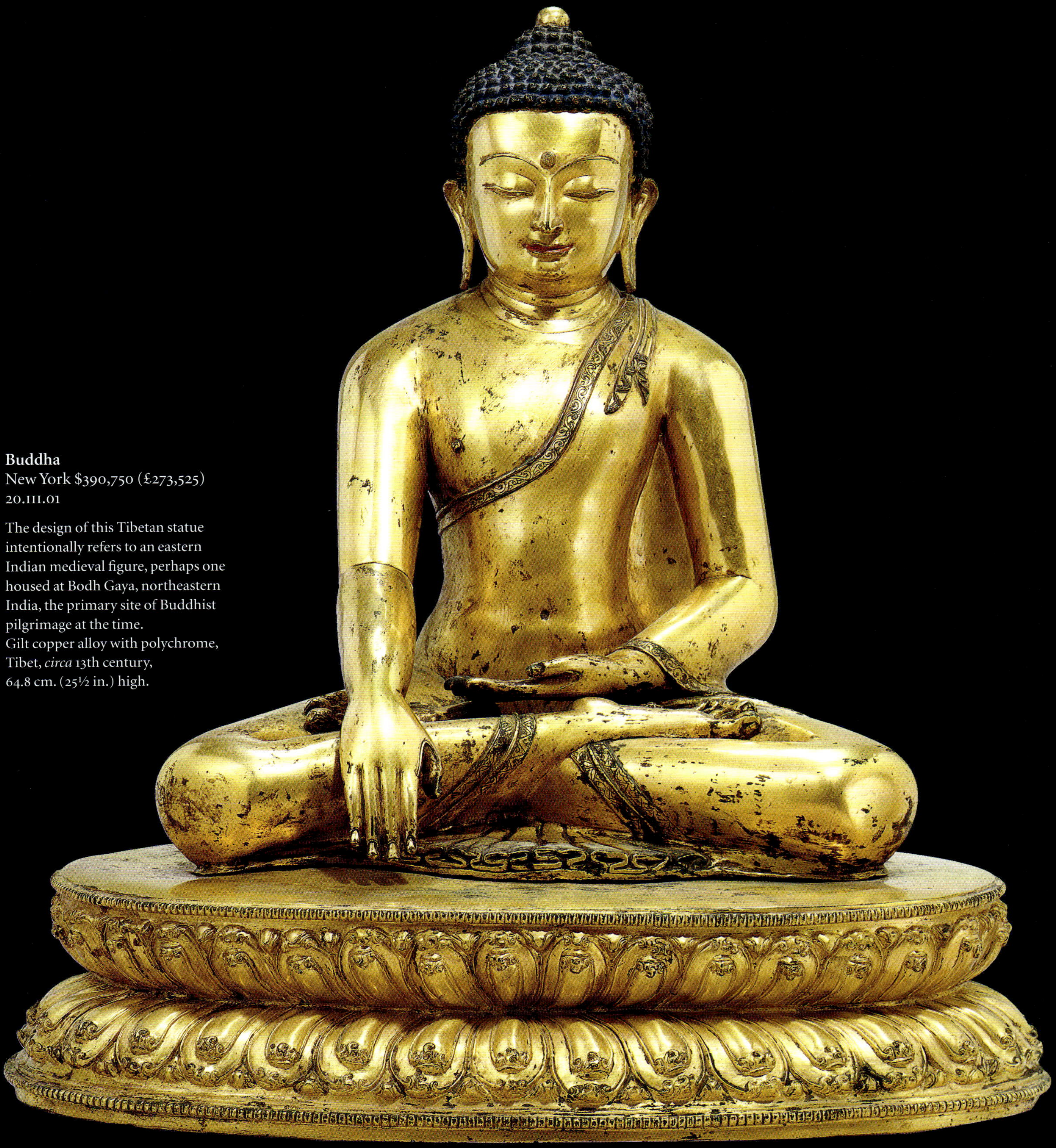

**Buddha**
New York $390,750 (£273,525)
20.III.01

The design of this Tibetan statue intentionally refers to an eastern Indian medieval figure, perhaps one housed at Bodh Gaya, northeastern India, the primary site of Buddhist pilgrimage at the time.
Gilt copper alloy with polychrome, Tibet, *circa* 13th century, 64.8 cm. (25½ in.) high.

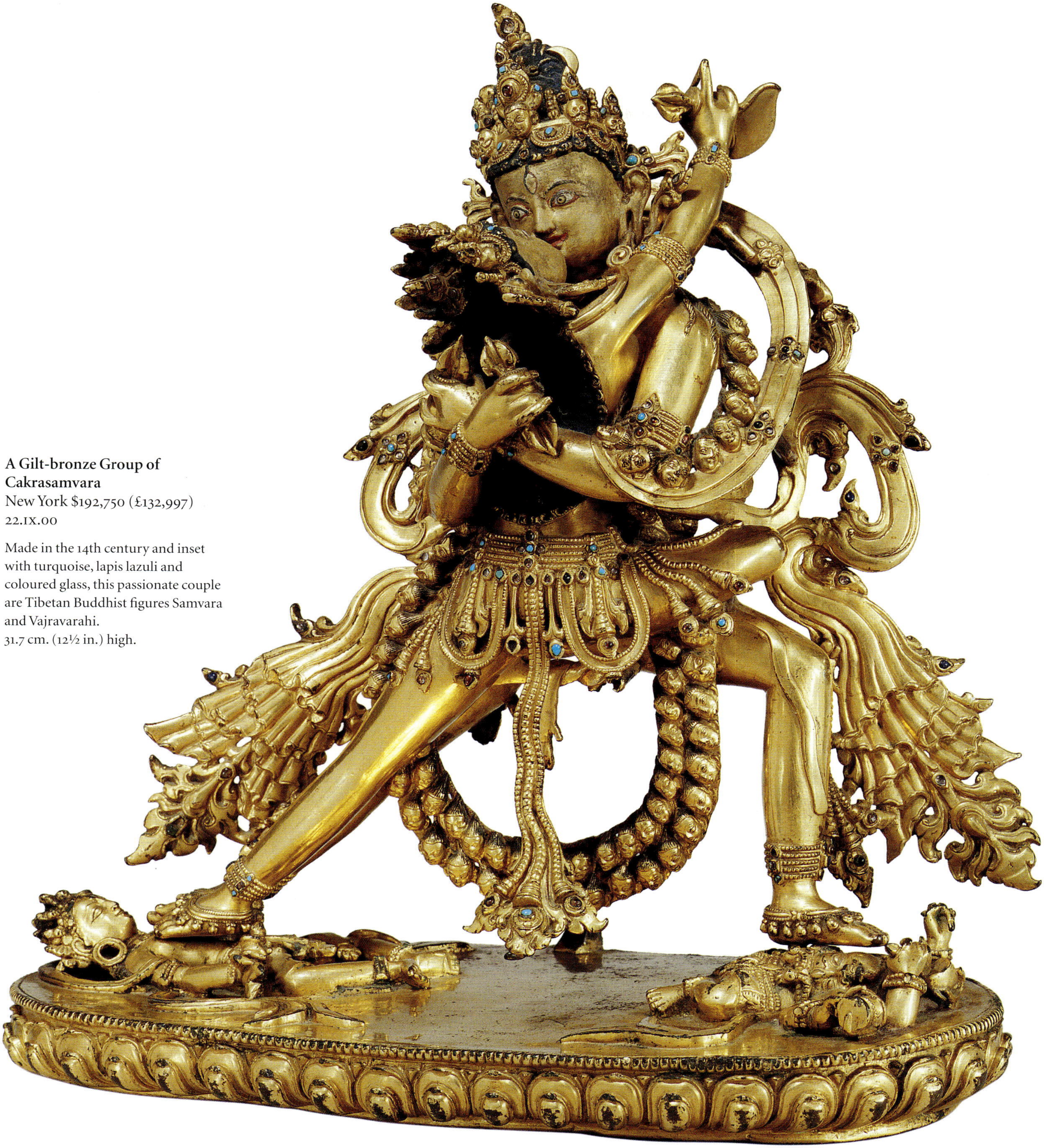

**A Gilt-bronze Group of Cakrasamvara**
New York $192,750 (£132,997)
22.IX.00

Made in the 14th century and inset with turquoise, lapis lazuli and coloured glass, this passionate couple are Tibetan Buddhist figures Samvara and Vajravarahi.
31.7 cm. (12½ in.) high.

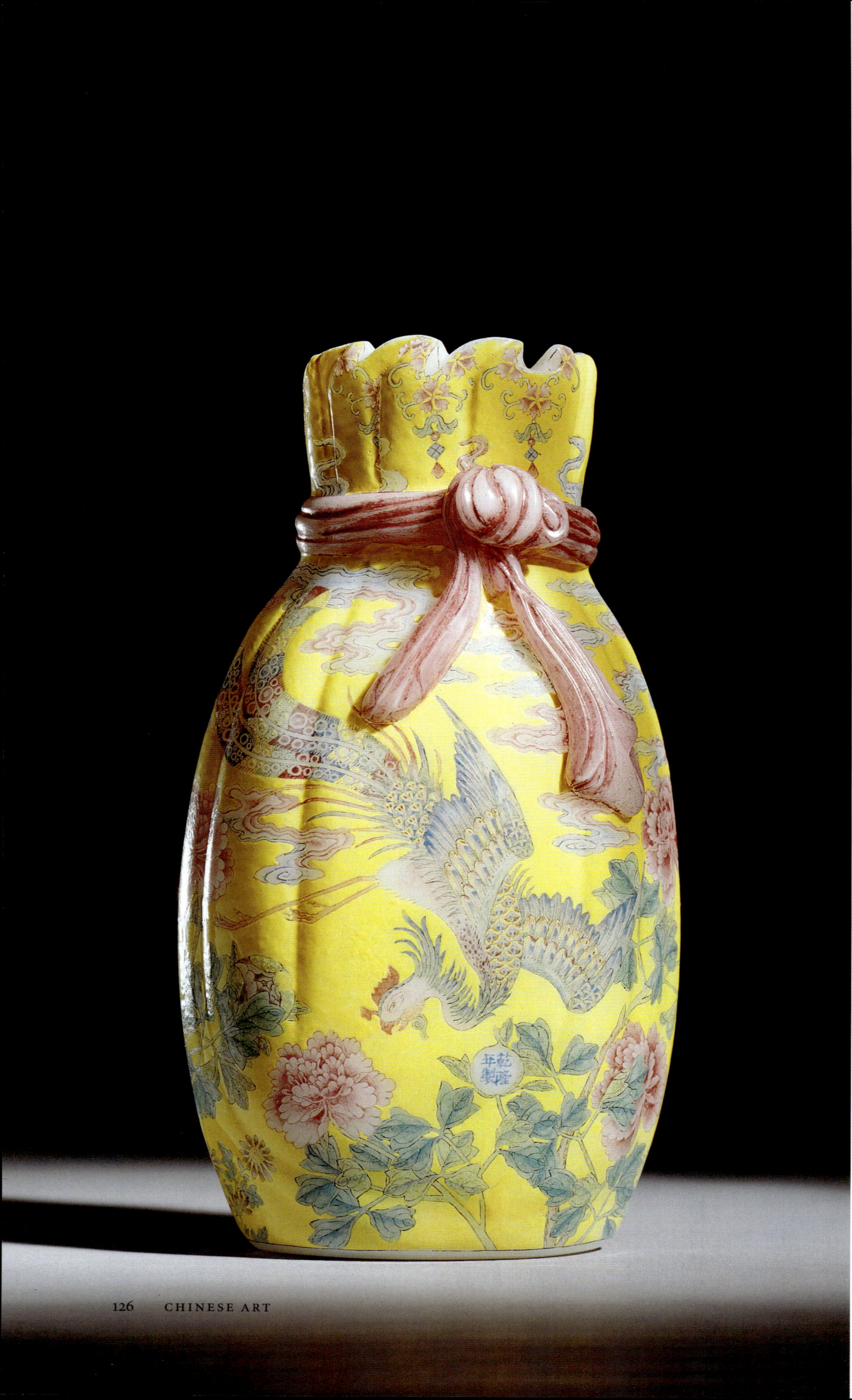

**An Enamelled Pouch-shaped Beijing Glass Vase**
Hong Kong HK$24,244,750 ($3,151817; £2,182,027) 29.x.00

Enamelled at the Imperial workshops in the Forbidden City, Beijing, this vase is an important and rare survivor. Showing a phoenix flying among peonies, it achieved an auction record for enamel ware.
Blue-enamel mark and period of Qianlong (1736–95), 18.2 cm. (7⅛ in.) high.

→

**A Blue-and-white 'Nine Dragon' Vase**
Hong Kong HK$9,064,750 ($1,178,417; £815,827) 29.x.00

Reaching an auction record for Qing blue-and-white porcelain, this *tianqiuping*-shaped vase shows the 'nine dragons' drawn in exceptional detail. Nine dragons were an Imperial symbol having, among other powers, the power to ward off evil spirits.
Seal mark and period of Qianlong (1736–95), 52.2. cm. (20½ in.) high.

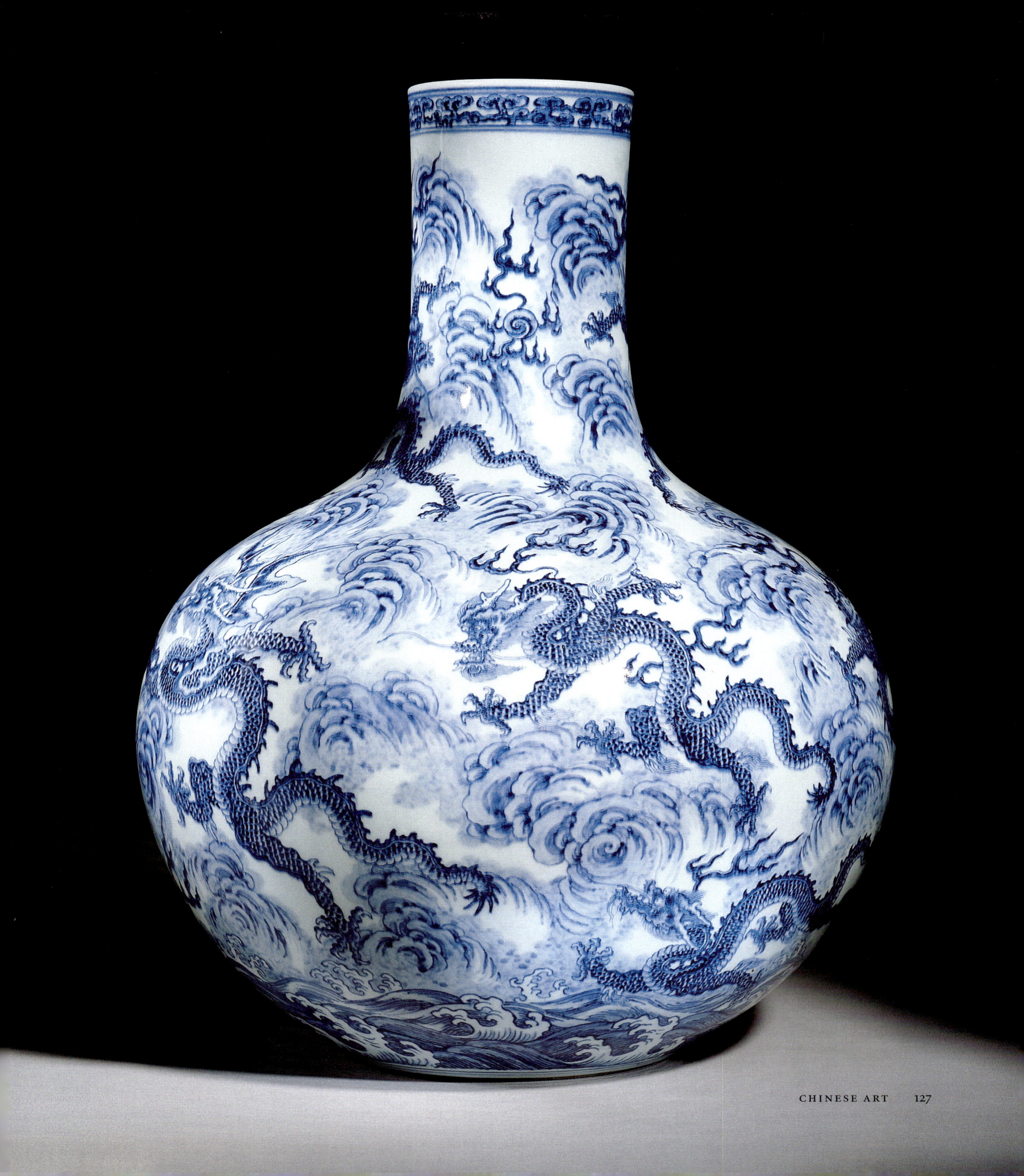

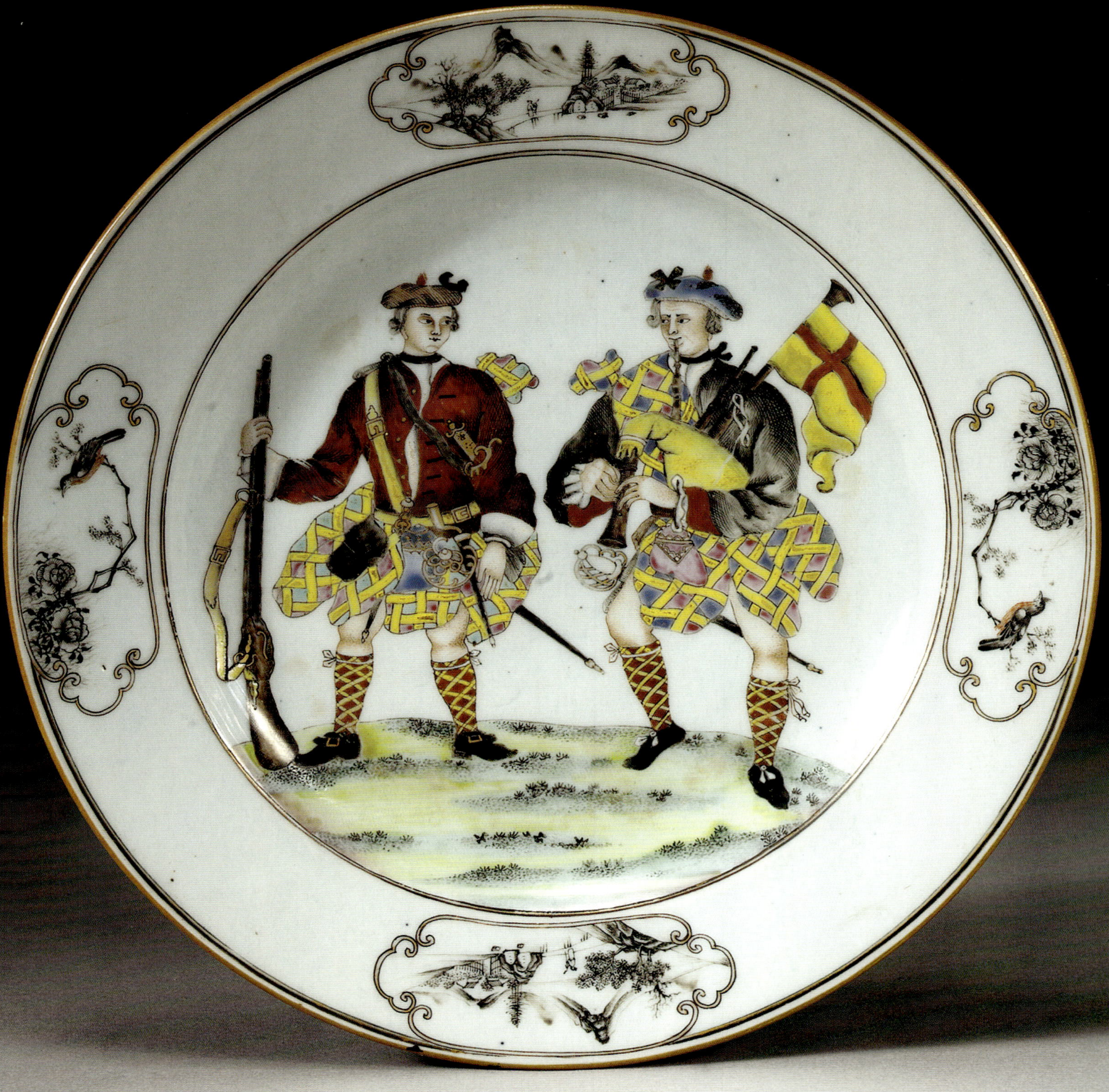

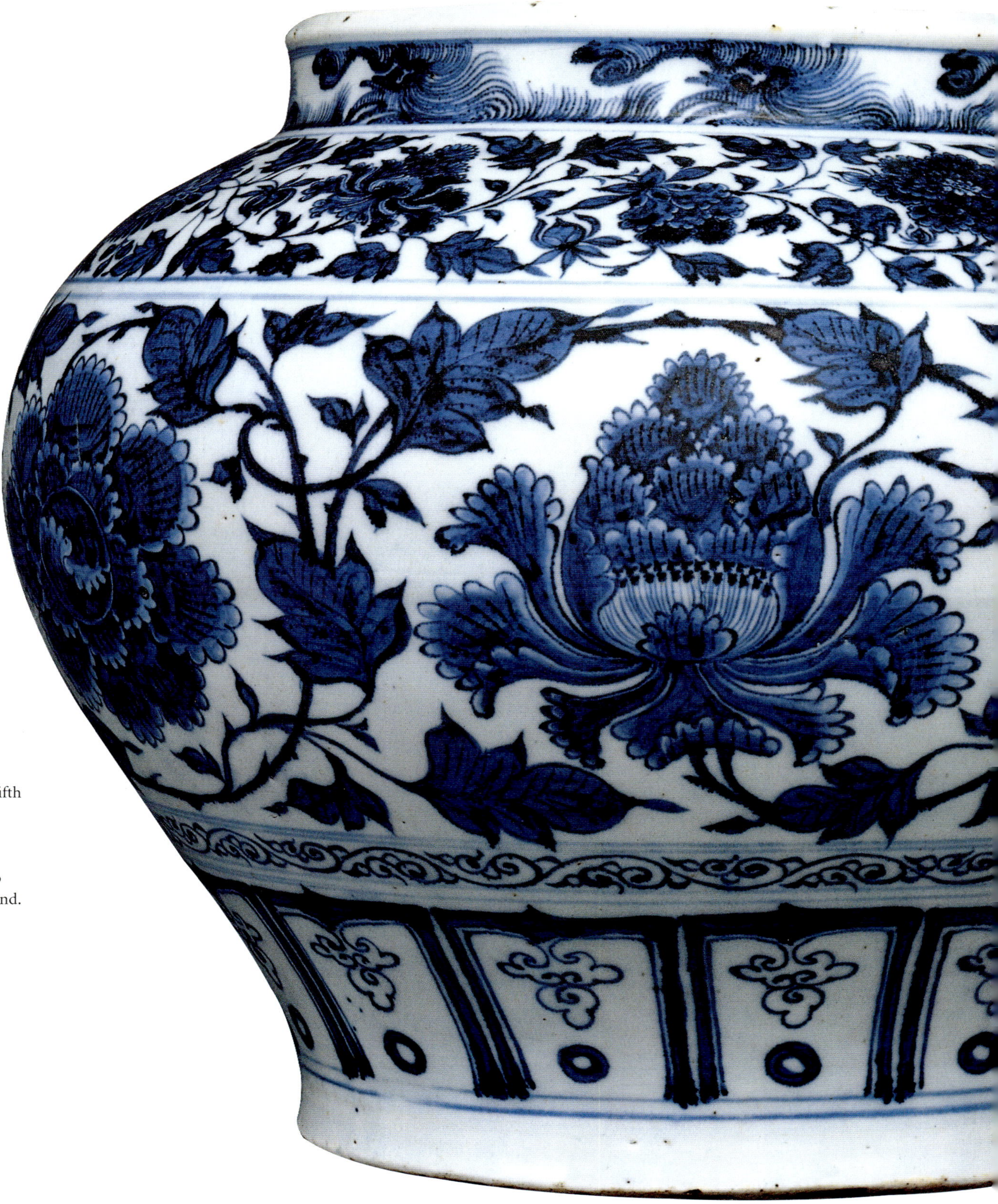

←

**A 'Famille-rose' Jacobite-subject Plate**
London £30,400 ($42,560)
22.XI.00

The plate was made for export in China around 1745, the date of the fifth Jacobite uprising, when Roman Catholic Bonnie Prince Charlie, strongly supported by Scottish lowlanders, fought – and failed – to become king of England and Scotland. 23 cm. (9 in.) diameter.

**A Blue-and-white Jar (*Guan*)**
New York $830,750 (£581,525)
20.IX.00

Originally part of the collection of newspaper editor Charles A. Dana, this jar, one of the finest surviving examples of its type, is probably the earliest piece of Yuan blue-and-white known to have reached the US in the 19th century.
Yuan dynasty (1260–1368), 27.9 cm. (11 in.) high.

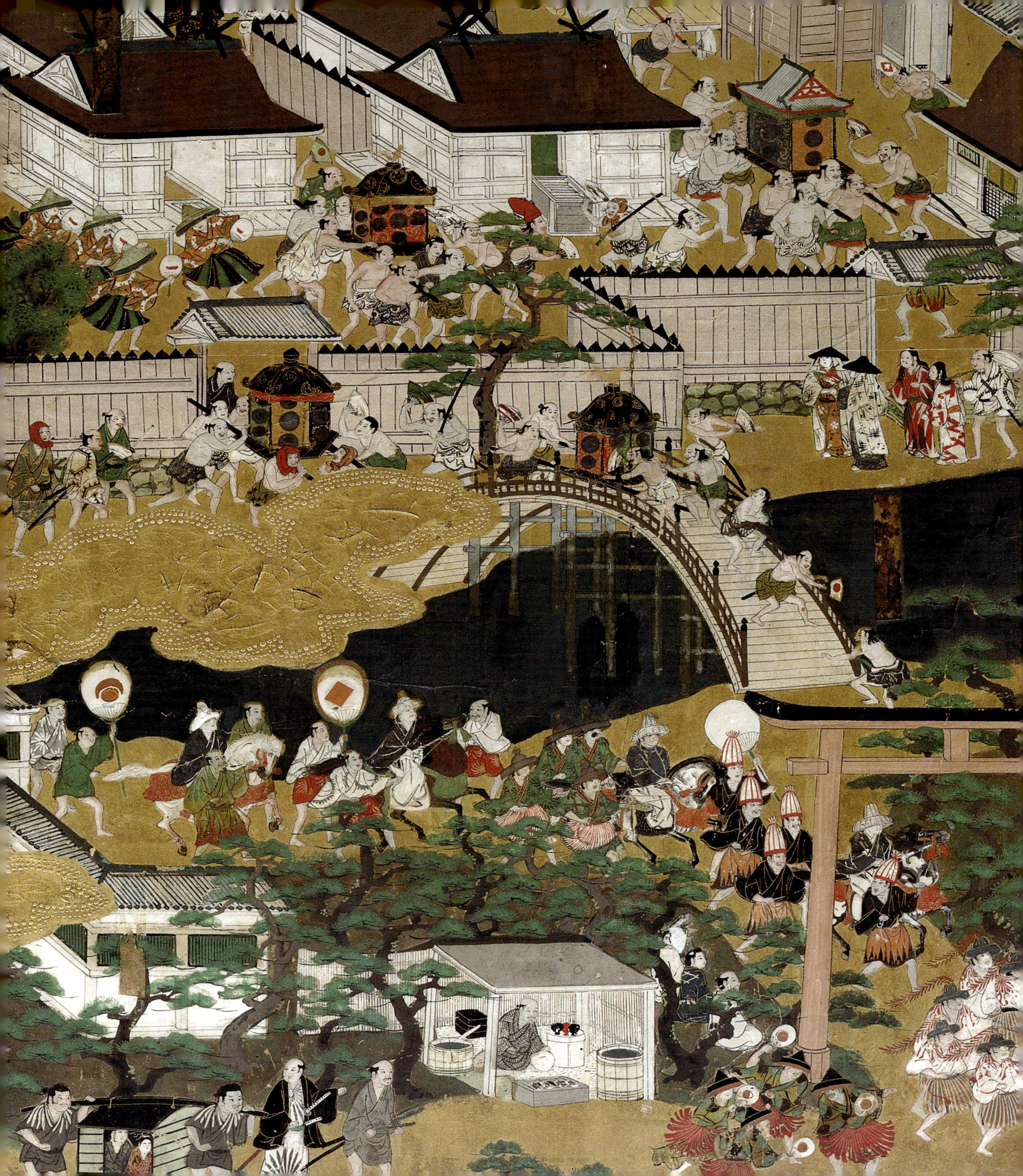

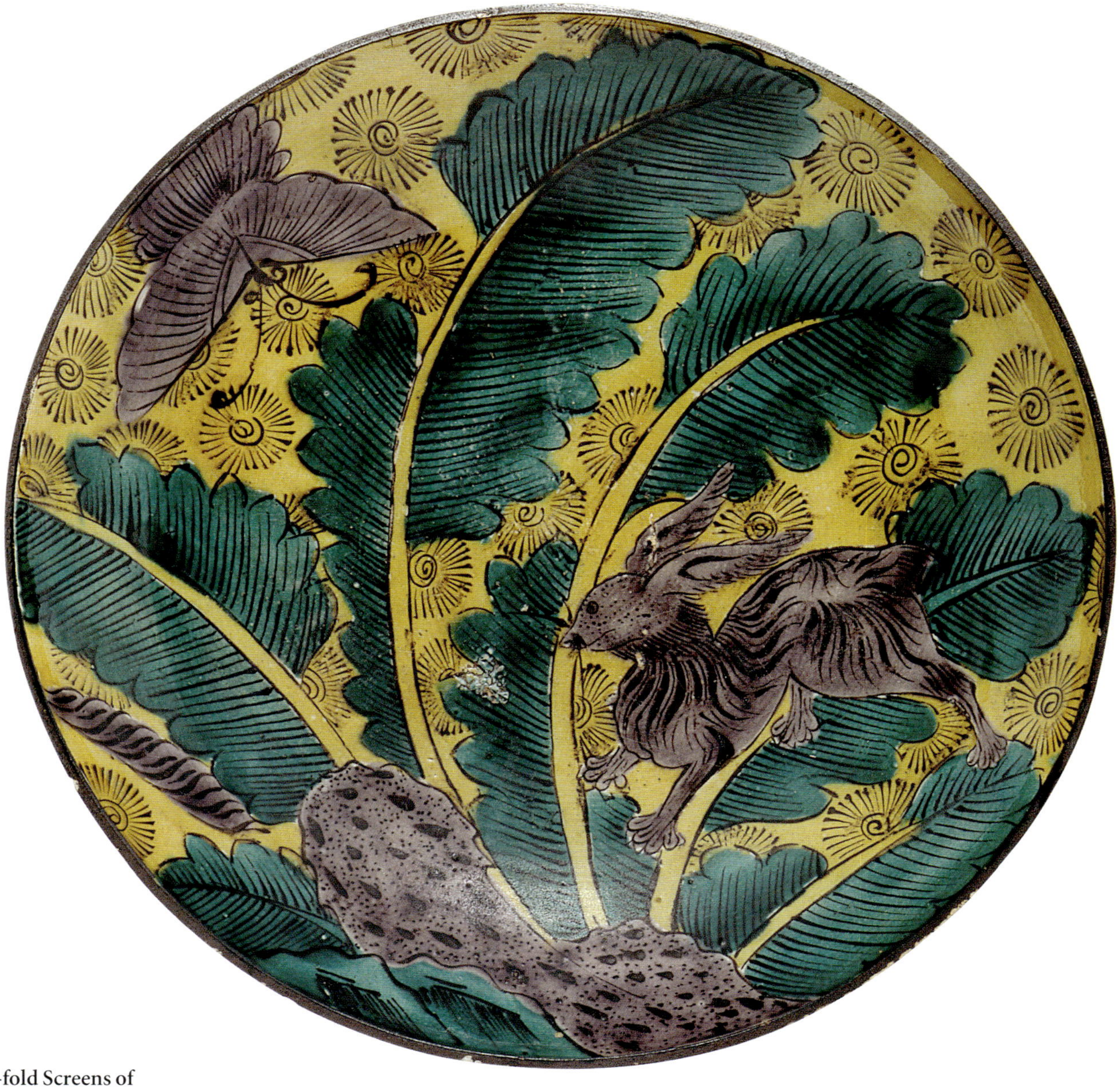

←

**A Pair of Six-fold Screens of Miyajima and the Sumiyoshi Festival (detail)**
London £190,500 ($266,700)
19.VI.01

These screens were probably made in the Genna era (1615–23). One shows the Sumiyoshi Shrine Festival, dedicated to the four patron gods of seafarers. The other screen shows celebrations at the Itsukushima Shrine Festival, dedicated to Princess Itsukushima.
Anonymous, early 17th century, ink, colour, gofun and gold on gilded paper mounted on brocade, each: 121 by 286 cm. (47½ by 112½ in.).

**An Aode Ko-Kutani dish**
New York $104,250 (£74,017)
21.II.01

The bold hare and butterfly design is coloured in fine purple enamel, one of the most difficult colours for the artist to control. Unlike the Kakiemon or Imari wares, Aode Ko-Kutani enamels were filled with designs and background motifs, which were rarely repeated on other pieces.
*Fuku* mark within a ring foot, late 17th century, 34.1 cm. (13⅜ in.) diameter.

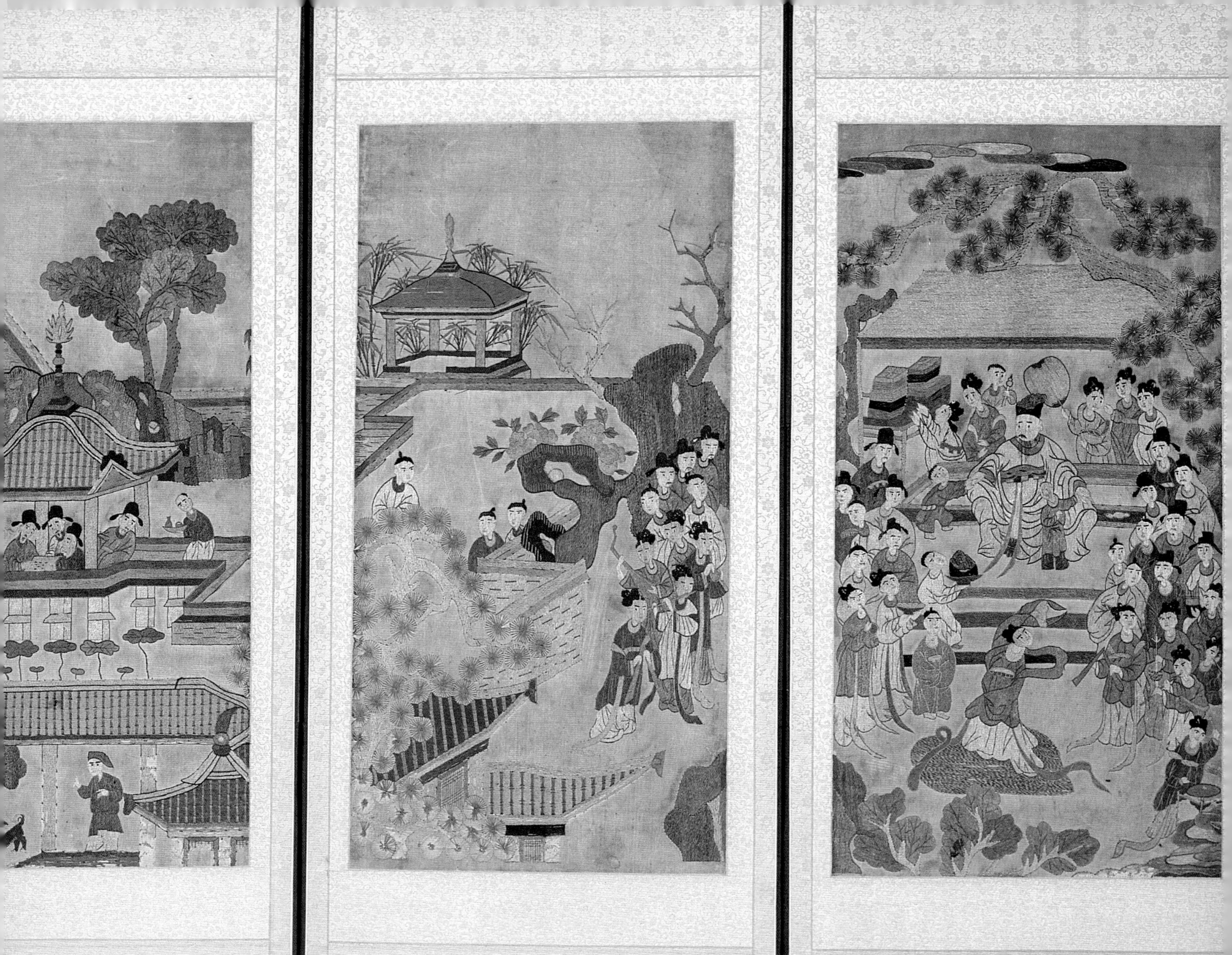

**Guo Ziyi's Banquet (detail)**
New York $55,375 (£39,316)
21.IX.00

The illustration on this pair of embroidered four-fold screens depicts the legendary Chinese general and strategist Guo Ziyi (697–781) and his descendants enjoying a banquet. It is a common theme in Korean art; however, its depiction in embroidery is rare. Anonymous, 19th century. Each panel: 60 by 30 cm. (23⅝ by 11¾ in.).

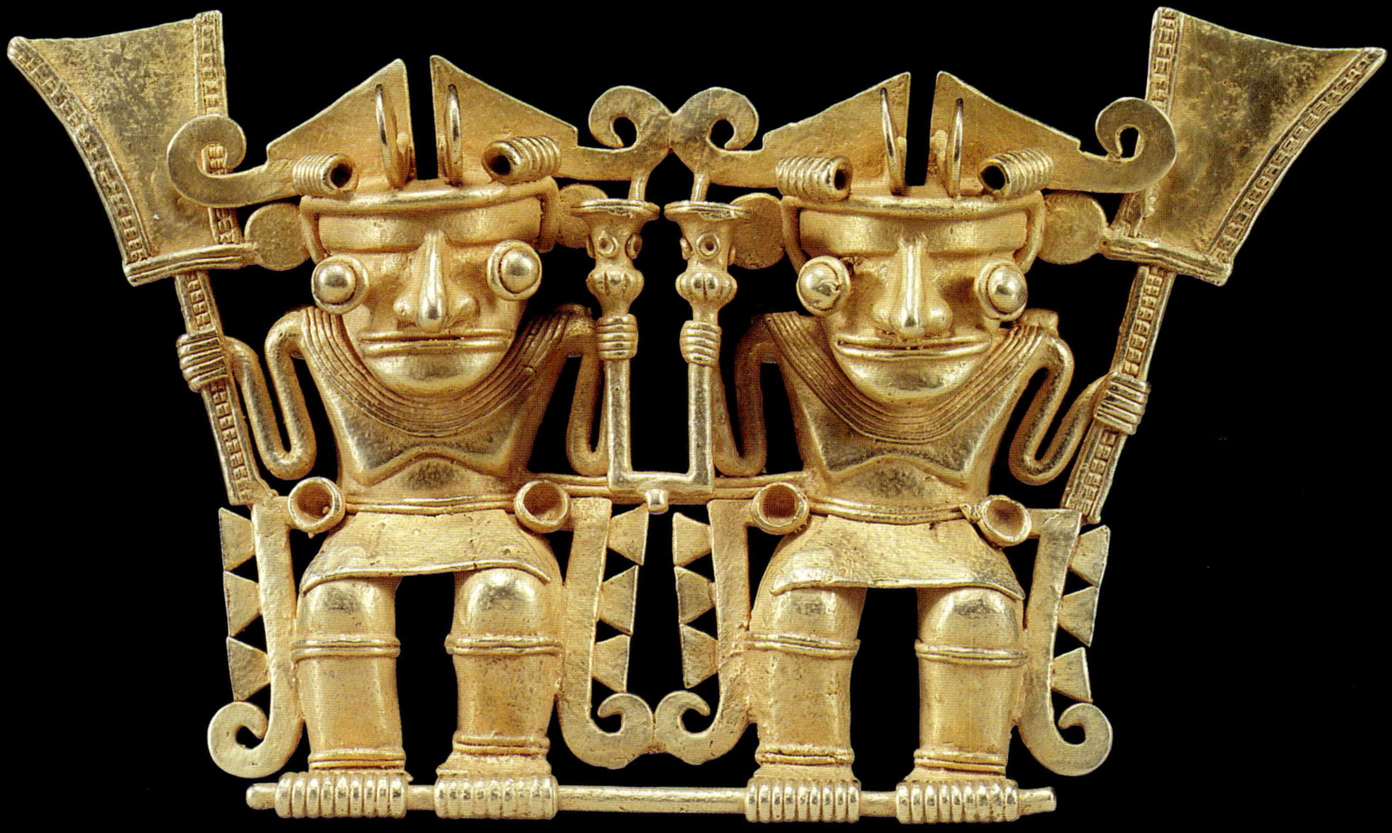

**A Coclé Gold Double-figural Pendant**
New York $92,750 (£64,910)
19.v.01

A classic example of the Coclé appreciation of, and indulgence in, fine-grade gold, this remarkable pendant weighs more than 370 g. (14¾ oz.). The finely and densely cast twin warriors dramatically portray the supernatural attributes of a warrior or chief.
Parita, Azuero Peninsula, *circa* AD 800–1500, 15.9 cm. (6¼ in.) wide.

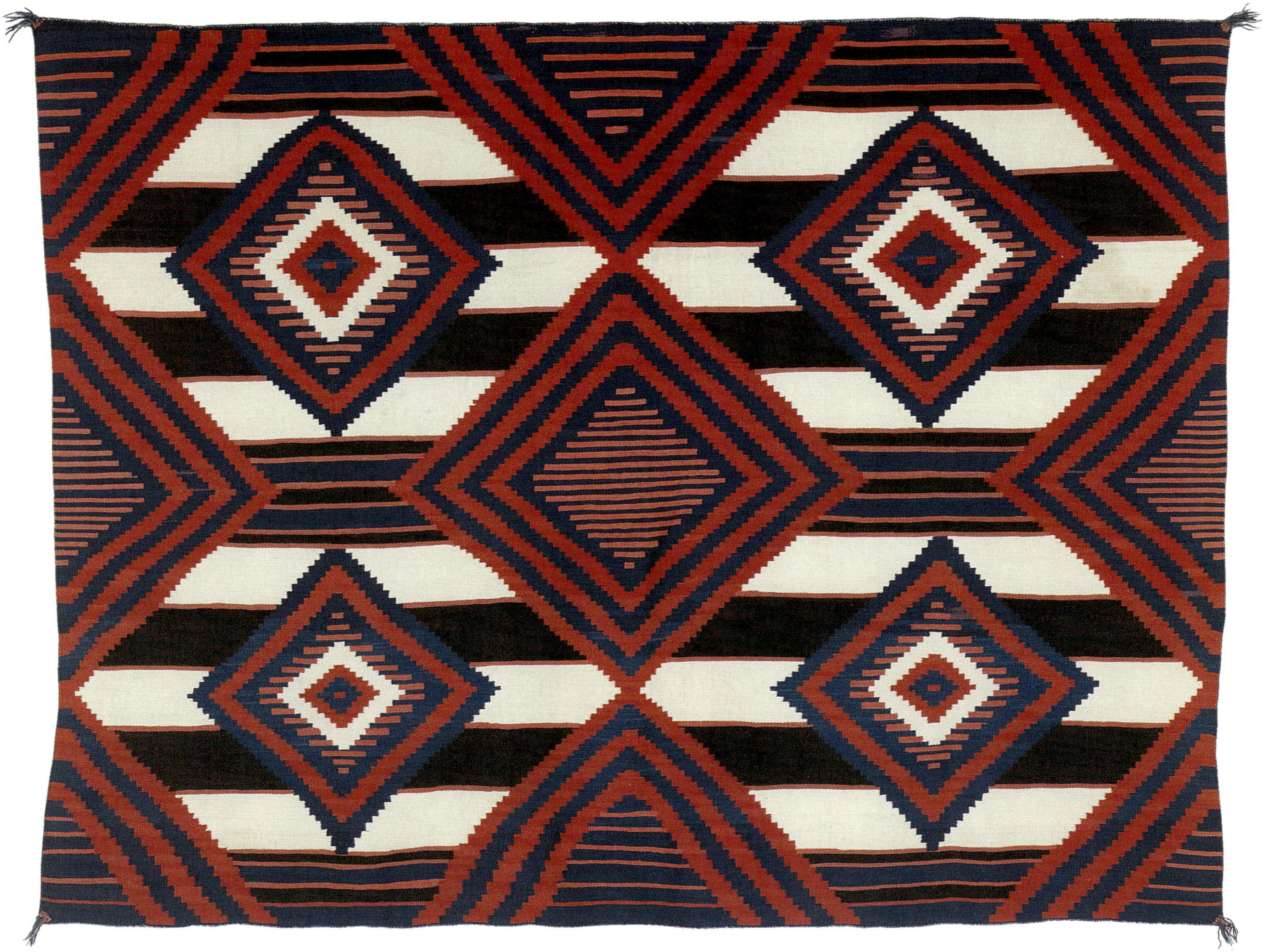

**A Navajo Man's Wearing Blanket**
New York $401,750 (£277,208)
19.V.01

The materials used to weave this textile could indicate an earlier date of manufacture than its variant Chief's Third Phase design suggests. This possibility, and the consequent art-historical significance of the piece, ignited competitive bidding that vaulted the selling price to more than ten times its pre-sale high estimate of $30,000 (£20,000). 144.7 by 182.8 cm. (57 by 72 in.).

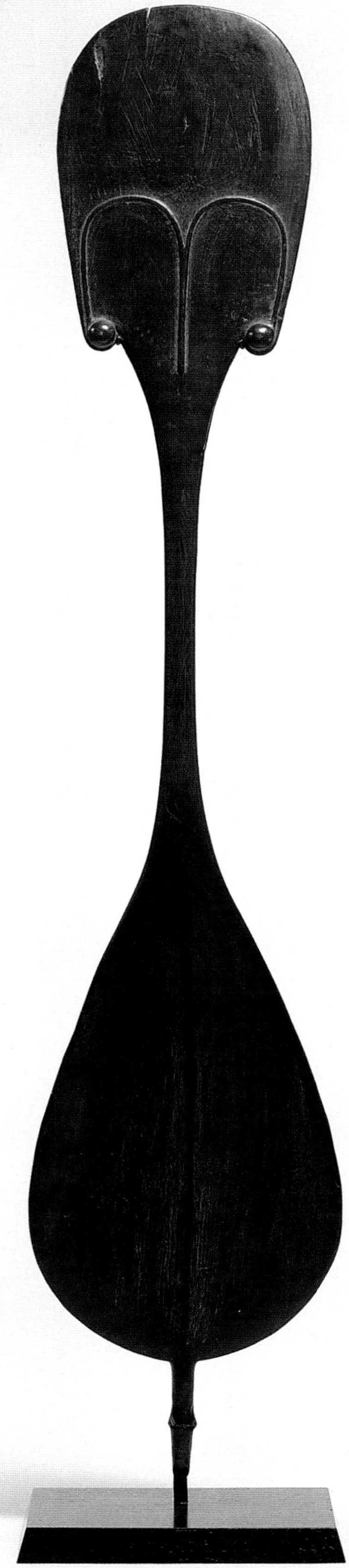

**An Easter Island Dance Paddle**
New York $423,750 (£296,540)
19.v.01

Easter Island dance paddles, or *rapa*, were most likely reserved for important ceremonial occasions. Scholars suggest that the paddles were incorporated in ceremonies involving jurisprudence. This paddle was formerly in the James T. Hooper Collection, one of the premier English collections of the 20th century.
83.8 cm. (33 in.) high.

**A Limestone Figure of a Lion**
New York $154,250 (£112,602)
12.VI.01

This lion may have been inspired by monumental granite lions, now in the Vatican, that were carved during the reign of Nectanedo I (380–342 BC). Ancient graffiti are visible on top of this lion's left leg, including Roman numerals.
30th Dynasty/Ptolemaic Period, 380–30 BC. 124.5 by 69.8 cm. (49 by 27½ in.).

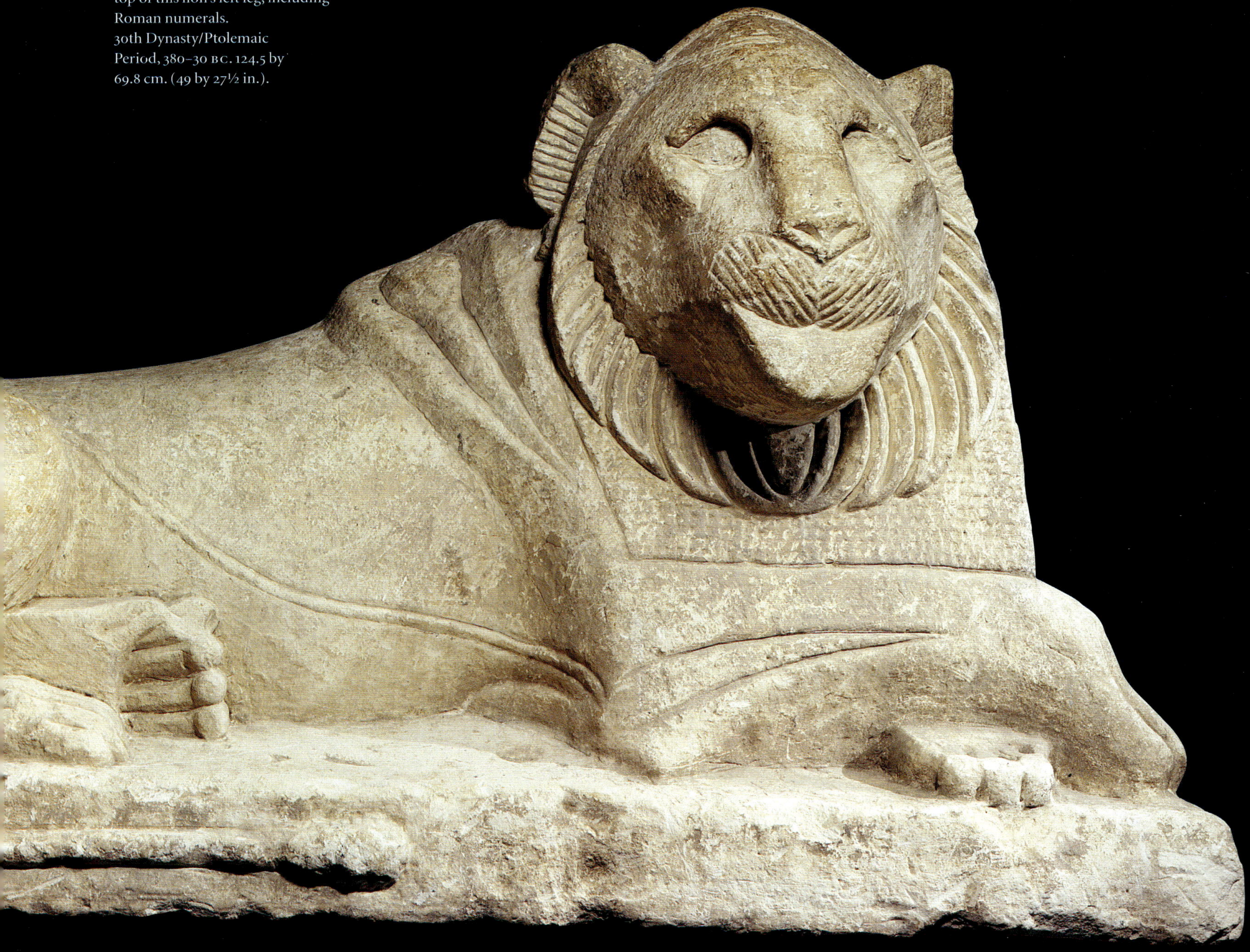

**A Florentine Bronze Pacing Bull, from the Giambologna-Susini Workshop**
New York $420,000 (£285,600)
25.I.01

This is an excellent example of the popular model that emanated from the Giambologna workshop. The thoroughly chased surface, exquisite detail, brilliant colour of original varnish, and thinly walled cast are all characteristics of the bronzes produced in the Florentine mannerist studios of Giambologna and Antonio Susini.
Late 16th–early 17th century,
22.5 by 24.8 cm. (8⅞ by 9¾ in.).

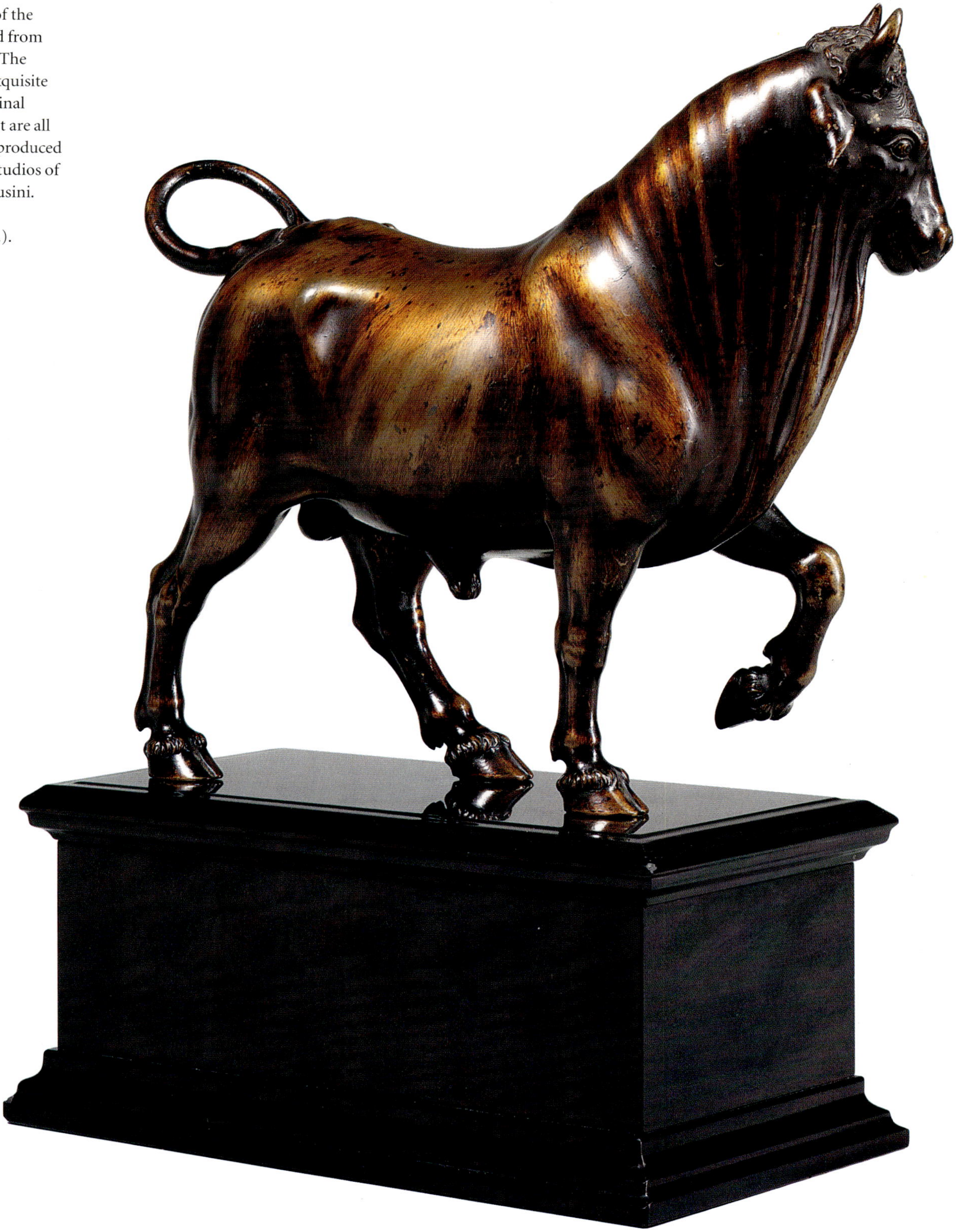

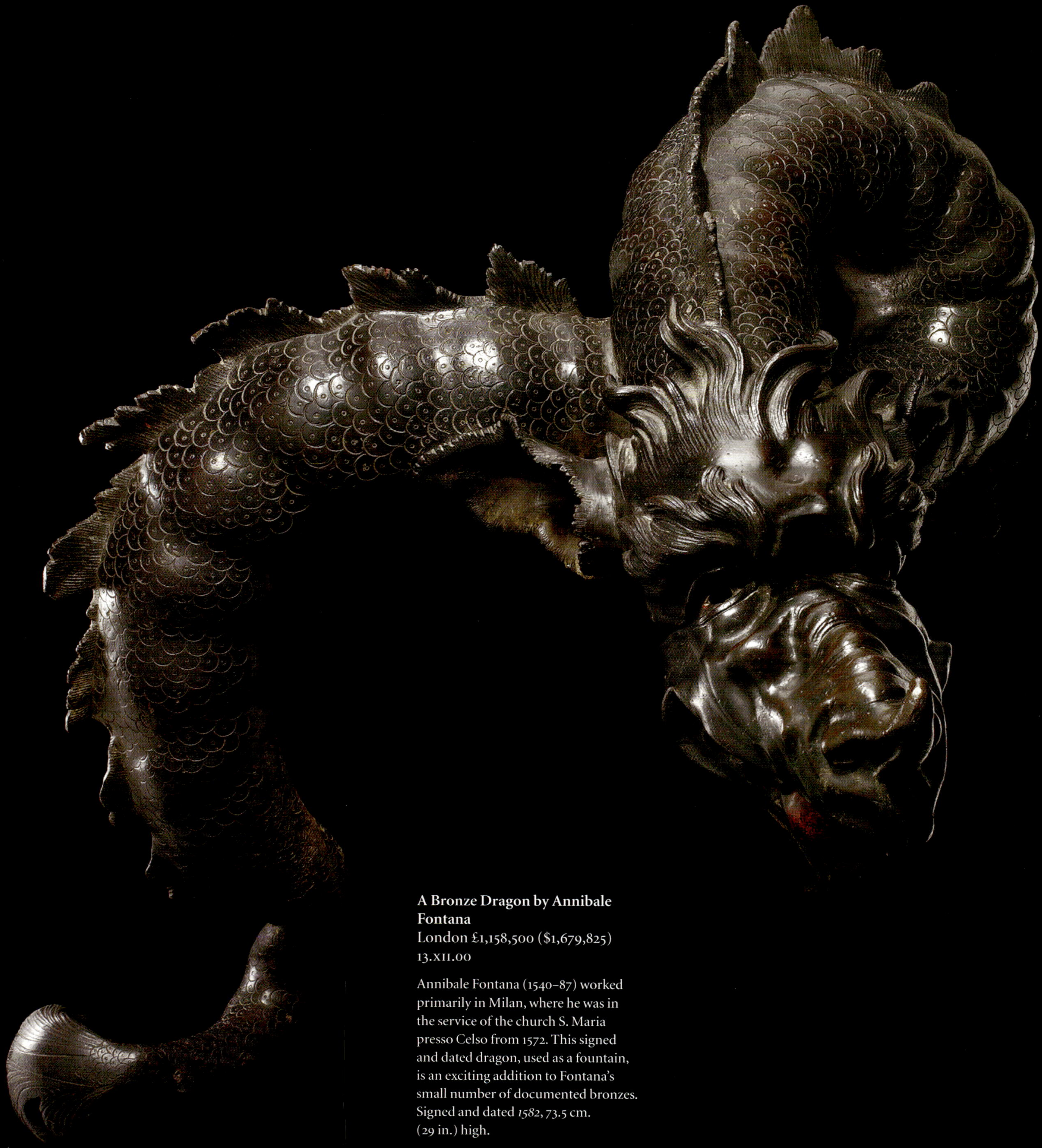

**A Bronze Dragon by Annibale Fontana**
London £1,158,500 ($1,679,825)
13.XII.00

Annibale Fontana (1540–87) worked primarily in Milan, where he was in the service of the church S. Maria presso Celso from 1572. This signed and dated dragon, used as a fountain, is an exciting addition to Fontana's small number of documented bronzes. Signed and dated *1582*, 73.5 cm. (29 in.) high.

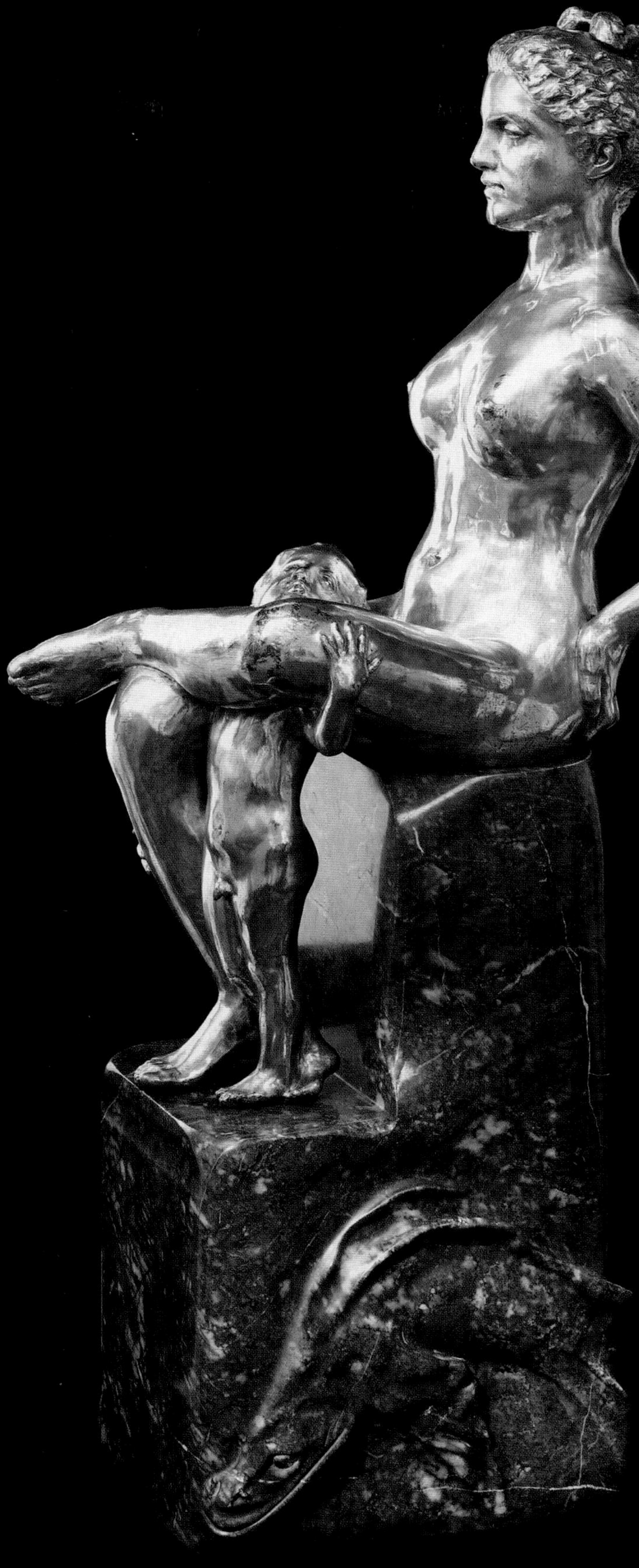

**Max Klinger**
*Galatea*
London £245,500 ($346,155)
11.VII.01

This unique silver cast of the sea nymph Galatea shows the fascination that the contrast between polished marble and reflective silver held for Klinger (1857–1920).
Silver and mottled grey marble, 111 cm. (43 ¾ in.) high.

**A James I Walnut and Inlaid Chest**
Thornton Manor £350,000 ($493,500) 26.VI.01

The earliest piece in the Leverhulme Collection (see pages 36–7), this 1604 chest was probably made to celebrate a marriage. The three panels represent Mercy, Justice and Prudence, and the chest is decorated in marquetry. With a label reading LORD LEVERHULME *March 23, 1920*, 79 by 142 by 61 cm. (2 ft. 7 in. by 2 ft. by 4 ft. 8 in.).

→

**A Chinese *Paktong* 12-light Chandelier**
New York $335,750 (£231,668) 19.IV.01

This chandelier is probably the largest piece of *paktong* – an alloy of copper, zinc and nickel – ever recorded. Probably made in the mid 18th century, it was possibly intended for a merchant's house in the Far East. 88.9 cm. (35 in.) high; 104.1 cm. (41 in.) diameter.

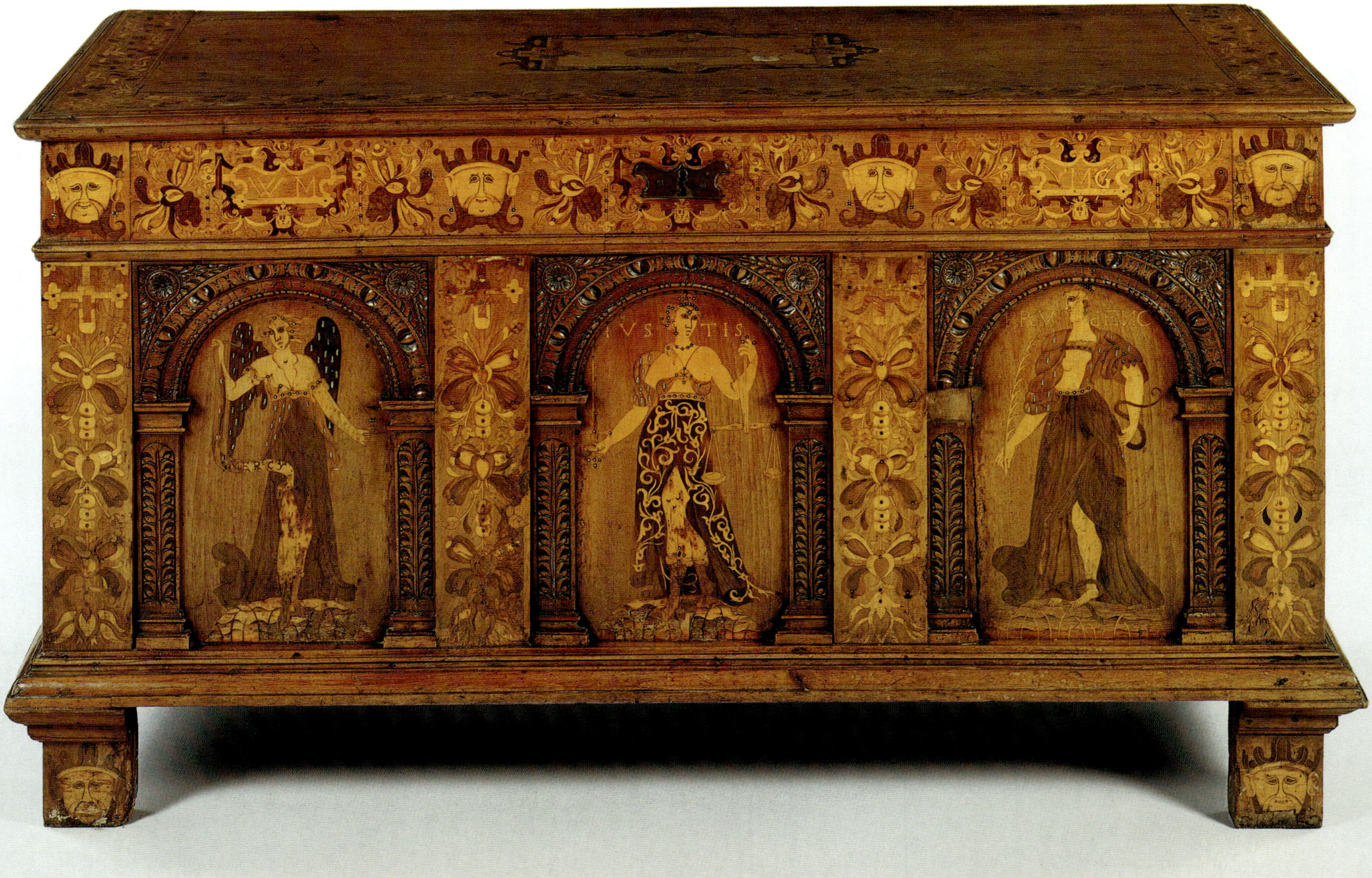

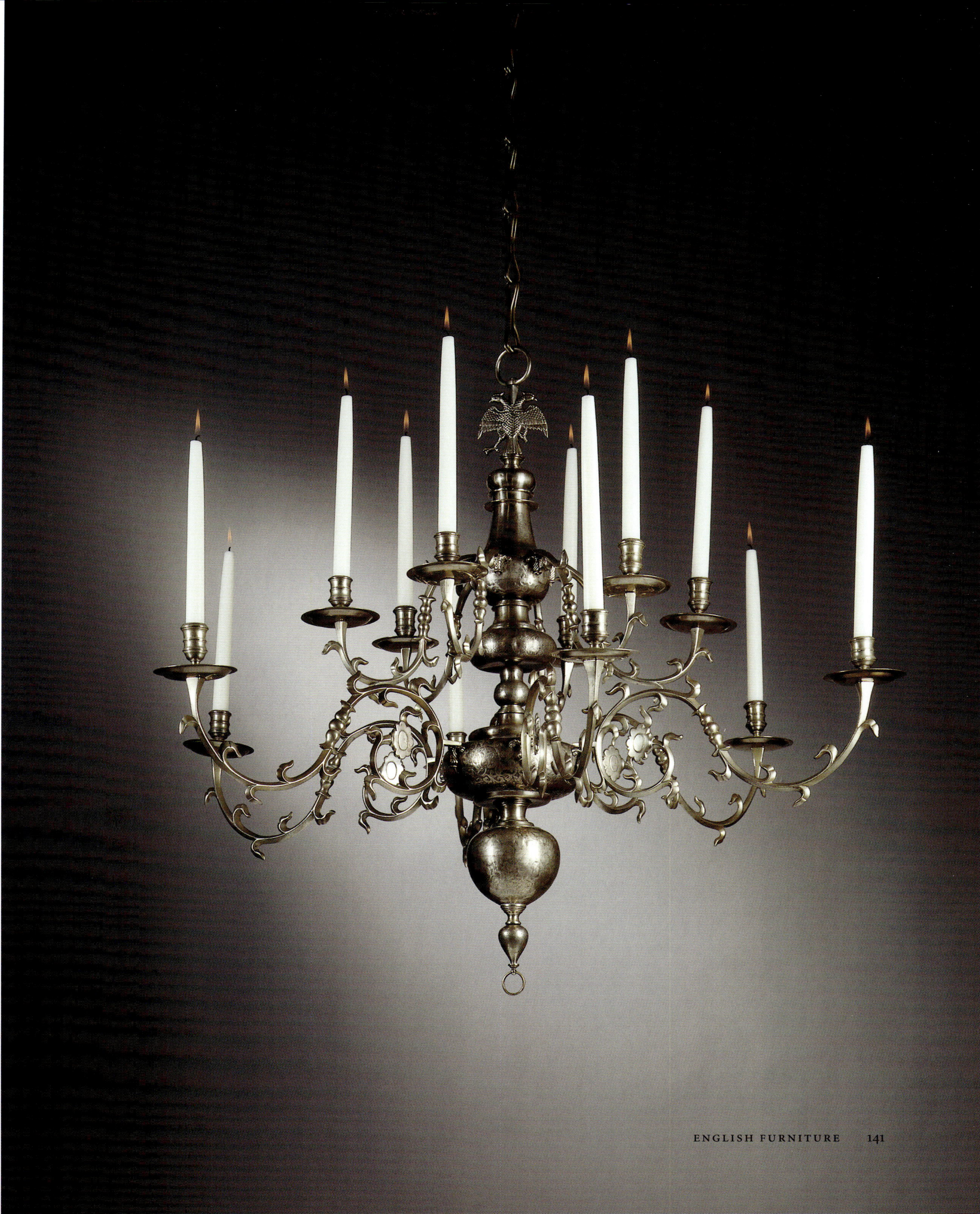

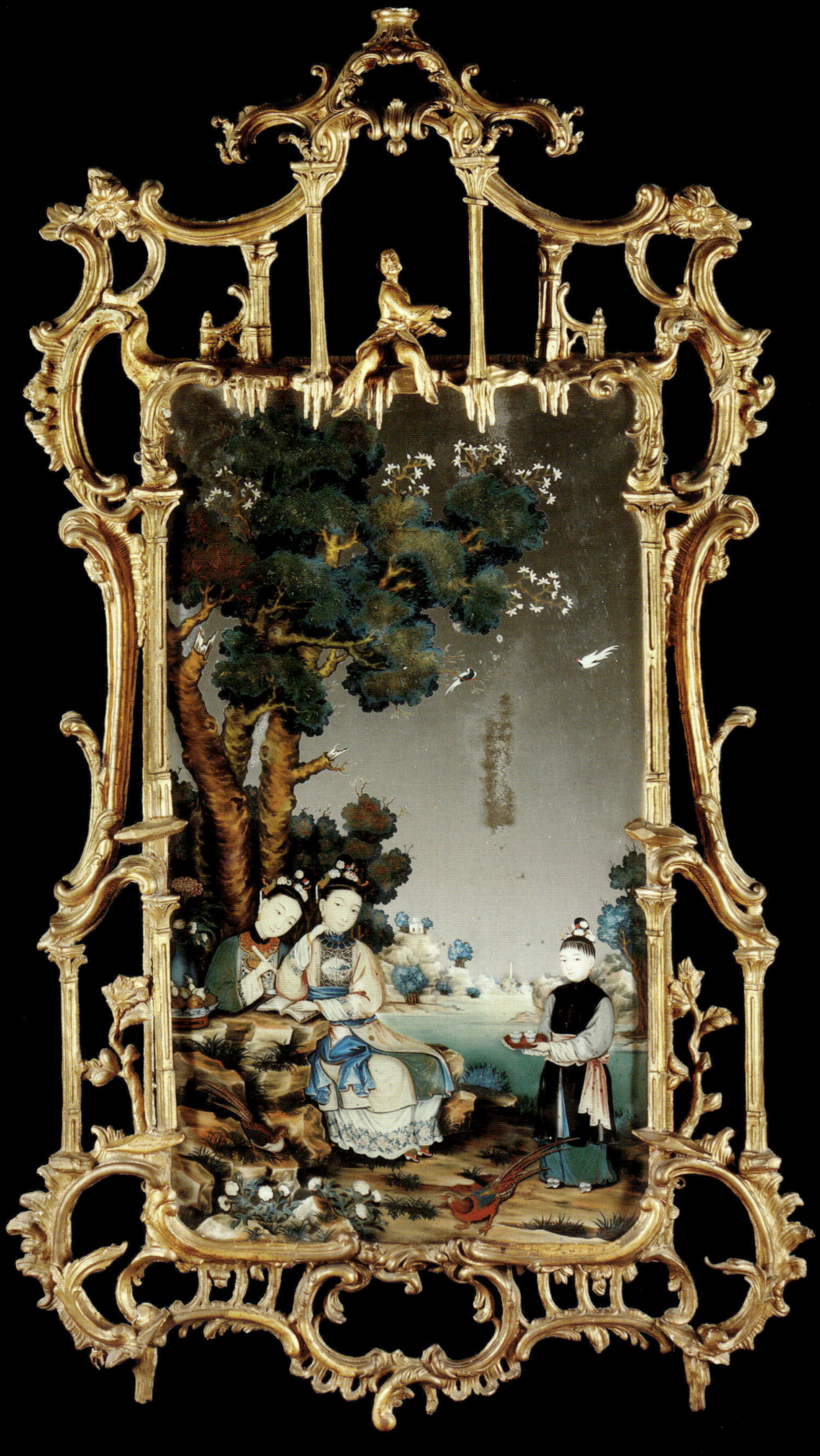

created from paper pulp, this mirror painting was executed in Canton, *circa* 1760, on plate possibly exported for the purpose from France.
166.5 by 89 cm. (5 ft. 5½ in by 2 ft. 11 in.).

**A George II Walnut Side Chair**
London £100,300 ($139,417)
13.VI.01

Sold as part of the collection of businessman Frederick Poke, this chair, made around 1730, features a carved female mask and contemporary *petit point* ribbon-tied floral needlework upholstery.

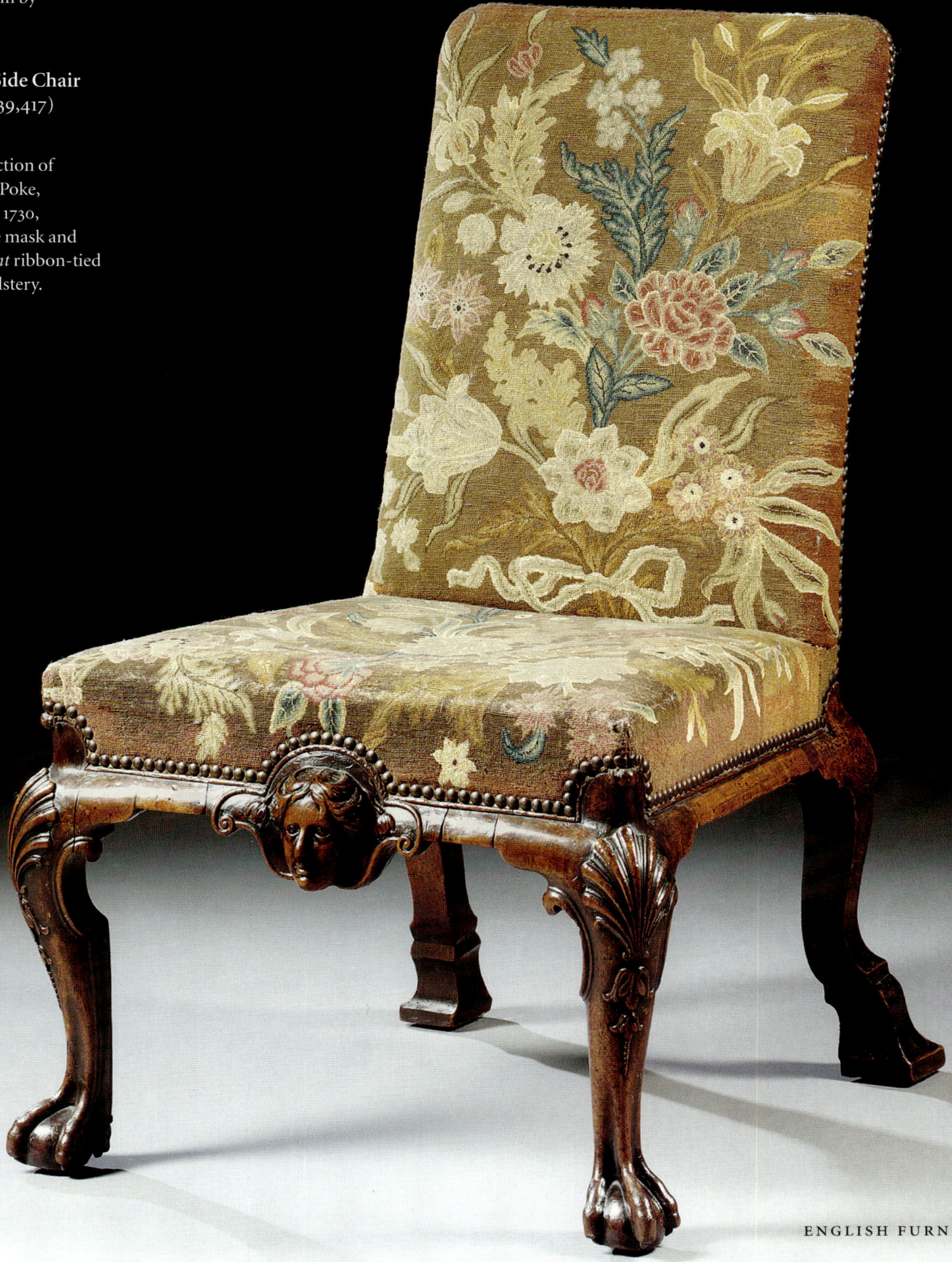

**A Pair of Italian Gilt-bronze-mounted, *brèche violette* Marble-topped, Kingwood, Tulipwood, Parquetry Commodes**
London £443,500 ($608,370)
13.VI.01

This surviving pair from a set of six commodes were commissioned for the Princes Carafa di Roccella. A commission of such scale is unprecedented in the history of furniture-making.
Neapolitan, second quarter 18th century, 94 by 130 by 65 cm.
(3 ft. 1 in. by 4 ft. 3¼ in. by 2 ft. 1½ in.).

→
**A Roman Table Top Inlaid with Coloured Marbles and Hardstones**
London £1,136,500 ($1,655,260)
13.XII.00

The art of inlaid decoration has its origins in ancient Rome, where it was known as *opus sectile*. The technique was so refined by the 16th century that intricate pieces such as this were being produced.
*Circa* 1625, 123.5 by 148 cm.
(48⅝ by 58¼ in.).

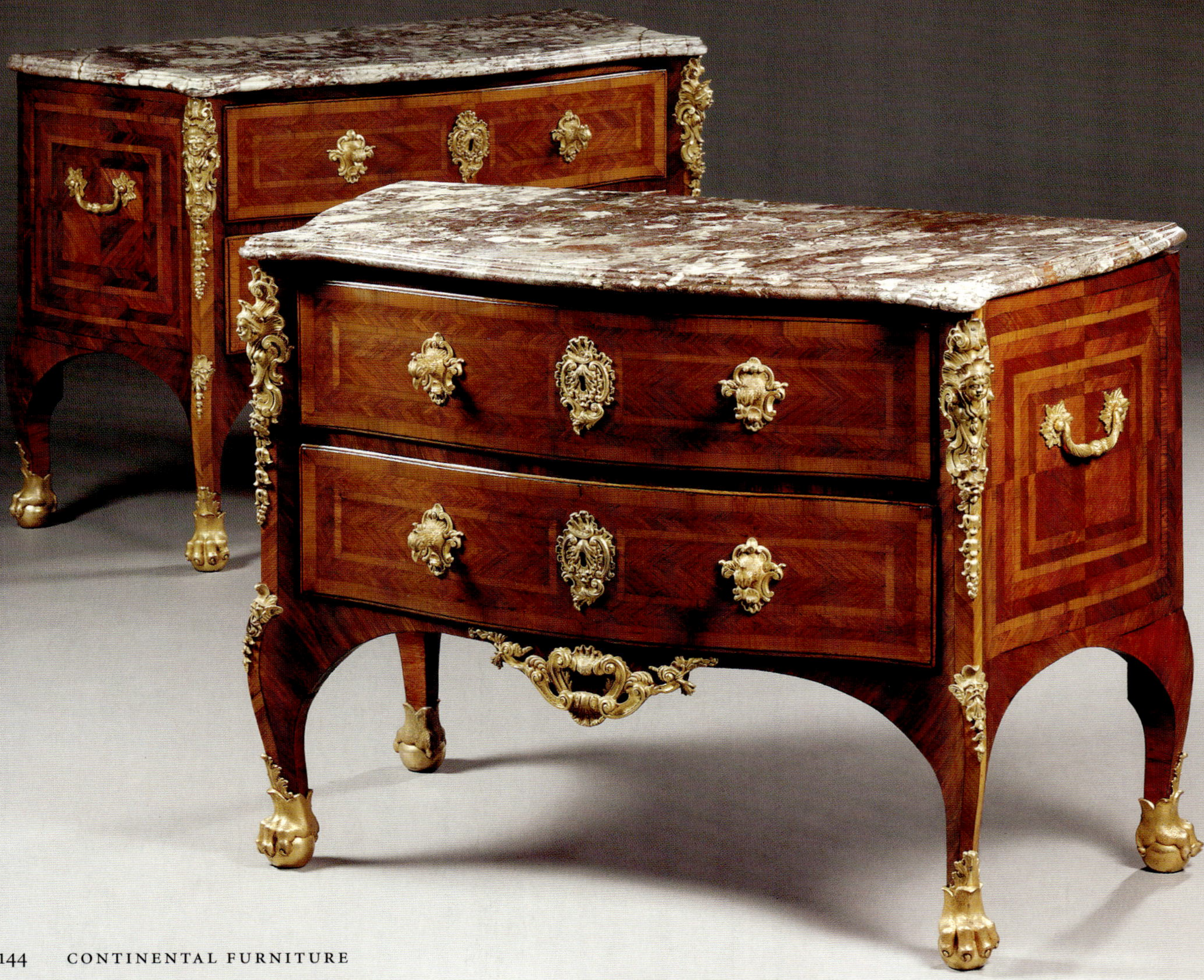

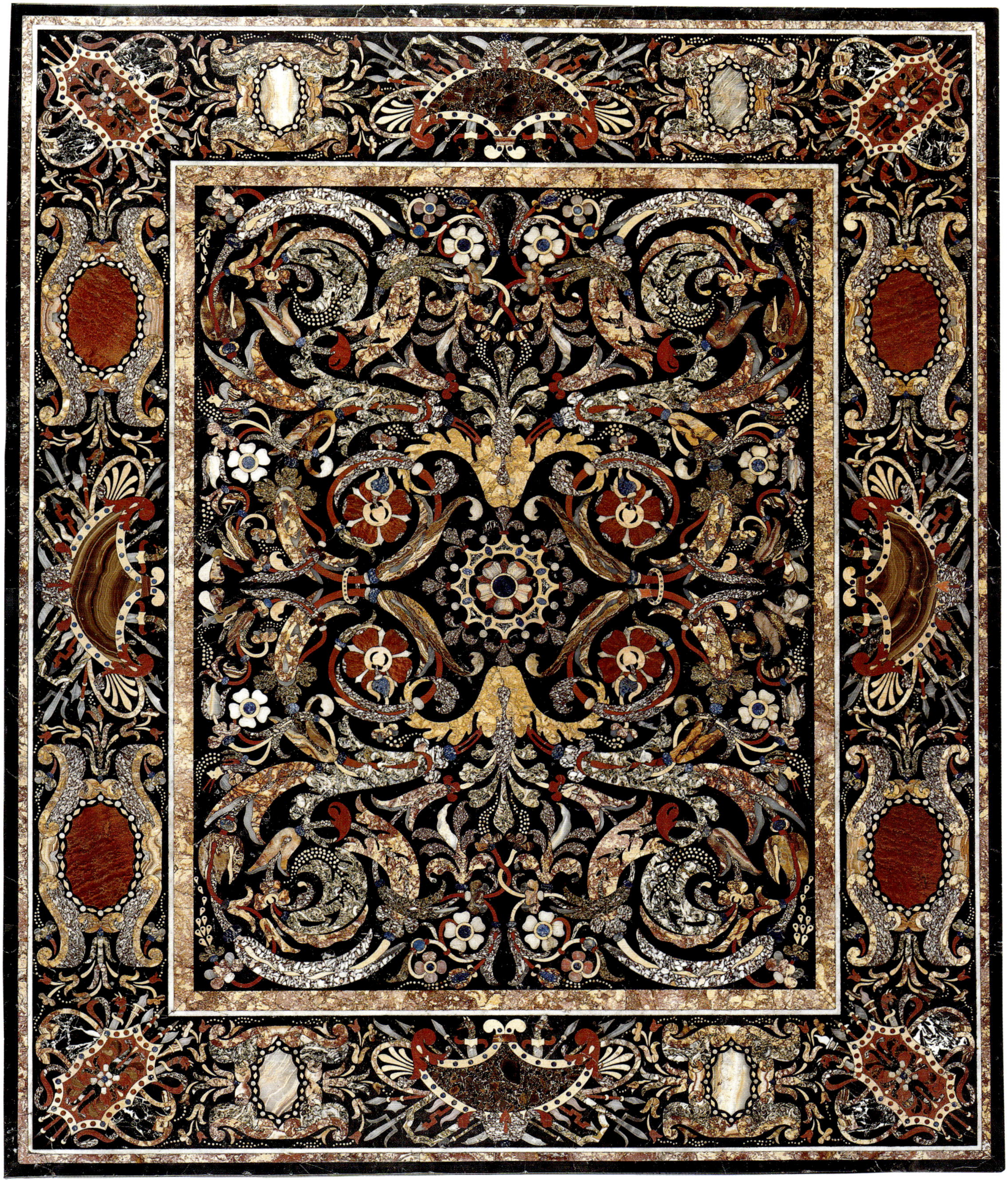

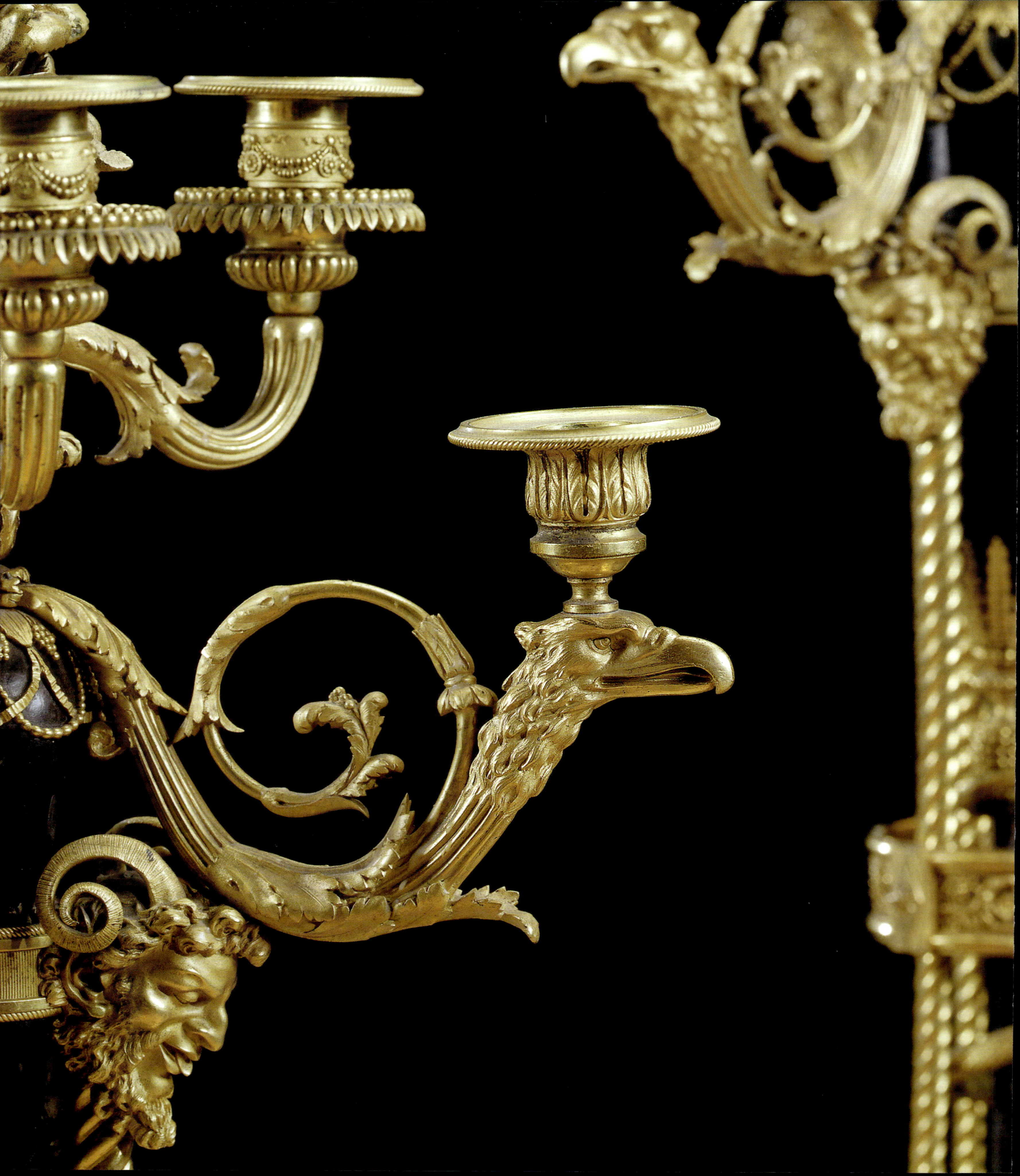

←

**A Pair of Gilt-bronze and Blue-steel, Seven-branch Candelabra (detail)**
Paris FF4,469,000 ($573,040; £402,210) 5.VII.01

A snake coils up through the legs of these tripods, which are ornamented with the heads of fauns and eagles. Louis XVI, *circa* 1785–88, attributed to Gouthière, the model probably made by the *marchand-mercier* Dominique Daguerre, 81 cm. (31⅞ in.) high.

**A Louis XV Ormolu and Stained Green Horn Bracket Clock**
New York $203,750 (£142,625) 11.XI.00

Made in the mid 18th century, the striking movement is contained within a cartouche-shaped case surmounted by the figure of Venus with an attendant putto.
Bearing numerous crowned *C* marks, 12.8 cm. (4ft 2¼ in.) high.

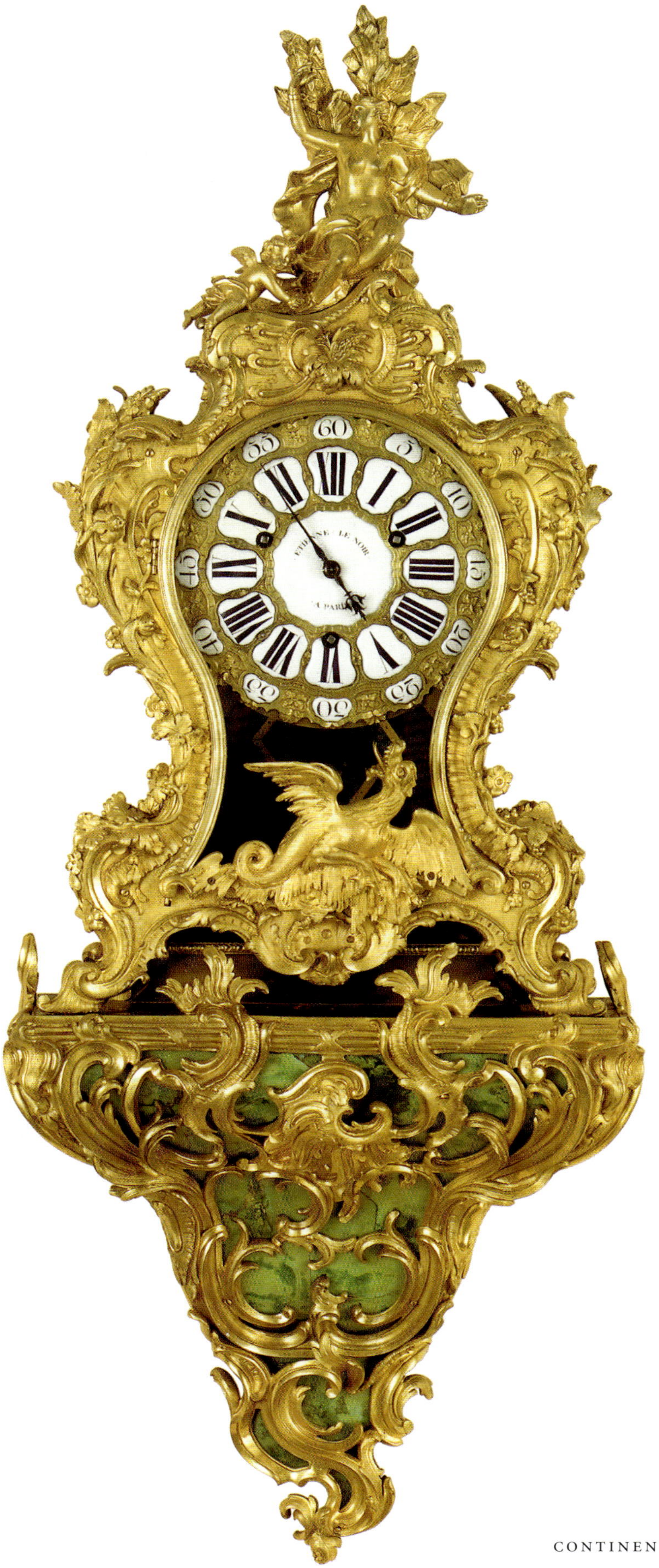

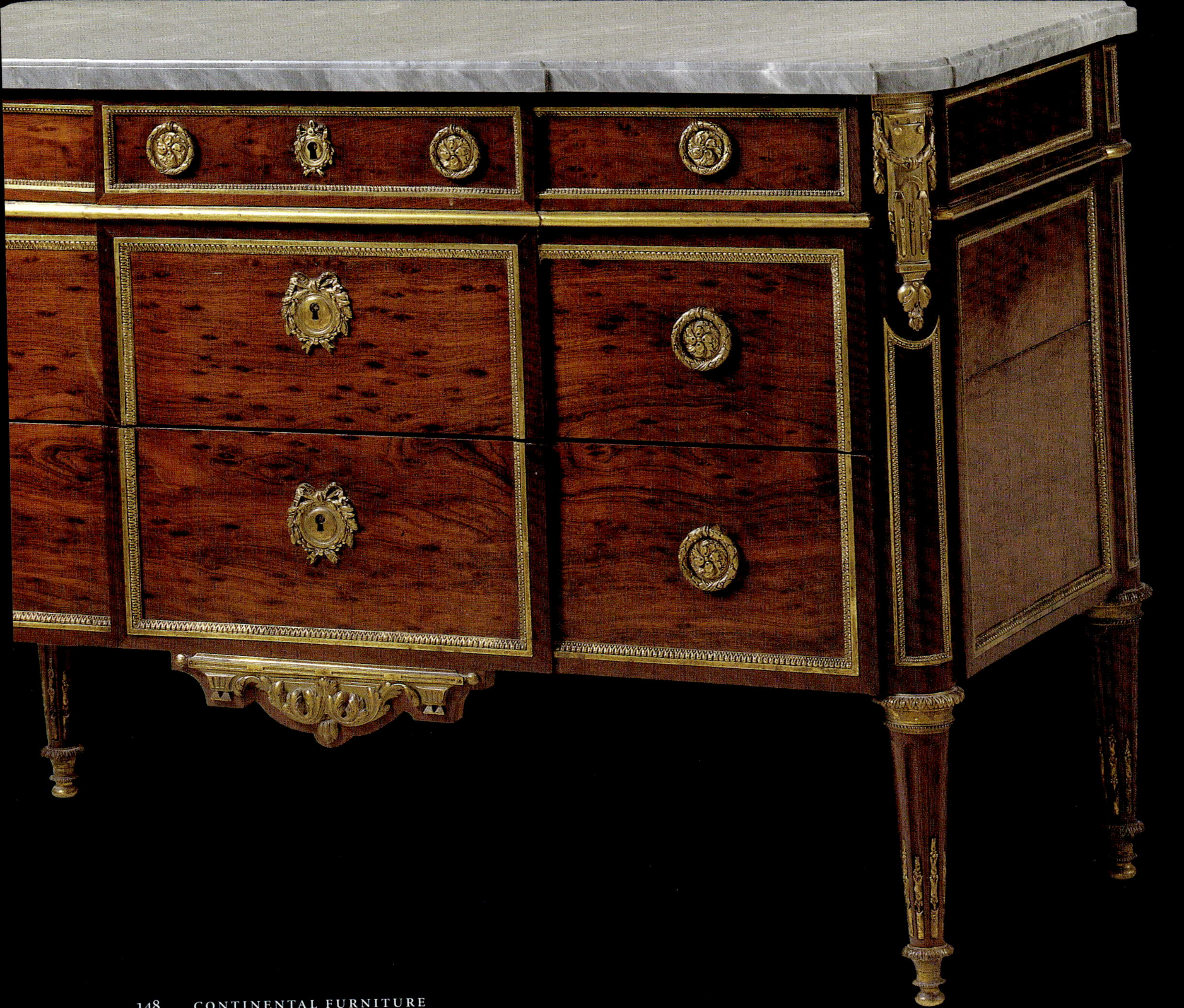

**A Pair of Monumental Sèvres Porcelain Gilt-bronze Mounted Covered Urns**
New York $170,750 (£121,232)
6.VI.01

Each of these urns has a panel with 18th-century figures, signed *Pailev*, and on the reverse a landscape panel. The foliate, angular handles are topped by figures of youths, and on the domed top of each are love birds.
Late 19th century, 140 cm. (4 ft. 7 in.) high.

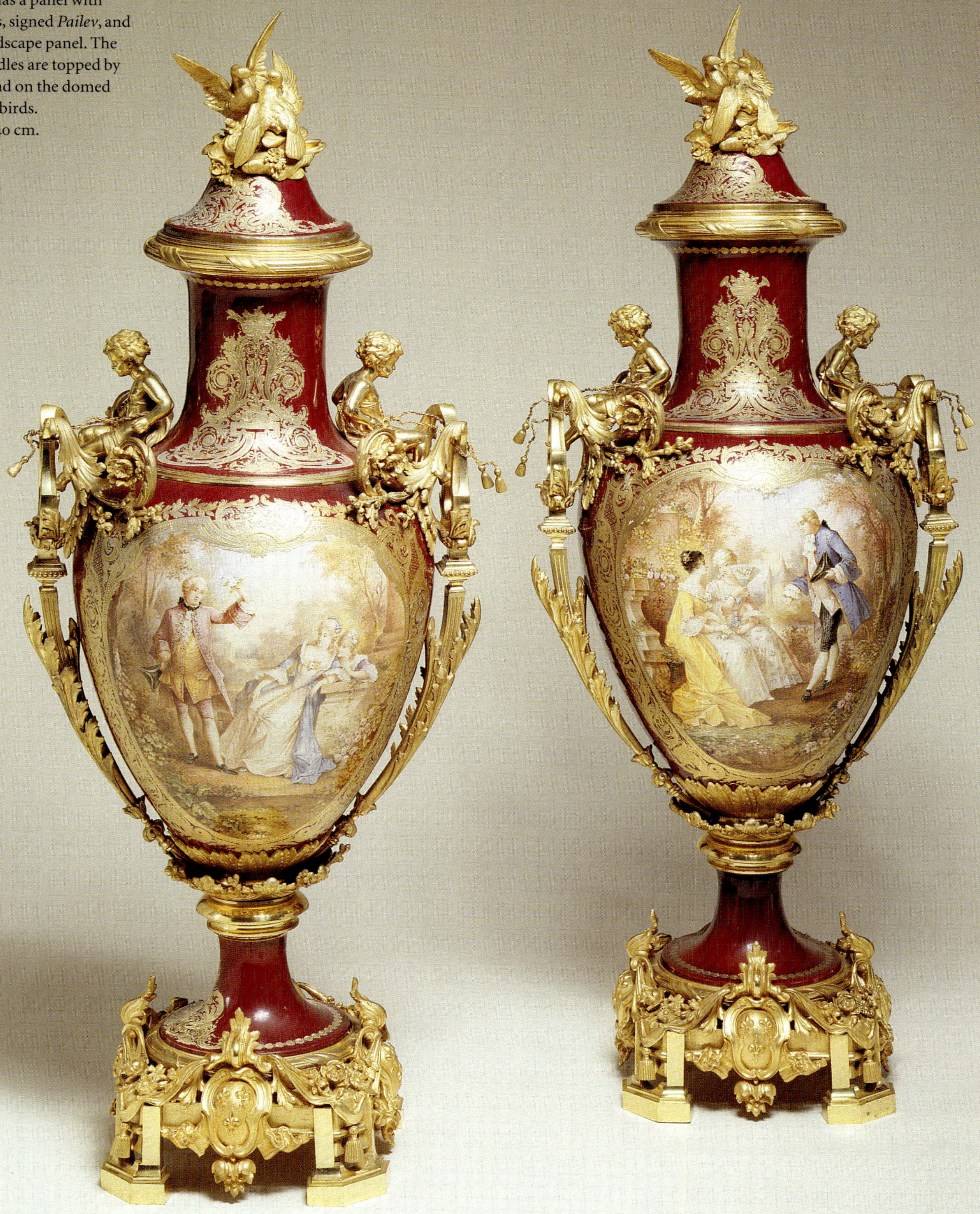

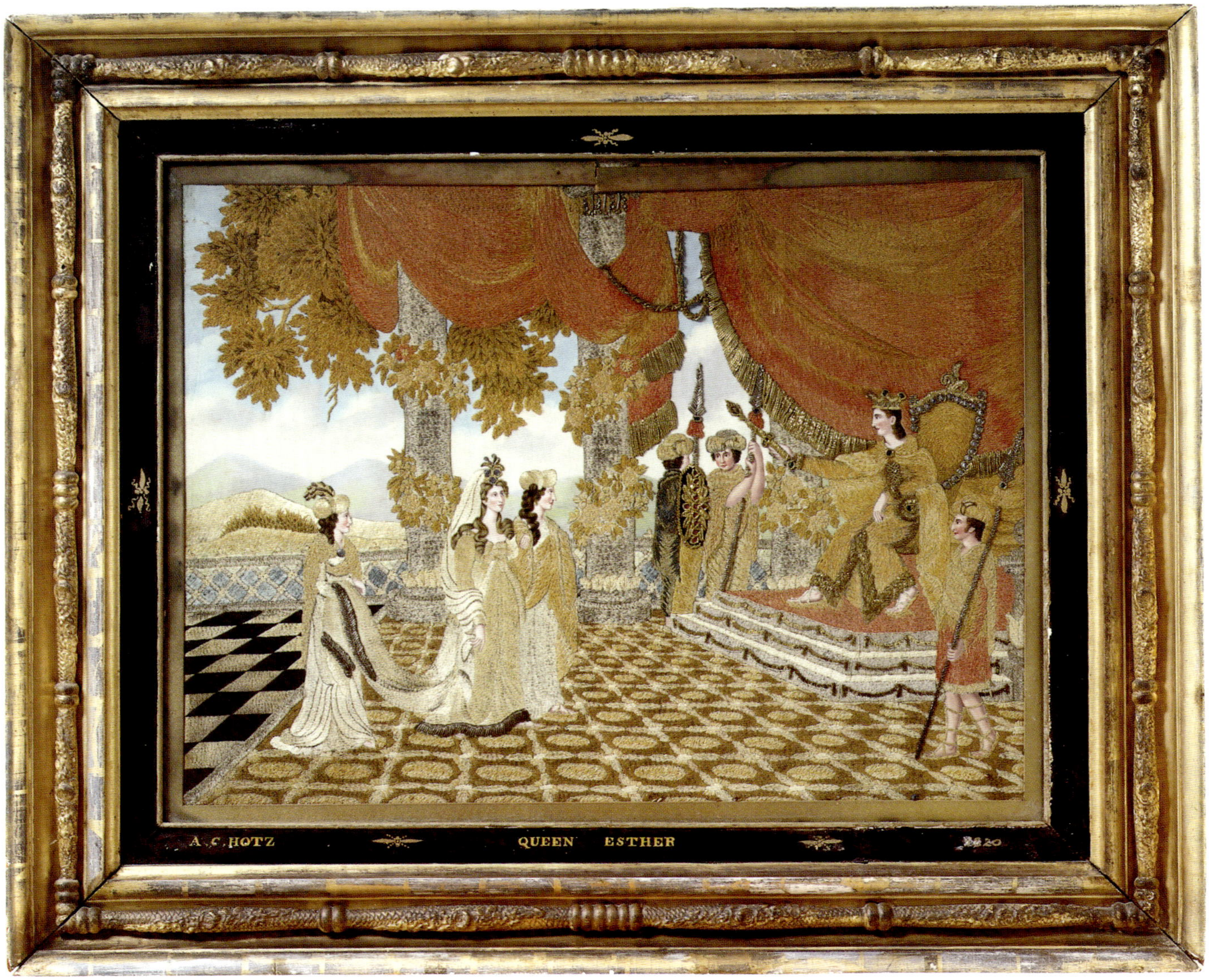


**An Embroidered Picture Depicting Queen Esther before King Ahasueras**
New York $81,250 (£55,250)
19.1.01

This embroidered picture in the style of Samuel Folwell (1764–1813) was probably worked at Mrs Folwell's school by an unknown artist using silk, chenille, gold and silver threads, glass stones, spangles, beads and paint on silk. It is still within the original Philadelphia giltwood and gesso frame.
C. Hotz, Philadelphia, dated *1820*, size of needlework: 76.2 by 91. 4 cm. (30 by 36 in.).

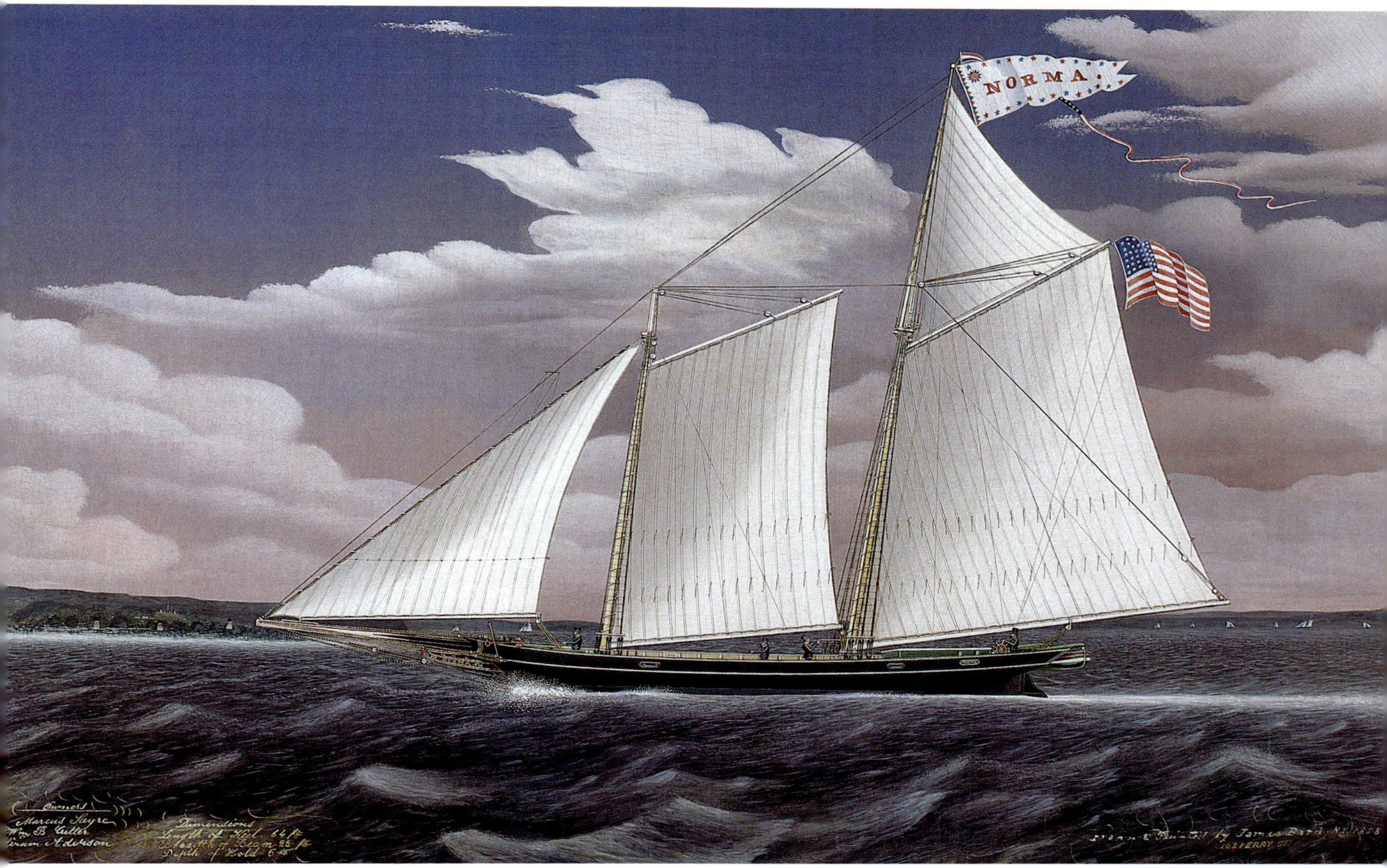


**James Bard**
*The Schooner Norma*
New York $247,750 (£168,470)
19.1.01

Only 19 of the 459 known paintings by Bard are of sailing vessels, all of them built in the Nyack, New York area where the *Norma* was built in 1852. This painting comes from Bard's middle period, when he moved from painting in watercolours to oils.
Oil on canvas, 76.2 by 132.1 cm. (30 by 52 in.).

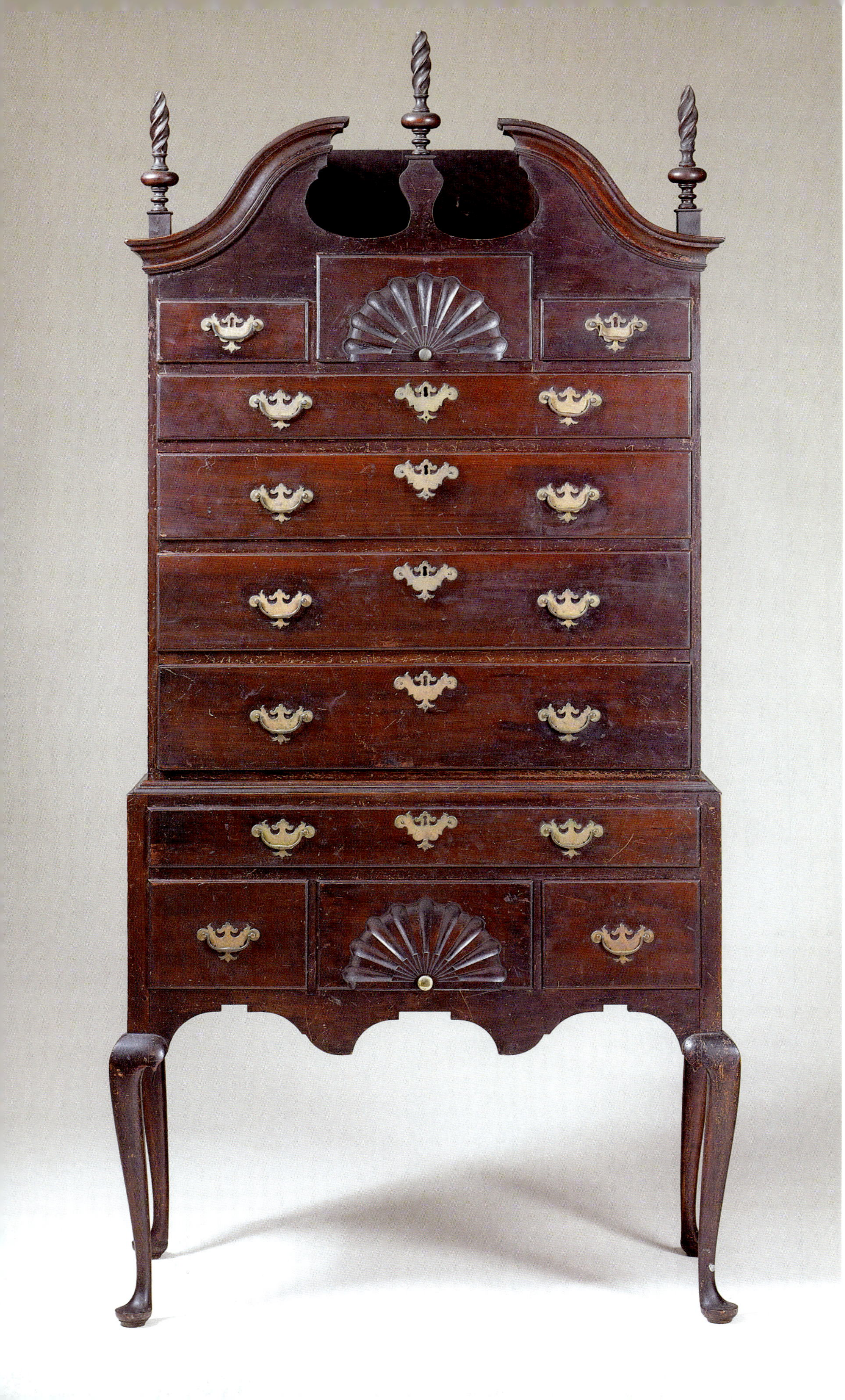

**A Queen Anne Carved and Figured Cherrywood Bonnet-top High Chest of Drawers**
New York $225,750 (£153,510)
19.1.01

The Massachusetts cabinetmaker who created this chest was probably inspired by other, similar pieces. The fluted shell design, the leg profile, in-curving knee returns and the ovoid openings in the pediment are all characteristics of the North Shore area. Ipswich/Salem, Massachusetts, *circa* 1740–60, 226.1 by 99.7 by 52.7 cm. (7ft. 5 in. by 39¼ in. by 20¾ in.).

**A Chippendale Figured Mahogany Bombé Chest of Drawers**
New York $401,750 (£273,190) 19.1.01

Believed to have been the property of the Perkins family of Boston from 1750, this extremely rare chest of drawers had never before been offered at auction. The final price achieved is a reflection both of its provenance and quality.
Boston, Massachusetts, *circa* 1770,
83.8 by 88.9 by 54 cm. (33 by 35 by 21¼ in.).

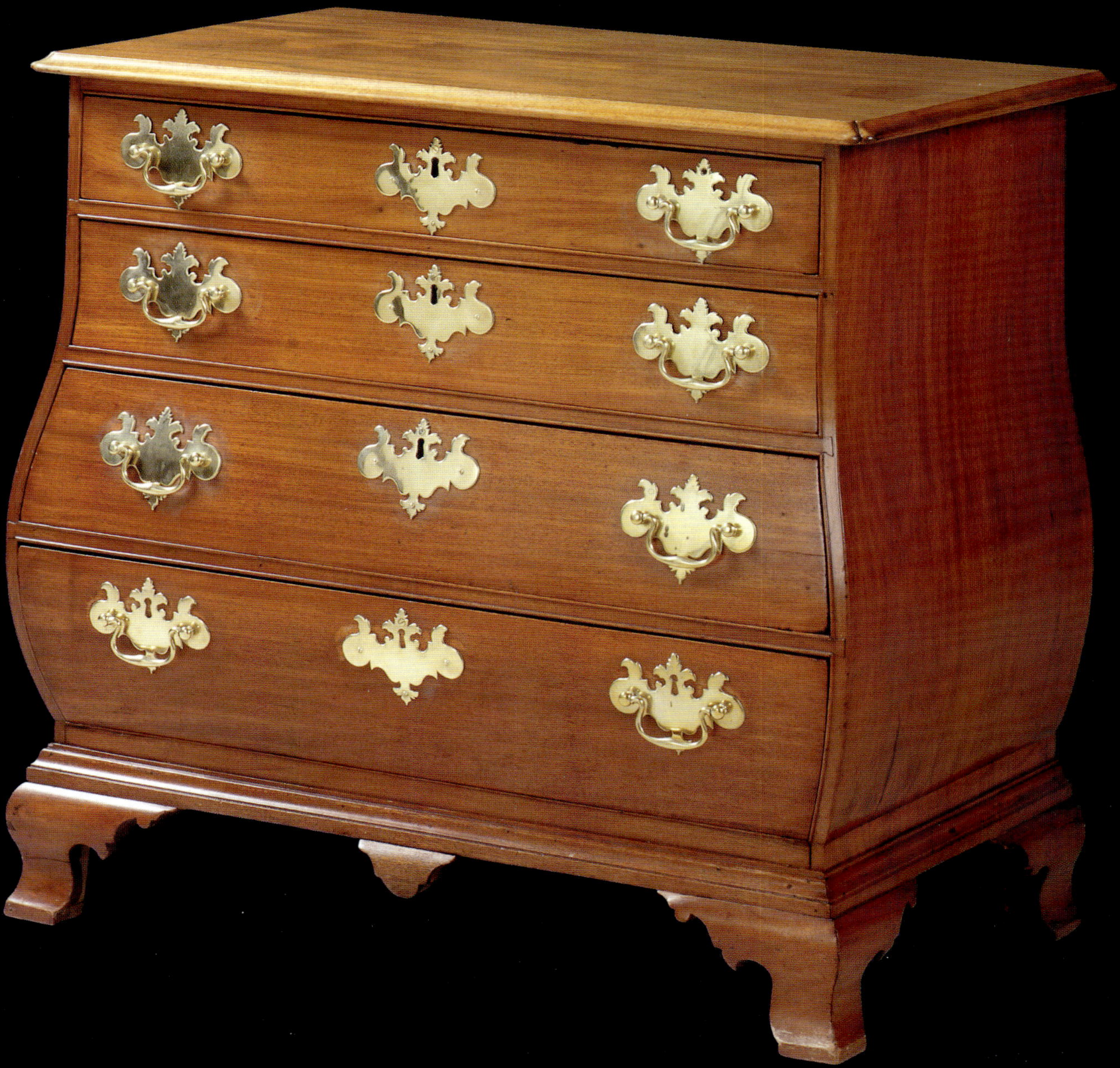

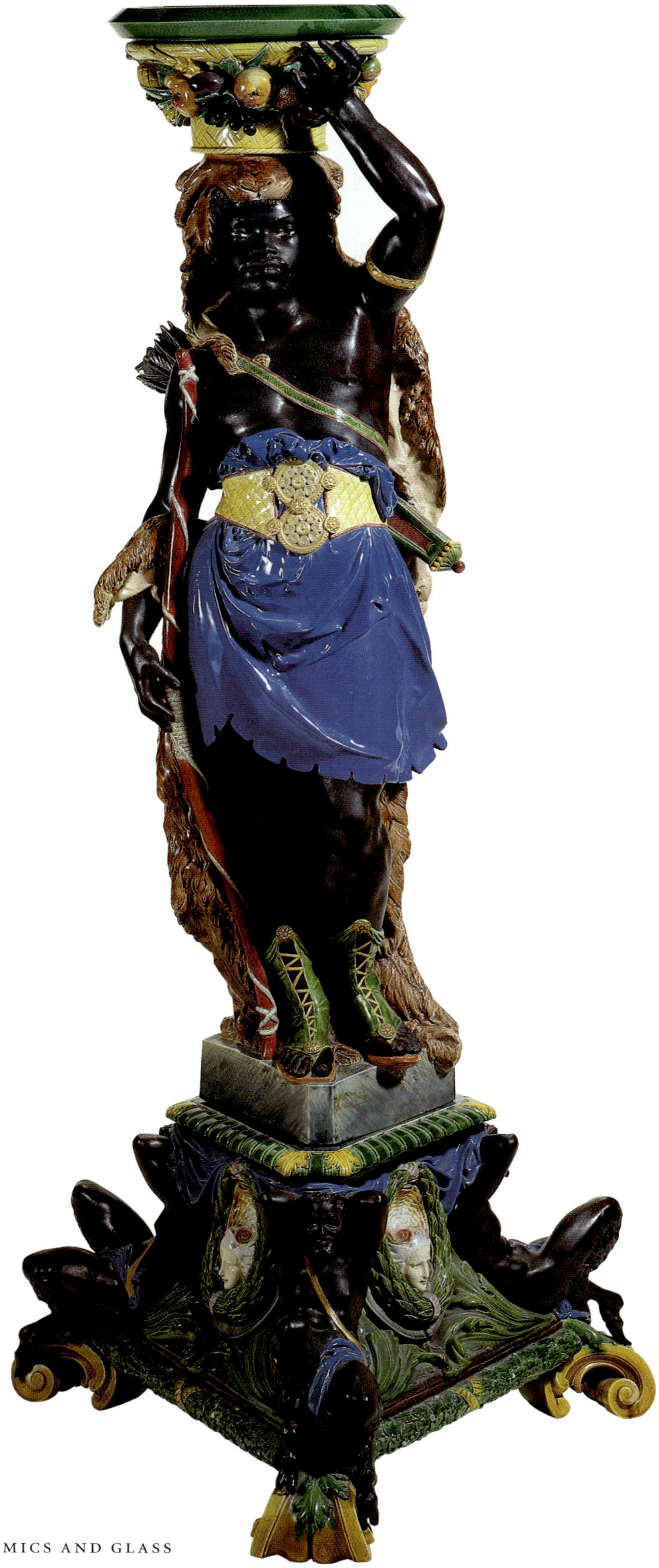

**A Minton Majolica Stand of an African Male Figure**
New York $115,750 (£78,710)
22.I.01

Part of the Harriman Judd Collection of British Art Pottery, this figure appears to have gained its original inspiration from a 17th-century engraving by Jean le Pautre, and was modelled in its present form in 1864 by A. Carrier de Belleuse.
185 cm. (72¾ in.) high.

→

**A London Delftware Oval Polychrome Pill Tile**
London £82,700 ($118,261)
21.XI.00

Painted with the arms of the Worshipful Society of Apothecaries and the arms of the City of London, this pill tile is previously unrecorded. Current research suggests that there are only two other recorded pill tiles of this oval shape, both of which are painted in blue, this being the only polychrome example known.
32 by 24.5 cm. (12⅝ by 9⅝ in.).

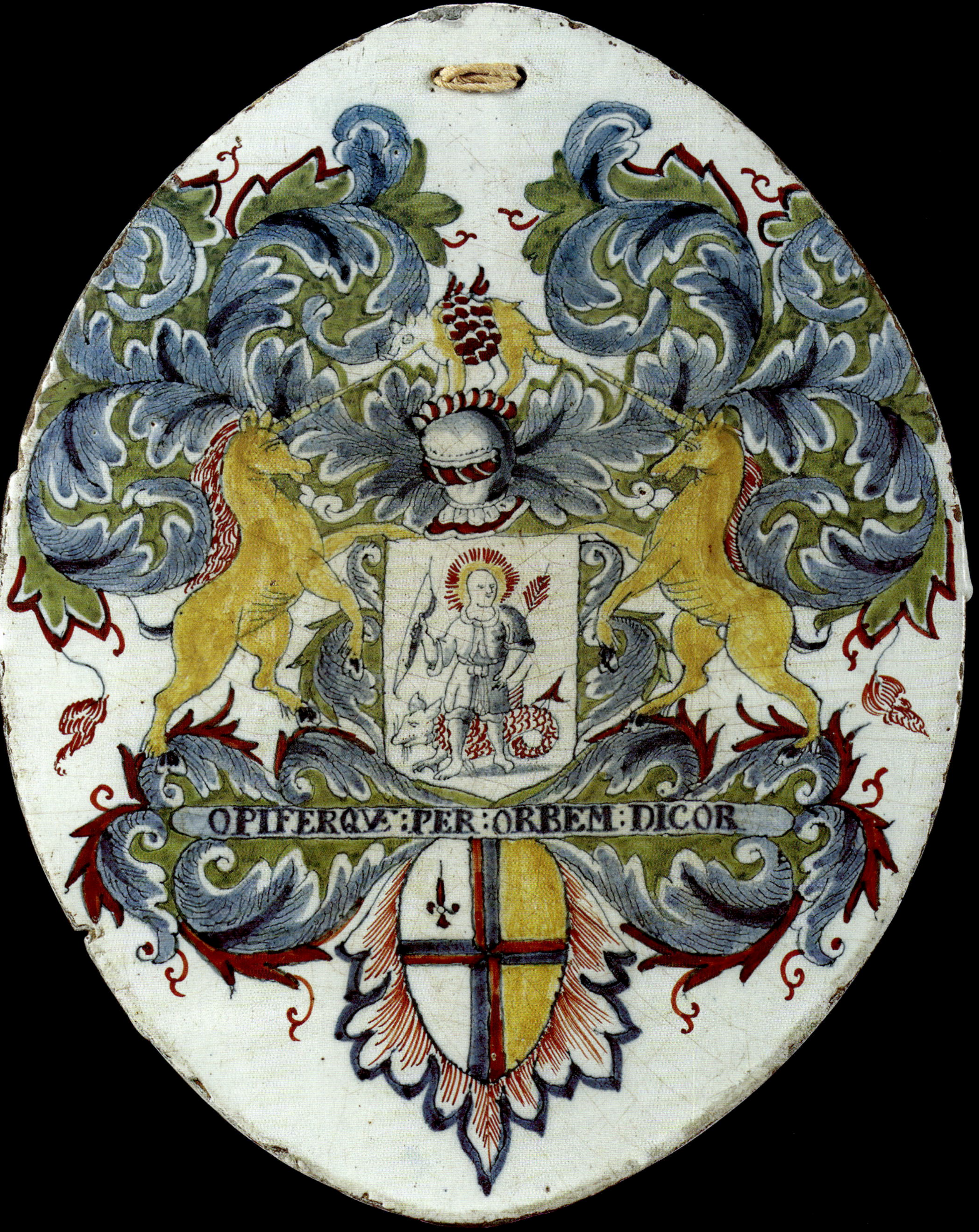
OPIFERQVE : PER : ORBEM : DICOR

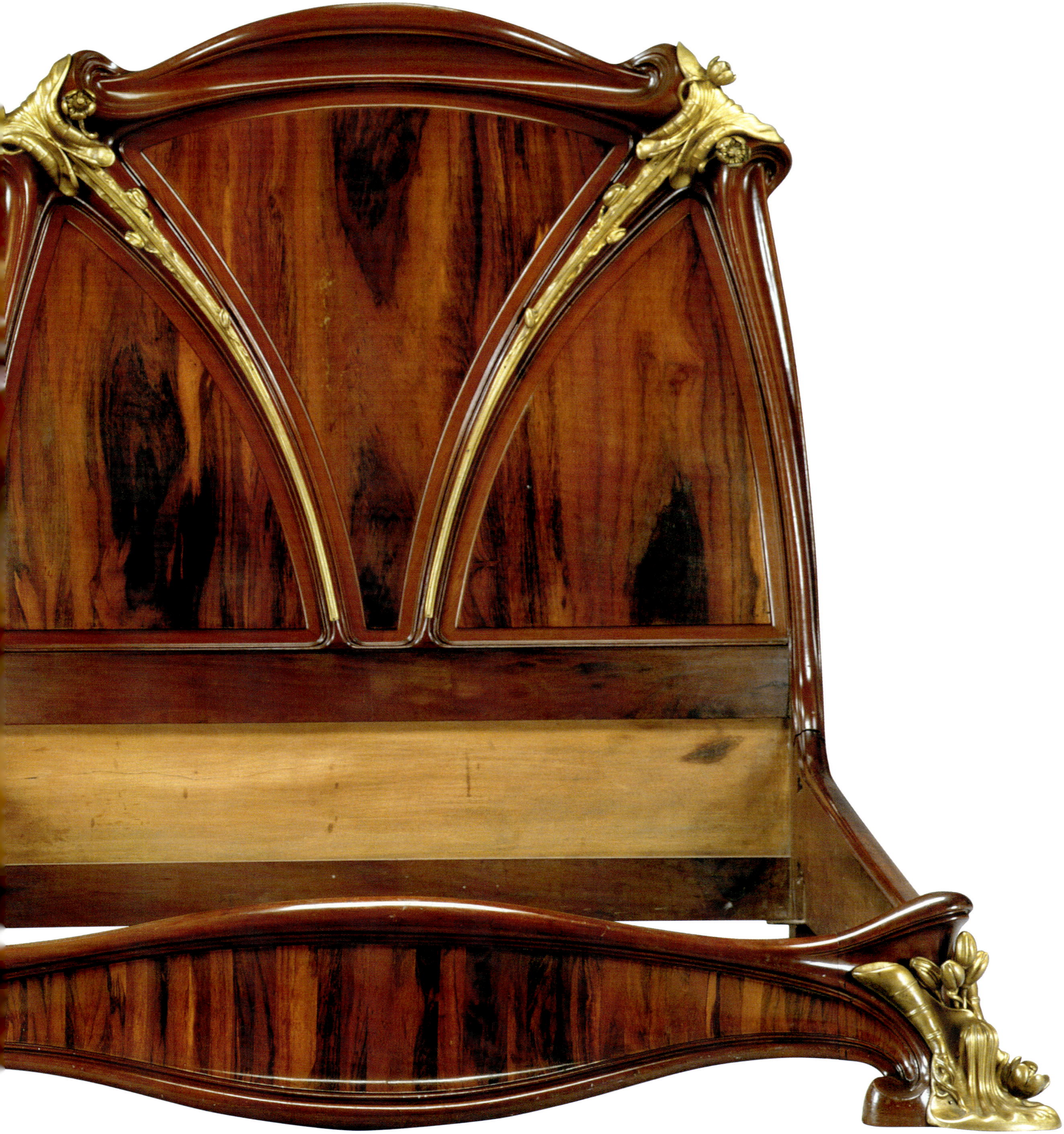

←

**Louis Majorelle, Bedroom '*Aux Nénuphars*' (detail)**
London £619,500 ($898,275)
19.x.00

Furniture designer Louis Majorelle was one of the greatest exponents of Art Nouveau. This bedroom suite, *circa* 1905, one of his rarest and most extravagant creations, features gilt-bronze lily-pads and flowers draped over a voluptuous mahogany structure.
Comprising: double bed, two bedside tables and armoire in mahogany and rosewood.

**A Gabriel Argy-Rousseau *pâte-de-verre* and wrought-iron lamp**
New York $143,250 (£100,275)
2.xii.00

The production of *pâte-de-verre* is complex and laborious and for this reason very few artists have chosen to work with it. This piece illustrates Gabriel Argy-Rousseau's use of rich, often unusual colours that complement both the design and pattern.
*Circa* 1922, 38.7 by 20.3 cm. (15⅝ by 8 in.).

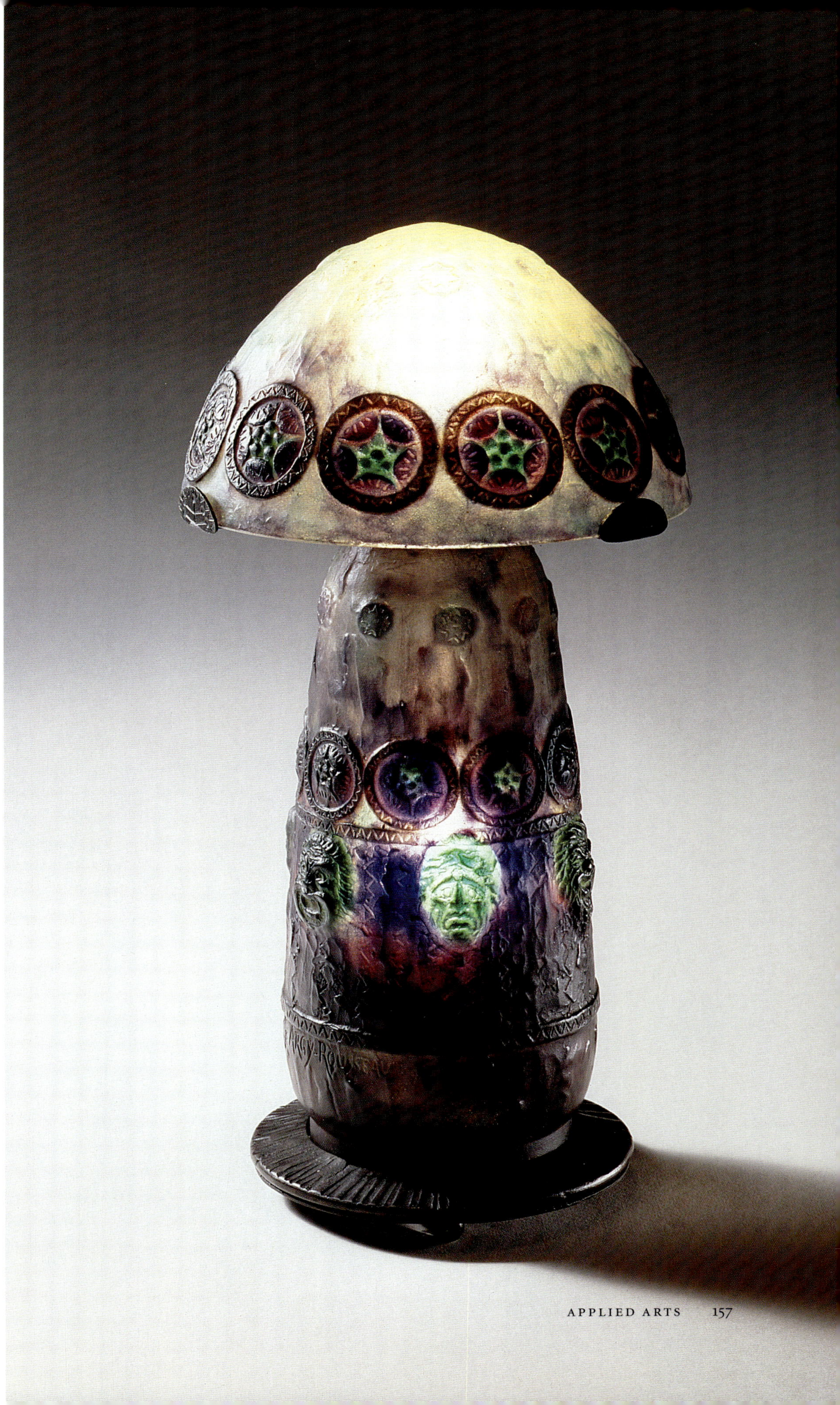

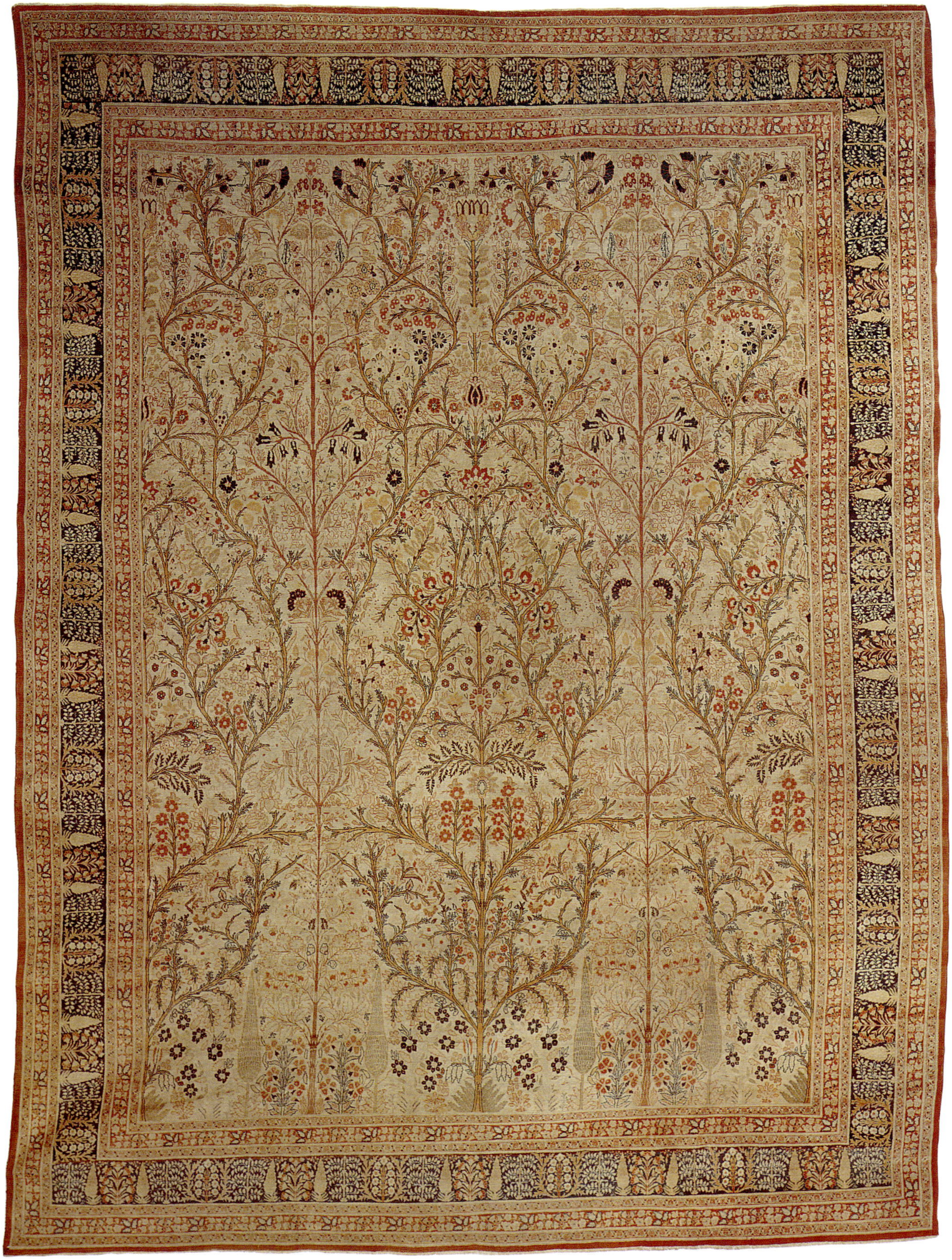

←

**A Tabriz Carpet**
London £53,400 ($77,964)
11.x.00

Tabriz is one of the most prolific and respected weaving centres of northwest Persia. Produced in the late 19th/early 20th century, this piece has the distinctive subtle colours and curvilinear, organic design that characterize the best of Tabriz workshop production during this period.
Northwest Persia, *circa* 1900,
484 by 347 cm. (15 ft. 11 in. by 11 ft. 5 in.).

**The Costikyan Garden Carpet**
New York $170,750 (£116,110)
27.IX.00

This exquisite garden carpet shares its design with the Palace gardens at Isphahan, a walled garden divided by two intersecting watercourses. Unlike other examples, which suggest an endless repeat, here the emphasis is on strict formality with an accent on singularity, as if based upon a real garden.
Northwest Persia, late 18th century,
approximately 663 by 284 cm.
(21 ft. 9 in. by 9 ft. 4 in.).

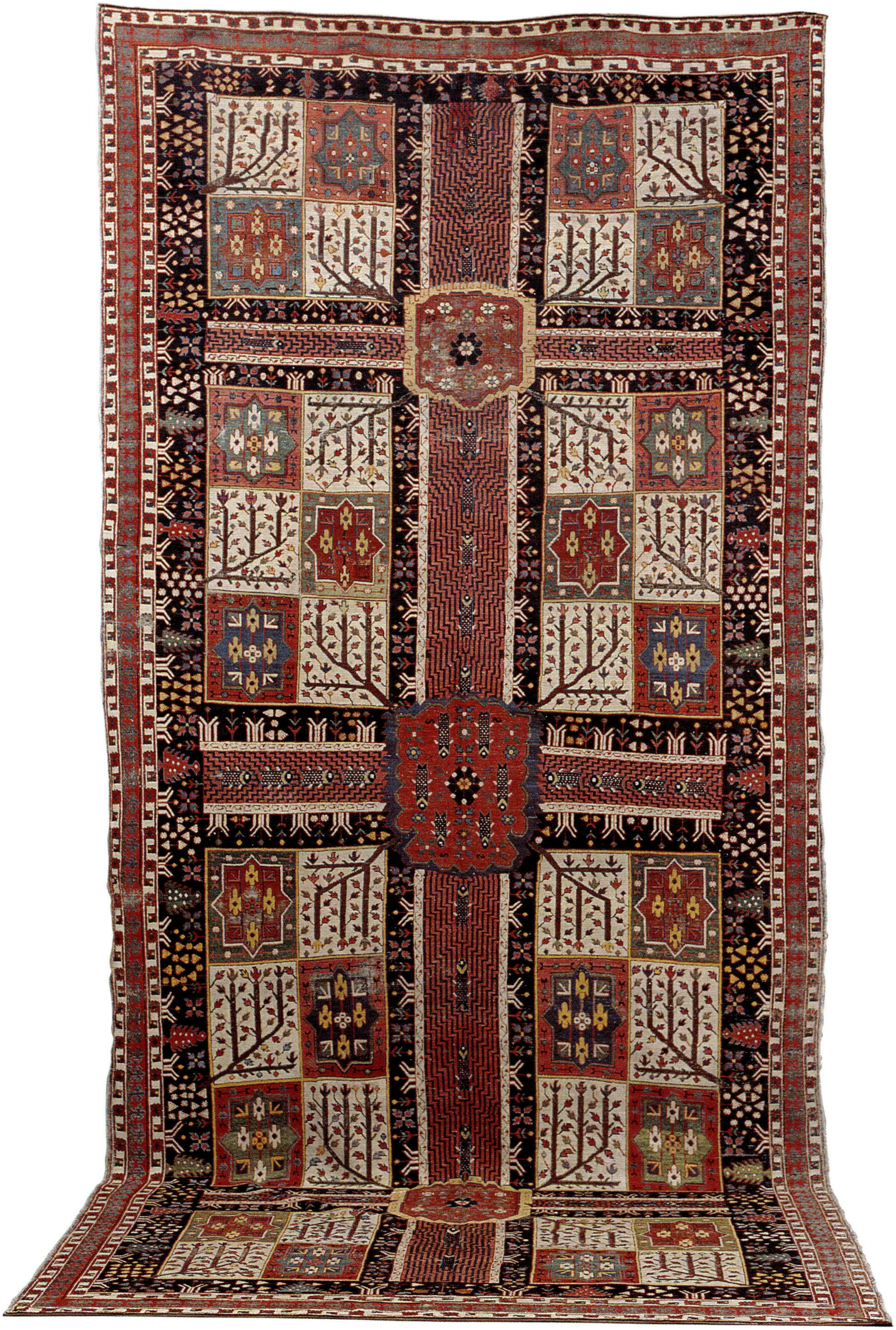

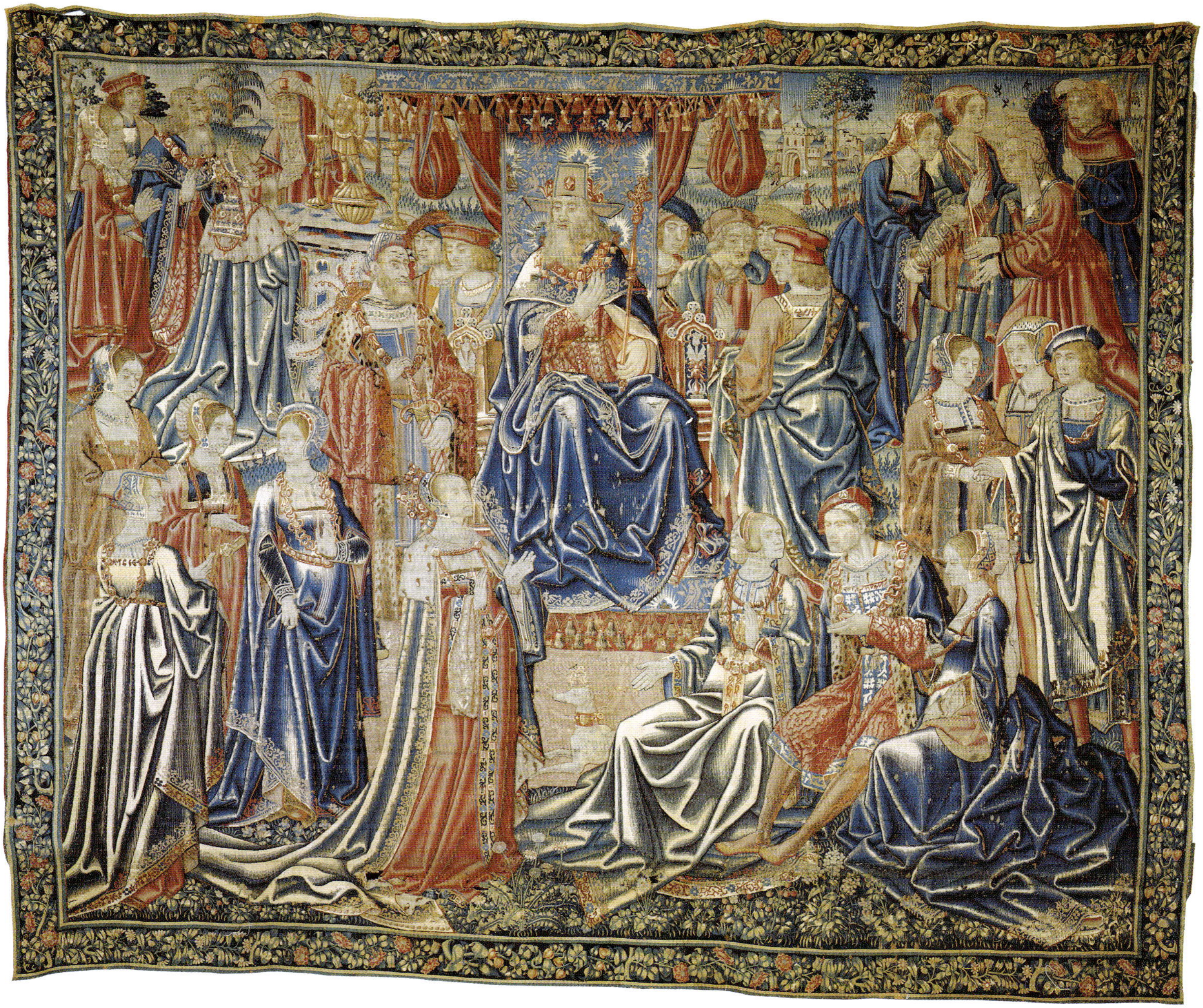

**A Late Gothic Mythological Narrative Tapestry in the Manner of Jan van Roome**
London £135,500 ($191,055)
11.VII.01

At the centre of this tapestry, depicting the story of Oedipus, is Laïus, King of Thebes, enthroned and surrounded by courtiers. Around this central group of figures are depictions of scenes from the story including, top left, Jocasta, the king's wife, before the oracle who foretold that her son would kill his father. Brussels, *circa* 1500–15, 340 by 405 cm. (11 ft. 2 in. by 13 ft. 3½ in.).

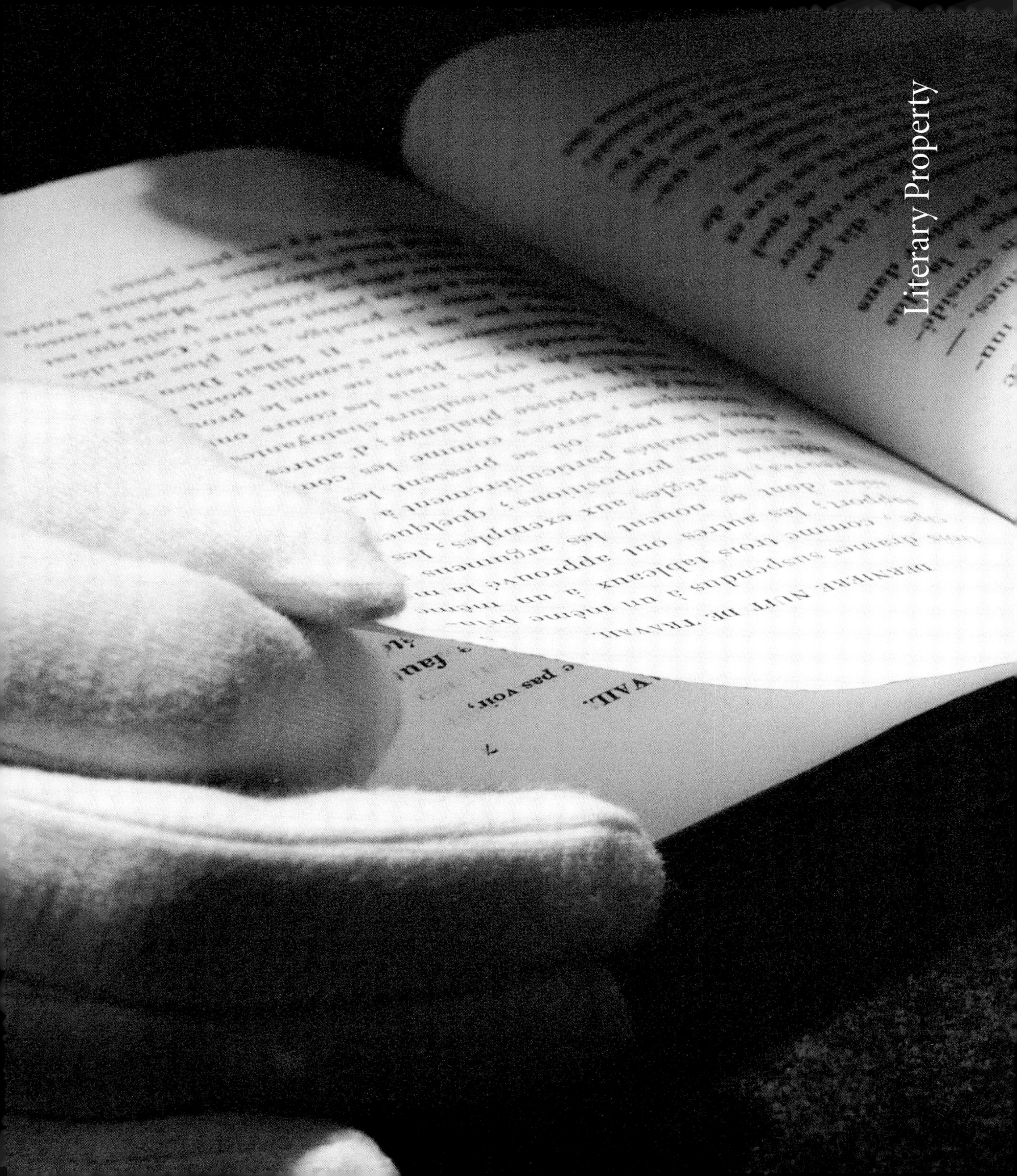

# Literary Property

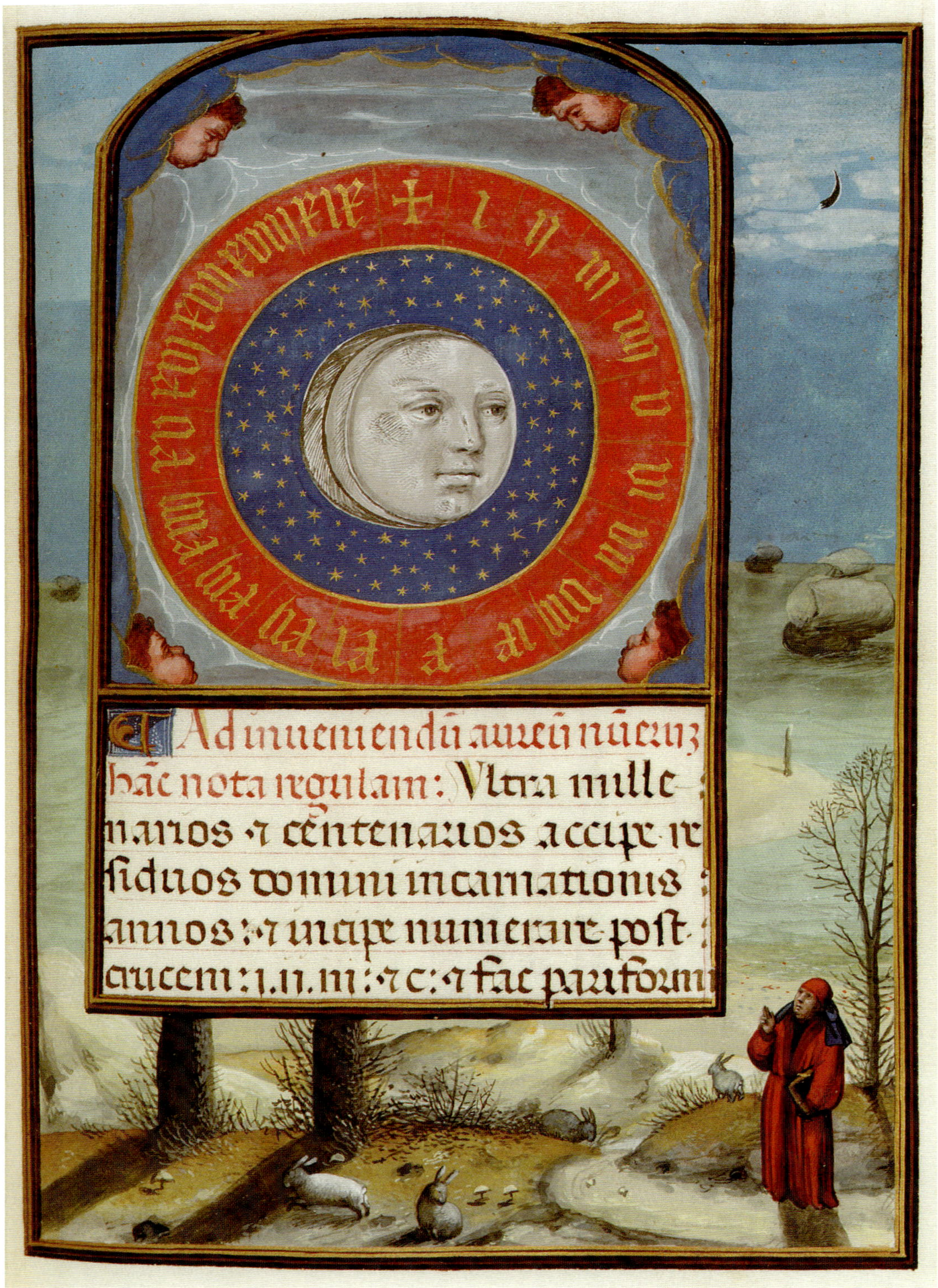

**The Hours of Albrecht of Brandenburg**
**Illuminated by Simon Bening**
London £2,973,500 ($4,162,900)
19.VI.01

This Book of Hours was produced in Bruges in 1522–23 for art patron Cardinal Albrecht of Brandenburg and painted by the greatest illuminator of the early 16th century.
Illuminated manuscript on vellum, two volumes, 294 and 298 leaves, 21.6 by 14.5 cm. (8½ by 5¾ in.).

→

**The Album de Croÿ**
**Illuminated by Adrien de Montigny**
London £1,213,500 ($1,698,900)
19.VI.01

Each measuring *circa* 52 by 38.5 cm. (20½ by 15⅜ in.) these large paintings, created in 1596–8, are views of properties owned by Charles, duc de Croÿ.
Illuminated manuscript on vellum, 86 leaves.

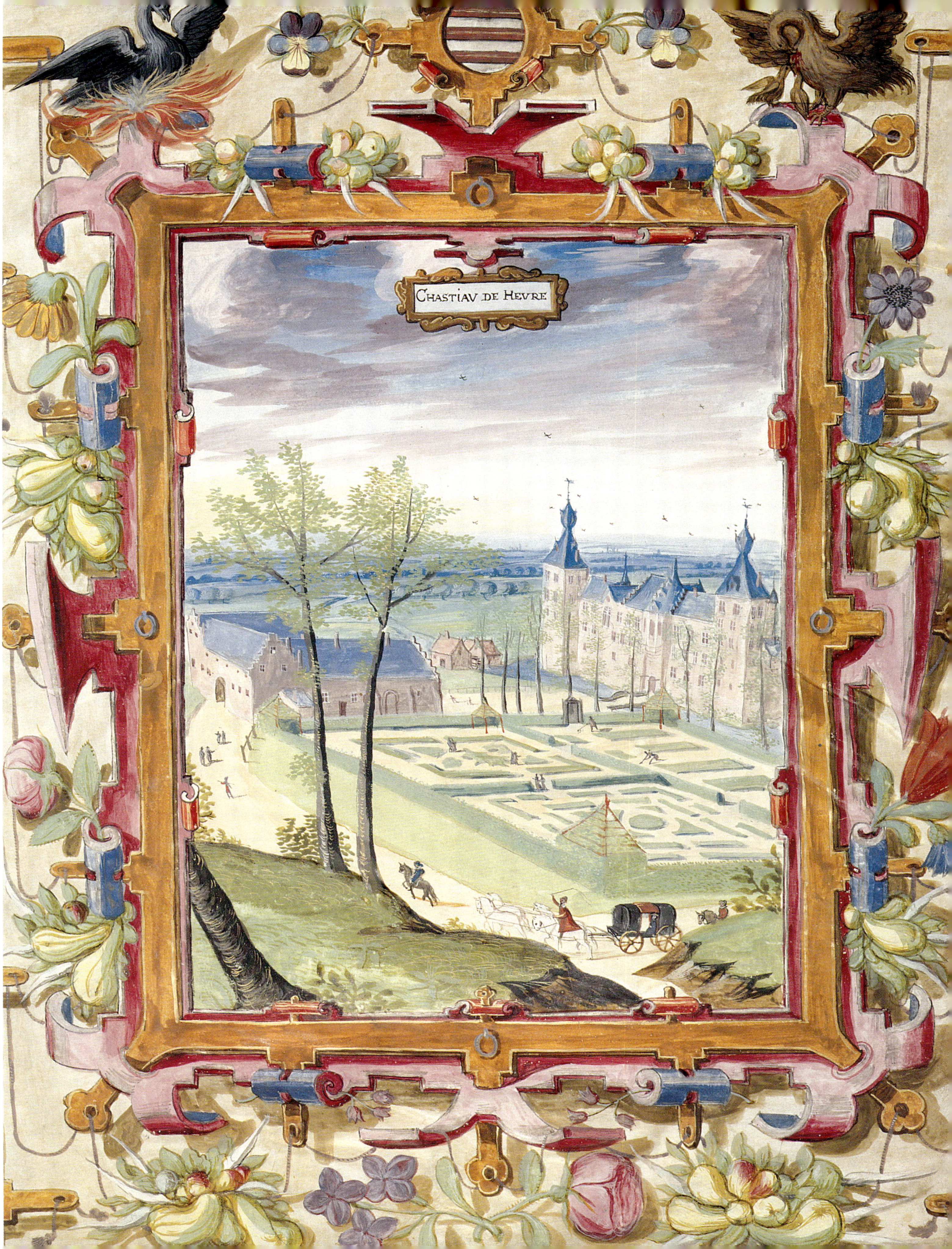
CHASTIAV DE HEVRE

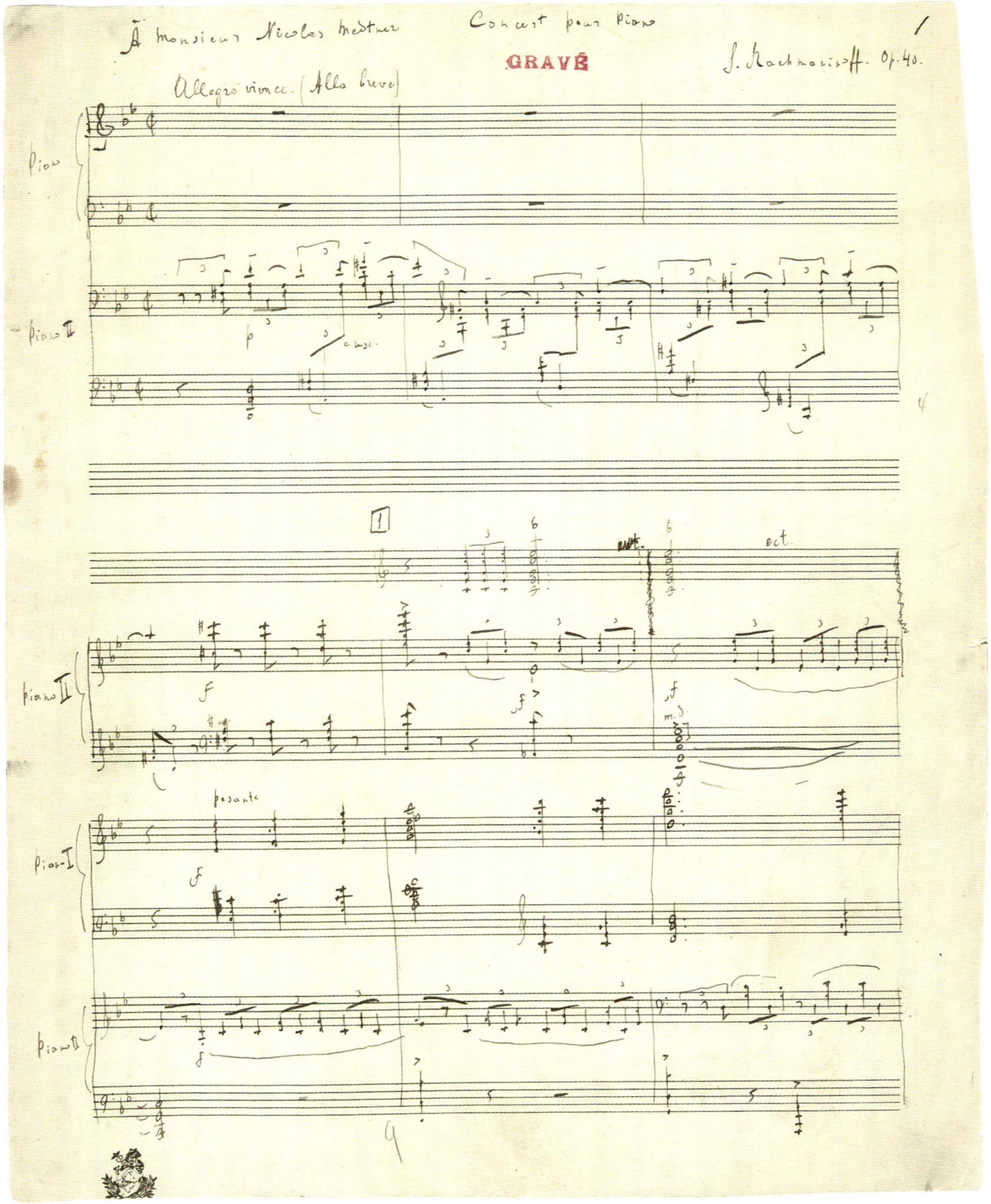


**Sergei Rakhmaninov**
An autograph manuscript of the Fourth Piano Concerto in G Minor, Op. 40
London £201,250 ($289,800) 8.XII.00

Probably the only major autograph of Rakhmaninov ever to be offered for sale at auction, this manuscript is the only surviving autograph evidence of the changes Rakhmaninov made to the concerto after its completion in 1925 and before its first publication in 1928. 102 pages, approximately 33.5 by 26.5 cm. (13⅛ by 10½ in.).

→

**An Autograph Letter by Wolfgang Amadeus Mozart and Leopold Mozart**
London £179,250 ($256,327) 25.V.01

Signed by father and son, this letter was sent by Leopold Mozart to his wife while he was touring Italy with his son between December 1769 and March 1771. The price achieved represents the auction record for an autograph letter in the United Kingdom, and the world record for such a letter by a musician. Three pages, folio, Bologna, 21st August 1770.

stuck hergschnitten wird, so sieht es sehr gut aus, denn es ist blass roth; nemlich das innere des kern. man nennt diese frucht angurie; auch Cocumero oder Kirbs, aber das sind die guten und nicht die wilden Kirbs. man isst sie mit Zucker und Zimmet. Ich schliesse; denn ich habe noch 2 briefe, nach Meyland und Rom zu schreiben. Wir küssen euch beyde 1000 mahl und bin der alte

Mozart mpa

unsre Empf: an alle freund und freundinen in und ausser dem Hause

Ich bin auch noch lebendig und zwar sehr lustig. heunt kam mir die lust auf einen esel zu reiten, denn in italien ists der brauch, und also habe ich gedacht ich muss es doch auch probiren. wir haben die ehre mit einen gewissen dominicaner umzugehen, welcher für heilig gehalten wird, ich zwar glaube es nicht recht, denn er nimt zum frühstück oft eine tassa cioccolata, gleich darauf ein gutes glas starcken spanischen wein, und ich habe selbsten die ehre gehabt mit diesen heiligen zu speisen, welcher brav wein und auf die lezt ein ganzes glas voll starcken wein bey der tafel getruncken hat, zwey gutte schnitz melone, pfersig, birn, 5 schallen caffe, ein ganzen teller voll vögeln, zwey teller voll mit limonien; doch dieses könnte er mit fleiss thun, aber ich glaube nicht, denn dieses wäre zu viel, und aber nimt vielle sachen zur jausen auf nachmittags. addio. lebe wohl küsse der mamma statt meiner die hände. an alle die mich kennen mein compliment.

Wolfgang Mozart. 1770

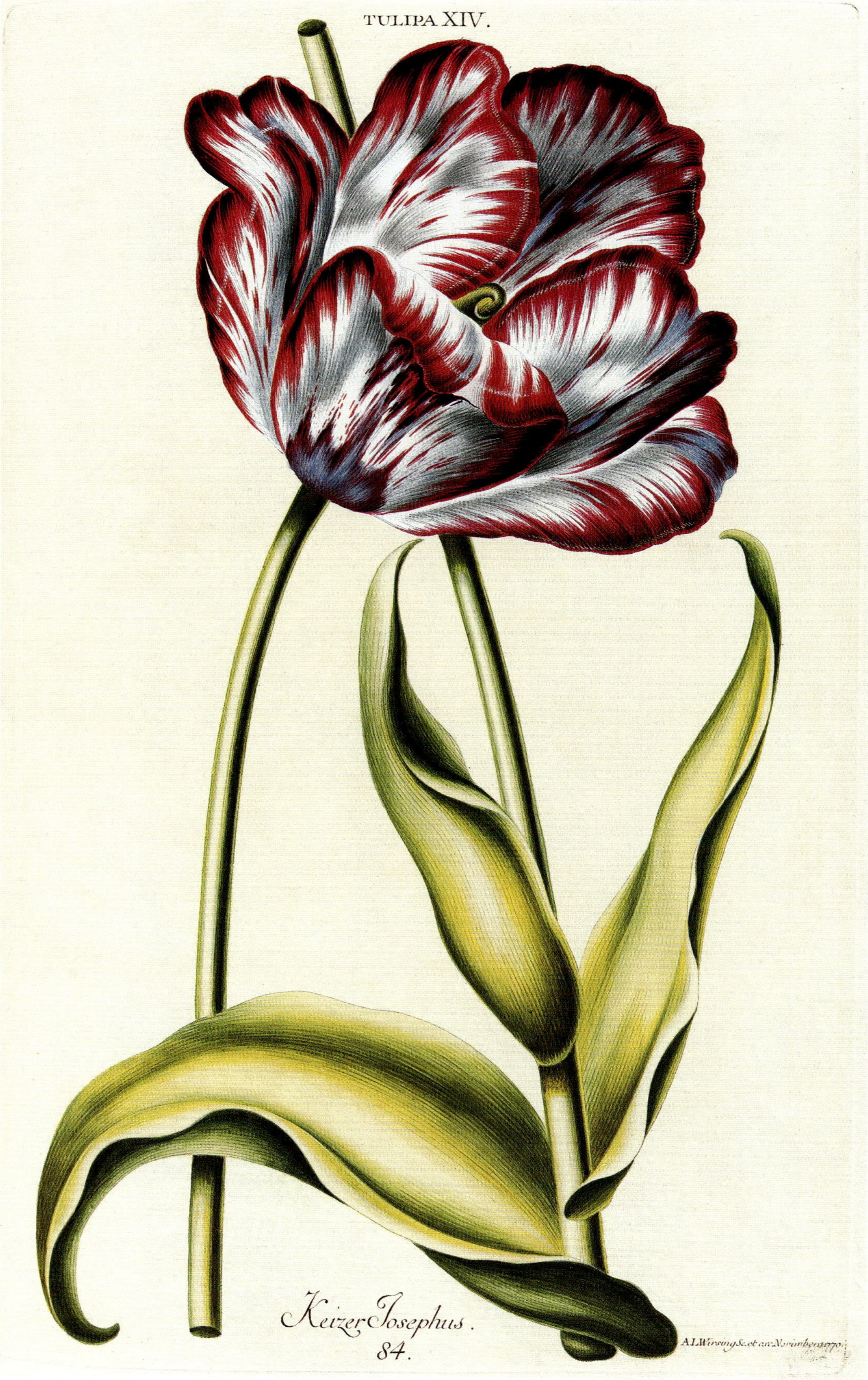


**Christoph Jakob Trew**
*Hortus nitidissimis . . . floribus*
London £553,250 ($791,147) 10.v.01

The stylized plates of this sought-after botanical work show the most luxurious flowers that can be grown in European gardens at the height of their beauty. It is the only 'complete as issued' copy of the book ever to be offered at auction, and was bound up between 1786 and 1792.
Three volumes, folio, Latin and German text, 178 hand-coloured plates.

→
**Charles Perrault**
*Histoires ou contes du temps passé*
Paris FF2,080,405 ($279,452; £187,236) 28.vi.01

An especially rare highlight of the sale of the library of Belgian bibliophile Charles Hayoit (1901–84), this is the first edition of the first printed collection of such classic fairy tales as *Cinderella* and *Sleeping Beauty*.
Paris, 1697.

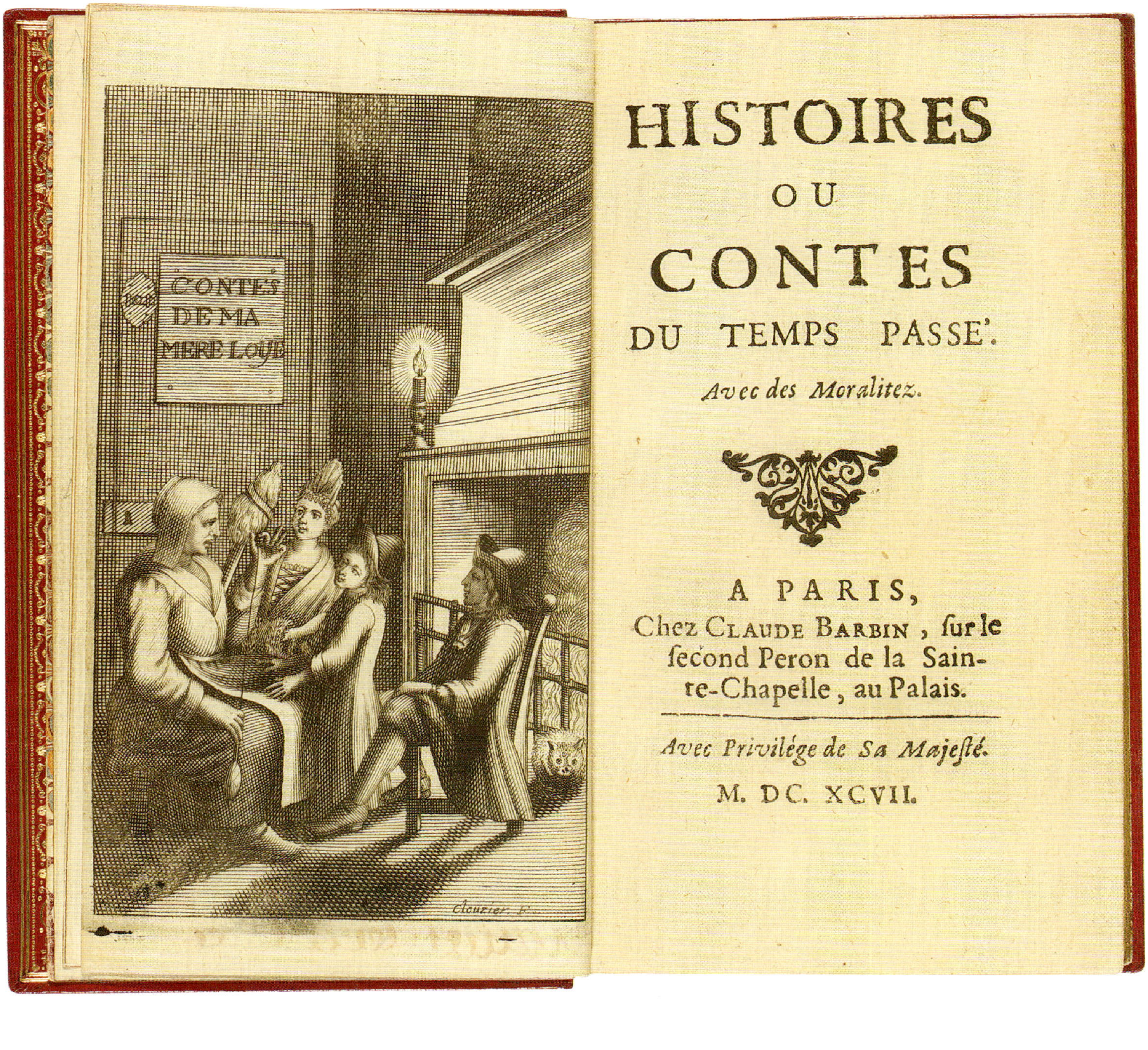


HISTOIRES
OU
CONTES
DU TEMPS PASSE'.
*Avec des Moralitez.*

A PARIS,
Chez CLAUDE BARBIN, ſur le
ſecond Peron de la Sain-
te-Chapelle, au Palais.

*Avec Privilége de Sa Majeſté.*
M. DC. XCVII.

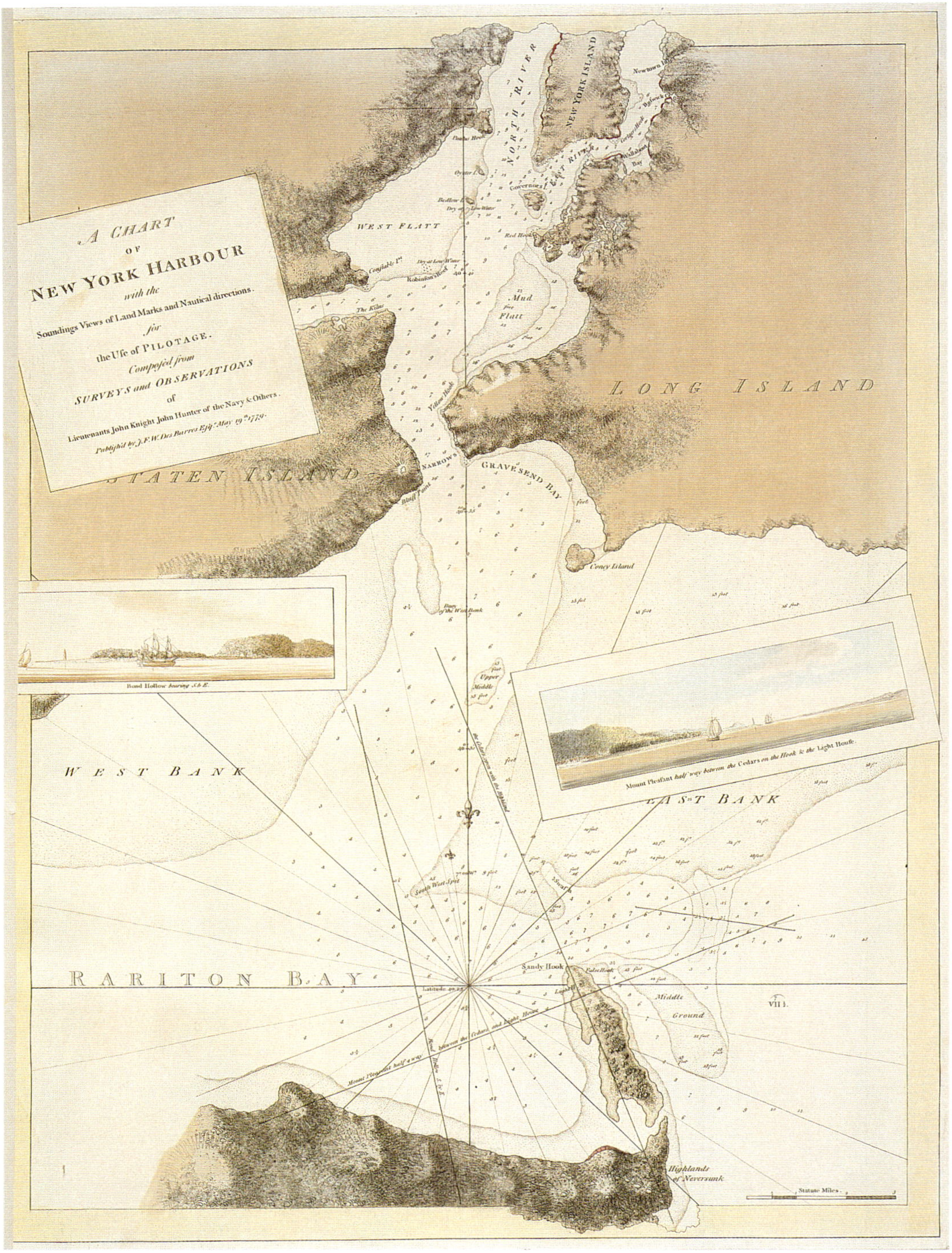


**Joseph Frederick Wallet Des Barres**
*The Atlantic Neptune*
New York $357,750 (£246,848)
13.XII.00

Des Barres was a British military engineer who devoted 16 years to this meticulous survey of the coast of North America, published in 1780–81. It was intended for the use of the British navy, is largely hand-coloured, and no two known copies contain precisely the same charts.
Five volumes, 83.8 by 61 cm.
(33 by 24 in.).

→

**A Vellum Copy of the Stone Facsimile of the *Declaration of Independence***
New York $192,750 (£134,925)
5.VI.01

William J. Stone was commissioned in 1820 to engrave a facsimile of the *Declaration of Independence*. Due to the very poor quality of the original *Declaration*, this facsimile remains the basis for all later ones, and the best indication of the appearance of the document. This is one of the 31 known vellum copies of the facsimile.

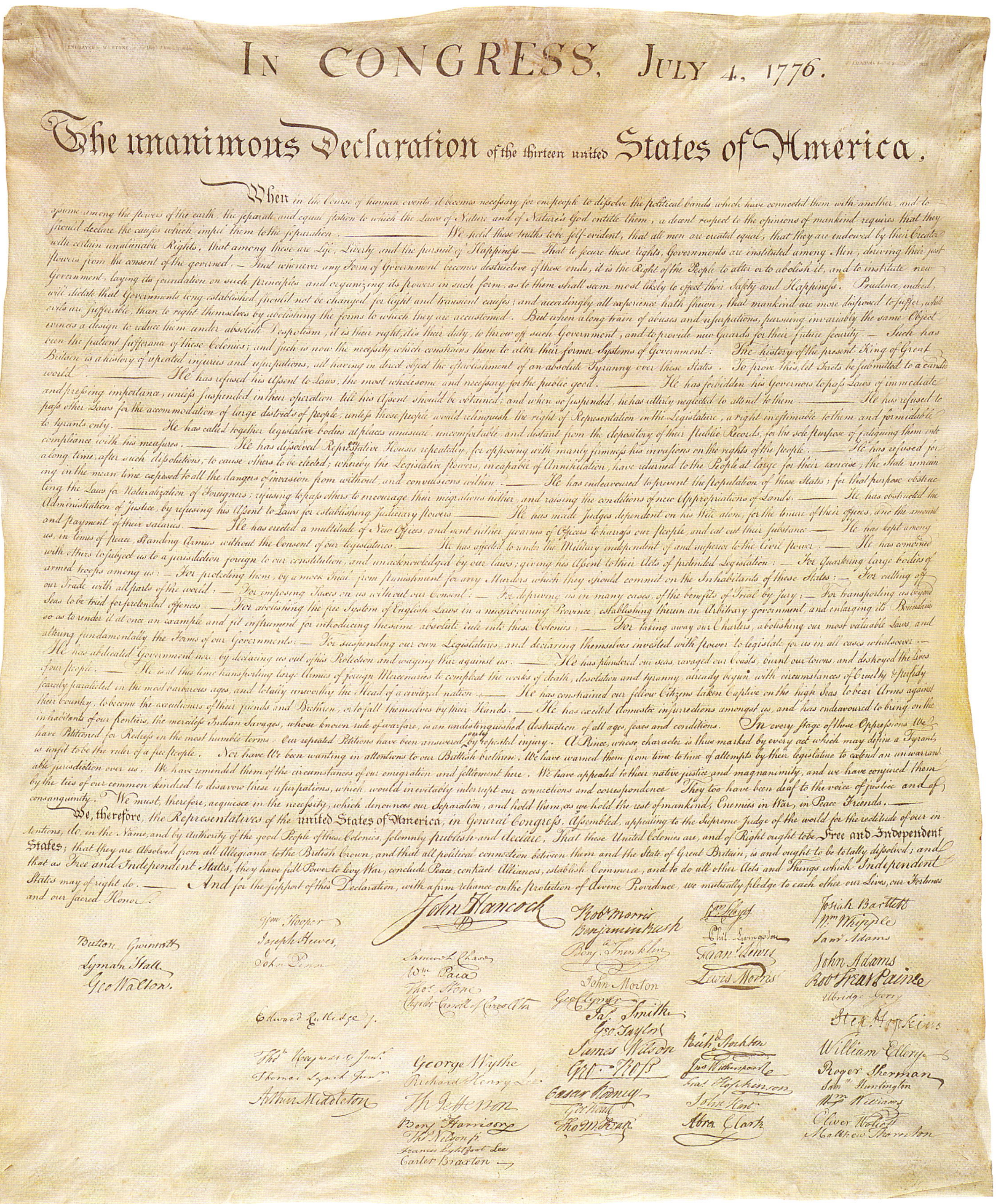

IN CONGRESS, JULY 4, 1776.

The unanimous Declaration of the thirteen united States of America,

When in the Course of human events, it becomes necessary for one people to dissolve the political bands which have connected them with another, and to assume among the powers of the earth, the separate and equal station to which the Laws of Nature and of Nature's God entitle them, a decent respect to the opinions of mankind requires that they should declare the causes which impel them to the separation. —— We hold these truths to be self-evident, that all men are created equal, that they are endowed by their Creator with certain unalienable Rights, that among these are Life, Liberty and the pursuit of Happiness. — That to secure these rights, Governments are instituted among Men, deriving their just powers from the consent of the governed, — That whenever any Form of Government becomes destructive of these ends, it is the Right of the People to alter or to abolish it, and to institute new Government, laying its foundation on such principles and organizing its powers in such form, as to them shall seem most likely to effect their Safety and Happiness. Prudence, indeed, will dictate that Governments long established should not be changed for light and transient causes; and accordingly all experience hath shewn, that mankind are more disposed to suffer, while evils are sufferable, than to right themselves by abolishing the forms to which they are accustomed. But when a long train of abuses and usurpations, pursuing invariably the same Object evinces a design to reduce them under absolute Despotism, it is their right, it is their duty, to throw off such Government, and to provide new Guards for their future security. — Such has been the patient sufferance of these Colonies; and such is now the necessity which constrains them to alter their former Systems of Government. The history of the present King of Great Britain is a history of repeated injuries and usurpations, all having in direct object the establishment of an absolute Tyranny over these States. To prove this, let Facts be submitted to a candid world. —— He has refused his Assent to Laws, the most wholesome and necessary for the public good. —— He has forbidden his Governors to pass Laws of immediate and pressing importance, unless suspended in their operation till his Assent should be obtained; and when so suspended, he has utterly neglected to attend to them. —— He has refused to pass other Laws for the accommodation of large districts of people, unless those people would relinquish the right of Representation in the Legislature, a right inestimable to them and formidable to tyrants only. —— He has called together legislative bodies at places unusual, uncomfortable, and distant from the depository of their public Records, for the sole purpose of fatiguing them into compliance with his measures. —— He has dissolved Representative Houses repeatedly, for opposing with manly firmness his invasions on the rights of the people. —— He has refused for a long time, after such dissolutions, to cause others to be elected; whereby the Legislative powers, incapable of Annihilation, have returned to the People at large for their exercise; the State remaining in the mean time exposed to all the dangers of invasion from without, and convulsions within. —— He has endeavoured to prevent the population of these States; for that purpose obstructing the Laws for Naturalization of Foreigners; refusing to pass others to encourage their migrations hither, and raising the conditions of new Appropriations of Lands. —— He has obstructed the Administration of Justice, by refusing his Assent to Laws for establishing Judiciary powers. —— He has made Judges dependent on his Will alone, for the tenure of their offices, and the amount and payment of their salaries. —— He has erected a multitude of New Offices, and sent hither swarms of Officers to harrass our people, and eat out their substance. —— He has kept among us, in times of peace, Standing Armies without the Consent of our legislatures. —— He has affected to render the Military independent of and superior to the Civil power. —— He has combined with others to subject us to a jurisdiction foreign to our constitution, and unacknowledged by our laws; giving his Assent to their Acts of pretended Legislation: — For Quartering large bodies of armed troops among us: — For protecting them, by a mock Trial, from punishment for any Murders which they should commit on the Inhabitants of these States: — For cutting off our Trade with all parts of the world: — For imposing Taxes on us without our Consent: — For depriving us in many cases, of the benefits of Trial by Jury: — For transporting us beyond Seas to be tried for pretended offences: — For abolishing the free System of English Laws in a neighbouring Province, establishing therein an Arbitrary government, and enlarging its Boundaries so as to render it at once an example and fit instrument for introducing the same absolute rule into these Colonies: — For taking away our Charters, abolishing our most valuable Laws, and altering fundamentally the Forms of our Governments: — For suspending our own Legislatures, and declaring themselves invested with power to legislate for us in all cases whatsoever. — He has abdicated Government here, by declaring us out of his Protection and waging War against us. —— He has plundered our seas, ravaged our Coasts, burnt our towns, and destroyed the lives of our people. —— He is at this time transporting large Armies of foreign Mercenaries to compleat the works of death, desolation and tyranny, already begun with circumstances of Cruelty & perfidy scarcely paralleled in the most barbarous ages, and totally unworthy the Head of a civilized nation. —— He has constrained our fellow Citizens taken Captive on the high Seas to bear Arms against their Country, to become the executioners of their friends and Brethren, or to fall themselves by their Hands. —— He has excited domestic insurrections amongst us, and has endeavoured to bring on the inhabitants of our frontiers, the merciless Indian Savages, whose known rule of warfare, is an undistinguished destruction of all ages, sexes and conditions. In every stage of these Oppressions We have Petitioned for Redress in the most humble terms: Our repeated Petitions have been answered only by repeated injury. A Prince, whose character is thus marked by every act which may define a Tyrant, is unfit to be the ruler of a free people. Nor have We been wanting in attentions to our Brittish brethren. We have warned them from time to time of attempts by their legislature to extend an unwarrantable jurisdiction over us. We have reminded them of the circumstances of our emigration and settlement here. We have appealed to their native justice and magnanimity, and we have conjured them by the ties of our common kindred to disavow these usurpations, which, would inevitably interrupt our connections and correspondence. They too have been deaf to the voice of justice and of consanguinity. We must, therefore, acquiesce in the necessity, which denounces our Separation, and hold them, as we hold the rest of mankind, Enemies in War, in Peace Friends.

We, therefore, the Representatives of the united States of America, in General Congress, Assembled, appealing to the Supreme Judge of the world for the rectitude of our intentions, do, in the Name, and by Authority of the good People of these Colonies, solemnly publish and declare, That these United Colonies are, and of Right ought to be Free and Independent States; that they are Absolved from all Allegiance to the British Crown, and that all political connection between them and the State of Great Britain, is and ought to be totally dissolved; and that as Free and Independent States, they have full Power to levy War, conclude Peace, contract Alliances, establish Commerce, and to do all other Acts and Things which Independent States may of right do. —— And for the support of this Declaration, with a firm reliance on the protection of divine Providence, we mutually pledge to each other our Lives, our Fortunes and our sacred Honor.

John Hancock

Button Gwinnett
Lyman Hall
Geo Walton.

Wm Hooper
Joseph Hewes,
John Penn

Edward Rutledge 1.
Thos Heyward Junr.
Thomas Lynch Junr.
Arthur Middleton

Samuel Chase
Wm. Paca
Thos. Stone
Charles Carroll of Carrollton

George Wythe
Richard Henry Lee
Th Jefferson
Benja. Harrison
Thos Nelson jr.
Francis Lightfoot Lee
Carter Braxton

Robt Morris
Benjamin Rush
Benja. Franklin
John Morton
Geo Clymer
Jas. Smith
Geo. Taylor
James Wilson
Geo. Ross
Caesar Rodney
Geo Read
Tho M:Kean

Wm Floyd
Phil. Livingston
Frans. Lewis
Lewis Morris
Richd. Stockton
Jno Witherspoon
Fras. Hopkinson
John Hart
Abra Clark

Josiah Bartlett
Wm. Whipple
Saml. Adams
John Adams
Robt Treat Paine
Elbridge Gerry
Step. Hopkins
William Ellery
Roger Sherman
Samel Huntington
Wm. Williams
Oliver Wolcott
Matthew Thornton

but his love

talent for quality

I hate violence

ideas reaches any

thing a stops

any thing

revolution

must come

gradually but

but

useful

accepted

alternative

first

the case

←

**James Joyce**
Autograph Manuscript of the 'Eumaeus' Episode of *Ulysses*
London £861,250 ($1,205,750) 10.VII.01

This previously unknown autograph draft of one of the closing episodes of *Ulysses* (1922) is an important literary discovery. In Joyce's handwriting it shows a prolific reworking of an early version of this episode, substantially different from later manuscript and published versions.
48 pages, octavo.

**Lewis Carroll (Charles Lutwidge Dodgson)**
*Alice's Adventures Underground*
London £157,250 ($224,868) 6.VI.01

Sold in the specialist 'Alice' sale in London, this book, published 23 years after *Alice's Adventures in Wonderland*, is a facsimile of the original adventures Dodgson wrote for Alice Liddell. It was Alice Liddell's own copy, inscribed by Dodgson *To her whose namesake one happy summer day inspired his story: from the Author. Xmas. 1886.*, Macmillan and Co., 1886.

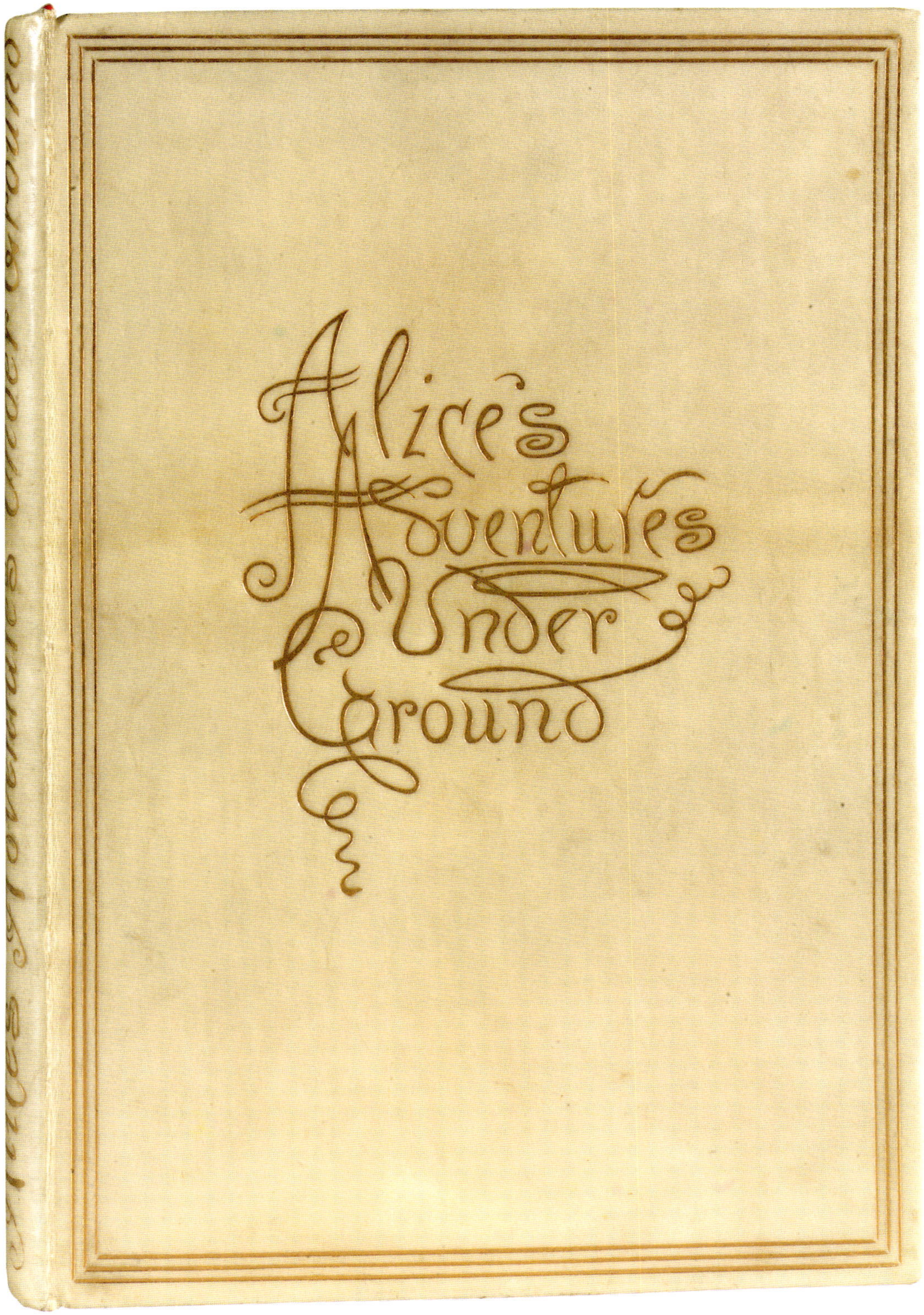

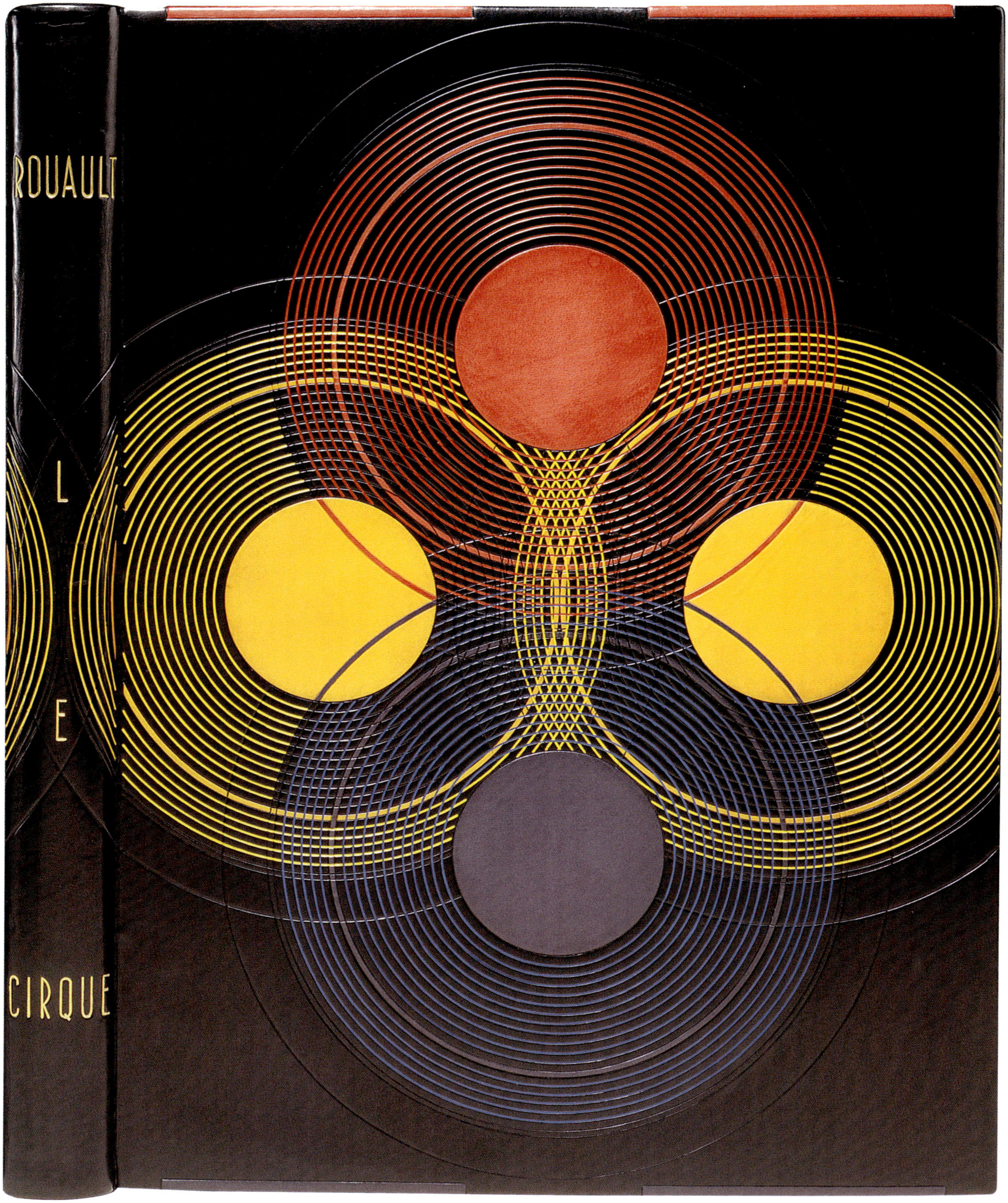
ROUAULT
L
E
CIRQUE

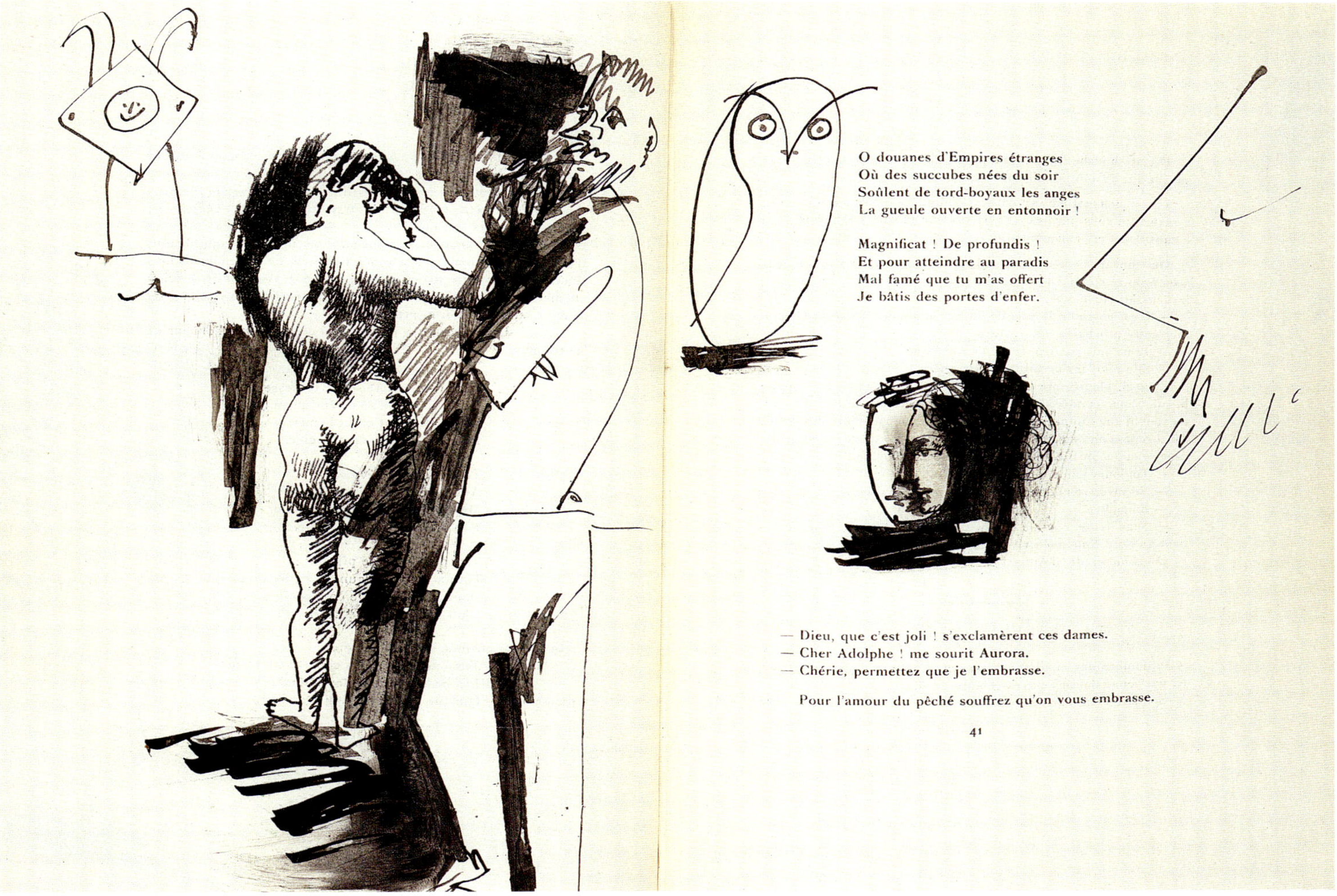


←

**George Rouault**
*Le Cirque*, Binding by Creuzevault
New York $126,750 (£88,725)
25.VI.01

One of only 35 copies on japon imperial, for this design Rouault used an abstract image inspired by the circus in order to symbolize the grotesqueness and decadence of life in the 1920s. An aquatint process has been used to create a more painterly and glossy effect.

**André Salmon**
*Le Manuscrit trouvé dans un chapeau*
New York $258,750 (£181,125)
25.VI.01

Picasso decorated this copy of the book for his close friend Paul Eluard. These exuberant drawings combine ornithological subjects and beautiful young women, which forms a playful commentary on that period of Picasso's life.
Inscribed *Pour Paul Eluard. Picasso*, drawings in ink and coloured crayons by Picasso on 70 pages.

→ →

**Wallasse Ting**
*1¢ Life*
London £118,750 ($169,812) 23.V.01

*1¢ Life* is the most important, but least known, Pop Art publication. With poems by writer and artist Wallasse Ting, 100 editions of the book had signed lithographs by the 28 artists who illustrated it, including Andy Warhol, Sam Franics and Roy Lichtenstein. A few copies, this one included, had magnificent, unique Pop Art bindings by Georges Leroux. Bern, E.W. Kornfeld, 1964.

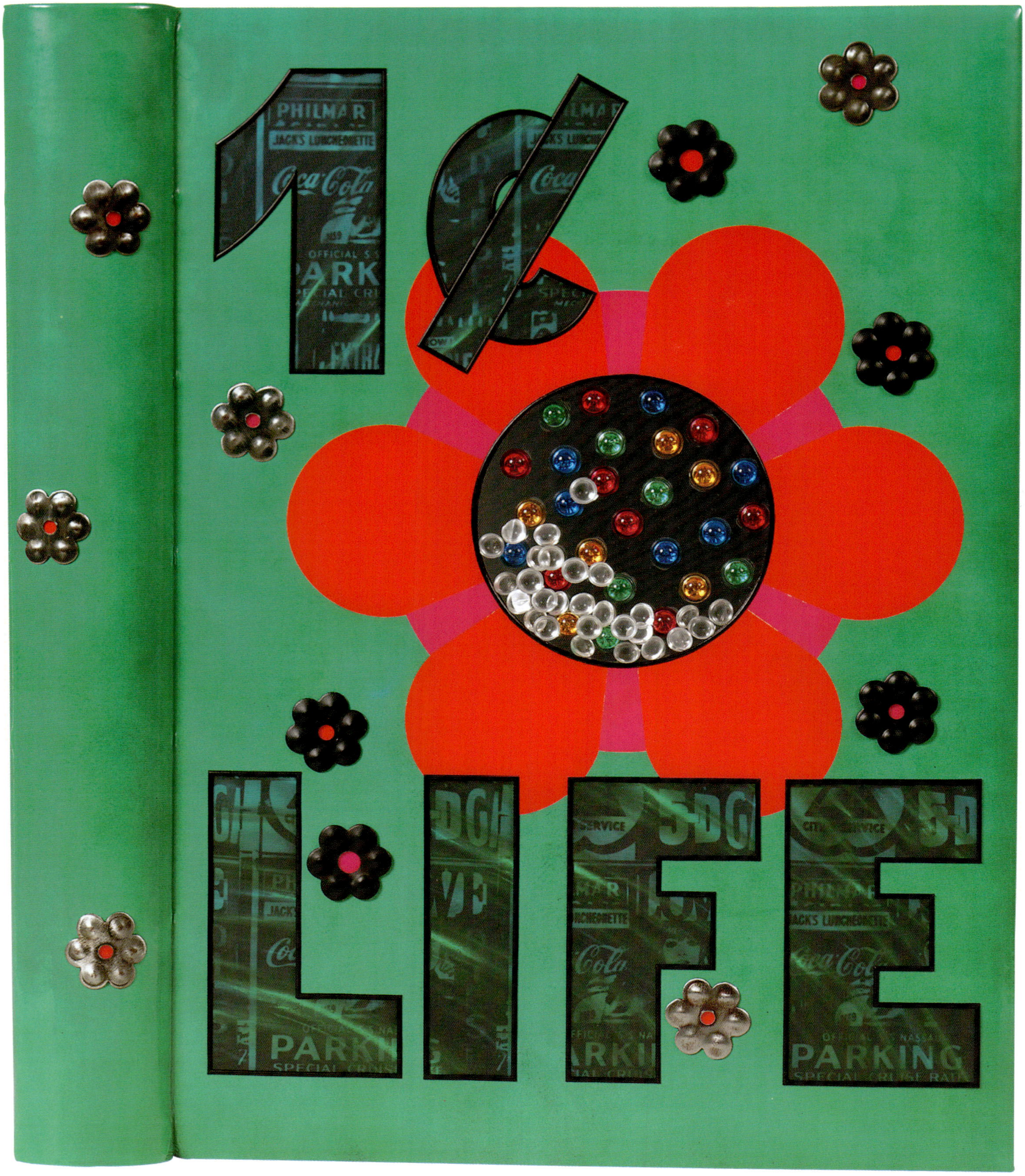
1¢
LIFE

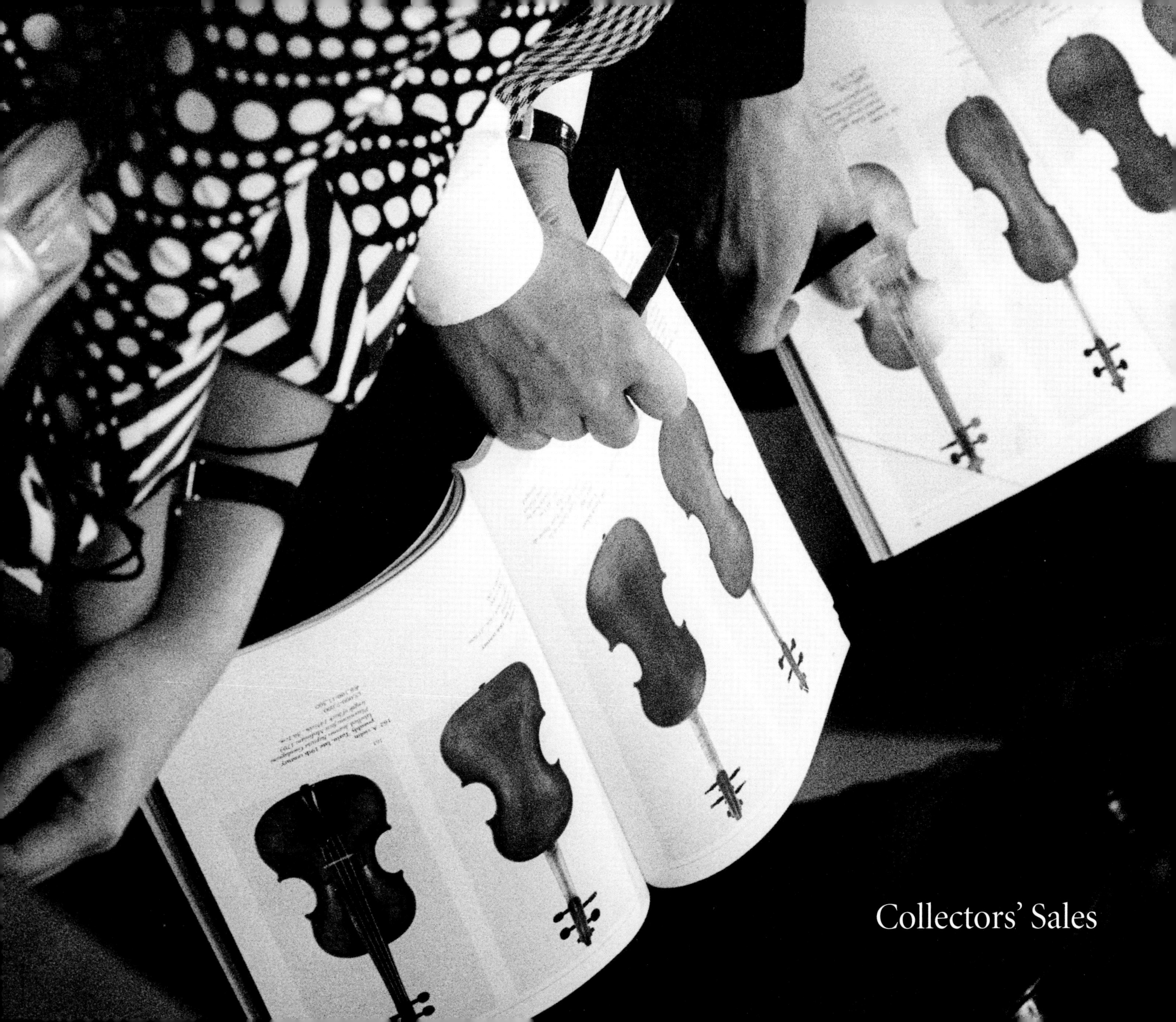

# Collectors' Sales

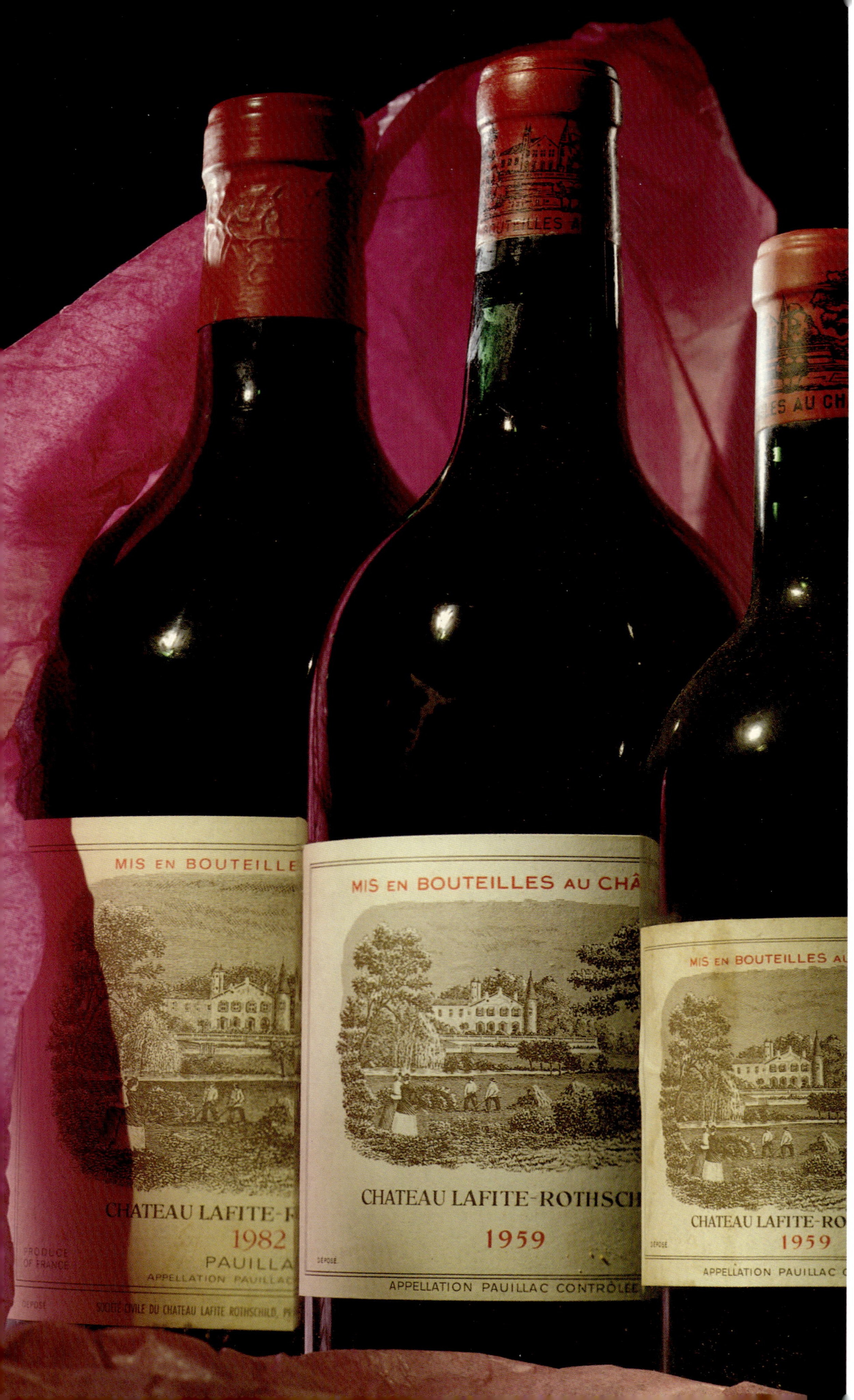


**Six magnums of Château Lafite, 1959**
London £12,100 ($17,545)
27–28.VI.01

This sale of an outstanding private collection included significant quantities of top red Bordeaux from the excellent vintages of the 1980s. These six magnums of Château Lafite sold for twice their estimate of £5,500–7,500 ($8,000–10,000).

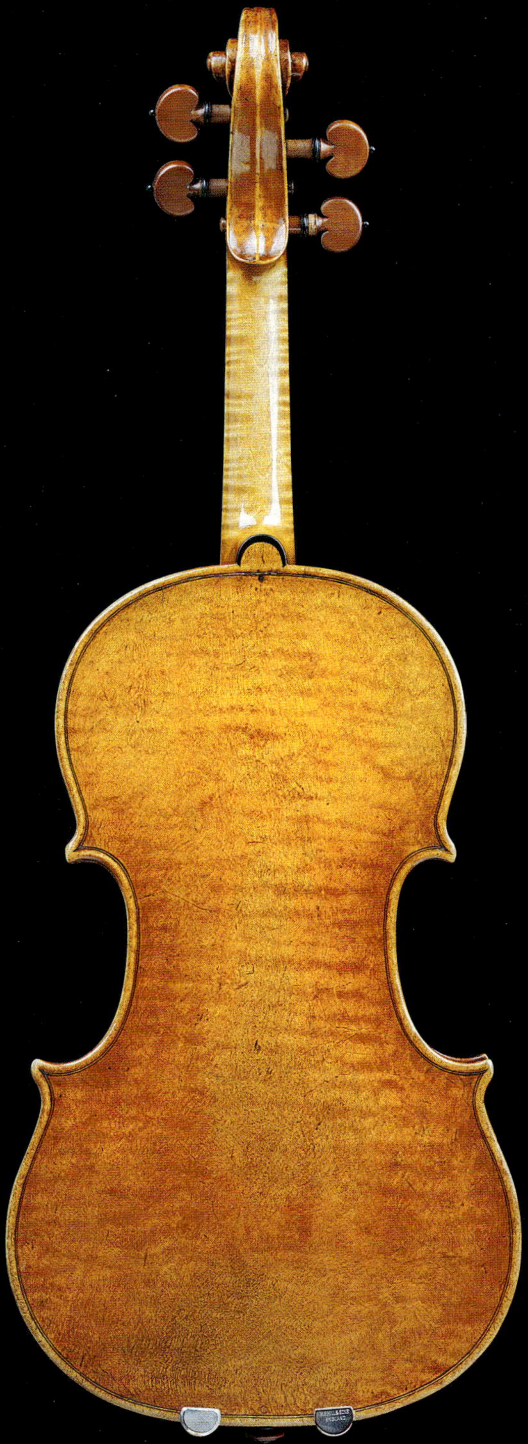

**A Violin by Carlo Tononi**
Chicago $173,625 (£119,801) 6.x.00

Labelled *Carlo Tononi Bolognese fece in Venezia l'an 1725*, this instrument achieved an auction record for the maker. Tononi was trained in his family's workshop and was among the foremost instrument makers of his day. Venice, 1725, length of back: 35.5 cm. (13⅞ in.).

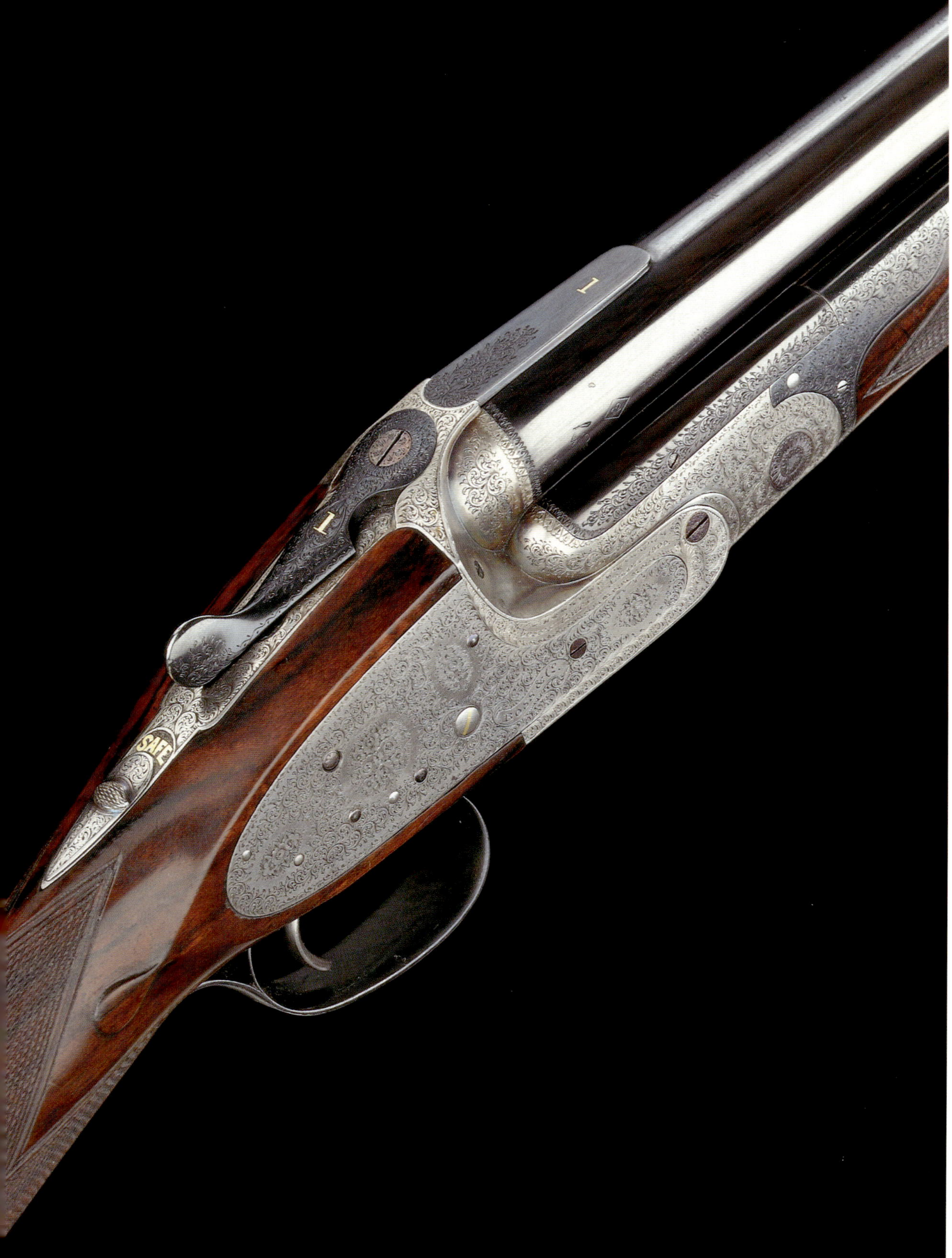


**A Pair of Boss & Co. 12-bore single trigger, sidelock ejector, over/under guns (one shown)**
Sussex £57,000 ($81,648) 11.IV.01

In 1909 Boss & Co introduced its influential over-and-under gun, which had the barrels placed one above the other. Although not the first, the Boss design was revolutionary, and, still manufactured today, continues to be regarded as the finest of all English over-and-under guns.
Nos. 6245/6.

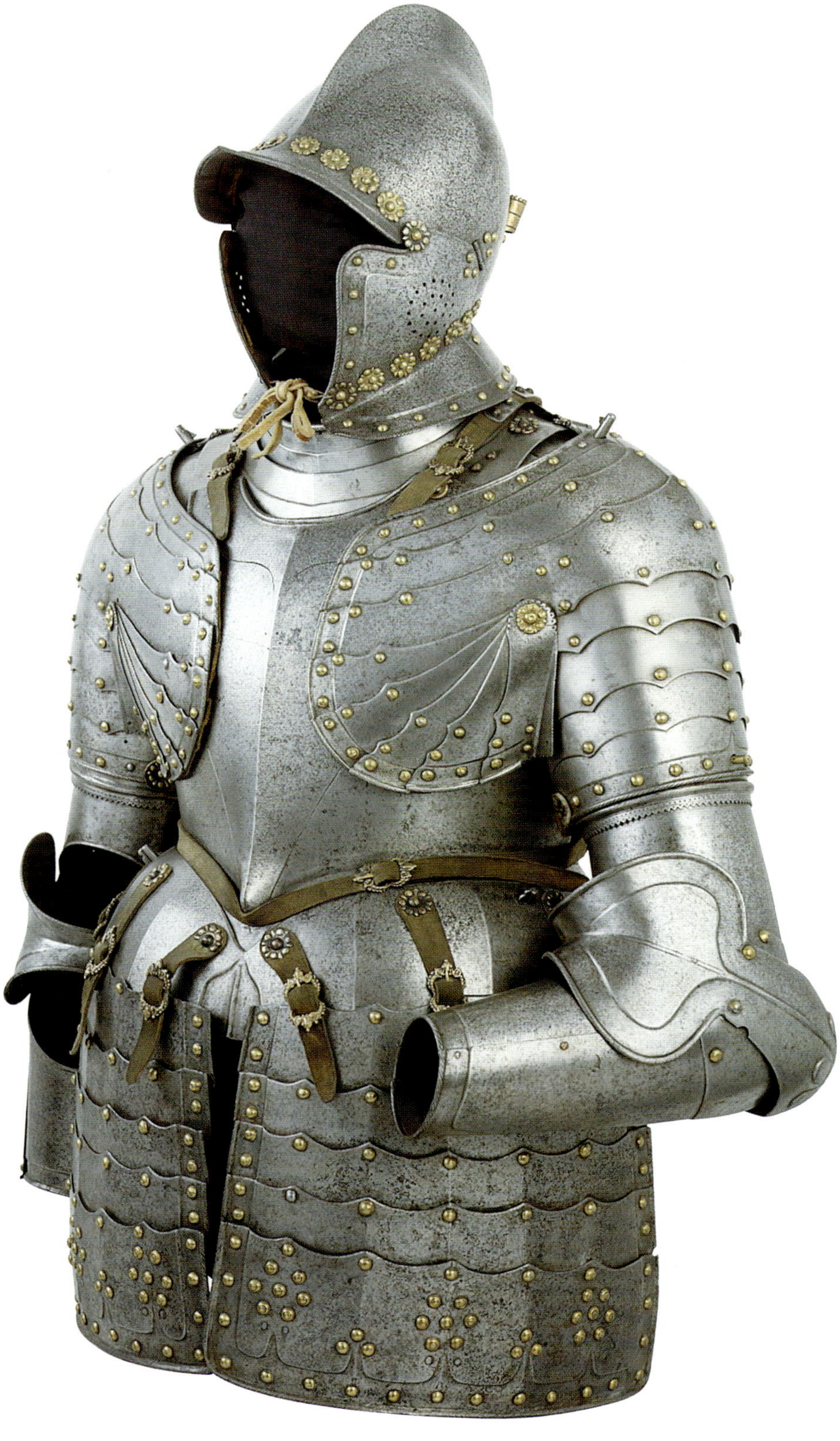

**A Swiss Officer's Half-armour,**
***circa* 1630**
Zurich SF47,200 ($18,730; £26,971)
14.XII.00

This characteristically Swiss half-armour is struck with the Freiburg in Uechtland control mark and was produced in either Bern or Freiburg. The maker was probably Heinrich Burenküng, who came to Freiburg in around 1575. The high quality of the materials used in production indicate it was the armour of an officer.

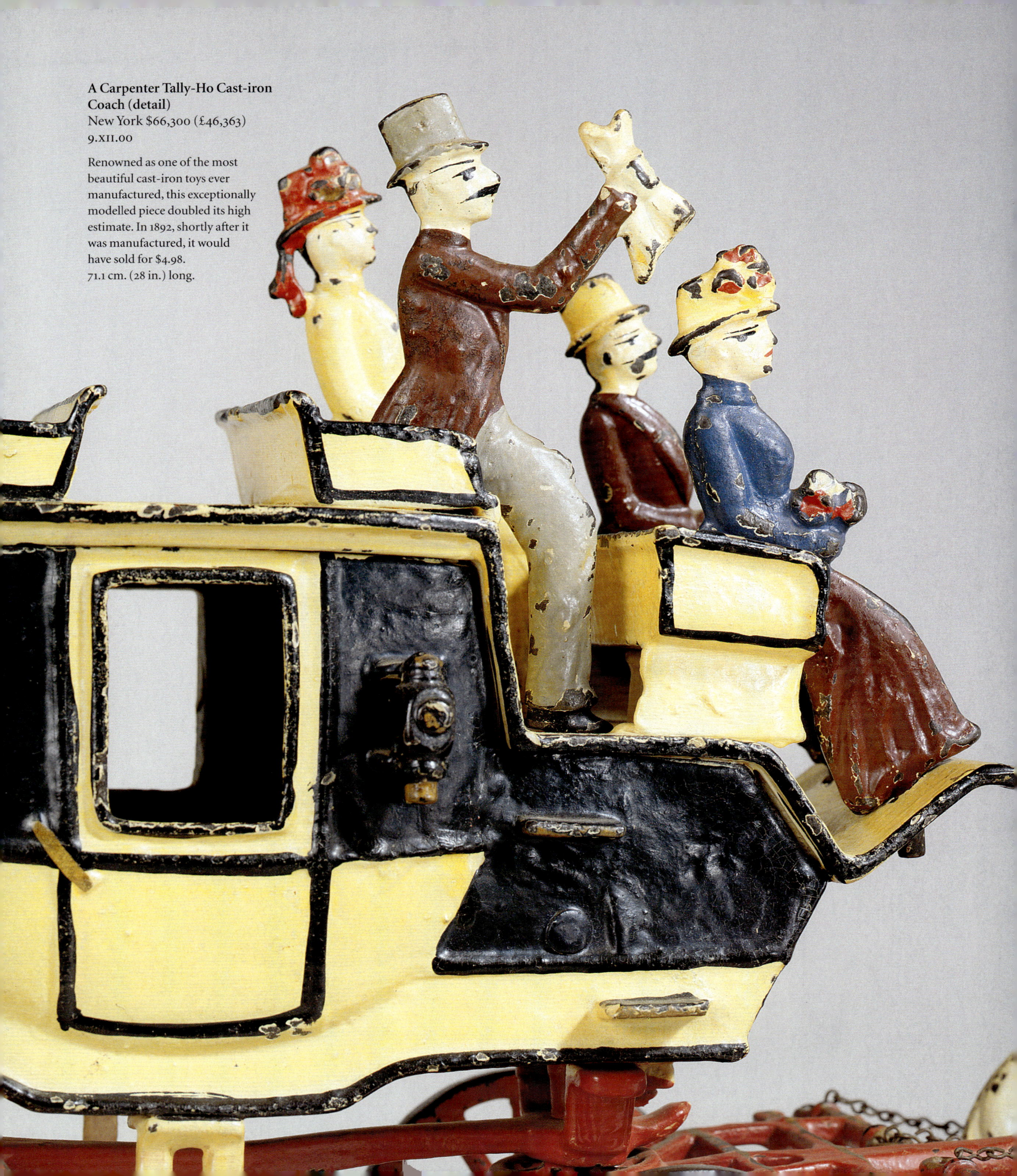

**A Carpenter Tally-Ho Cast-iron Coach (detail)**
New York $66,300 (£46,363)
9.XII.00

Renowned as one of the most beautiful cast-iron toys ever manufactured, this exceptionally modelled piece doubled its high estimate. In 1892, shortly after it was manufactured, it would have sold for $4.98.
71.1 cm. (28 in.) long.

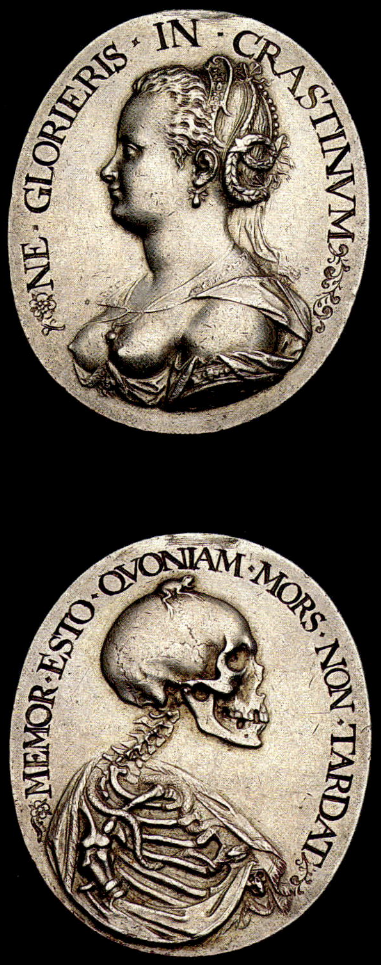


**A Silver Medal depicting Vanitas by Jan de Vos**
London £30,250 ($44,165) 3.v.01

Made in Germany and dated *1618*, this is surely Jan de Vos' most memorable medallic work. The likeness is thought to be that of a mistress of the Emperor Rudolph II. The legend may be translated as: 'Do not boast for the morrow: Be mindful that death does not delay'.
5.9 by 4.76 cm. (2⅜ by 1⅞ in.).

**Cape of Good Hope 1861 triangular 'Woodblock' 4d. vermilion 'error of colour'**
London £91,500 ($132,675)
25–26.IV.01

One of the most desired of all British African stamps is the famous Cape of Good Hope 'triangular' stamp. Known as the celebrated Sir Maxwell Joseph cover, this letter features a legendary 'error of colour' issued in 1861: the 4d. in red instead of blue. Together with two normal 1d. within a block of three.

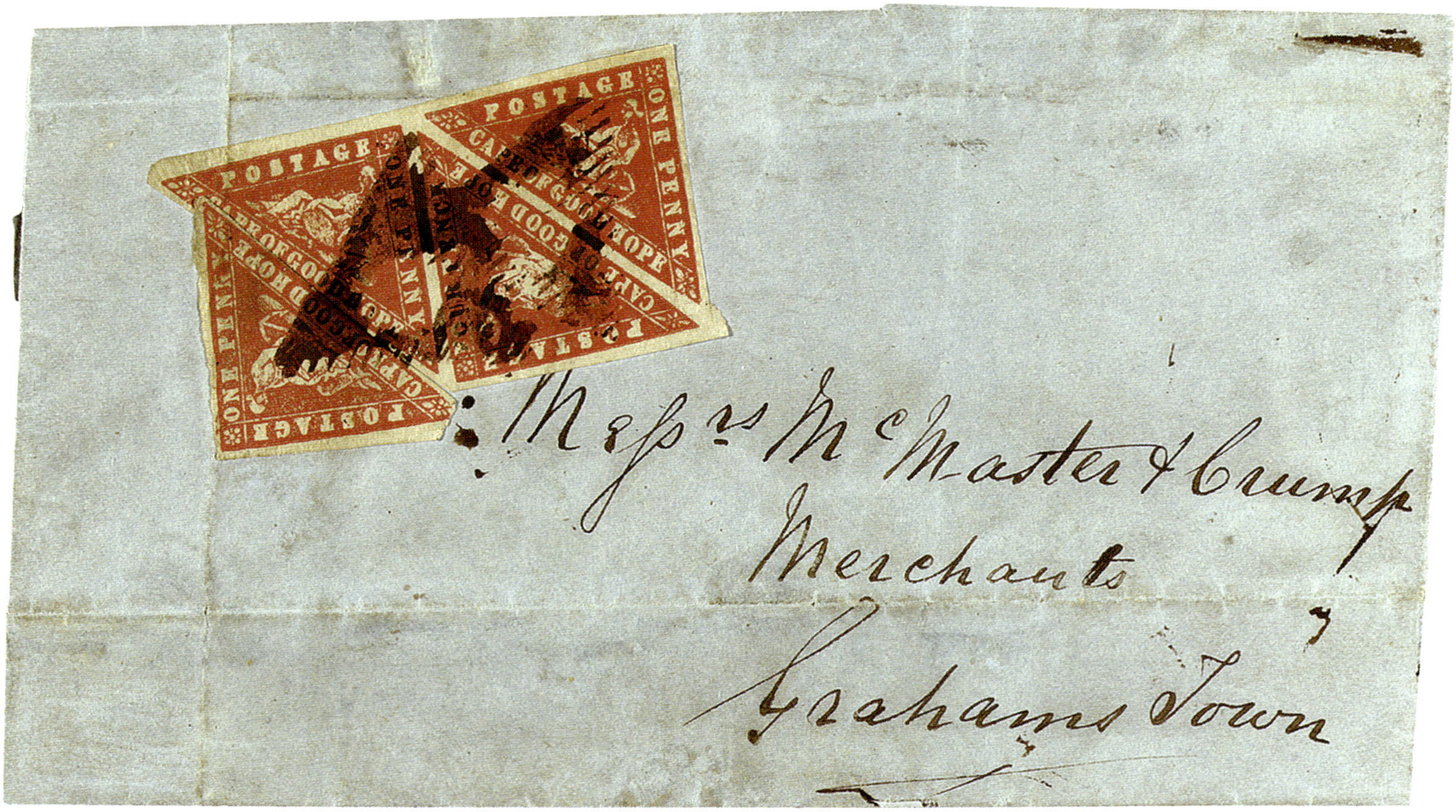

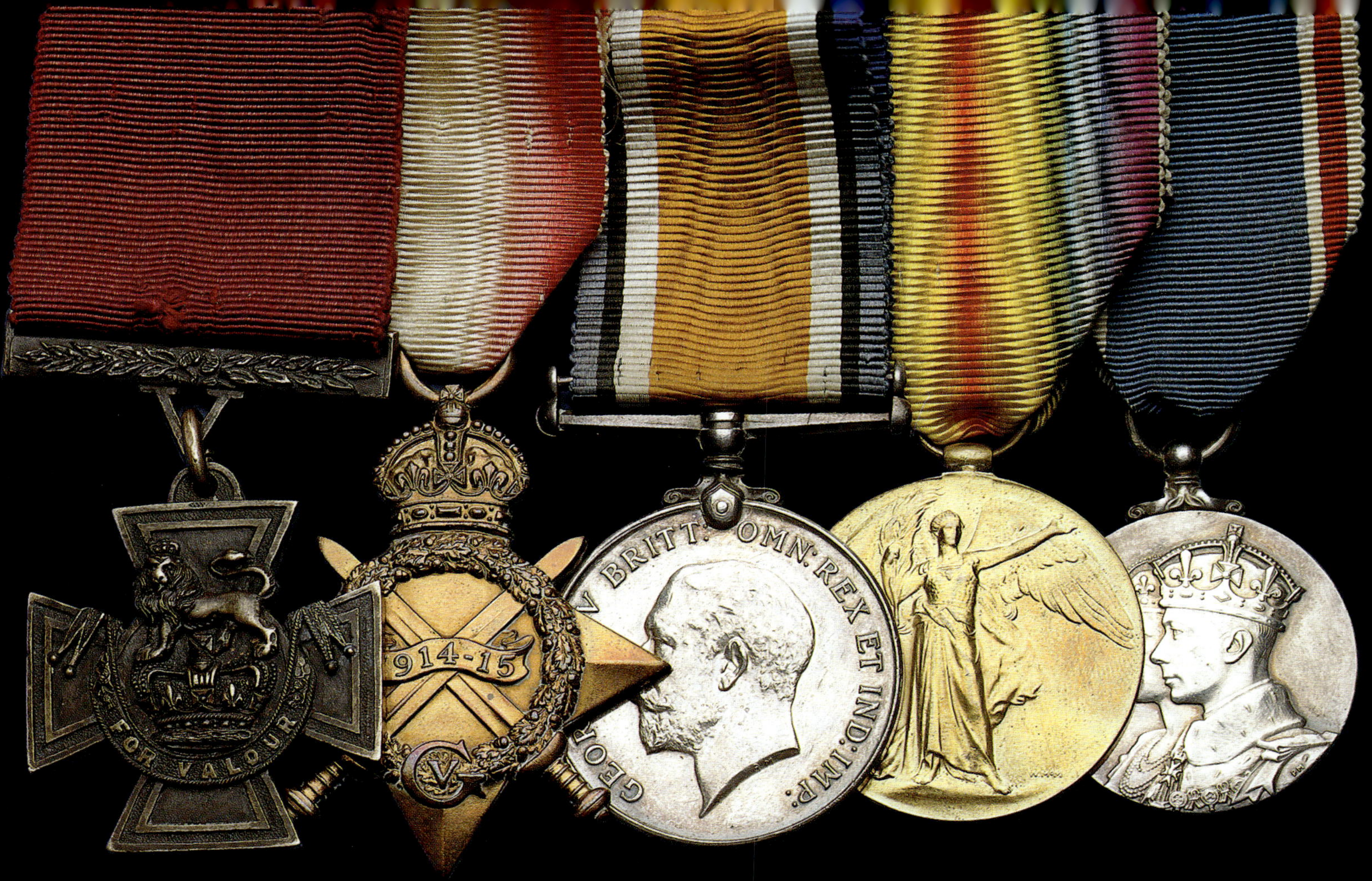


**A Great War Victoria Cross Group, Captain Samuel Meekosha, First 6th Battalion, West Yorkshire Regiment (Bradford Territorials)**
London £101,200 ($143,704) 3.v.01

This group of medals, sold with a group of Second World War medals belonging to the recipient's son, were awarded to Samuel Meekosha for his bravery in the trenches in 1915. Under heavy bombardment Meekosha, then a corporal, took charge when his senior officers were badly wounded and, with another three men, saved the lives of several comrades.

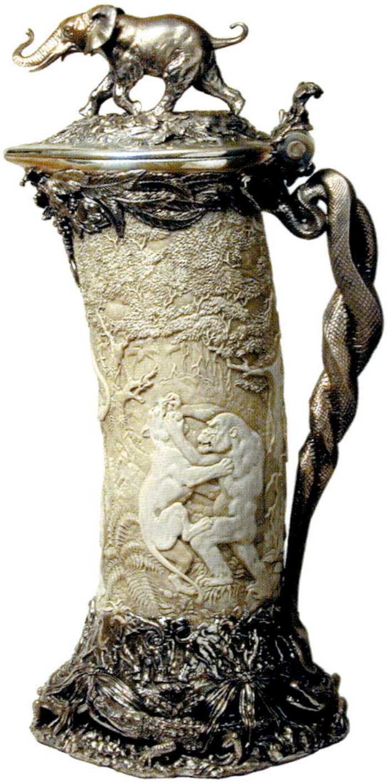

**The Pabst Brewing Company Stein Collection**
$220,750 (£152,317) 26.IV.01

This collection of steins and tankards was sold in a highly successful one-day online auction. Among the items on offer was a silver-mounted ivory tankard by Tiffany & Co., which achieved a record price for a decorative object in an online auction. Other highlights included a moulded pottery stein with an elaborate village scene, weighing 40 pounds and thought to be among the largest beer steins in the world.

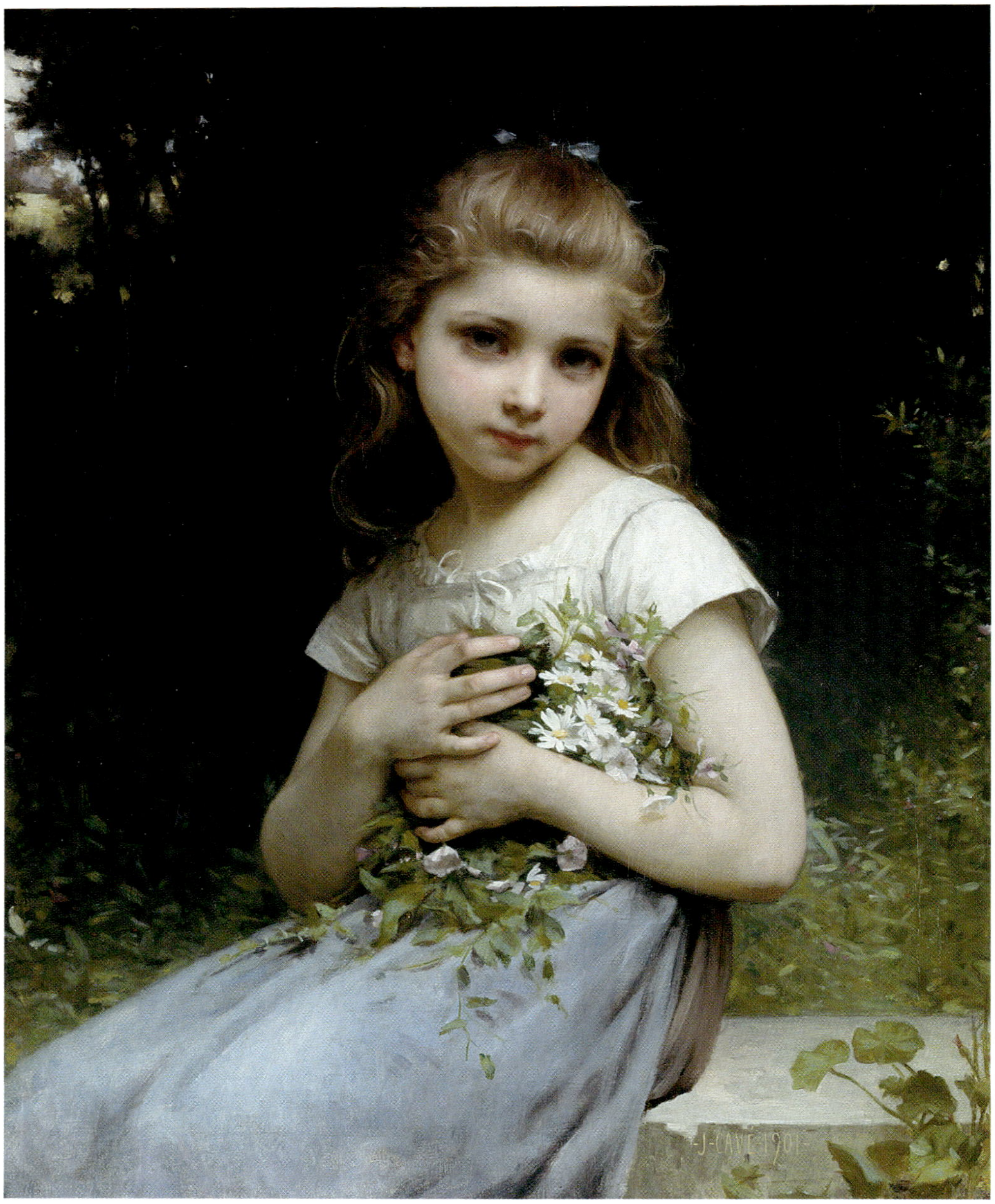

**19th Century Art**
$55,750 (£38,971) 9.V.01

In May, Sothebys.com along with several Associates, presented an online auction of '19th Century Art: The Real and the Ideal'. This sale of European art brought strong results with many works well exceeding their pre-sale estimates. One particular highlight was a lovely oil on canvas, posted for sale on the website by the Odon Wagner Gallery of Toronto, evoking the essence of rural France by Jules-Cyrille Cavé entitled *My Daisies*.

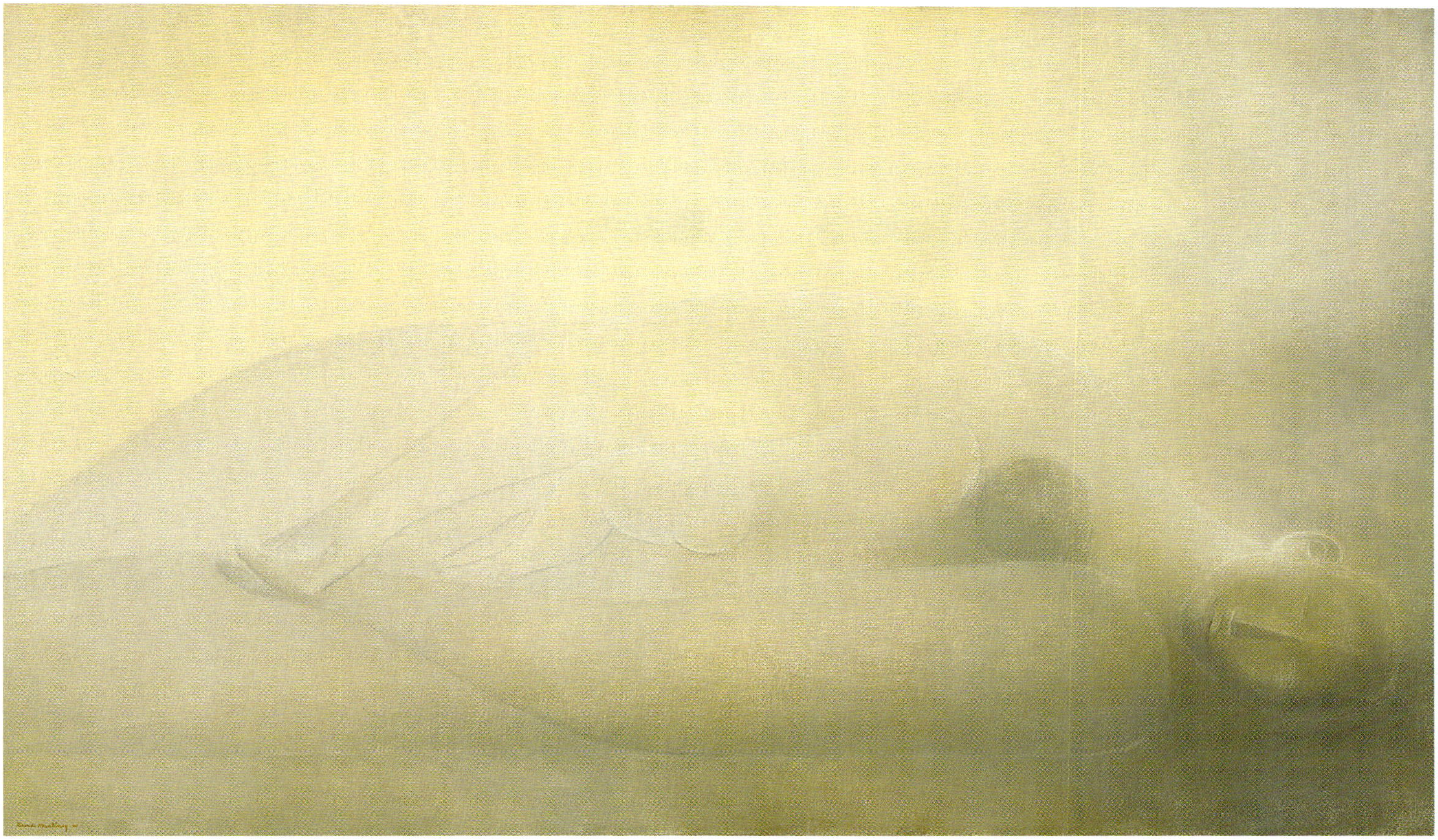

**Gutenberg Bible Leaf**
$48,400 (£33,880) 21.XII.00

Printed in 1454–55, the Gutenberg Bible was the first substantial European book printed with moveable type. Approximately 48 copies of the Gutenberg Bible exist today, in varying states of completeness and single leaves periodically appear on the market. This particular leaf, in fine condition, contains the opening verses of Isaiah 11, one of the Old Testament prophecies of the birth of Jesus of Nazareth as the Messiah.

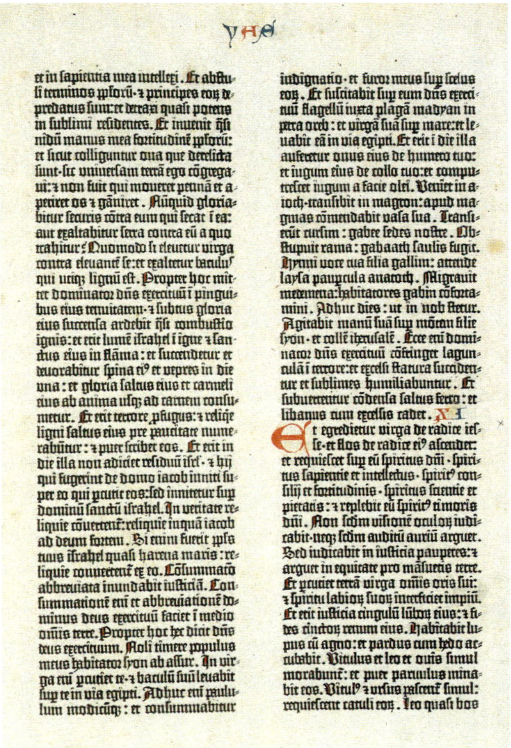

**Contemporary Latin American Art**
$44,000 (£30,562) 4.XII.00

Last December, Sotheby's held its first online auction devoted to Contemporary Latin American art. With more than 150 lots posted by Sothebys.com Associates, this sale offered a selection of artists' works in a number of categories including drawings, sculpture, prints and photographs. Viewed as a whole, the collection illustrated the evolution of this artistic tradition created from a fusion of European, African and indigenous influences. The top-selling lot was Ricardo Martinez's iconic *Mother and Child*, a work that was posted on the site by noted New York dealer, Mary-Ann Martin Fine Art.

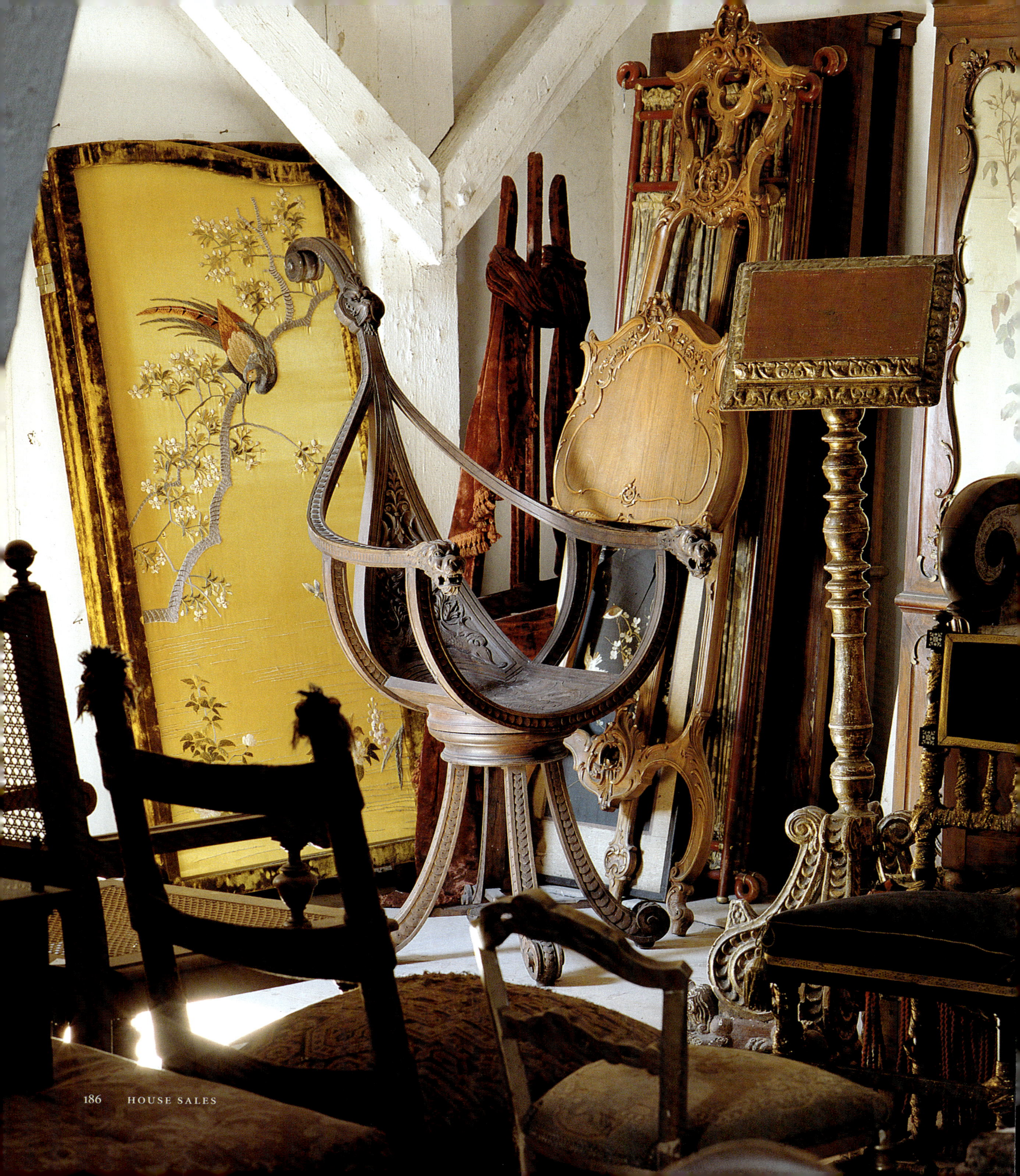

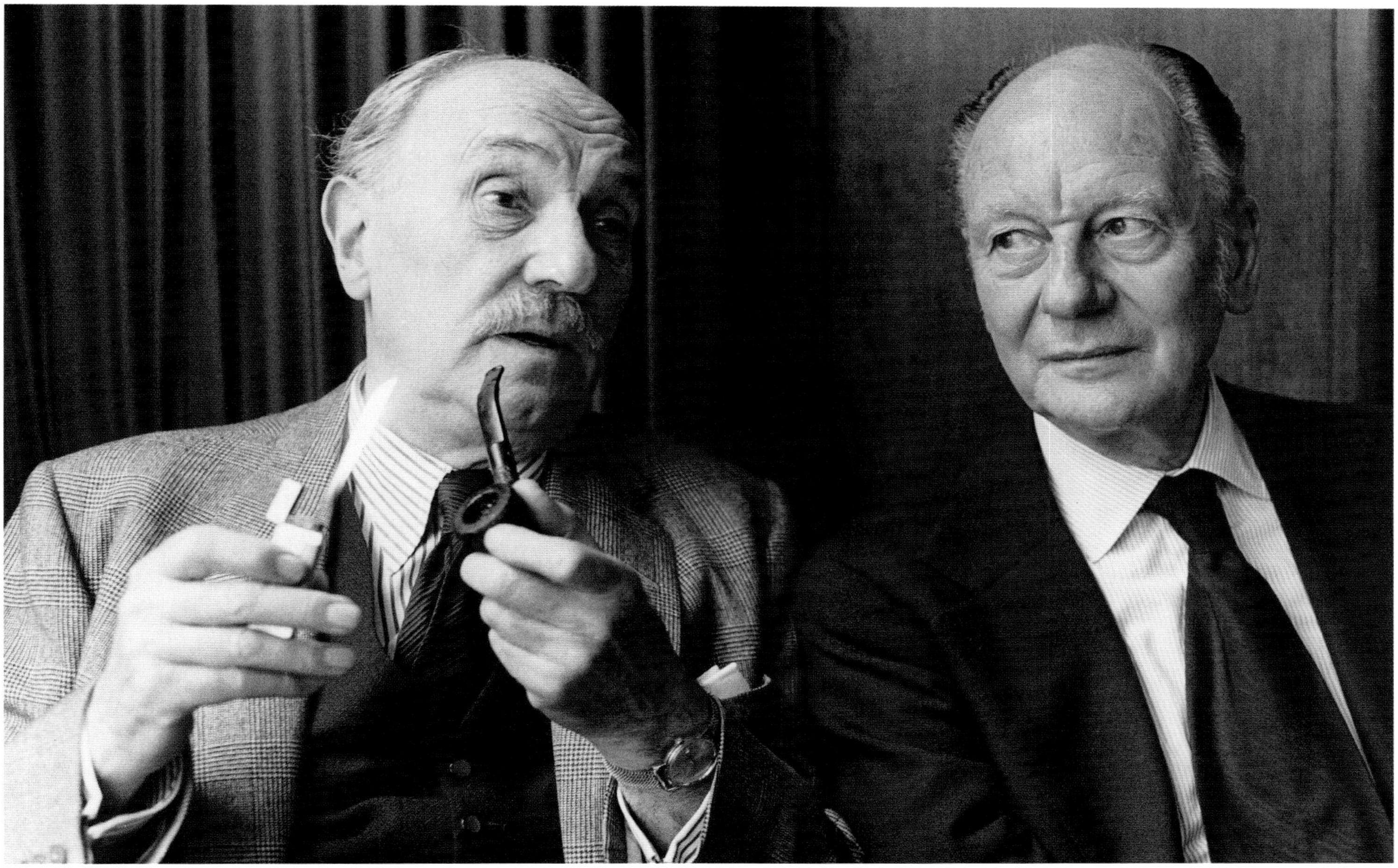

←

**Ancestral Attics**

Comprising offerings from 30 German noble families, the Ancestral Attics sale in October 2000, hosted by Sotheby's at Schloss Monrepos near Ludwigsburg in southwest Germany, was to help restore and conserve the art collections and buildings belonging to the various vendors. This sale was appropriately named, as many of the 2,800 objects offered had been hidden in vaults or attics for decades, emerging to reveal something of the original ambience of the aristocratic homes they once graced. The total for the six days was DM 19,758,344 ($8,496,087; £5,927,503), the highest-selling lot being a *circa* 1575 terracotta bust of Giulio Contarini, Procurator of St Mark's in Venice, attributed to Alessandro Vittoria, which sold for more than seven times its high estimate, at DM 1,534,000 ($659,620; £460,200).

**Sir John Gielgud and Sir Ralph Richardson**

The lives and work of these two giants of theatre were celebrated at separate sales in April 2001. The sale, on 5th April, of Sir John Gielgud's Collection benefited his favourite actors' and animal welfare charities, while the sale of Sir Ralph Richardson's Collection, on 27th April, saw the establishment of the Ralph and Meriel Richardson Foundation to help actors who have fallen on hard times in later life. The top lots in both sales featured fine English furniture, editions of Shakespeare and paintings by Sir William Nicholson (1872–1949).

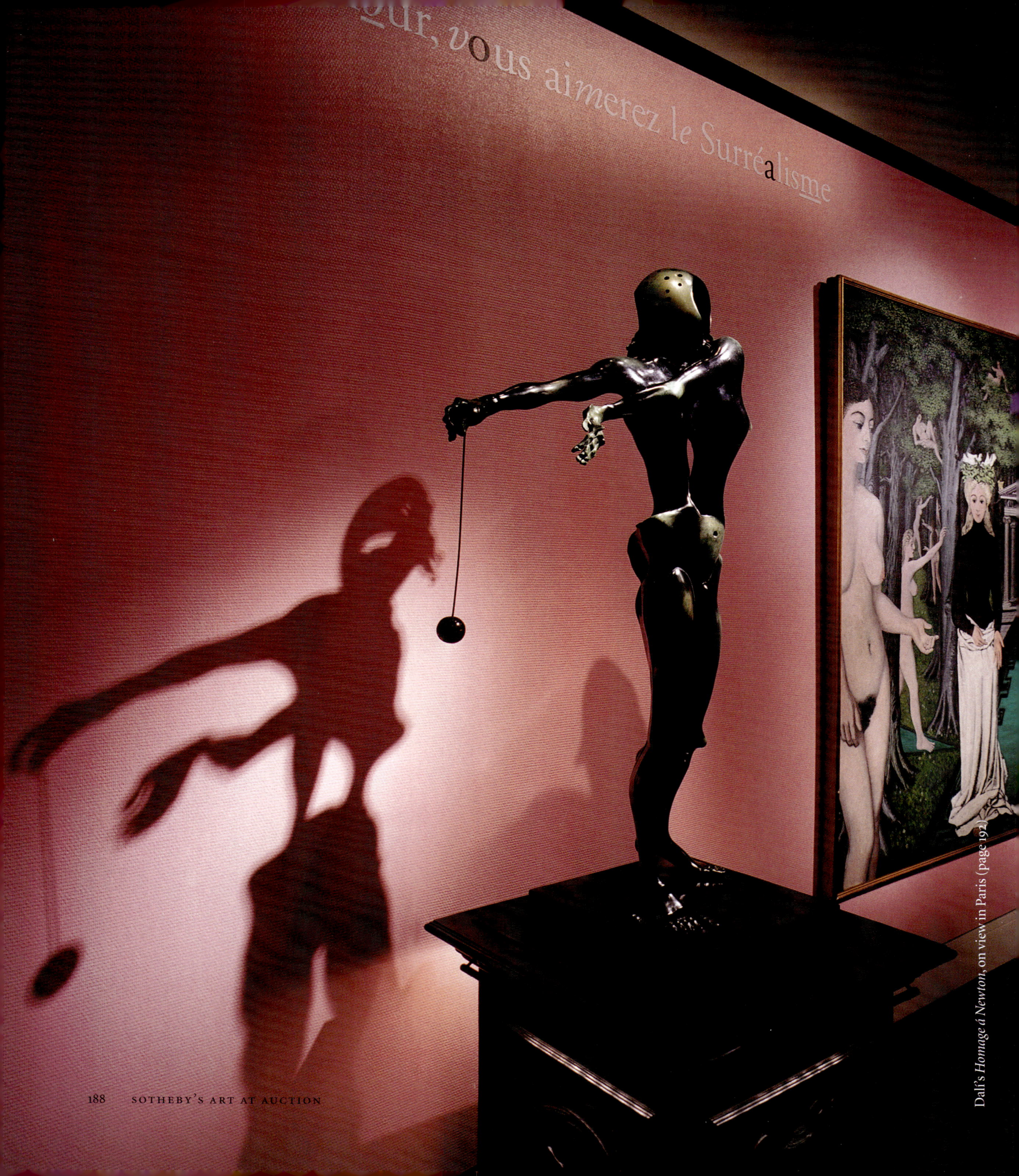


Dalí's *Homage à Newton*, on view in Paris (page 192)

# Contributors

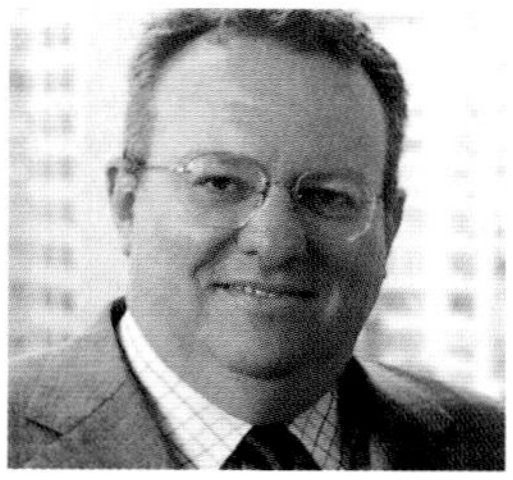

**William F. Ruprecht**
*President & chief executive officer, Sotheby's*

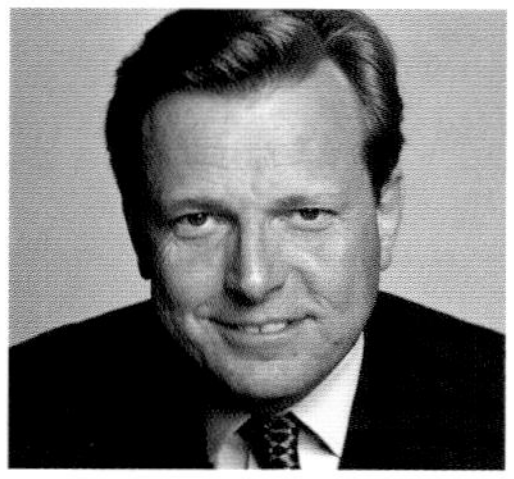

**Robin Woodhead**
*Chief executive officer, Sotheby's Europe & Asia*

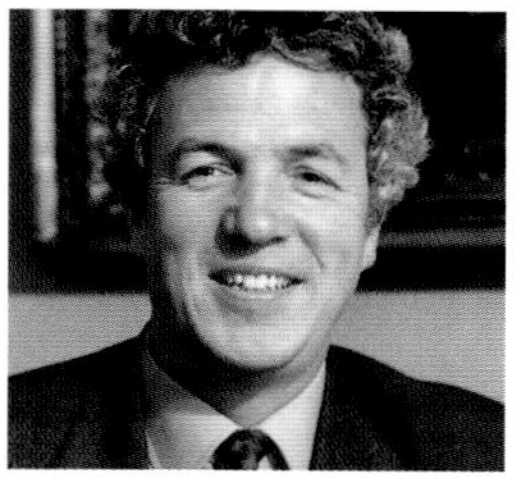

**Henry Wyndham**
*Chairman, Sotheby's Europe*

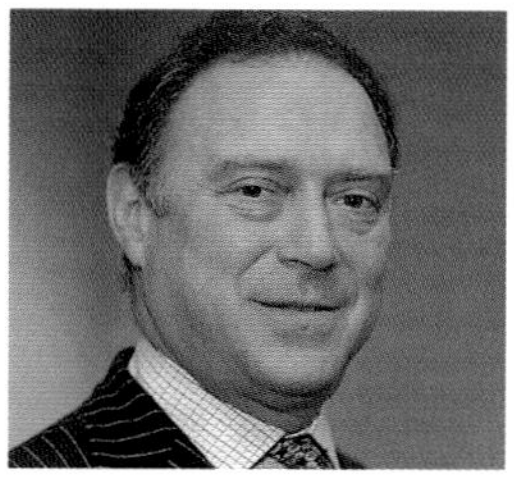

**Warren P. Weitman, Jr.**
*Chairman, Sotheby's North & South America*

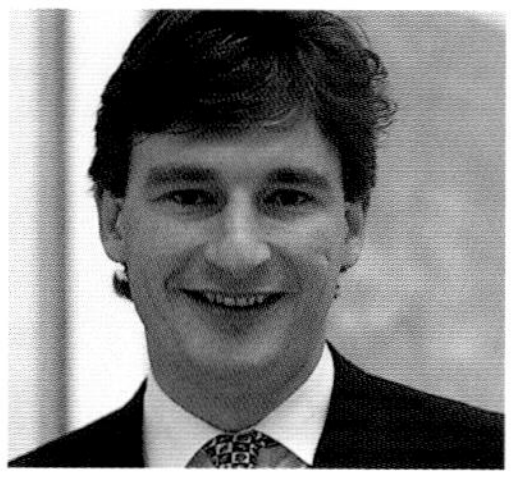

**Henry Howard-Sneyd**
*Managing director, Sotheby's Asia*

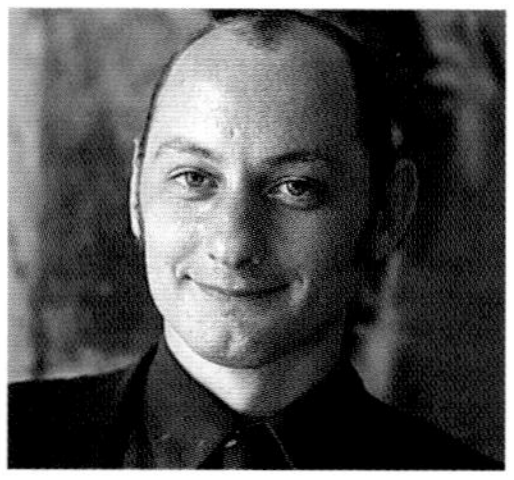

**Richard Aronowitz-Mercer**
*Head of research, Sotheby's Europe & deputy director in the Impressionist & Modern Art department, Sotheby's Europe*

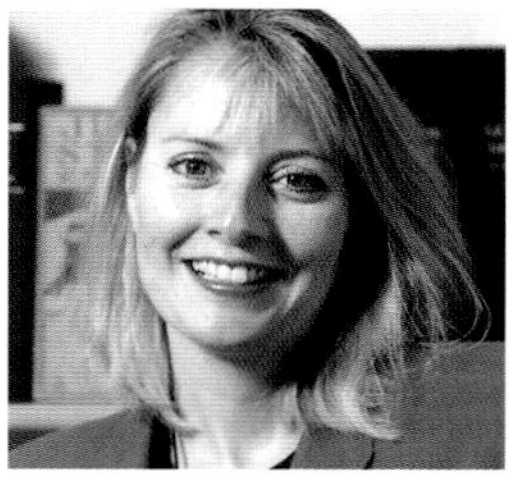

**Catherine Porter**
*Head of the Children's & Illustrated Books department, Sotheby's London*

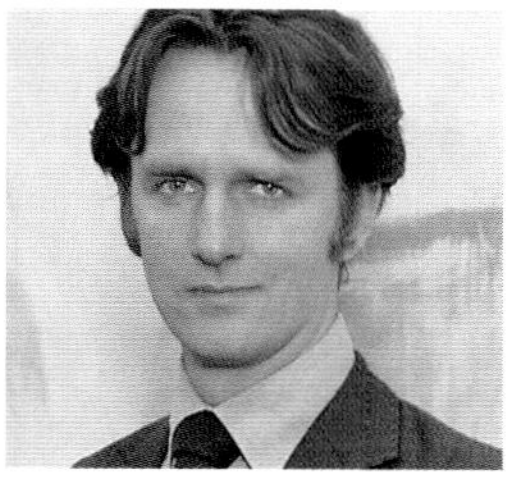

**Tobias Meyer**
*Head of Contemporary Art, Sotheby's Worldwide*

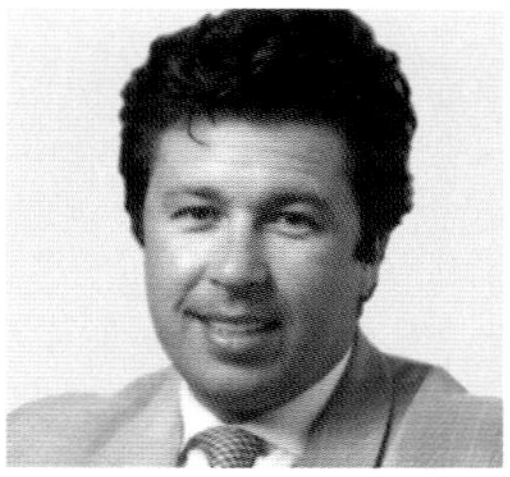

**Stephane Cosman Connery**
*Senior vice president in the Impressionist & Modern Art department, Sotheby's New York*

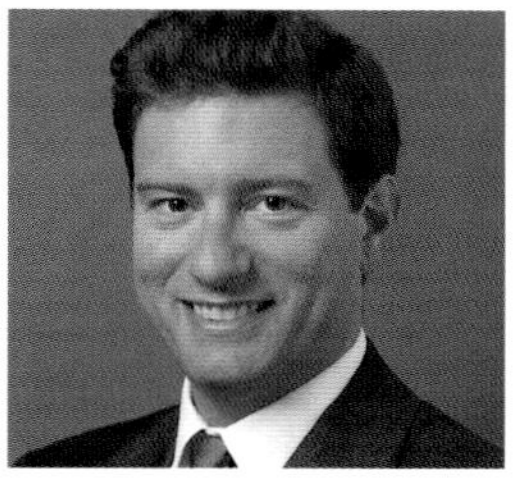

**Carlton C. Rochell, Jr.**
*Executive vice president & head of Jewellery, Sotheby's Worldwide*

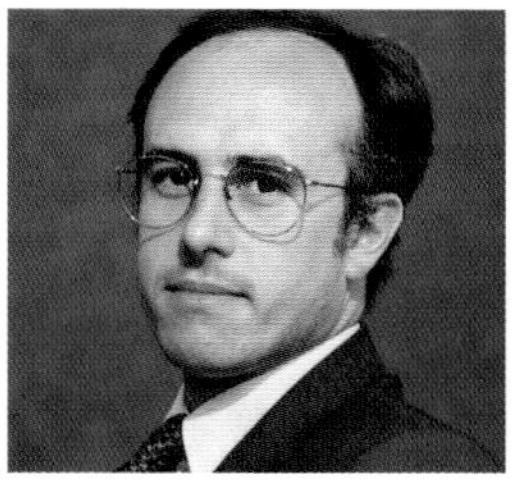

**Gregory Rubinstein**
*Director & head of Old Master Drawings, Sotheby's Worldwide*

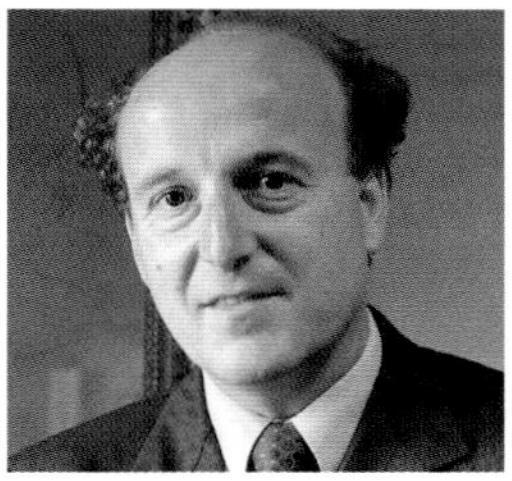

**Henry Wemyss**
*Director of the British Paintings department, Sotheby's London*

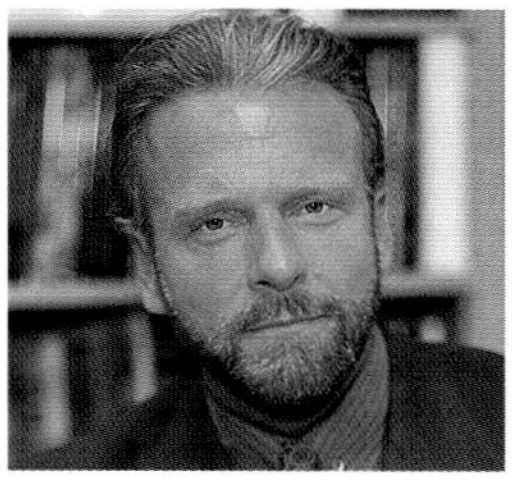

**Phillips Hathaway**
*Senior vice president & director of Business Development for European Decorative Arts, Sotheby's New York*

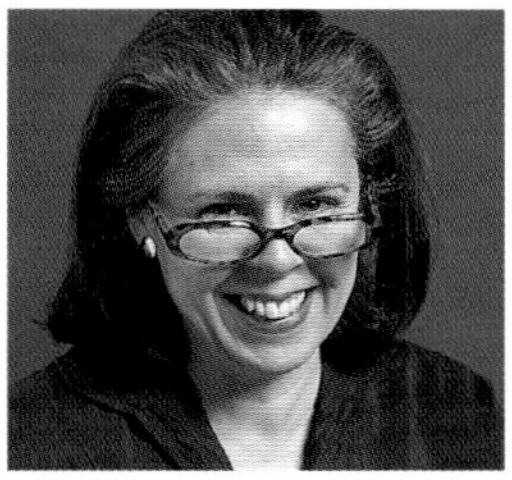

**Denise Bethel**
*Director in the Photographs department, Sotheby's New York*

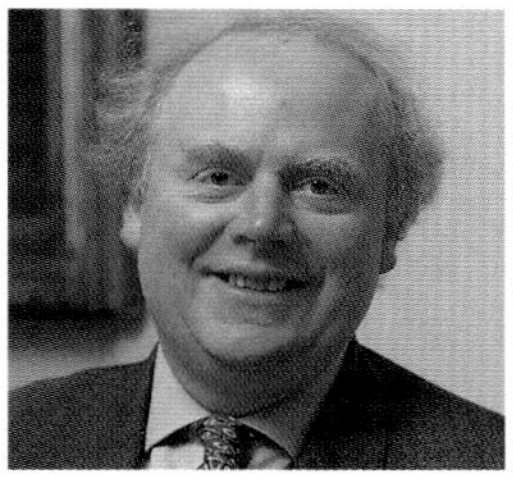

**James Miller**
*Deputy chairman, Sotheby's United Kingdom*

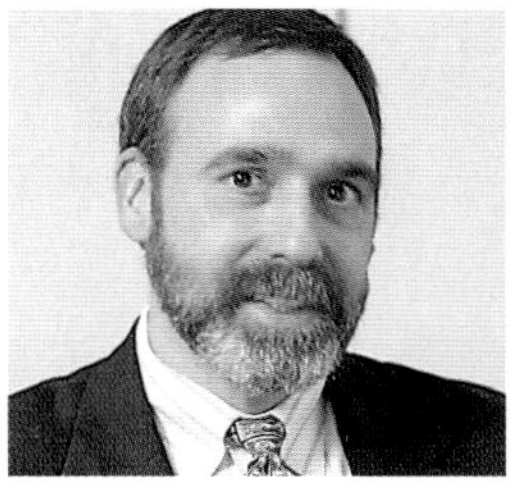

**Selby Kiffer**
*Head of the Books & Manuscripts department, Sotheby's New York*

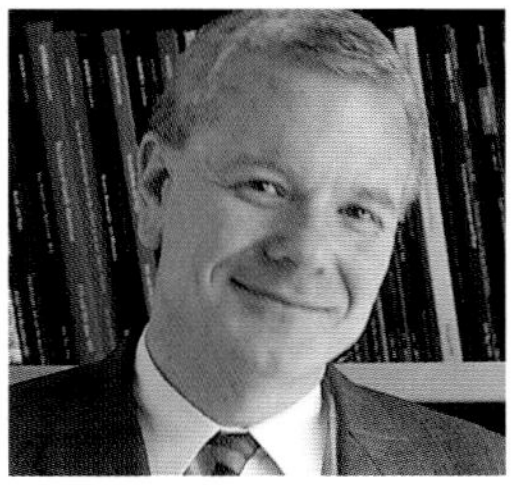

**Justin Caldwell**
*Assistant vice president in the Books & Manuscripts department, Sotheby's New York*

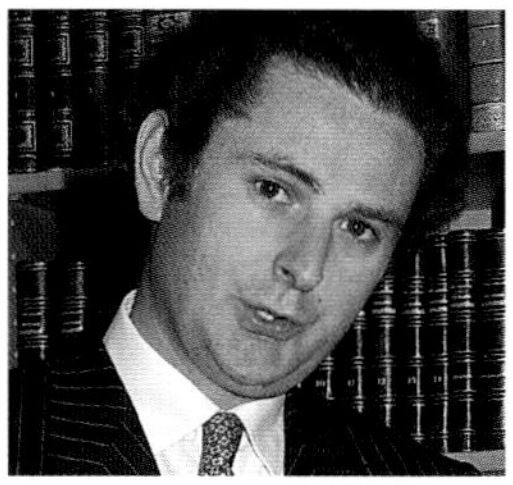

**Jean-Baptiste de Proyart**
*Vice-president, Sotheby's France*

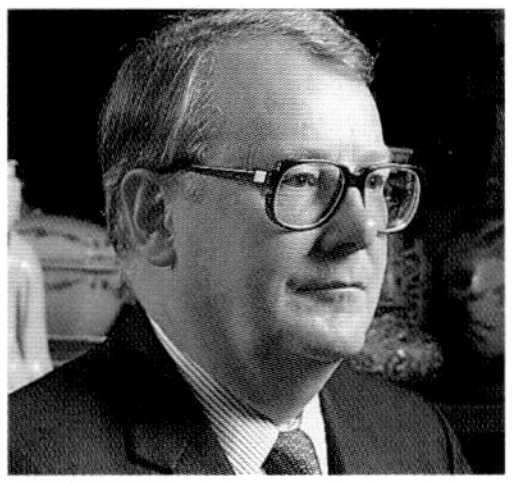

**Julian Thompson**
*Chairman of Sotheby's Asia*

# Principal Officers and Specialists

**William F. Ruprecht**
*President & Chief Executive Officer*

NORTH AMERICA

**Warren P. Weitman, Jr.**
*Chairman, Sotheby's North & South America*

**Richard E. Oldenburg**
*Honorary Chairman, Sotheby's North America*

**John L. Marion**
*Honorary Chairman, Sotheby's North America*

**James G. Niven**
**David N. Redden**
**William W. Stahl, Jr.**
**George Wachter**
*Vice Chairmen, Sotheby's North America*

**William S. Cottingham**
**C. Hugh Hildesley**
**Carlton C. Rochell, Jr.**
*Executive Vice Presidents, Sotheby's North America*

EUROPE

**Robin Woodhead**
*Chief Executive, Sotheby's Europe & Asia*

**The Marquess of Hartington**
*Deputy Chairman, Sotheby's Holdings*

**Henry Wyndham**
*Chairman, Sotheby's Europe*

**Princess de Beauvau Craon**
*Deputy Chairman, Sotheby's Europe*
*President, Sotheby's France*

**Melanie Clore**
*Deputy Chairman, Sotheby's Europe*

**Guy Jennings**
*Deputy Chairman, Sotheby's Europe*
*Chairman, Sotheby's Switzerland*

**Tobias Meyer**
*Deputy Chairman, Sotheby's Europe*

**The Hon. James Stourton**
*Deputy Chairman, Sotheby's Europe*

**James Miller**
*Deputy Chairman, Sotheby's United Kingdom*

**George Bailey**
*Managing Director, Sotheby's Europe*

**Simon Taylor**
*Deputy Managing Director, Sotheby's Europe*

ASIA

**Julian Thompson**
*Chairman, Sotheby's Asia*

**Henry Howard-Sneyd**
*Managing Director, Sotheby's Asia*

---

The telephone numbers for Sotheby's offices are:
Amsterdam 31 (20) 550 2200
Geneva 41 (22) 908 4800
Hong Kong (852) 2524 8121
London 44 (020) 7293 5000
Milan 39 (02) 2950 01
Munich 49 (89) 291 3151
New York 1 (212) 606 7000
Paris 33 (1) 5305 5305
Sussex 44 (1403) 833 500
Tel Aviv 972 (3) 560 1666
Zurich 41 (1) 226 2200
www.sothebys.com

All London departments are based at 34–35 New Bond Street unless specified

**African & Oceanic Art**
LONDON AND NEW YORK
Jean G. Fritts

**American Decorative Arts & Furniture**
NEW YORK
Wendell Garrett
Leslie B. Keno
John B. A. Nye
William W. Stahl, Jr.

**American Folk Art**
NEW YORK
Nancy Druckman

**American Indian Art**
NEW YORK
David Roche

**American Paintings, Drawings & Sculpture**
NEW YORK
Dara Mitchell Offit
Peter B. Rathbone

**Antiquities**
LONDON AND NEW YORK
Richard M. Keresey

**Arms & Armour**
LONDON OLYMPIA
Thomas Del Mar (UK & USA)

**Books & Manuscripts**
LONDON
Dr Stephen Roe
NEW YORK
Selby Kiffer
Marsha Malinowski
David N. Redden
PARIS
Jean-Baptiste de Proyart

**British Pictures**
LONDON
Grant Ford (*Victorian*)
David Moore-Gwyn (*Paintings to 1850*)
Susannah Pollen (*20th Century*)
Henry Wemyss (*Watercolours*)

**Ceramics**
LONDON OLYMPIA
Simon Cottle
NEW YORK
Christina Prescott-Walker

**Chinese Art**
HONG KONG AND LONDON
Henry Howard-Sneyd
HONG KONG
Jason Tse
LONDON
Alastair Gibson
Julian King
NEW YORK
Joe-Hynn Yang

**Clocks & Watches**
HONG KONG
Tim Bourne
LONDON OLYMPIA
Jonathan Darracott
Michael Turner
NEW YORK
Daryn F. Schnipper

**Collectibles**
LONDON OLYMPIA
Kerry Taylor
NEW YORK
Leila Dunbar
Dana Hawkes

**Contemporary Art**
LONDON
Oliver Barker
Valentina Castellani
Francis Outred
Cheyenne Westphal
MILAN
Claudia Dwek
NEW YORK
Matthew Carey-Williams
Wendy Cromwell
Tobias Meyer
Laura Paulson
Leslie Prouty
PARIS
Florence de Botton

**English Furniture & Decorations**
LONDON
Fergus Lyons
Daniel Morris
NEW YORK
Peter Lang
Simon Redburn

**European Works of Art & Sculpture**
LONDON
Alexander Kader
Elizabeth Wilson
NEW YORK
Margaret Schwartz

**French & Continental Furniture & Decorations**
LONDON
Mario Tavella
NEW YORK
Gillian Arthur
Mary Frances Cunningham
Phillips Hathaway
PARIS
Brice Foisil
ZURICH
Thomas Böller

**Garden Statuary & Architectural Items**
SUSSEX
Rupert van de Werff

**Glass & Paperweights**
LONDON OLYMPIA
Simon Cottle

**Impressionist & Modern Art**
GENEVA
Guy Jennings
Caroline Lang
LONDON
Richard Aronowitz-Mercer
Melanie Clore
Emmanuel Di Donna
Philip Hook
Helena Newman
NEW YORK
Lavinia Calza
Stephane Cosman Connery
Blake Koh
Charles S. Moffett
David Norman
John L. Tancock
PARIS
Simon Shaw
Andrew Strauss

**Indian & Southeast Asian Art**
NEW YORK
Edward Wilkinson

**Islamic Art**
LONDON
Marcus Fraser
NEW YORK
Richard M. Keresey

**Japanese Art**
LONDON OLYMPIA
Neil Davey
Max Rutherston
NEW YORK
Sachiko Hori
Ryoichi Iida

**Jewellery**
CHICAGO
Eve Reppen Rogers
GENEVA
Michael Hall
Alexandra Rhodes
HONG KONG
Quek Chin Yeow
LONDON
Martyn Downer
Daniela Mascetti
LOS ANGELES
Lisa Hubbard
MIAMI
Tracy Sherman
MILAN
Stefano Papi
NEW YORK
Hoda Esphahani
Carlton C. Rochell, Jr.
Gary Schuler
SINGAPORE
Esther Seet

**Judaica**
LONDON
Camilla Previté
NEW YORK
Selby Kiffer (*Books*)
Kevin L. Tierney (*Silver*)
TEL AVIV
Rivka Saker

**Korean Art**
NEW YORK
Ryoichi Iida

**Latin American Art**
NEW YORK
Kirsten Hammer

**Musical Instruments**
LONDON AND NEW YORK
Tim Ingles

**19th Century European Furniture & Decorations**
LONDON OLYMPIA
Jonathan Meyer
NEW YORK
Elaine Whitmire

**19th Century European Paintings & Drawings**
AMSTERDAM
Eveline van Oirschot
LONDON
Adrian Biddell
Claude Piening
MILAN
Dominique Reiner
NEW YORK
Benjamin Doller
Constantine Frangos
Polly Sartori
PARIS
Pascale Pavageau

**Old Master Paintings & Drawings**
LONDON
Alexander Bell
Richard Charlton-Jones
George Gordon
Gregory Rubinstein (*Drawings*)
Cristiana Romalli (*Drawings*)
Julien Stock
NEW YORK
Christopher Apostle
Ben Hall
George Wachter
PARIS
Nicolas Joly

**Manuscripts**
LONDON
Marcus Fraser (*Oriental*)
Peter Kidd (*Western*)

**Photographs**
LONDON
Lydia Cresswell-Jones
Philippe Garner
NEW YORK
Denise Bethel

**Portrait Miniatures & Vertu**
NEW YORK
Gerard Hill

MUNICH
Heinrich Graf von Spreti

**Pre-Columbian Art**
NEW YORK
Stacy Goodman

**Prints**
LONDON
Susan Harris
Jonathan Pratt
NEW YORK
Mary Bartow (*19th & 20th century*)
Dr Nancy Bialler (*Old Master*)
Christopher Gaillard (*Contemporary*)

**Rugs & Carpets**
LONDON AND NEW YORK
Mary Jo Otsea

**Russian Paintings & Works of Art**
LONDON
Joanna Vickery
NEW YORK
Gerard Hill

**Silver**
LONDON OLYMPIA
Harry Charteris (*Continental*)
Peter Waldron (*English*)
NEW YORK
Ian Irving
Kevin L. Tierney
PARIS
Thierry de Lachaise

**Sporting Guns**
SUSSEX
Gavin Gardiner

**20th Century Applied Arts**
LONDON
Lydia Cresswell-Jones
Philippe Garner
NEW YORK
Barbara E. Deisroth

**Wine**
LONDON
Stephen Mould
Serena Sutcliffe, MW
NEW YORK AND CHICAGO
Michael Davis
Paul Hart
Jamie Ritchie
Robert Sleigh

**Sotheby's Institute**
LONDON
Steven Parissien
NEW YORK
Tom Savage

**Tax & Heritage**
LONDON
James Jowitt

**Trusts & Estates**
NEW YORK
Amy Corcoran
Jennifer Davis
Deborah Schmidt Robinson

**Valuations / Appraisals**
LONDON
William Lucy
NEW YORK
Libby Alexander

**Sotheby's Financial Services**
LONDON
Ann-Marie Casey-Jones
NEW YORK
Catherine Chiarella
Shelley Fischer
Mitchell Zuckerman

**Sotheby's International Realty**
LONDON
Paul Tayler
NEW YORK
Stuart N. Siegel *President*

**Sothebys.com**
NEW YORK
Richard C. Buckley
*Managing Director*
David N. Redden
*Chairman*

First published in 2001 by
Sotheby's
34–35 New Bond Street
London W1A 2AA



British Library Cataloguing in Publication Data

A catalogue record for this book is available from the British Library.

ISBN 0–9622588–0–6

*Project Editor* Malcolm Cossons; *Deputy Editor* Sarah Day; *Associate Editor* Matthew Robbins; *Desk Editor* Kate Quarry; *Assistant Editor* Daniella Wood; *Art Editors* Sally Jeffery and Beate Stöckert, Jeffery Design; *Art Director* Ruth Blacksell; *Production Control* Ken Adlard; *Production Co-ordinator* Sandra Orme

Colour reproduction by Precise @ Icon Reproduction

Printed in Germany by
MOHN MEDIA · Mohndruck GmbH, Gütersloh

**Acknowledgements**
Prices given throughout include the buyer's premium applicable in the saleroom concerned. These prices are shown in the currency in which they were realized. The sterling and dollar equivalent figures, shown in brackets, are based upon the rates of exchange on the day of the sale.

The editor would like to thank Kate Quarry, Jennifer Conner, Kate Johnson and all the Sotheby's departments for their help.

The editor would like to thank the following photographers and organizations for their kind permission to reproduce these works in *Sotheby's Art at Auction 2000–2001*: © Estate of Patrick Heron, 2001, All rights reserved, DACS p 2; © Gerhard Richter, *180 Farben* p 4; *Drei Kerzen* p 92; © ADAGP, Paris and DACS 2001 pp 19, 80 & 81 ; © Estate of Francis Bacon/ARS, NY and DACS, London p 23; © DACS 2001 cover & p 25, 85, 91, 96, 97 & 102; © Estate of Stanley Spencer 2001. All Rights Reserved, DACS p 63; © Kit Orpen Casey p 64; © The Sir Alfred Munnings Art Museum, Castle House, Dedham, Essex, England p 65; © Andrew Wyeth, 2001 p 73; © Banco de México, Diego Rivera & Frida Kahlo Museums Trust, Av. Cinco de Mayo No. 2, Col. Centro, Del. Cuauhtémoc 06059 México, D.F. p 76; © Fundación Olga y Rufino Tamayo pp 78–9; © Succession H. Matisse/DACS 2001 pp 86 & 87. © Kingdom of Spain, Gala-Salvador Dali Foundation, DACS, London 2001 pp 88 & 188; © Man Ray Trust/ADAGP, Paris and DACS, London 2001 p 89; © ARS, NY and DACS, London 2001 p 90; © Kate Rothko Prizel & Christopher Rothko/DACS 1998 p 93;© ADAGP, Paris and DACS 2001 p 94; © Sigmar Polke p 95; © Succession Picasso/ DACS 2001 pp 101 & 173; © Copyright in the manuscript is owned by the Joyce Estate. Any related queries should be referred to the Literary Trustees of the Joyce Estate p 170; © Jane Bown p 187; © Ken Adlard/ Sotheby's pp 2, 4, 43, 103, 119, 161, 175 & 188; © Bonnie Morrison/ Sotheby's p 15

Every effort has been made to trace the copyright of the images used in this book. Sotheby's apologizes for any errors or omissions.

PAGE 2 The sale of British works from the Collection of Stanley J. Seeger in London on 14th June, mirrored the success of Contemporary works from the same collection that had sold in New York in May. On the evening of the sale many new world auction records were set, including one for Patrick Heron's *Lux Eterna: May–June 1958* (illustrated), that sold for £289,500 ($402,530)

PAGE 4 Gerhard Richter's stunning *180 Farben* (*180 Colours*), the culmination of a series of experiments in colour conducted by the artist, sold in London in the summer for £1,818,500 ($2,582,360)

PAGE 188 Works from the first ever sale devoted to Surrealist art were exhibited at Sotheby's Paris, prior to auction in London. The sculpture shown here is Salvador Dalí's *Homage à Newton*, which sold for £190,500 ($274,320)